Financial and Management Accounting

An Introduction

Volume I Financial Accounting

Financial and Management Accounting
An Introduction

Volume I Financial Accounting

Third Edition

Pauline Weetman

Professor of Accounting
University of Strathclyde

 Prentice Hall
FINANCIAL TIMES

An imprint of **Pearson Education**
Harlow, England • London • New York • Boston • San Francisco • Toronto • Sydney • Singapore • Hong Kong
Tokyo • Seoul • Taipei • New Delhi • Cape Town • Madrid • Mexico City • Amsterdam • Munich • Paris • Milan

**To my parents,
Harry and Freda Weetman**

Pearson Education Limited

Edinburgh Gate
Harlow
Essex CM20 2JE

and Associated Companies throughout the world.

Visit us on the World Wide Web at:
www.pearsoned.co.uk

First edition published under the
Financial Times Pitman Publishing imprint in 1996
Second edition published in 1999
Third edition published in 2003

ISBN 0 273 65783 6

British Library Cataloguing-in-Publication Data
A catalogue record for this book is available from the British Library

Library of Congress Cataloging-in-Publication Data
A catalog record for this book is available from the Library of Congress

10   9   8   7   6   5   4   3
07   06   05   04

Typeset in 10/12pt Palatino by 35
Printed and bound by Ashford Colour Press Ltd, Gosport

Contents

Chapter 3   Financial statements from the accounting equation   54

Chapter 4   Ensuring the quality of financial statements   76

For *Volume I Financial Accounting* supporting material, visit the website that accompanies both volumes:

A Companion Website accompanies
FINANCIAL AND MANAGEMENT ACCOUNTING
by Pauline Weetman

Visit the *Financial and Management Accounting* Companion Website at ***www.booksites.net/weetman*** to find valuable teaching and learning material including:

For Students:
- Additional problem questions and case-study questions to help you test your learning
- Multiple-choice questions with answers for revision
- Notes on using the World Wide Web to find further relevant information

For Lecturers, comprehensive resources including:

For each chapter, lecturer support material comprising
- Student handouts to accompany lectures
- Overhead transparencies to match student handouts
- Multiple-choice questions
- Application questions
- Problem-solving and evaluation questions
- Full solutions to all end-of-chapter questions and additional problems

For Financial Accounting
- Annual report of 'Craigielaw plc'
- Questions with each chapter drawing on Craigielaw example

For Management Accounting
Additional material on bookkeeping records in a job-costing system

For course planning
- Guidance on mapping the textbook to 8- or 12-week lecture courses
- Benchmarking to quality standards in learning outcomes and assessment
- Additional questions for end-of-course assessment
- Student project design
- Notes on using the World Wide Web to find further relevant information
- A syllabus manager that will build and host your very own course web page.

Preface to the third edition

Introduction

In order to make this book available as a self-contained introduction for students taking financial accounting courses not requiring management accounting, the author's third edition of *Financial and Management Accounting* has been divided into two volumes, *Volume I Financial Accounting* and *Volume II Management Accounting*, while retaining the same pagination and numbering system.

As institutions come under increasing scrutiny for the quality of the teaching and learning experience offered, a textbook must do more than present the knowledge and skills of the chosen subject. It must make explicit to the students what targets are to be achieved and it must help them to assess realistically their own achievements of those targets. It must help the class lecturer prepare, deliver, explain and assess the knowledge and skills expected for the relevant level of study.

This book is written for the first level of undergraduate degree study in accounting and business studies, or equivalent introductory accounting courses for any professional training where an understanding of accounting is a basic requirement. The third edition is thoroughly revised, both in content and in aspects of pedagogy, responding to helpful suggestions from reviewers while retaining the positive aspects that have been encouraged by those already using the book. In particular the revision has added an international perspective to each of the chapters on financial accounting, reflecting the European Union's target that by 2005 all listed companies in Member States will use standards issued by the International Accounting Standards Board.

An accompanying website at *www.booksites.net/weetman* provides the lecturer with a complete resource pack for each chapter. Student handouts containing a skeleton outline of each chapter, leaving slots for students to complete; overhead-projector masters that match the lecture handouts, additional multiple-choice questions and further graded questions in application of knowledge and in problem solving; all are new features for this third edition.

End-of-chapter questions are graded according to the skills being assessed. There are tests of retained knowledge, tests of application of knowledge in straightforward situations and tests of problem solving and evaluation using the acquired knowledge in less familiar situations.

Overall the aim of the third edition is to provide an introduction to financial accounting which engages the interest of students and encourages a desire for further study. It also contributes to developing the generic skills of application, problem solving, evaluation and communication, all emphasised by employers.

Subject coverage

Financial reporting is an essential component in the process of communication between a business and its stakeholders. The importance of communication increases as organisations become larger and more complex. Reporting financial information to external stakeholders not involved in the day-to-day management of the business requires a carefully balanced process of extracting the key features while preserving the essential core of information. The participants in the communication process cover a wide range of expertise and educational background, so far as accounting is concerned. The range begins with the preparers of financial statements, who may have a special training in accounting techniques, but it ends with those who may be professional investors, private investors, investment advisers, bankers, employee representatives, customers, suppliers and journalists.

First-level degree courses in accounting are increasingly addressed to this broad base of potential interest and this book seeks to provide such a broad base of understanding while also supplying a sound technical base for those intending to pursue specialised study of the subject further. In particular it makes use of the *Statement of Principles for Financial Reporting* which is used by the UK Accounting Standards Board in developing and reviewing accounting standards. That statement is intended to help preparers, users and auditors of financial statements to understand better the general nature and function of information reported in financial statements.

Aim of the book

The third edition has been updated throughout. It aims to provide a full understanding of the key aspects of the annual report, concentrating in particular on companies in the private sector but presenting principles of wider application which are relevant also to organisations operating in the public sector.

The international perspective on financial accounting becomes increasingly important under targets for convergence by 2005. The third edition gives a taste of what is to come, by including an international note at the end of each chapter and giving an international flavour to the final chapter.

In particular

An international perspective reflects the target of convergence in accounting standards across the European Union by the year 2005.

Concepts of financial accounting are identified by applying the principles enunciated by the UK Accounting Standards Board in its *Statement of Principles* document. The *Statement of Principles* emphasises the desirability of meeting the needs of users of financial statements and it takes a balance sheet-oriented approach. That approach is applied consistently throughout the book, with some indication of the problems which may arise when it is clear that the established emphasis on the matching of revenues and costs may give a more rational explanation of existing practice.

User needs are explained in every chapter and illustrated by including first-person commentary from a professional fund manager, holding a conversation with an audit manager. The conversations are based on the author's research in the area of communication through the annual report.

The *accounting equation* is used throughout the financial accounting section for analysis and processing of transactions. It is possible for students who do not seek a technical specialism to complete the text without any reference to debit and credit bookkeeping. It is, however, recognised that particular groups of students may wish to understand the basic aspects of debit and credit bookkeeping and for this purpose the end-of-chapter supplements revisit, on a debit and credit recording basis, material already explored in the chapter. Debit and credit aspects of management accounting are not covered since these are regarded as best reserved for later specialist courses if the student so chooses.

Practical illustration is achieved by drawing on the financial information of a fictitious major listed company, taking an overview in early chapters and then developing the detailed disclosures as more specific matters are explored.

Interpretation of financial statements is a feature of all financial reporting chapters, formally brought together in Chapters 13 and 14. The importance of the Operating and Financial Review is emphasised throughout and reinforced in Chapter 14.

Future developments in financial reporting are outlined in Chapter 15 on the basis of selecting those aspects which are most likely to impact on the reader of this text over the next five to ten years. The impact will be on all stakeholders and it will be important for future users of accounts, as well as the preparers, to be aware of the major changes in financial reporting which are now under way.

Self-evaluation is encouraged by setting learning outcomes at the start of each chapter and reviewing these in the chapter summaries. Activity questions are placed at various stages throughout each chapter. Self-testing questions at the end of the chapter may be answered by referring again to the text. Group activities are suggested at the end of each chapter with the particular aim of encouraging participation and interaction. Further end-of-chapter questions provide a range of practical applications. Answers are available to all computational questions, either at the end of the book or on the website.

A *sense of achievement* is engendered in the reader of the financial accounting section by providing a general understanding of the entire annual report by the end of Chapter 7. Thereafter specific aspects of the annual report are explored in Chapters 8–12. Lecturers who wish to truncate a first-level course or leave specific aspects to a later level will find Chapters 8–12 may be used on a selective basis.

A *spreadsheet* approach to financial accounting transactions is used in the body of the relevant chapters to show processing of transactions using the accounting equation. The author is firmly convinced, after years of trying every conceivable approach, that the spreadsheet encourages students to apply the accounting equation analytically, rather than trying to memorise T-account entries. Furthermore students now use spreadsheets as a tool of analysis on a regular basis and will have little difficulty in applying suitable software in preparing spreadsheets. In the bookkeeping supplementary sections, the three-column ledger account has been adopted in the knowledge that school teaching is moving increasingly to adopt this approach which cuts out much of the bewilderment of balancing T-accounts. Computerised accounting systems also favour the three-column presentation with continuous updating of the balance.

Flexible course design

There was once a time when the academic year comprised three terms and we all knew the length of a typical course unit over those three terms. Now there are semesters, trimesters, modules and half-modules so that planning a course of study becomes an exercise in critical path analysis. This text is written for the 12-teaching-week semester but may need selective guidance to students for a module of lesser duration. Chapters 1–4 provide an essential conceptual framework which sets the scene. For a general appreciation course, Chapters 5 and 6 are practical so that one or both could be omitted, leading directly to Chapter 7 as a guide to published accounts. Chapters 8–12 are structured so that the explanation of principles is contained early in each chapter, but the practical implementation is later in each chapter. For a general appreciation course, it would be particularly important to refer to the section of each chapter which analyses users' needs for information and discusses information provided in the financial statements. However, the practical sections of these chapters could be omitted or used on a selective basis rather than attempting full coverage. Chapters 13 and 14 are important to all readers for a sense of interpretation. Chapter 15 encourages interest in future developments, which could be studied selectively.

Approaches to teaching and learning

Learning outcomes

Targets for student achievement in relation to knowledge and understanding of the subject are numbered in each chapter as **LO1**, **LO2**, etc.

Learning outcomes are measurable achievements for students, stated at the start of each chapter. In the Summary section the student is invited to carry out self-evaluation of learning outcomes and then to test this against graded questions. The achievement of some learning outcomes may be confirmed by Activities set out at the appropriate stage within the chapter. Others may be confirmed by end-of-chapter questions.

Skills outcomes

The end-of-chapter questions test not only subject-specific knowledge and technical skills but also the broader general skills that are transferable to subsequent employment or further training.

S01 Application of technical skills

These are skills specific to the subject of accounting and add to the specialist expertise of the student. More generally they show the student's capacity to acquire and apply a technical skill of this type.

S02 Problem-solving and evaluation skills

These are skills that are relevant to many subjects and many activities in life, especially in subsequent employment. Some initiative is required in deciding how to apply relevant knowledge and in solving problems.

S03 Communication skills

Communication may involve writing or speaking, or both. It may require, for example, explanation of a technical matter to a non-technical person, or discussion with other students to explore a controversial issue, or presentation of a report to a business audience.

End-of-chapter questions are graded and each is matched to one or more learning outcomes. The grades of question are:

Test your understanding (Series A questions)

The answers to these questions can be found in the chapter.

Application (Series B questions)

These are questions that apply the knowledge gained from reading and practising the material of the chapter. They resemble closely in style and content the technical material of the chapter. Confidence is gained in applying knowledge in a situation that is very similar to that illustrated. Answers are given in Appendix II or on the website.

Problem solving and evaluation (Series C questions)

These are questions that apply the knowledge gained from reading the chapter, but the style of each question is different. Problem-solving skills are required in selecting relevant data or in using knowledge to work out what further effort is needed to solve the problem. Evaluation means giving an opinion or explanation of the results of the problem-solving exercise. Some answers are given in Appendix II but others are on the website so that they can be used in tutorial preparation or class work.

Supplementary section: Test your understanding (Series S questions)

These are questions on the accounting records system (bookkeeping entries) to test understanding for those who wish to study the supplementary bookkeeping sections.

Interpretation of company accounts

In the textbook there is a running example of the fictitious company Safe and Sure plc, which is in the service sector. The website contains a parallel example, Craigielaw plc, in the manufacturing sector. On the website there are questions on Craigielaw to accompany most of the chapters. These test application, problem solving and evaluation. They are labelled Series D questions.

Website

A website is available at *www.booksites.net/weetman* by password access to lecturers adopting this textbook. It contains additional problem questions for each chapter, with full solutions to these additional questions as well as any solutions not provided in the textbook. The website includes basic tutorial instructions and overhead-projector masters to support each chapter.

Target readership

This book is targeted at a broad-ranging business studies type of first-level degree course. It is intended to support the equivalent of one semester of 12 teaching weeks. There is sufficient basic bookkeeping (ledger accounts) in the end-of-chapter supplements to make the book suitable for those intending to pursue a specialised study of accounting beyond the first level but the book-keeping material is optional for those who do not have such special intentions. The book has been written with undergraduate students particularly in mind, but may also be suitable for professional and postgraduate business courses where financial reporting is taught at an introductory level.

Acknowledgements

I am grateful to academic colleagues and to reviewers of the text for helpful comments and suggestions. I am also grateful to undergraduate students of five universities who have taken my courses and thereby helped in developing an approach to teaching and learning the subject. Professor Graham Peirson and Mr Alan Ramsay of Monash University provided a first draft of their text based on the conceptual framework in Australia which gave valuable assistance in designing the structure of this book. I am grateful to Pat Bond at my publishers for his considerable patience, to Julianne Mulholland who was responsible for the editing of the first edition text, and to Ron Harper at Longman Australia for initiating the project.

For this latest edition I am grateful to colleagues and students who have used the book in their teaching and learning. I have also been helped by constructive comments from reviewers and by guidance from Catherine Newman, Stuart Hay and Liz Tarrant.

Part 1

A conceptual framework: setting the scene

Chapter 1

Who needs accounting?

Learning outcomes

After studying this chapter you should be able to:

LO1 Define, and explain the definition of, accounting.

LO2 Explain what is meant by a *conceptual framework*.

LO3 Explain the distinguishing features of a sole trader, a partnership and a limited company.

LO4 List the main users of financial information and their particular needs.

LO5 Discuss the usefulness of financial statements to the main users.

Additionally, for those who choose to study the Supplement:

LO6 Define the basic terminology of business transactions.

LO1

1.1 Introduction

LO1

Activity 1.1

Before starting to read this section, write down one paragraph stating what you think the word 'accounting' means. Then read this section and compare it with your paragraph.

There is no single 'official' definition of accounting but for the purposes of this text the following wording will be used:

Definition

Accounting is the process of identifying, measuring and communicating financial information about an entity to permit informed judgements and decisions by users of the information.[1]

This definition may appear short but it has been widely quoted over a number of years and is sufficient to specify the entire contents of this introductory textbook.

Taking the definition word by word, it leads to the following questions:

1 What is the process?
2 How is financial information identified?
3 How is financial information measured?
4 How is financial information communicated?
5 What is an entity?
6 Who are the users of financial information about an entity?
7 What types of judgements and decisions do these users make?

Writing the questions in this order is slightly dangerous because it starts by emphasising the process and waits until the final question to ask about the use of the information. The danger is that accountants may design the process first and then hope to show that it is suitable to allow judgements and decisions by users. This is what has often happened over many years of development of the process by accountants.

In order to learn about, and understand, accounting by taking a critical approach to the usefulness of the current processes and seeing its limitations and the potential for improvement, it is preferable to reverse the order of the questions and start by specifying the users of financial information and the judgements and decisions they make. Once the users and their needs have been identified, the most effective forms of communication may be determined and only then may the technical details of measurement and identification be dealt with in a satisfactory manner.

Reversing the order of the questions arising from the definition of accounting is the approach to be used in this book because it is the approach which has been taken by those seeking to develop a *conceptual framework* of accounting.

This chapter outlines the meaning of the words 'conceptual framework' and in particular the *Statement of Principles* which has been developed for use in United Kingdom accounting practice. It explains the nature of three common types of business *entity* and concludes by drawing on various views relating to the users of accounting information and their information needs.

Because the understanding of users' needs is essential throughout the entire text, the chapter introduces David Wilson, a *fund manager* working for a large insurance company. In order to balance the demands of users with the restrictions and constraints on preparers of financial information, the chapter also introduces Leona Rees who works as an *audit manager* with an *accountancy firm*. Both of them will offer comments and explanations as you progress through the text.

L01 **Activity 1.2**

> *How does this section compare with your initial notions of what 'accounting' means? If they are similar, then it is likely that the rest of this textbook will meet your expectations. If they are different, then it may be that you are hoping for more than this textbook can achieve. If that is the case, this may be a useful point at which to consult your lecturer or tutor or some other expert in the subject to be sure that you are satisfied that this book will meet your personal learning outcomes.*

L02 ## 1.2 The development of a conceptual framework

A conceptual framework for accounting is a statement of principles which provide generally accepted guidance for the development of new reporting practices and for challenging and evaluating the existing practices. Conceptual frameworks have been developed in several countries around the world, with the United Kingdom arriving a little late on the scene. However, arriving late does give the advantage of learning from what has gone before. It is possible to see a pattern emerging in the various approaches to developing a conceptual framework.

The conceptual frameworks developed for practical use by the *accountancy profession* in various countries all start with the common assumption that *financial statements* must be useful. The structure of most conceptual frameworks is along the following lines:

- Who are the users of financial statements?
- What are the information needs of users?
- What types of financial statements will best satisfy their needs?
- What are the characteristics of financial statements which meet these needs?
- What are the rules for defining and recognising items in financial statements?
- What are the rules for measuring items in financial statements?

The most widely applicable conceptual framework is that of the International Accounting Standards Board (IASB). It was issued in 1989 and either reflects, or is reflected in, national conceptual frameworks of the United States, Canada and Australia, as well as that of the UK. The thinking in all those documents can be traced to two discussion papers of the 1970s in the UK and the United States. In the United Kingdom, *The Corporate Report*[2] was a slim but highly influential document setting out the needs of users and how these might be met. Two years earlier the *Trueblood Report*[3] in the United States had taken a similar approach of identifying the needs of users, although perhaps coming out more strongly in support of the needs of shareholders and creditors than of other user groups. In the United Kingdom, various documents have been prepared by persons invited to help the process[4] or those who took it on themselves to propose radical new ideas.[5] The United Kingdom now has a conceptual framework which it can call its own, in the form of the *Statement of Principles* issued by the Accounting Standards Board.[6]

L02 **Activity 1.3**

Most conceptual frameworks start with the question: 'Who are the users of financial statements?' Write down a list of the persons or organisations you think would be interested in making use of financial statements, and their possible reasons for being interested. Have you included yourself in that list? Keep your list available for comparing with a later section of this chapter.

L02 ## 1.3 The Statement of Principles

The *Statement of Principles* has eight chapters:

1 The objectives of financial statements.
2 The reporting entity.
3 The qualitative characteristics of financial statements.
4 The elements of financial statements.
5 Recognition in financial statements.
6 Measurement in financial statements.
7 Presentation of financial information.
8 Accounting for interests in other entities.

Chapters 1 and 3 of the *Statement of Principles* are written at a general level and a reader would find no difficulty in reviewing those immediately to gain a flavour of what is expected of financial statements. The remaining chapters are a mixture of general principles, which are appropriate to first-level study of the subject, and some quite specific principles which deal with more advanced problems.

Some of those problems need an under
a first level of study. This textbook wil
of the *Statement of Principles*, as appropri
You should be aware, however, that th
of the *Statement of Principles* and does

A conceptual framework is particu
developed for reporting to those who
the business. This is called *external rep*
of *Financial Accounting*. For those wh
day basis, special techniques have be
as *internal reporting* or *management*
Accounting.

Before continuing with the them
pause and consider the types of bu
be required.

LO3

Web activity

Activity 1.4

Visit the website of the Accounting Standards Board at **www.asb.org.uk** *and find the
link to the Statement of Principles. What does the ASB say about the purpose of the
Statement of Principles? How was it developed?*

Visit the website of the International Accounting Standards Board at **www.iasb.org.uk**
*and find the link to the IASB Framework (you may have to follow the link to 'standards'
although the Framework is not a formal Standard). What does the IASB say about
the purpose of the Framework? How was it developed? What are the similarities and
differences between the ASB and IASB in the way each describes its conceptual
framework?*

LO3

1.4 Types of business entity

The word 'entity' means 'something that exists independently'. A business entity
is a business that exists independently of those who own the business. There are
three main categories of business which will be found in all countries of the world,
although with different titles in different countries. This chapter uses the terminology common to the United Kingdom. The three main categories are: *sole
trader, partnership* and *limited liability company*. This list is by no means exhaustive
but provides sufficient variety to allow explanation of the usefulness of most
accounting practices and their application.

LO3

Activity 1.5

*Before reading the next sections, take out a newspaper with business advertisements,
or a business telephone directory, or else take a walk down your local high street or
drive round the trading estate. Write down the names of five businesses or shops or
other organisations. Then read the sections and attempt to match your list against the
information provided in each.*

ole trader

dividual may enter into business alone, either selling goods or providing a vice. Such a person is described as a sole trader. The business may be started because the sole trader has a good idea which appears likely to make a profit, and has some cash to buy the equipment and other resources to start the business. If cash is not available, the sole trader may borrow from a bank to enable the business to start up. Although this is the form in which many businesses have started, it is one which is difficult to expand because the sole trader will find it difficult to arrange additional finance for expansion. If the business is not successful and the sole trader is unable to meet obligations to pay money to others, then those persons may ask a court of law to authorise the sale of the personal possessions, and even the family home, of the sole trader. Being a sole trader can be a risky matter and the cost of borrowing from banks may be a relatively unfavourable rate of interest because the bank fears a risk of losing its money.

From this description it will be seen that the sole trader's business is very much intertwined with the sole trader's personal life. However, for accounting purposes, the business is regarded as a separate economic entity, of which the sole trader is the owner who takes the risk of the bad times and the benefit of the good times. Take as an example the person who decides to start working as an electrician and advertises his or her services in a newspaper. The electrician travels to jobs from home and has no business premises. Tools are stored in the loft and the business records are in a cupboard in the kitchen. Telephone calls from customers are received on the domestic phone and there are no clearly defined working hours. The work is inextricably intertwined with family life. For accounting purposes that person is seen as the owner of a business which provides electrical services and the business is seen as being separate from the person's other interests and private life. The owner may hardly feel any great need for accounting information because he or she knows the business very closely, but accounting information will be needed by other persons, mainly the government (in the form of the *Inland Revenue*) for tax collecting purposes. It may also be required by a bank for the purposes of lending money to the business or by another sole trader who is intending to buy the business when the existing owner retires.

1.4.2 Partnership

One method by which the business of a sole trader may expand is to enter into partnership with one or more other persons. This may permit a pooling of skills to allow more efficient working, or may allow one person with ideas to work with another who has the money to provide the resources needed to turn the ideas into a profit. There is thus more potential for being successful. If the business is unsuccessful, then the consequences are similar to those for the sole trader. Persons to whom money is owed by the business may ask a court of law to authorise the sale of the personal property of the partners in order to meet the obligation. Even more seriously, one partner may be required to meet all the obligations of the partnership if the other partner does not have sufficient personal property, possessions and cash. This is described in law as *joint and several liability* and the risks have to be considered very carefully by those entering into partnership.

Partnership may be established as a matter of fact by two persons starting to work together with the intention of making a profit and sharing it between them. More often there is a legal agreement, called a *partnership deed*, which sets out the rights and duties of each partner and specifies how they will share the profits. There is also *partnership law* which governs the basic relationships between partners and which they may use to resolve their disputes in a court of law if there is no partnership deed, or if the partnership deed has not covered some aspect of the partnership.

For accounting purposes the partnership is seen as a separate economic entity, owned by the partners. The owners may have the same intimate knowledge of the business as does the sole trader and may therefore feel that accounting information is not very important for them. On the other hand, each partner may wish to be sure that he or she is receiving a fair share of the partnership profits. There will also be other persons requesting accounting information, such as the Inland Revenue, banks who provide finance, and individuals who may be invited to join the partnership so that it may expand even further.

1.4.3 Limited liability company

The main risk attached to either a sole trader or a partnership is that of losing their personal property and possessions, including the family home, if the business fails. That risk would inhibit many persons from starting or expanding a business. Historically, as the United Kingdom changed from a predominantly agricultural to a predominantly industrial economy in the nineteenth century, it became apparent that the owners needed the protection of *limited liability*. This meant that if the business failed, then the owners might lose all the money they had put into the business but their personal wealth would be safe.

There are two forms of limited liability company. The *private limited company* has the word 'Limited' (abbreviated as 'Ltd') in its title. The *public limited company* has the abbreviation 'plc' in its title. The private limited company is prohibited by law from offering its *shares* to the public, so it is a form of limited liability which is appropriate to a family-controlled business. The public limited company is permitted to offer its shares to the public. In return it has to satisfy more onerous regulations. Where the shares of a public limited company are bought and sold on a *stock exchange*, the public limited company is called a *listed plc* because the shares of the company are on a list of share prices.

In either type of company the owners are called *shareholders* because they share the ownership and share the profits of the good times and the losses of the bad times (to the defined limit of liability). Once they have paid in full for their shares, the owners face no further risk of being asked to contribute to meeting any obligations of the business. Hopefully, the business will prosper and the owners may be able to receive a share of that prosperity in the form of a cash *dividend*. A cash dividend returns to the owners, on a regular basis and in the form of cash, a part of the profit created by the business.

If the company is very small, the owners may run the business themselves. If it is larger, then they may prefer to pay someone else to run the business. In either case the persons running the business on a day-to-day basis are called the *directors*.

Because limited liability is a great privilege for the owners, the company must meet regulations set out by Parliament in the form of a *Companies Act*. At present the relevant law is the Companies Act 1985.

For accounting purposes the company is an entity with an existence separate from the owners. In the very smallest companies the owners may not feel a great need for accounting information, but in companies of medium or larger size, accounting information will be very important for the shareholders as a report

Exhibit 1.1
Differences between a partnership and a limited liability company

	Partnership	**Limited liability company**
Formation	Formed by two or more persons, usually with written agreement but not necessarily in writing.	Formed by a number of persons registering the company under the Companies Act, following legal formalities. In particular there must be a written *memorandum* and *articles of association* setting out the powers allowed to the company.
Running the business	All partners are entitled to share in the running of the business.	Shareholders must appoint directors to run the business (although shareholders may appoint themselves as directors).
Accounting information	Partnerships are not obliged to make accounting information available to the wider public.	Companies must make accounting information available to the public through the *Registrar of Companies*.
Meeting obligations	All members of a general partnership are jointly and severally liable for money owed by the firm.	The personal liability of the owners is limited to the amount they have agreed to pay for shares.
Powers to carry out activities	Partnerships may carry out any legal business activities agreed by the partners.	The company may only carry out the activities set out in its memorandum and articles of association.
Status in law	The partnership is not a separate legal entity (under English law), the partnership property being owned by the partners. (Under Scots law the partnership is a separate legal entity.)	The company is seen by law as a separate person, distinct from its members. This means that the company can own property, make contracts and take legal action or be the subject of legal action.

on how well the directors have run the company on their behalf. As with other forms of business there will be a need to provide accounting information to the Inland Revenue for tax-collecting purposes. The list of other users will expand considerably because there will be a greater variety of sources of finance, the company may be seeking to attract more *investors*, employees will have a concern for the well-being of the business, and even the customers and suppliers may want to know more of the financial strength of the company.

Although the law provides the protection of limited liability, this has little practical meaning for many small family-controlled companies because a bank lending money to the business will ask for personal guarantees from the shareholder directors. Those personal guarantees could involve a mortgage over the family home, or an interest in life assurance policies. The potential consequences of such personal guarantees, where a company fails, are such that the owners may suffer as much as the sole trader whose business fails.

Exhibit 1.1 summarises the differences between a partnership and a company which are relevant for accounting purposes.

Exhibit 1.2 identifies the differences between the private limited company and the public limited company which are relevant for accounting purposes.

Exhibit 1.2
Brief comparison of private and public companies

	Public company	Private company
Running the business	Minimum of two directors.	Minimum of one director.
	Must have a company secretary who holds a relevant qualification (responsible for ensuring the company complies with requirements of company law).	The sole director may also act as the company secretary and is not required to have a formal qualification.
Ownership	Shares may be offered to the public, inviting subscription. Minimum share capital £50,000.	Shares must not be offered to the public. May only be sold by private arrangements. No minimum share capital.
Accounting information	Extensive information required on transactions between directors and the company.	Less need for disclosure of transactions between directors and the company.
	Information must be made public through the Registrar of Companies. Provision of financial information to the public is determined by size of company, more information being required of medium and large companies.	
	Accounting information must be sent to all shareholders.	

L03 **Activity 1.6**

Look at the list of five organisations which you prepared before reading this section. Did the list match what you read in the section? If not, there are several possible explanations. One is that you have written down organisations which are not covered by the work of this textbook. That would apply if you have written down 'museum', 'town hall' or 'college'. These are examples of public sector bodies which require specialised financial statements not covered by this text. Another is that you did not discover the name of the business enterprise. Perhaps you wrote down 'Northern Hotel' but did not find the name of the company owning the hotel. If your list does not match the section, ask for help from your lecturer, tutor or other expert in the subject so that you are satisfied that this book will continue to meet your personal learning outcomes.

L04 ## 1.5 Users and their information needs

Who are the users of the information provided by these reporting entities? This section shows that there is one group, namely the *management* of an organisation, whose information needs are so specialised that a separate type of accounting has evolved called management accounting. However, there are other groups, each of which may believe it has a reasonable right to obtain information about an organisation, that do not enjoy unrestricted access to the business and so have to rely on management to supply suitable information. These groups include the owners, where the owners are not also the managers, but extend further to employees, lenders, suppliers, customers, government and its branches, and the public interest.

1.5.1 Management

Many would argue that the foremost users of accounting information about an organisation must be those who manage the business on a day-to-day basis. This group is referred to in broad terms as *management*, which is a collective term for all those persons who have responsibilities for making judgements and decisions within an organisation. Because they have close involvement with the business, they have access to a wide range of information (much of which may be confidential within the organisation) and will seek those aspects of the information which are most relevant to their particular judgements and decisions. Because this group of users is so broad and because of the vast amount of information potentially available, a specialist branch of accounting has developed, called management accounting, to serve the particular needs of management.

It is management's responsibility to employ the resources of their business in an efficient way and to meet the objectives of the business. The information needed by management to carry out this responsibility ought to be of high quality and in an understandable form so far as the management is concerned. If that is the case, it would not be unreasonable to think that a similar quality (although not necessarily quantity) of information should be made available more widely to those *stakeholders* who do not have the access available to management.[7] Such an idea would be regarded as somewhat revolutionary in nature by some of those who manage companies, but more and more are beginning to realise that sharing information with investors and other stakeholders adds to the general atmosphere of confidence in the enterprise.

1.5.2 Owners as investors

Where the owners are the managers, as is the case for a sole trader or a partnership, they have no problem in gaining access to information and will select information for their own needs on matters of judgement and decision. They may be asked to provide information for other users, such as the Inland Revenue or a bank which has been approached to provide finance, but that information will be designed to meet the needs of those particular users rather than the owners.

Where the ownership is separate from the management of the business, as is the case with a limited liability company, the owners are more appropriately viewed as investors who entrust their money to the company and expect something in return, usually a dividend and a growth in the value of their investment as the company prospers. Providing money to fund a business is a risky act to take and investors are concerned with the *risk* inherent in, and *return* provided by, their investments. They need information to help them decide whether they should buy, hold or sell. They are also interested in information on the entity's financial performance and financial position that helps them to assess its cash-generation abilities and that helps them to assess the stewardship of management.[8]

Much of the investment in shares through the Stock Exchange in the UK is carried out by *institutional investors*, such as pension funds, insurance companies, unit trusts and investment trusts. The day-to-day business of buying and selling shares is carried out by a *fund manager* employed by the institutional investor. Private investors are in the minority as a group of investors in the UK. They will often take the advice of an *equities analyst* who investigates and reports on share investment. The fund managers and the equities analysts are also regarded as users of accounting information.

The kinds of judgements and decisions made by investors could include any or all of the following:

(a) Evaluating the performance of the entity.
(b) Assessing the effectiveness of the entity in achieving objectives (including compliance with *stewardship* obligations) established previously by its management, its members or owners.
(c) Evaluating managerial performance, efficiency and objectives, including investment and dividend distribution plans.
(d) Ascertaining the experience and background of company directors and officials including details of other directorships or official positions held.
(e) Ascertaining the economic stability and vulnerability of the reporting entity.
(f) Assessing the liquidity of the entity, its present or future requirements for additional fixed capital or working capital, and its ability to raise long-term and short-term finance.
(g) Assessing the capacity of the entity to make future reallocations of its resources for economic purposes.

(h) Estimating the future prospects of the entity, including its capacity to pay dividends, and predicting future levels of investment.

(i) Making economic comparisons, either for the given entity over a period of time or with other entities.

(j) Estimating the value of present or prospective interests in or claims on the entity.

(k) Ascertaining the ownership and control of the entity.[9]

That list was prepared in 1975 and, while it is a valid representation of the needs of investors, carries an undertone which implies that the investors have to do quite a lot of the work themselves in making estimates of the prospects of the entity. Today there is a stronger view that the management of a business should share more of its thinking and planning with the investors. The list may therefore be expanded by suggesting that it would be helpful for investors (and all external users) to know:

(a) the entity's actual performance for the most recent accounting period and how this compares with its previous plan for that period;

(b) management's explanations of any significant variances between the two; and

(c) management's financial plan for the current and forward accounting periods and explanations of the major assumptions used in preparing it.[10]

If you look through some annual reports of major listed companies you will see that this is more a 'wish list' than a statement of current practice, but it is indicative of the need for a more progressive approach. In the annual reports of large companies you will find a section called the *Operating and Financial Review* (or similar title). This is where the more progressive companies will include forward-looking statements which stop short of making a *forecast* but give help in understanding which of the trends observed in the past are likely to continue into the future.

1.5.3 Employees

Employees and their representatives are interested in information about the stability and profitability of their employers. They are also interested in information that helps them to assess the ability of the entity to provide remuneration, retirement benefits and employment opportunities.[11] Employees continue to be interested in their employer after they have retired from work because in many cases the employer provides a pension fund.

The matters which are likely to be of interest to past, present and prospective employees include: the ability of the employer to meet wage agreements; management's intentions regarding employment levels, locations and working conditions; the pay, conditions and terms of employment of various groups of employees; job security; and the contribution made by employees in other divisions of the organisation. Much of this is quite specialised and detailed information. It may be preferable to supply this to employees by means of special purpose reports on a frequent basis rather than waiting for the annual report, which is slow to arrive and more general in nature. However, employees may look to financial statements to confirm information provided previously in other forms.

1.5.4 Lenders

Lenders are interested in information that enables them to determine whether their loans, and the related interest, will be paid when due.[12]

Loan creditors provide finance on a longer-term basis. They will wish to assess the economic stability and vulnerability of the borrower. They are particularly concerned with the risk of *default* and its consequences. They may impose conditions (called *loan covenants*) which require the business to keep its overall borrowing within acceptable limits. The financial statements may provide evidence that the loan covenant conditions are being met.

Some lenders will ask for special reports as well as the general financial statements. Banks in particular will ask for *cash flow projections* showing how the business plans to repay, with interest, the money borrowed.

1.5.5 Suppliers and other trade creditors

Suppliers of goods and services (also called *trade creditors*) are interested in information that enables them to decide whether to sell to the entity and to determine whether amounts owing to them will be paid when due. Trade creditors are likely to be interested in an entity over a shorter period than lenders unless they are dependent upon the continuation of the entity as a major customer.[13]

Trade creditors supply goods and services to an entity and have very little protection if the entity fails because there are insufficient assets to meet all *liabilities*. They are usually classed as *unsecured creditors*, which means they are a long way down the queue for payment. So they have to exercise caution in finding out whether the business is able to pay and how much risk of non-payment exists. This information need not necessarily come from accounting statements. It could be obtained by reading the local press and trade journals, joining the Chamber of Trade, and generally listening in to the stories and gossip circulating in the geographical area or in the industry. However, the financial statements of an entity may confirm the stories gained from other sources.

In recent years there has been a move for companies to work more closely with their suppliers and to establish 'partnership' arrangements where operational and financial plans of both may be dovetailed by specifying the amount and the timing of goods and services required. Such arrangements depend heavily on confidence, which in turn may be derived partly from the strength of financial statements.

1.5.6 Customers

Customers have an interest in information about the continuance of an entity, especially when they have a long-term involvement with, or are dependent upon, the entity.[14] In particular, customers need information concerning the current and future supply of goods and services offered, price and other product details and conditions of sale. Much of this information may be obtained from sales literature or from sales staff of the enterprise, or from trade and consumer journals.[15]

The financial statements provide useful confirmation of the reliability of the enterprise itself as a continuing source of supply, especially when the customer is making payments in advance. They also confirm the capacity of the entity in terms of *fixed assets* and working capital and give some indication of the strength of the entity to meet any obligations under guarantees or warranties.[16]

1.5.7 Governments and their agencies

Governments and their agencies are interested in the allocation of resources and, therefore, in the activities of entities. They also require information in order to regulate the activities of entities, assess taxation and provide a basis for national income and economic statistics.[17]

Acting on behalf of the United Kingdom government's Treasury Department, the Inland Revenue collects taxes from businesses based on profit calculated according to commercial accounting practices (although there are some specific rules in the taxation legislation which modify the normal accounting practices). The Inland Revenue has the power to demand more information than appears in published financial statements, but will take these as a starting point.

Other agencies include the regulators of the various utility companies. Examples are OFTEL (The Office of Telecommunications) and OFGEM (The Office of Gas and Electricity Markets). They use accounting information as part of the package by which they monitor the prices charged by these organisations to consumers of their services. They also demand additional information designed especially to meet their needs.

1.5.8 Public interest

Enterprises affect members of the public in a variety of ways. For example, enterprises may make a substantial contribution to the local economy by providing employment and using local suppliers. Financial statements may assist the public by providing information about the trends and recent developments in the prosperity of the entity and the range of its activities.[18]

A strong element of public interest has been aroused in recent years by environmental issues and the impact of companies on the environment. There are costs imposed on others when a company pollutes a river or discharges harmful gases into the air. It may be perceived that a company is cutting corners to prune its own reported costs at the expense of other people. Furthermore, there are activities of companies today which will impose costs in the future. Where an oil company has installed a drilling rig in the North Sea, it will be expected one day to remove and destroy the rig safely. There is a question as to whether the company will be able to meet that cost. These costs and future liabilities may be difficult to identify and quantify, but that does not mean that companies should not attempt to do so. More companies are now including descriptions of environmental policy in their annual reports, but regular accounting procedures for including environmental costs and obligations in the financial statements have not yet been developed.

L04 **Activity 1.7**

Look back to the list of users of financial statements which you prepared earlier in this chapter. How closely does your list compare with the users described in this section? Did you have any in your list which are not included here? Have you used names which differ from those used in the chapter? Are there users in the chapter which are not in your list? If your list does not match the section, ask for help from your lecturer, tutor or other expert in the subject so that you are satisfied that this book will continue to meet your personal learning outcomes.

L05 ## 1.6 General purpose or specific purpose financial statements?

Some experts who have analysed the needs of users in the manner set out in the previous section have come to the conclusion that no single set of general purpose financial statements could meet all these needs. It has been explained in the previous section that some users already turn to special reports to meet specific needs. Other experts hold that there could be a form of general purpose financial statements which would meet all the needs of some user groups and some of the needs of others.

This textbook is written on the assumption that it *is* possible to prepare a set of general purpose financial statements which will have some interest for all users. The existence of such reports is particularly important for those who cannot prescribe the information they would like to receive from an organisation. That is perhaps because they have no bargaining power, or because they are many in number but not significant in economic influence.

Preparers of general purpose financial statements tend to regard the owners and long-term lenders as the primary users of the information provided. There is an expectation or hope that the interests of these groups will overlap to some extent with the interests of a wider user group and that any improvements in financial statements will be sufficient that fewer needs will be left unmet.[19]

The primary focus of the *Statement of Principles* is on general purpose financial statements.[20] It is based on the assumption that all potential users are interested, to varying degrees, in the financial performance and financial position of the entity as a whole.[21]

L05 ## 1.7 Stewards and agents

In an earlier section, the needs of investors as users were listed and the word 'stewardship' appeared. In the days before an industrial society existed, 'stewards' were the people who looked after the manor house and lands while the lord of the manor enjoyed the profits earned. Traditionally, accounting has been regarded as having a particular role to play in confirming that those who manage a business on behalf of the owner take good care of the resources entrusted to them and earn a satisfactory profit for the owner by using those resources. The *Statement of Principles* regards stewardship as being not merely about the safe-keeping and proper use of an entity's resources but also about their efficient and profitable use.[22]

As the idea of a wider range of users emerged, this idea of the 'stewardship' objective of accounting was mentioned less often (although its influence remains strong in legislation governing accounting practice). In the academic literature it has been reborn under a new heading – that of *agency*. Theories have been developed about the relationship between the owner, as 'principal', and the manager, as 'agent'. A conscientious manager, acting as an agent, will carry out his or her duties in the best interest of the owners, and is required by the law of agency to do so. However, not all agents will be perfect in carrying out this role and some principals will not trust the agent entirely. The principal will incur costs in monitoring (enquiring into) the activities of the agent and may lose some wealth if the interests of the agent and the interests of the principal diverge. The view taken in *agency theory* is that there is an inherent conflict between the two parties and so they spend time agreeing contracts which will minimise that conflict. The contracts will include arrangements for the agent to supply information on a regular basis to the principal.

While the study of agency theory in all its aspects could occupy a textbook in itself, the idea of conflicts and the need for compromise in dealing with pressures of demand for, and supply of, accounting information may be helpful in later chapters in understanding why it takes so long to find answers to some accounting issues.

L05 1.8 Who needs financial statements?

In order to keep the flavour of debate on accounting issues running through this text, two people will give their comments from time to time. The first of these is David Wilson, a fund manager of seven years' experience working for an insurance company. He manages a United Kingdom equity portfolio (collection of company shares) and part of his work requires him to be an *equities analyst*. At university he took a degree in history and has subsequently passed examinations to qualify as a member of the Institute of Investment Management and Research (IIMR).

The second is Leona Rees, an audit manager with a big accountancy firm. She has five years' experience as a qualified accountant and had previously spent three years in training with the same firm. Her university degree is in accounting and economics and she has passed the examinations to qualify for membership of one of the major accountancy bodies.

David and Leona had been at school together but then went to different universities. More recently they have met again at workout sessions at a health club, relaxing afterwards at a nearby wine bar. David is very enthusiastic about his work, which demands long hours and a flexible attitude. He has absorbed a little of the general scepticism of audit which is expressed by some of his fund manager colleagues.

Leona's main role at present is in company audit and she is now sufficiently experienced to be working on the audit of one listed company as well as several private companies of varying size. For two years she worked in the corporate recovery department of the accountancy firm, preparing information to help companies find sources of finance to overcome difficult times. She feels that a great deal of accounting work is carried out behind the scenes and the careful procedures are not always appreciated by those who concentrate only on the relatively few well-publicised problems.

We join them in the wine bar at the end of a hectic week for both.

DAVID: *This week I've made three visits to companies, attended four presentations of preliminary announcements of results, received copies of the projector slides used for five others that I couldn't attend, and collected around 20 annual reports. I have a small mound of brokers' reports, all of which say much the same thing but in different ways. I've had to read all those while preparing my monthly report to the head of Equities Section on the performance of my fund and setting out my strategy for three months ahead consistent with in-house policy. I think I'm suffering from information overload and I have reservations about the reliability of any single item of information I receive about a company.*

LEONA: *If I had to give scores for reliability to the information crossing your desk, I would give top marks to the 20 annual reports. They have been through a very rigorous process and they have been audited by reputable audit firms using established standards of auditing practice.*

DAVID: *That's all very well, but it takes so long for annual reports to arrive after the balance sheet date that they don't contain any new information. I need to get information at the first available opportunity if I'm to keep up the value of the share portfolio I manage. The meetings which present the preliminary announcements are held less than two months after the accounting year-end. It can take another six weeks before the printed annual report appears. If I don't manage to get to the meeting I take a careful look at what the company sends me in the way of copies of projector slides used.*

LEONA: *Where does accounting information fit in with the picture you want of a company?*

DAVID: *It has some importance, but accounting information is backward-looking and I invest in the future. We visit every company in the portfolio once each year and I'm looking for a confident management team, a cheerful-looking workforce and a general feeling that things are moving ahead. I'll also ask questions about prospects – how is the order book; which overseas markets are expanding; have prices been increased to match the increase in raw materials?*

LEONA: *Isn't that close to gaining insider information?*

DAVID: *No – I see it as clarification of information which is already published. Companies are very careful not to give an advantage to one investor over another – they would be in trouble with the Stock Exchange and perhaps with the Financial Services Authority if they did give price-sensitive information. There are times of the year (running up to the year-end and to the half-yearly results) when they declare a 'close season' and won't even speak to an investor.*

LEONA: *So are you telling me that I spend vast amounts of time auditing financial statements which no one bothers to read?*

DAVID: *Some people would say that, but I wouldn't. It's fairly clear that share prices are unmoved by the issue of the annual report, probably because investors already have that information from the preliminary announcement. Nevertheless, we like to know that there is a regulated document behind the information we receive – it allows us to check that we're not being led astray. Also I find the annual report very useful when I want to find out about a company I don't know. For the companies I understand well, the annual report tells me little that I don't already know.*

LEONA: *I'll take that as a very small vote of confidence for now. If your offer to help me redecorate the flat still stands, I might try to persuade you over a few cans of emulsion that you rely on audited accounts more than you realise.*

S01

Activity 1.8

As a final activity for this chapter, go back to the start of the chapter and make a note of every word which you have encountered for the first time. Look to the Glossary at the end of the book for the definition of each technical word. If the word is not in the Glossary it is probably in sufficiently general use to be found in a standard dictionary.

1.9 Summary

Now score your view of your confidence in achieving the learning outcomes of the chapter.

1 = Very confident about knowledge, application, problem solving and evaluation.

2 = Confident about knowledge and application, less sure about problem solving and evaluation.

3 = Need to read again to be more certain of basic knowledge and application.

L01 You have learned the definition of accounting and seen that the questions raised by the definition may be reversed in order to establish questions for a conceptual framework.   1   2   3 □ □ □

L02 You have learned that in the UK this conceptual framework is called the *Statement of Principles*, issued by the Accounting Standards Board (ASB). The *Statement of Principles* is designed to help the ASB to be consistent in setting accounting standards but it is also helpful to you in understanding current practice and thinking about new ideas in accounting.   1   2   3 □ □ □

L03 You are now able to explain the nature of three basic types of business entity: the sole trader; the partnership; and the limited liability company.   1   2   3 □ □ □

L04 You have read about the various users of accounting information and their needs for accounting information.   1   2   3 □ □ □

L05 You have read a discussion of whether some needs of users would be better served by special purpose financial statements, so that you are aware that there may be different views of what kinds of financial statements are best. This textbook will concentrate on the general purpose statements which are produced most widely. You have seen that themes common to all users are a need for information on: resources available to the business; obligations of the business to others; and adequate cash to support continuation of the business. Of particular interest to the owner is the profit earned by the business which will increase the owner's wealth.

1 2 3
□ □ □

LO6 If you wish to study the bookkeeping sections of the later chapters, you should now read the Supplement to this chapter which sets out the terminology of business transactions.

1 2 3
□ □ □

If your scores are all 1 or 2, try the questions in the series A, B and C. This will give you feedback on your assessment of how well you have achieved the learning outcomes. Read again any sections of the chapter where you find your knowledge and understanding are less comprehensive than you first estimated.

If your scores include some at 3, try the series A questions to find where the problems lie. Read the relevant sections again, work through any illustrative examples and case studies, then try the questions in the series B. Once you feel confident at that level of knowledge and application, move on to try some or all of the series C questions.

International perspective

A conceptual framework, called the *Framework for the Preparation and Presentation of Financial Statements*, has been adopted or adapted in many countries within a programme of following the guidance of the International Accounting Standards Board (IASB). In some countries this applies to large listed companies but not to the larger number of small companies and businesses. To understand national accounting practices it is important to identify the users of accounting and their information needs, which will depend on the political and economic environment of the country, and its cultural traditions.

Further reading

ASB (1999) *Statement of Principles for Financial Reporting*, chs 1 and 3, Accounting Standards Board.

ASSC (1975) *The Corporate Report*, Accounting Standards Steering Committee.

Beattie, V. (ed.) (1999) *Business Reporting: The Inevitable Change?*, Research Committee of The Institute of Chartered Accountants of Scotland.

ICAS (1988) *Making Corporate Reports Valuable*, discussion paper of the Research Committee of The Institute of Chartered Accountants of Scotland.

Marston, C. (1999) *Investor Relations Meetings: Views of Companies, Institutional Investors and Analysts*, Research Committee of The Institute of Chartered Accountants of Scotland.

Weetman, P. and Beattie, A. (eds) (1999) *Corporate Communication: Views of Institutional Investors and Lenders*, Research Committee of The Institute of Chartered Accountants of Scotland.

Note: Test your understanding *Series A* questions – answers can be found from the text. Application *Series B* questions and Problem solving and evaluation *Series C* questions – solutions to many of these are given in Appendix II.

Test your understanding

Skills outcomes
S01 Application of technical skills   S02 Problem solving and evaluation skills   S03 Communication skills

L01, S01 **A1.1** Define 'accounting' and identify the separate questions raised by the definition.

L01–L05, S01 **A1.2** The following technical terms appear for the first time in this chapter. Check that you know the meaning of each. (If you can't find them again in the text, there is a glossary at the end of the book.)

- accounting standards
- agency
- annual report
- broker
- business entity
- capital
- cash flow projections
- conceptual framework
- directors
- entity
- equities analyst
- external reporting
- financial accounting
- financial information
- financial statements
- fund manager
- general purpose financial statements

- Inland Revenue
- limited liability company
- liquidity
- loan covenants
- management accounting
- partnership
- portfolio [of investment]
- portfolio of shares
- Registrar of Companies
- share capital
- shareholders
- sole trader
- specific purpose financial statements
- stakeholders
- stewardship
- unsecured creditors

Application

L03, S01, S03 **B1.1** Brian and Jane are planning to work in partnership as software consultants. Write a note (100–200 words) to explain their responsibilities for running the business and producing accounting information about the financial position and performance of the business.

L03, L04, L05, S01, S03 **B1.2** Jennifer has inherited some shares in a public company which has a share listing on the Stock Exchange. She has asked you to explain how she can find out more about the financial position and performance of the company. Write a note (100–200 words) answering her question.

L03, L05, S01, S03 **B1.3** Martin is planning to buy shares in the company that employs him. He knows that the directors of the company are his employers but he wonders what relationship exists between the directors and the shareholders of the company. Write a note (100–200 words) answering his question.

Problem solving and evaluation

L01, L04,
S01, S02

C1.1 The following extracts are typical of the annual reports of large listed companies. Which of these extracts satisfy the definition of 'accounting'? What are the user needs that are most closely met by each extract?

(a) Suggestions for improvements were made by many employees, alone or in teams. Annual savings which have been achieved total €15m. The best suggestion for improvement will save around €0.3m per year for the next five years.

(b) As of 31 December, 3,000 young people were learning a trade or profession with the company. This represents a studentship rate of 3.9%. During the reporting period we hired 1,300 young people into training places. This is more than we need to satisfy our employment needs in the longer term and so we are contributing to improvement of the quality of labour supplied to the market generally.

(c) During the year to 31 December our turnover (sales) grew to £4,000 million compared to £2,800 million last year. Our new subsidiary contributed £1,000 million to this increase.

(d) It is our target to pay our suppliers within 30 days. During the year we achieved an average payment period of 33 days.

(e) The treasury focus during the year was on further refinancing of the group's borrowings to minimise interest payments and reduce risk.

(f) Our plants have emission rates that are 70% below the national average for sulphur dioxide and 20% below the average for oxides of nitrogen. We will tighten emissions significantly over the next 10 years.

L03, S01, S02

C1.2 Explain how you would class each of the following – as a sole trader, partnership or limited company. List any further questions you might ask for clarification about the nature of the business.

(a) Miss Jones works as an interior decorating adviser under the business name 'U-decide'. She rents an office and employs an administrative assistant to answer the phone, keep files and make appointments.

(b) George and Jim work together as painters and decorators under the business name 'Painting Partners Ltd'. They started the business 10 years ago and work from a rented business unit on a trading estate.

(c) Jenny and Chris own a hotel jointly. They operate under the business name 'Antler Hotel Company' and both participate in the running of the business. They have agreed to share profits equally.

Activities for study groups (4 or 5 per group)

Obtain the annual report of a listed company. Each member of the group should choose a different company. (Most large companies will provide a copy of the annual report in response to a polite request – or you may know someone who is a shareholder and receives a copy automatically.)

1 Look at the contents page. What information does the company provide?

2 Find the financial highlights page. What are the items of accounting information which the company wants you to note? Which users might be interested in this highlighted information, and why?

3 Is there any information in the annual report which would be of interest to employees?

4 Is there any information in the annual report which would be of interest to customers?

5 Is there any information in the annual report which would be of interest to suppliers?

6 Find the auditors' report. To whom is it addressed? What does that tell you about the intended readership of the annual report?

7 Note the pages to which the auditors' report refers. These are the pages which are regulated by company law, accounting standards and Stock Exchange rules. Compare these pages with the other pages (those which are not regulated). Which do you find more interesting? Why?

8 Each member of the group should now make a 5-minute presentation evaluating the usefulness of the annual report examined. When the presentations are complete the group should decide on five criteria for judging the reports and produce a score for each. Does the final score match the initial impressions of the person reviewing it?

9 Finally, as a group, write a short note of guidance on what makes an annual report useful to the reader.

Notes and references

1   AAA (1966) *A Statement of Basic Accounting Theory*, American Accounting Association, Evanston, Ill., p. 1.
2   ASSC (1975) *The Corporate Report*, Accounting Standards Steering Committee.
3   AICPA (1973) *Report of a Study Group on the Objectives of Financial Statements* (The Trueblood Committee), American Institute of Certified Public Accountants.
4   Solomons, D. (1989) *Guidelines for Financial Reporting Standards*, Research Board of The Institute of Chartered Accountants in England and Wales.
5   ICAS (1988) *Making Corporate Reports Valuable*, Research Committee of The Institute of Chartered Accountants of Scotland.
6   ASB (1999) *Statement of Principles for Financial Reporting*, Accounting Standards Board.
7   ICAS (1988), para. 3.3.
8   ASB (1999), ch. 1, 'The objective of financial statements', para. 1.3(a).
9   ASSC (1975), para. 2.8.
10   ICAS (1988), para. 3.12.
11   ASB (1999), para. 1.3(d).
12   *Ibid.*, para. 1.3(b).
13   *Ibid.*, para. 1.3(c).
14   *Ibid.*, para. 1.3(e).
15   ASSC (1975), para. 2.25.
16   *Ibid.*, para. 2.26.
17   ASB (1999), para. 1.3(f).
18   *Ibid.*, para. 1.3(g).
19   ICAS (1988), para. 3.7.
20   ASB (1999), Introduction, para. 7.
21   ASB (1999), para. 1.5.
22   ASB (1999), Appendix III, para. 13(a).

Introduction to the terminology of business transactions

The following description explains the business terminology which will be encountered frequently in describing transactions in this textbook. The relevant words are italicised. Other technical terms of accounting will be found in the text but these will be defined where they are used for the first time.

Most businesses are established with the intention of earning a *profit*. Some do so by selling goods at a price greater than that paid to buy or manufacture the goods. Others make a profit by providing a service and charging a price greater than the cost to them of providing the service. By selling the goods or services the business is said to earn *sales revenue*.

Profit arising from transactions relating to the operation of the business is measured by deducting from sales revenue the expenses of earning that revenue.

Sales revenue (often abbreviated to 'sales' and sometimes referred to as 'turnover') means the value of all goods or services provided to customers, whether for *cash* or for *credit*. In a *cash sale* the customer pays immediately on receipt of goods or services. In a *credit sale* the customer takes the goods or service and agrees to pay at a future date. By agreeing to pay in the future the customer becomes a *debtor* of the business. The name *debtor* is given to anyone who owes money to the business. The business will send a document called a *sales invoice* to the credit customer, stating the goods or services provided by the business, the price charged for these and the amount owing to the business.

Eventually the credit customer will pay cash to settle the amount shown on the invoice. If he pays promptly the business may allow him to deduct a discount for prompt payment. This deduction is called *discount allowed* by the business. As an example, if the customer owes £100 but is allowed a 5 per cent discount by the business, he will pay £95. The business will record cash received of £95 and discount allowed of £5.

The business itself must buy goods in order to manufacture a product or provide a service. When the business buys goods it *purchases* them and holds them as a stock of goods (sometimes referred to as 'inventory') until they are used or sold. The goods will be purchased from a supplier, either for *cash* or for *credit*. In a *credit purchase* the business takes the goods and agrees to pay at a future date. By allowing the business time to pay, the supplier becomes a *creditor* of the business. The name *creditor* is given to anyone who is owed money by the business. The business will receive a purchase invoice from the supplier describing the goods supplied, stating the price of the goods and showing the amount owed by the business.

Eventually the business will pay cash to settle the amount shown on the purchase invoice. If the business pays promptly the supplier may permit the business to deduct a discount for prompt payment. This is called *discount received* by the business. As an example, if the business owes £200 but is permitted a 10 per cent discount by the supplier, the business will pay £180 and record the remaining £20 as *discount received* from the supplier.

The purchase price of goods sold is one of the *expenses* of the business, to be deducted from sales revenue in calculating profit. Other expenses might include wages, salaries, rent, rates, insurance and cleaning. In each case there will be a document providing evidence of the expense, such as a wages or salaries slip, a landlord's bill for rent, a local authority's demand for rates, an insurance renewal note or a cleaner's time sheet. There will also be a record of the cash paid in each case.

Sometimes an expense is incurred but is not paid for until some time later. For example, electricity is consumed during a quarter but the electricity bill does not arrive until after the end of the quarter. An employee may have worked for a week but not yet have received a cash payment for that work. The unpaid expense of the business is called an *accrued expense* and must be recorded as part of the accounting information relevant to the period of time in which the expense was incurred.

On other occasions an expense may be paid for in advance of being used by the business. For example, a fire insurance premium covering the business premises is paid annually in advance. Such expenditure of cash will benefit a future time period and must be excluded from any profit calculation until that time. In the meantime it is recorded as *a prepaid expense* or a *prepayment*.

Dissatisfaction may be expressed by a customer with the quantity or quality of goods or service provided. If the business accepts that the complaint is justified it may replace goods or give a cash refund. If the customer is a credit customer who has not yet paid, then a cash refund is clearly inappropriate. Instead the customer would be sent a *credit note* for sales returned, cancelling the customer's debt to the business for the amount in dispute. The credit note would record the quantity of goods or type of service and the amount of the cancelled debt.

In a similar way the business would expect to receive a *credit note* from a supplier for *purchases returned* where goods have been bought on credit terms and later returned to the supplier because of some defect.

LO6, S01 | Test your understanding

S1.1 The following technical terms appear for the first time in this Supplement. Check that you know the meaning of each.

- Profit
- Sales revenue
- Cash sale
- Credit sale
- Debtor
- Discount allowed
- Purchases
- Cash purchase

- Credit purchase
- Creditor
- Discount received
- Expense
- Accrued expense
- Prepaid expense
- Credit note for sales returned
- Credit note for purchases returned

Chapter 2

A systematic approach to financial reporting: the accounting equation

After studying this chapter you should be able to:

LO1 Define and explain the accounting equation.

LO2 Define assets.

LO3 Apply the definition to examples of assets.

LO4 Explain and apply the rules for recognition of assets.

LO5 Define liabilities.

LO6 Apply the definition to examples of liabilities.

LO7 Explain and apply the rules for recognition of liabilities.

LO8 Define ownership interest.

LO9 Explain how the recognition of ownership interest depends on recognition of assets and liabilities.

LO10 Use the accounting equation to show the effect of changes in the ownership interest.

LO11 Explain how users of financial statements can gain assurance about assets and liabilities.

Additionally, for those who choose to study the Supplement:

LO12 Explain how the rules of debit and credit recording are derived from the accounting equation.

2.1 Introduction

Chapter 1 considered the needs of a range of users of financial information and summarised by suggesting that they would all have an interest in the resources available to the business and the obligations of the business to those outside it. Many of these users will also want to be reassured that the business has an adequate flow of cash to support the continuation of the business. The owners of the business have a claim to the resources of the business after all other obligations have been satisfied. This is called the *ownership interest* or the *equity* interest. They will be particularly interested in how that ownership interest grows from one year to the next and whether the resources of the business are being applied to the best advantage.

Accounting has traditionally applied the term *assets* to the resources available to the business and has applied the term *liabilities* to the obligations of the business to persons other than the owner. Assets and liabilities are reported in a financial statement called a *balance sheet*. The balance sheet is a statement of the financial position of the entity at a particular point in time. It may be described by a very simple equation.

L01 2.2 The accounting equation

The accounting equation as a statement of financial position may be expressed as:

Assets minus **Liabilities**	equals	**Ownership interest**

The ownership interest is the residual claim after liabilities to third parties have been satisfied. The equation expressed in this form emphasises that residual aspect.

Another way of thinking about an equation is to imagine a see-saw on which two containers are balanced. In one container are the assets (A) minus liabilities (L). In the other is the ownership interest (OI).

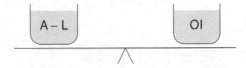

If anything happens to disturb the assets then the see-saw will fall out of balance unless some matching disturbance is applied to the ownership interest. If anything happens to disturb the liabilities then the see-saw will fall out of balance unless some matching disturbance is applied to the ownership interest. If a disturbance applied to an asset is applied equally to a liability, then the see-saw will remain in balance.

2.2.1 Form of the equation: national preferences

If you have studied simple equations in a maths course you will be aware that there are other ways of expressing this equation. Those other ways cannot change the magnitudes of each item in the equation but can reflect a different emphasis being placed on the various constituents. The form of the equation used in this chapter is the sequence which is applied in most balance sheets reported to external users of accounting information in the United Kingdom. In some Continental European countries the balance sheets reported to external users are better represented by another form of the equation:

Assets	equals	**Liabilities** plus **Ownership interest**

The see-saw analogy remains applicable here but the participants have moved to different parts of the see-saw.

A disturbance on one side of the balance will require a corresponding disturbance on the other side if the balance is to be maintained.

The form of the equation used in any particular situation is a matter of preference related to the choice of presentation of the balance sheet. That is a communication issue which will be discussed later. This chapter will concentrate on the nature of the various elements of the equation, namely assets, liabilities and ownership interest.

L01 | **Activity 2.1**

Make a simple see-saw from a ruler balanced on a pencil and put coins on each side. Satisfy yourself that the ruler only remains in balance if any action on one side of the balance is matched by an equivalent action on the other side of the balance. Note also that rearranging the coins on one side will not disturb the balance. Some aspects of accounting are concerned with taking actions on each side of the balance. Other aspects are concerned with rearranging one side of the balance.

L02 | ## 2.3 Defining assets

Assets are defined as: '*rights or other access to future economic benefits controlled by an entity as a result of past transactions or events*'.[1] To understand this definition fully, each phrase must be considered separately.

2.3.1 Rights or other access

The strongest form of right over an asset is the right of ownership. Sometimes, however, the entity does not have ownership but does have the right to use an item. This right may be very similar to the right of ownership. So far as the user of accounting information is concerned, what really matters is the availability of the item to the entity and how well the item is being used to earn profits for the business. Forms of 'other access' may include an agreement to lease or rent a resource, and a licence allowing exclusive use of a resource.

2.3.2 Future economic benefits

Most businesses use resources in the expectation that they will eventually generate cash. Some resources generate cash more quickly than others. If the business manufactures goods in order to sell them to customers, those goods carry a future economic benefit in terms of the expectation of sale. That benefit comes to the entity relatively quickly. The business may own a warehouse in which it stores the goods before they are sold. There is a future economic benefit associated with the warehouse because it helps create the cash flow from sale of the goods (by keeping them safe from damage and theft) and also because at some time in the future the warehouse could itself be sold for cash.

The example of the warehouse is relatively easy to understand, but in other cases there may be some uncertainty about the amount of the future economic benefit. When goods are sold to a customer who is allowed time to pay, the customer becomes a *debtor* of the business (a person who owes money to the business) and is regarded as an asset. There may be some uncertainty as to whether the customer will eventually pay for the goods. That uncertainty does not prevent the item being regarded as an asset but may require some caution as to how the asset is measured in money terms.

2.3.3 Controlled by the entity

Control means the ability to obtain the economic benefits and to restrict the access of others. The items which everyone enjoys, such as the benefit of a good motorway giving access to the business or the presence of a highly skilled workforce in a nearby town, provide benefits to the business which are not reported in financial statements because there would be considerable problems of identifying the entity's share of the benefits. If there is no control, the item is omitted.

The condition of control is also included to prevent businesses from leaving out of the balance sheet some items which ought to be in there. In past years, practices emerged of omitting an asset and a corresponding liability from a balance sheet on the grounds that there was no effective obligation remaining in respect of the liability. At the same time, the business carefully retained effective control of the asset by suitable legal agreements. This practice of omitting items from the balance sheet was felt to be unhelpful to users because it was concealing some of the resources used by the business and concealing the related obligations.

2.3.4 Past transactions or events

Accounting depends on finding some reasonably objective way of confirming that the entity has gained control of the resource. The evidence provided by a past transaction is an objective starting point. A transaction is an agreement between two parties which usually involves exchanging goods or services for cash or a promise to pay cash. (The supplement to Chapter 1 explains basic business transactions in more detail.) Sometimes there is no transaction but there is an event which is sufficient to give this objective evidence. The event could be the performance of a service which, once completed, gives the right to demand payment.

L02 **Activity 2.2**

Write down five items in your personal possession which you regard as assets. Use the definition given in this section to explain why each item is an asset from your point of view. Then read the next section and compare your list with the examples of business assets. If you are having difficulty in understanding why any item is, or is not, an asset you should consult your lecturer, tutor or other expert in the subject area for a discussion on how to apply the definition in identifying assets.

L03 ## 2.4 Examples of assets

The following items are commonly found in the assets section of the balance sheets of companies:

- land and buildings owned by the company
- buildings leased by the company on a 50-year lease
- plant and machinery owned by the company
- equipment leased (rented) by the company under a finance lease
- vehicles
- raw materials
- goods for resale
- finished goods
- work-in-progress
- trade debtors (customers who have promised to pay for goods sold on credit)
- prepaid insurance and rentals
- investments in shares of other companies
- cash held in a bank account.

Do all these items meet the definition of an asset? Exhibits 2.1 and 2.2 test each item against the four aspects of the definition which have already been discussed. Two tables have been used because it is conventional practice to separate assets into fixed assets and current assets. *Fixed assets* are held by the business for

Exhibit 2.1

Analysis of some frequently occurring fixed assets

	Rights or other access	Future economic benefits	Controlled by the entity by means of	Past transaction or event
Land and buildings owned by the company	Ownership.	Used in continuing operations of the business; potential for sale of the item.	Ownership.	Signing the contract as evidence of purchase of land and buildings.
Buildings leased (rented) by the company on a 50-year lease	Contract for exclusive use as a tenant.	Used in continuing operations of the business.	Contract for exclusive use.	Signing a lease agreeing the rental terms.
Plant and machinery owned by the company	Ownership.	Used in continuing operations of the business.	Ownership.	Purchase of plant and equipment, evidenced by receiving the goods and a supplier's invoice.
Equipment used under a finance lease	Contract for exclusive use.	Used in continuing operations of the business.	Contract for exclusive use.	Signing lease agreeing rental terms.
Vehicles owned by the company	Ownership.	Used in continuing operations of the business.	Ownership.	Purchase of vehicles, evidenced by taking delivery and receiving a supplier's invoice.

Exhibit 2.2
Analysis of some frequently occurring current assets

	Rights or other access	Future economic benefits	Controlled by the entity by means of	Past transaction or event
Raw materials	Ownership.	Used to manufacture goods for sale.	Ownership.	Receiving raw materials into the company's store, evidenced by goods received note.
Goods purchased from supplier for resale	Ownership.	Expectation of sale.	Ownership.	Receiving goods from supplier into the company's store, evidenced by the goods received note.
Finished goods (manufactured by the entity)	Ownership.	Expectation of sale.	Ownership.	Transfer from production line to finished goods store, evidenced by internal transfer form.
Work-in-progress (partly finished goods)	Ownership.	Expectation of completion and sale.	Ownership.	Evaluation of the state of completion of the work, evidenced by work records.
Trade debtors (customers paying on credit)	Firm contract where customer agrees to pay.	Expectation that the customer will pay cash.	Contract for payment.	Delivery of goods to the customer, obliging customer to pay for goods at a future date.
Prepaid insurance premiums	Contract for continuing benefit of insurance cover.	Expectation of continuing insurance cover.	Contract for insurance cover.	Paying insurance premiums in advance, evidenced by cheque payment.
Investments in shares of other companies	Ownership.	Expectation of dividend income and growth in value of investment, for future sale.	Ownership.	Buying the shares, evidenced by broker's contract note.
Cash held in a bank account	Ownership.	Expectation of using the cash to buy resources which will create further cash.	Ownership.	Depositing cash with the bank, evidenced by bank statement or certificate.

continuing use in the business while *current assets* are held with the intention of converting them into cash within the business cycle. The business cycle is the period (usually twelve months) during which the peaks and troughs of activity of a business form a pattern which is repeated on a regular basis. For a business selling swimwear, production will take place all winter in preparation for a rush of sales in the summer. Painters and decorators work indoors in the winter and carry out exterior work in the summer. Because many businesses are affected by the seasons of the year, the business cycle is normally twelve months. Some of the answers are fairly obvious but a few require a little further comment here.

First, there are the items of buildings and equipment which are rented under a lease agreement. The benefits of such leases are felt to be so similar to the benefits of ownership that the items are included in the balance sheet as assets. Suitable wording is used to describe the different nature of these items so that users, particularly creditors, are not misled into believing that the items belong to the business.

Second, it is useful to note at this stage that partly finished items of output may be recorded as assets. The term 'work-in-progress' is used to describe work of the business which is not yet completed. Examples of such work-in-progress might be: partly finished items in a manufacturing company; a partly completed motorway being built by a construction company; or a continuing legal case being undertaken by a firm of lawyers. Such items are included as assets because there has been an event in the partial completion of the work and there is an expectation of completion and eventual payment by a customer for the finished item.

Finally, it is clear that the relative future economic benefits of these assets have a wide variation in potential risk. This risk is a matter of great interest to those who use accounting information, but this text will show that there are generally no accounting techniques for quantifying this risk. Consequently, it is very important to have adequate descriptions of assets. Accounting information is concerned with the words used to describe items in financial statements, as well as the numbers attributed to them.

Definitions

Assets are rights or other access to future economic benefits controlled by an entity as a result of past transactions or events.[2]

A *fixed asset* is an asset that is held by an enterprise for use in the production or supply of goods or services, for rental to others, or for administrative purposes, on a continuing basis in the reporting entity's activities.[3]

A *current asset* is an asset that is expected to be converted into cash within the trading cycle (normally within twelve months of the date of the balance sheet).[4]

L04 2.5 Recognition of assets

When an item has passed the tests of definition of an asset, it has still not acquired the right to a place in the balance sheet. To do so it must meet further tests of recognition. *Recognition* means reporting an item by means of words and amounts within the main financial statements in such a way that the item is included in the arithmetic totals. An item which is reported in the notes to the accounts is said to be *disclosed* but *not recognised*.

The conditions for recognition have been expressed in the following words:

An item that meets the definition of an asset should be recognised if:

(a) sufficient evidence exists that the new asset has been created or that there has been an addition to an existing asset; and

(b) the new asset or the addition to the existing asset can be measured at a monetary amount with sufficient reliability.[5]

Sufficient evidence

What evidence is sufficient? Usually more than one item of evidence is looked for. In the case of fixed assets which have a physical existence, looking at them to make sure they do exist is a useful precaution which some auditors have in the past regretted not taking. Checking on physical existence is not sufficient, however, because the enterprise may have no control over the future economic benefit associated with the item. Evidence of the benefit from fixed assets may lie in: title deeds of property; registration documents for vehicles plus the purchase invoice from the supplier; invoices from suppliers of plant and equipment or office furniture; a written lease agreement for a computer or other type of equipment; and also the enterprise's internal forecasts of the profits it will make by using these fixed assets. This is the kind of evidence which the auditor seeks in forming an opinion on the financial statements.

For current assets the evidence of future benefit comes when the assets are used within the trading cycle. A satisfactory sales record will suggest that the present stock of finished goods is also likely to sell. Analysis of the time that credit customers have taken to pay will give some indication of whether the debtors should be recognised as an asset. Cash can be counted, while amounts deposited in banks may be confirmed by a bank statement or bank letter. Internal projections of profit and cash flow provide supporting evidence of the expected benefit from using current assets in trading activities.

Reliable measurement

Reliable measurement of assets can be quite a problem. For the most part, this textbook will accept the well-tried practice of measuring an asset at the cost of acquiring it, allowing for any reduction in value through use of the asset (depreciation) or through it falling out of fashion (obsolescence). The suitability of this approach to measurement will be discussed in Chapter 15 as one of the main unresolved problems of accounting.

Non-recognition

Consider some items which pass the definition test but do not appear in a balance sheet:

- The workforce of a business (a human resource)
- The strength of the management team (another human resource)
- The reputation established for the quality of the product
- The quality of the regular customers
- A tax refund which will be claimable against profits in two years' time.

These items all meet the conditions of rights or other access, future economic benefits, control and a past transaction or event. But they all have associated with them a high level of uncertainty and it could be embarrassing to include them in a balance sheet of one year only to remove them the following year because something unexpected had happened.

All these items fail one of the recognition tests and some fail both. The workforce as a whole may be reliable and predictable, but unexpected circumstances can come to all and the illness or death of a member of the management team can have a serious impact on the perceived value of the business. A crucial member of the workforce might give notice and leave. In relation to the product, a reputation for quality may become well established and those who would like to include brand names in the balance sheet argue for the permanence of the reputation. Others illustrate the relative transience of such a reputation by bringing out a list of well-known biscuits or sweets of thirty years ago and asking who enjoys them today. Reliable customers of good quality are valuable to a business, but they are also fickle and may change their allegiance at a moment's notice. The tax refund may be measurable in amount, but will there be taxable profits in two years' time against which the refund may be claimed?

It could be argued that the assets which are not recognised in the financial statements should be reported by way of a general description in a note to the accounts. In practice, this rarely happens because accounting tries to avoid raising hopes which might subsequently be dashed. This cautious approach is part of what is referred to more generally as *prudence* in accounting practice.

L05 2.6 Defining liabilities

Liabilities are defined as: *'obligations of an entity to transfer economic benefits as a result of past transactions or events'.*[6] This wording reads somewhat tortuously but has been designed to mirror the definition of an asset.

The most familiar types of liabilities arise in those situations where specific amounts of money are owed by an entity to specific persons called *creditors*. There is usually no doubt about the amount of money owed and the date on which payment is due. Such persons may be *trade creditors*, the general name for those suppliers who have provided goods or services in return for a promise of payment later. They may be *bankers* or other *lenders* who have lent money to the entity.

There are also situations where an obligation is known to exist but the amount due is uncertain. That might be the case where a court of law has found an entity negligent in failing to meet some duty of care to a customer. The company will have to pay compensation to the customer but the amount has yet to be determined.

Even more difficult is the case where an obligation might exist if some future event happens. Neither the existence nor the amount of the obligation is known with certainty at the balance sheet date. An example would arise where one company has guaranteed the overdraft borrowing of another in the event of that other company defaulting on repayment. At the present time there is no reason to suppose a default will occur, but it remains a possibility for the future.

The definition of liabilities tries to encompass all these degrees of variation and uncertainty. It has to be analysed for each separate word or phrase in order to understand the full implications.

2.6.1 Obligations

A legal obligation is evidence that a liability exists because there is another person or entity having a legal claim to payment. Most liabilities arise because a legal obligation exists, either by contract or by statute law.

However, a legal obligation is not a necessary condition. There may be a commercial penalty faced by the business if it takes a certain action. For example, a decision to close a line of business will lead to the knowledge of likely redundancy costs long before the employees are actually made redundant and the legal obligation becomes due. There may be an obligation imposed by custom and practice, such as a condition of the trade that a penalty operates for those who pay bills late. There may be a future obligation caused by actions and events of the current period where, for example, a profit taken by a company now may lead to a taxation liability at a later date which does not arise at this time because of the wording of the tax laws.

2.6.2 Transfer of economic benefits

The resource of cash is the economic benefit transferable in respect of most obligations. The transfer of property in settlement of an obligation would also constitute a transfer of economic benefits. More rarely, economic benefits could be transferred by offering a resource such as labour in settlement of an obligation.

2.6.3 Past transactions or events

A decision to buy supplies or to acquire a new fixed asset is not sufficient to create a liability. It could be argued that the decision is an event creating an obligation, but it is such a difficult type of event to verify that accounting prefers not to rely too much on the point at which a decision is made.

Most liabilities are related to a transaction. Normally the transaction involves receiving goods or services, receiving delivery of new fixed assets, or borrowing money from a lender. In all these cases there is documentary evidence that the transaction has taken place.

Where the existence of a liability is somewhat in doubt, subsequent events may help to confirm its existence at the balance sheet date. For example, when a company offers to repair goods under a warranty arrangement, the liability exists from the moment the warranty is offered. It may, however, be unclear as to the extent of the liability until a pattern of customer complaints is established. Until that time there will have to be an estimate of the liability. In accounting this estimate is called a *provision*. Amounts referred to as *provisions* are included under the general heading of *liabilities*.

L05

Activity 2.3

Write down five items in your personal experience which you regard as liabilities. Use the definition given in this section to explain why each item is a liability from your point of view. Then read the next section and compare your list with the examples of business liabilities. If you are having difficulty in understanding why any item is, or is not, a liability you should consult your lecturer, tutor or other expert in the subject area for a discussion on how to apply the definition in identifying liabilities.

L06 2.7 **Examples of liabilities**

Here is a list of items commonly found in the liabilities section of the balance sheets of companies:

- bank loans and overdrafts
- trade creditors (suppliers of goods and services on credit terms)
- taxation payable
- accruals (amounts owing, such as unpaid expenses)
- provision for deferred taxation
- long-term loans.

The first five items in this list would be classified as current liabilities because they will become due for payment within one year of the balance sheet date. The last two items would be classified as long-term liabilities because they will remain due by the business for longer than one year.

Definitions   *Liabilities* are the obligations of an entity to transfer economic benefits as a result of past transactions or events.[7]

Long-term liabilities are those liabilities expected to extend beyond one year from the balance sheet date.

Current liabilities are those liabilities expected to be repaid within one year of the balance sheet date.

L07 2.8 **Recognition of liabilities**

As with an asset, when an item has passed the tests of definition of a liability it may still fail the test of recognition. In practice, because of the concern for prudence, it is much more difficult for a liability to escape the balance sheet.

The condition for recognition of a liability uses wording which mirrors that used for recognition of the asset. The only difference is that the economic benefits are now expected to flow *from* the enterprise:

An item that meets the definition of a liability should be recognised if:

(a) sufficient evidence exists that the new liability has been created or that there has been an addition to an existing liability; and

(b) the new liability or the addition to the existing liability can be measured as a monetary amount with sufficient reliability.[8]

What kind of evidence is acceptable? For short-term liabilities there will be a payment soon after the balance sheet date and a past record of making such payments on time. For long-term liabilities there will be a written agreement stating the terms and dates of repayment required. The enterprise will produce internal forecasts of cash flows which will indicate whether the cash resources will be adequate to allow that future benefit to flow from the enterprise.

Reliable measurement will normally be based on the amount owing to the claimant. If goods or services have been supplied there will be an invoice from the supplier stating the amount due. If money has been borrowed there will be a bank statement or some other document of a similar type, showing the lender's record of how much the enterprise owes.

In cases which fail the recognition test, the documentary evidence is likely to be lacking, probably because there is not sufficient evidence of the existence or the measurable amount. Examples of liabilities which are not recognised in the balance sheet are:

- a commitment to purchase new machinery next year (but not a firm contract)
- a remote, but potential, liability for a defective product, where no court action has yet commenced
- a guarantee given to support the bank overdraft of another company, where there is very little likelihood of being called upon to meet the guarantee.

Because of the prudent nature of accounting, the liabilities which are not recognised in the balance sheet may well be reported in note form under the heading 'contingent liabilities'. This is referred to as *disclosure* by way of a note to the accounts.

Looking more closely at the list of liabilities which are not recognised, we see that the commitment to purchase is not legally binding and therefore the outflow of resources may not occur. The claim based on a product defect appears to be uncertain as to occurrence and as to amount. If there has been a court case or a settlement out of court then there should be a provision for further claims of a similar nature. In the case of the guarantee the facts as presented make it appear that an outflow of resources is unlikely. However, such appearances have in the past been deceiving to all concerned and there is often interesting reading in the note to the financial statements which describes the contingent liabilities.

An analysis of some common types of liability is given in Exhibit 2.3.

Exhibit 2.3

Analysis of some common types of liability

Type of liability	Obligation	Transfer of economic benefits	Past transaction or event
Bank loans and overdrafts (repayable on demand or in the very short term)	The entity must repay the loans on the due date or on demand.	Cash, potentially within a short space of time.	Receiving the borrowed funds.
Trade creditors (suppliers of goods and services)	Suppliers must be paid for the goods and services supplied, usually about 1 month after the supplier's invoice is received.	Cash within a short space of time.	Taking delivery of the goods or service and receiving the supplier's invoice.
Taxation payable (tax due on company profits 9 months after the balance sheet date)	Cash payable to the Inland Revenue. Penalties are charged if tax is not paid on the due date.	Cash.	Making profits in the accounting year and submitting an assessment of tax payable.
Accruals (a term meaning 'other amounts owing', such as unpaid bills)	Any expense incurred must be reported as an accrued liability (e.g. electricity used, gas used, unpaid wages), if it has not been paid at the balance sheet date.	Cash.	Consuming electricity or gas, using employees' services, receiving bills from suppliers (note that it is not necessary to receive a gas bill in order to know that you owe money for gas used).
Provision for deferred taxation (tax due in respect of present profits but having a delayed payment date allowed by tax law)	Legislation allows companies to defer payment of tax in some cases. The date of future payment may not be known as yet.	Cash eventually, but could be in the longer term.	Making profits or incurring expenditure now which meets conditions of legislation allowing deferral.
Long-term loans (sometimes called debenture loans)	Balance sheet will show repayment dates of long-term loans and any repayment conditions attached.	Cash.	Received borrowed funds.

L08   2.9 Defining the ownership interest

The ownership interest is the residual amount found by deducting all of the entity's liabilities from all of the entity's assets.[9]

The term *net assets* is used as a shorter way of saying 'total assets less total liabilities'. Because the ownership interest is the residual item, it will be the owners of the business who benefit from any increase in assets after liabilities have been met. Conversely it will be the owners who bear the loss of any decrease in assets after liabilities have been met. The ownership interest applies to the entire net assets. It is sometimes described as the owners' wealth, although economists would take a view that the owners' wealth extends beyond the items recorded in a balance sheet.

If there is only one owner, as in the sole trader's business, then there is no problem as to how the ownership interest is shared. In a partnership, the partnership agreement will usually state the profit-sharing ratio, which may also be applied to the net assets shown in the balance sheet. If nothing is said in the partnership agreement, the profit sharing must be based on equal shares for each partner.

In a company the arrangements for sharing the net assets depend on the type of ownership chosen. The owners may hold *ordinary shares* in the company, which entitle them to a share of any dividend declared and a share in net assets on closing down the business. The ownership interest is in direct proportion to the number of shares held.

Some investors like to hold *preference shares*, which give them a preference (although not an automatic right) to receive a dividend before any ordinary share dividend is declared. The rights of preference shareholders are set out in the articles of association of the company. Some will have the right to share in a surplus of net assets on winding up, but others will only be entitled to the amount of capital originally contributed.

Definitions

> The *ownership interest* is the residual amount found by deducting all of the entity's liabilities from all of the entity's assets.
>
> *Net assets* means the difference between the total assets and the total liabilities of the business: it represents the amount of the ownership interest in the entity.

L09   2.10 Recognition

There can be no separate recognition criteria for the ownership interest because it is the result of recognising assets and recognising liabilities. Having made those decisions on assets and liabilities the enterprise has used up its freedom of choice.

2.11 Changes in the ownership interest

It has already been explained that the owner will become better off where the net assets are increasing. The owner will become worse off where the net assets are decreasing. To measure the increase or decrease in net assets, two accounting equations are needed:

At time $t = 0$	**Assets**$_{(t0)}$ − **Liabilities**$_{(t0)}$	equals	**Ownership interest**$_{(t0)}$
At time $t = 1$	**Assets**$_{(t1)}$ − **Liabilities**$_{(t1)}$	equals	**Ownership interest**$_{(t1)}$

Taking one equation away from the other may be expressed in words as:

Change in (assets − liabilities)	equals	**Change in ownership interest**

or, using the term 'net assets' instead of 'assets − liabilities':

Change in net assets	equals	**Change in ownership interest**

The change in the ownership interest between these two points in time is a measure of how much better off or worse off the owner has become, through the activities of the business. The owner is better off when the ownership interest at time $t = 1$ is higher than that at time $t = 0$. To calculate the ownership interest at each point in time requires knowledge of all assets and all liabilities at each point in time. It is particularly interesting to know about the changes in assets and liabilities which have arisen from the day-to-day operations of the business.

The term *revenue* is given to any increase in the ownership interest arising from the operations of the business and caused by an increase in an asset which is greater than any decrease in another asset (or increase in a liability). The term *expense* is given to any reduction in the ownership interest arising from the operations of the business and caused by a reduction in an asset to the extent that it is not replaced by a corresponding increase in another asset (or reduction in a liability).

In addition to the effect of operations of the business, the owner or owners of the business may change the amount of the ownership interest by deciding to contribute more cash or other resources in order to finance the business or to withdraw some of the cash and other resources previously contributed or accumulated. The amount contributed to the business by the owner is usually referred to as *capital*. Decisions about the level of capital to invest in the business are *financing decisions*. These financing decisions are normally distinguished separately from the results of operations.

So another equation may now be derived as a subdivision of the basic accounting equation, showing analysis of the changes in the ownership interest.

Change in ownership interest	equals	**Capital contributed/withdrawn by the owner** plus **Revenue** minus **Expenses**

The difference between revenue and expenses is more familiarly known as profit. So a further subdivision of the basic equation is:

Profit	equals	**Revenue** minus **Expenses**

2.11.1 Revenue and expense

Revenue is created by a transaction or event arising during the operations of the business which causes an increase in the ownership interest. It could be due to an increase in cash or debtors, received in exchange for goods or services. Depending on the nature of the business, revenue may be described as sales, turnover, fees, commission, royalties or rent.

An expense is caused by a transaction or event arising during the operations of the business which causes a decrease in the ownership interest. It could be due to an outflow or depletion of assets such as cash, trading stock or fixed assets. It could be due to a liability being incurred without a matching asset being acquired.

Finding a working definition of revenues and expenses for first-year level of study is not so easy because the conceptual frameworks which are available in the United Kingdom and elsewhere try to use wording which has the widest possible coverage for all complexities of transaction. The following wording is adapted from the definitions given by the International Accounting Standards Board.

Definitions

Revenue is created by a transaction or event arising during the ordinary activities of the business which causes an increase in the ownership interest.

An *expense* is caused by a transaction or event arising during the ordinary activities of the business which causes a decrease in the ownership interest.

2.11.2 Position after a change has occurred

At the end of the accounting period there will be a new level of assets and liabilities recorded. These assets and liabilities will have resulted from the activities of the business during the period, creating revenue and incurring expenses. The owner may also have made voluntary contributions or withdrawals of capital as a financing decision. The equation in the following form reflects that story:

Assets minus **Liabilities** at the end of the period	equals	**Ownership interest at the start of the period** plus **Capital contributed/withdrawn in the period** plus **Revenue of the period** minus **Expenses of the period**

2.12 Assurance for users of financial statements

The definitions of assets and liabilities refer to expected flows into or out of the business. The recognition conditions refer to the evidence that the expected flows in or out will occur. The directors of a company are responsible for ensuring that the financial statements presented by them are a faithful representation of the assets and liabilities of the business and of the transactions and events relating to those assets and liabilities. Shareholders need reassurance that the directors, as their agents, have carried out this responsibility with sufficient care. To give themselves this reassurance, the shareholders appoint a firm of auditors to examine the records of the business and give an opinion as to whether the financial statements correspond to the accounting records and present a true and fair view. (Chapter 1 explained the position of directors as agents of the shareholders. Chapter 4 explains the regulations relating to company financial statements and the appointment of auditors.)

Meet again David and Leona as they continue their conversation on the work of the auditor and its value to the shareholder as a user of accounting information provided by a company.

DAVID: *I've now coated your ceiling with apple green emulsion. In return you promised to convince me that I rely on audited accounting information more than I realise. Here is your chance to do that. I was looking today at the annual report of a company which is a manufacturing business. There is a production centre in the United Kingdom but most of the production work is carried out in Spain where the operating costs are lower. The distribution operation is carried out from Swindon, selling to retail stores all over the UK. There is an export market, mainly in France, but the company has only scratched the surface of that market. Let's start with something easy – the stocks of finished goods which are held at the factory in Spain and the distribution depot in Swindon.*

LEONA: *You've shown right away how limited your understanding is, by choosing the asset where you need the auditor's help the most. Everything can go wrong with stocks! Think of the accounting equation:*

$$Assets - Liabilities = Ownership\ interest$$

If an asset is overstated, the ownership interest will be overstated. That means the profit for the period, as reported, is higher than it should be. But you won't know that because everything will appear to be in order from the accounts. You have told me repeatedly that you buy the future, not the past, but I know you look to the current profit and loss account as an indicator of future trends of profit. And so do all your friends.

DAVID: *How can the asset of finished goods stock be overstated? It's quite a solid item.*

LEONA: *There are two types of error – the physical counting of the stock and the valuation placed on it. There are two main causes of error, one being carelessness and the other an intention to deceive. I've seen situations where the stocktakers count the same stack of goods twice because they don't have a marker pen to put a cross on the items counted. I've also heard of situations where items are counted twice deliberately. We always attend the end-of-year counting of the stock and observe the process carefully. I wish there weren't so many companies with December year-ends. Stock counting on 2 January is never a good start to the new year.*

DAVID: *I suppose I can believe that people lose count but how does the valuation go wrong? All companies say that they value stock at cost as the usual rule. How can the cost of an item be open to doubt?*

LEONA: *Answering that question needs a textbook in itself. The subject comes under the heading of 'management accounting'. Take the goods that you know are manufactured in Spain. There are costs of materials to make the goods, and labour to convert raw materials into finished goods. There are also the running costs of the production unit, which are called the overheads. There is an unbelievable variety of ways of bringing those costs together into one item of product. How much does the company tell you about all that? I know the answer – nothing.*

DAVID: *Well, I could always ask them at a briefing meeting. I usually ask about the profit margin on the goods sold, rather than the value of the goods unsold. But I can see that if the stock figure is wrong then so is the profit margin. Do you have a systematic procedure for checking each kind of asset?*

LEONA: *Our magic word is* **CEAVOP**. *That stands for:*

Completeness of information presented.
Existence of the asset or liability at a given date.
Amount of the transaction is correctly recorded.
Valuation reported for assets and liabilities is appropriate.
Occurrence of the transaction or event took place in the period.
Presentation and disclosure is in accordance with regulations and accounting standards or other comparable regulations.

Every aspect of that list has to be checked for each of the assets and liabilities you see in the balance sheet. We need good-quality evidence of each aspect before we sign off the audit report.

DAVID: *I probably believe that you do a great deal of work with your CEAVOP. But next time I come round to paint your kitchen I'll bring a list of the situations where the auditors don't appear to have asked all the questions in that list.*

2.13 Summary

This chapter has set out the accounting equation for a situation at any one point in time:

Assets minus **Liabilities**	equals	**Ownership interest**

and explained the definitions of each item.

'Recognition' means reporting an item in the financial statements, in words and in amounts, so that the amounts are included in the arithmetic totals of the financial statements. Any other form of reporting by way of note is called 'disclosure'. The conditions for recognition of assets and liabilities are similar in wording.

At the end of an accounting period the assets and liabilities are reported in a balance sheet. Changes in the assets and liabilities during the period have caused changes in the ownership interest through revenue and expenses of operations. The owner may also have voluntarily added or withdrawn capital. The final position is explained on the left-hand side of the equation and the movement to that position is explained on the right-hand side:

Assets minus Liabilities at the end of the period	equals	Ownership interest at the start of the period plus Capital contributed/withdrawn in the period plus Revenue of the period minus Expenses of the period

As with any equation, it is possible to make this version more complex by adding further details. That is not necessary for the purpose of explaining the basic processes, but the equation will be revisited later in the book when some of the problems of accounting are opened up. The helpful aspect of the accounting equation is that it can always be used as a basis for arguing a feasible answer. The limitation is that it cannot give an opinion on the most appropriate answer when more than one option is feasible.

In Chapter 3 there is an explanation of how the information represented by the accounting equation is displayed in a form which is useful to the user groups identified in Chapter 1.

Now score your view of your confidence in achieving the learning outcomes of the chapter.

1 = Very confident about knowledge, application, problem solving and evaluation.

2 = Confident about knowledge and application, less sure about problem solving and evaluation.

3 = Need to read again to be more certain of basic knowledge and application.

		1	2	3
LO1	You can now define and explain the accounting equation.	□	□	□
LO2	You know the definition of an asset.	□	□	□
LO3	You can apply the definition to examples of assets.	□	□	□
LO4	You can apply the rules for recognition of assets, explaining when an asset qualifies for recognition and when it fails the recognition test.	□	□	□
LO5	You know the definition of a liability.	□	□	□
LO6	You can apply the definition to examples of liabilities.	□	□	□
LO7	You can apply the rules for recognition of liabilities, explaining when a liability qualifies for recognition and when it fails the recognition test.	□	□	□

LO8 You can define ownership interest as the residual item in the accounting equation, and you know the alternative terminology of 'equity' and 'net assets'.

1 2 3 ☐ ☐ ☐

LO9 You can explain how the recognition of ownership interest depends on recognition of assets and liabilities, with the consequence that there are no separate recognition criteria for ownership interest.

1 2 3 ☐ ☐ ☐

LO10 You can use the accounting equation to show the effect of changes in the ownership interest, particularly the revenues and expenses that arise because of the operations of the business.

1 2 3 ☐ ☐ ☐

LO11 You can now explain how users of financial statements gain assurance about assets and liabilities through reliance on the work of the auditor.

1 2 3 ☐ ☐ ☐

LO12 If you wish to develop skills of knowing how the rules of debit and credit recording are derived from the accounting equation, you should now read the Supplement.

1 2 3 ☐ ☐ ☐

If your scores are all 1 or 2, try the questions in the series A, B and C. This will give you feedback on your assessment of how well you have achieved the learning outcomes. Read again any sections of the chapter where you find your knowledge and understanding are less comprehensive than you first estimated.

If your scores include some at 3, try the series A questions to find where the problems lie. Read the relevant sections again, work through any illustrative examples and case studies, then try the questions in the series B. Once you feel confident at that level of knowledge and application, move on to try some or all of the series C questions.

International perspective

The accounting equation is universal. The arrangement of items either side of the 'equals' sign varies from one country to another. In countries that have a strong capitalist economy and a well-established structure of private ownership of companies, the accounting equation is written:

Assets minus **Liabilities**	equals	**Ownership interest**

In this form the equation is emphasising the role of the shareholders as the primary stakeholders in the company.

In countries that have a tradition of bank financing rather than stock market finance, and a less well-established structure of private ownership, the accounting equation is written:

Assets	equals	**Liabilities** plus **Ownership interest**

In this form the equation is giving more balanced recognition to lenders and shareholders as having stakeholder claims on the assets of the business.

Further reading

ASB (1999) *Statement of Principles for Financial Reporting,* chs 4 and 5, Accounting Standards Board.

Test your understanding

Skills outcomes
S01 Application of technical skills   **S02** Problem solving and evaluation skills   **S03** Communication skills

L01, S01 **A2.1** Write out the basic form of the accounting equation.

L02, S01 **A2.2** Define an asset and explain each part of the definition.

L03, S01 **A2.3** Give five examples of items which are assets.

L02, S01 **A2.4** Use the definition to explain why each of the items in your answer to (**A.2.3**) is an asset.

L04, S01 **A2.5** Explain what 'recognition' means in accounting.

L04, S01 **A2.6** State the conditions for recognition of an asset.

L04, S01 **A2.7** Explain why an item may pass the definition test but fail the recognition test for an asset.

L04, S01 **A2.8** Give three examples of items which pass the definition test for an asset but fail the recognition test.

L04, S01 **A2.9** Some football clubs include the players in the balance sheet as an asset. Others do not. Give the arguments to support each approach.

L05, S01 **A2.10** Define a liability and explain each part of the definition.

L06, S01 **A2.11** Give five examples of items which are liabilities.

L05, S01 **A2.12** Use the definition to explain why each of the items in your answer to (**A2.11**) is a liability.

L07, S01 **A2.13** State the conditions for recognition of a liability.

L07, S01 **A2.14** Explain why an item may pass the definition test but fail the recognition test for a liability.

L07, S01 **A2.15** Explain why the recognition tests for an asset may appear stricter than those for a liability.

L08, S01 **A2.16** Define the term 'equity'.

L08, S01 **A2.17** Explain what is meant by 'net assets'.

L09, S01 **A2.18** Set out the accounting equation for a change in the ownership interest.

L09, S01 **A2.19** Define 'revenue' and 'expenses'.

L010, S01 **A2.20** Set out the accounting equation which represents the position after a change has occurred.

All L0s, S01 **A2.21** Explain the auditor's approach to giving assurance about assets and liabilities.

Application

LO2, LO3, LO5, LO6, SO1   **B2.1** Classify each of the items in the following list as: asset; liability; neither an asset nor a liability:

(a) cash at bank
(b) loan from the bank
(c) letter from the bank promising an overdraft facility at any time in the next three months
(d) trade debtor (a customer who has promised to pay later)
(e) trade debtor (a customer who has promised to pay later but has apparently disappeared without leaving a forwarding address)
(f) supplier of goods who has not yet received payment from the business
(g) stock of finished goods (fashion clothing stored ahead of the spring sales)
(h) stock of finished goods (fashion clothing left over after the spring sales)
(i) investment in shares of another company where the share price is rising
(j) investment in shares of another company where the share price is falling
(k) lender of 5-year loan to the business
(l) customer to whom the business has offered a 12-month warranty to repair goods free of charge
(m) a motor vehicle owned by the business
(n) a motor vehicle rented by the business for one year
(o) an office building owned by the business
(p) an office building rented by the business on a 99-year lease, with 60 years' lease period remaining.

LO4, LO7, SO1   **B2.2** Explain whether each of the items from question **B.2.1** above which you have identified as assets and liabilities would also meet the conditions for recognition of the item in the balance sheet.

LO2–7, SO1   **B2.3** Explain why each of the following items would not meet *either* the definition *or* the recognition conditions of an asset of the business:

(a) A letter from the owner of the business, addressed to the bank manager, promising to guarantee the bank overdraft of the business.
(b) A list of the customers of the business.
(c) An order received from a customer.
(d) The benefit of employing a development engineer with a high level of 'know-how' specifically relevant to the business.
(e) Money spent on an advertising campaign to boost sales.
(f) Structural repairs to a building.

Problem solving and evaluation

LO10, SO2   **C2.1** The following information has been gathered from the accounting records of Pets Parlour:

Assets and liabilities at 31 December Year 4

	£
Cash at bank	500
Borrowings	6,000
Amounts due from debtors for services supplied	5,000
Property, plant and equipment	29,000

Revenue and expenses for the year ended 31 December Year 4

	£
Fees charged for work done	20,000
Interest paid on borrowings	1,000
Administration costs incurred	1,500
Salaries paid to employees	14,000

Required

Using the accounting equation, calculate:

(a) The amount of ownership interest at 31 December Year 4.

(b) The amount of net profit for the year.

(c) The amount of the ownership interest at 1 January Year 4.

Activities for study groups

Obtain the annual report of a listed company. From the balance sheet list the items shown as assets and liabilities. (This will require you to look in detail at the notes to the accounts using the references on the face of the balance sheet.) Share out the list of assets and liabilities so that each person has four or five assets and four or five liability items.

1 Separately, using the definitions and recognition criteria, prepare a short statement explaining why each item on your list passes the tests of definition and recognition. State the evidence you would expect to see, as auditor, to confirm the expected future inflow of economic benefit from any asset and the expected future outflow of benefit from any liability.

2 Present your explanations to the group and together prepare a list of assets and a separate list of liabilities in order of the uncertainty which attaches to the expected future benefit.

3 Read the 'contingent liability' note, if there is one, to find examples of liabilities which have not been recognised but have been disclosed. Why will you not find a 'contingent asset' note?

Notes and references

1 ASB (1999) *Statement of Principles for Financial Reporting*, ch. 4, 'The elements of financial statements', para. 4.6.

2 *Ibid.*

3 ASB (1999) FRS 15, *Tangible Fixed Assets,* Accounting Standards Board, para. 2.

4 There is no 'official' definition of a current asset. It is assumed that any asset which is not fixed must be current. As a working guide, any expectation of benefit more than 12 months from the balance sheet date would need careful consideration as to whether it was preferable to classify it as a fixed asset.

5 ASB (1999), ch. 5, 'Recognition in financial statements', Principles section.

6 ASB (1999), ch. 4, para. 4.23.

7 ASB (1999), ch. 4, para. 4.23.

8 ASB (1999), ch. 5, Principles section.

9 ASB (1999), ch. 4, para. 4.37.

Debit and credit bookkeeping

You do not have to read this supplement to be able to progress through the rest of the textbook. In the main body of each chapter the explanations are all given in terms of changes in elements of the accounting equation. However, for those who would like to know how debits and credits work, each chapter will have a supplement putting into debit and credit form the material contained in the chapter.

Recording in ledger accounts

The double entry system of bookkeeping records business transactions in *ledger accounts*. It makes use of the fact that there are two aspects to every transaction when analysed in terms of the accounting equation.

A ledger account accumulates the increases and reductions either in a category of business activities such as *sales* or in dealings with individual *customers* and *suppliers*.

Ledger accounts may be subdivided. Sales could be subdivided into *home sales* and *export sales*. Separate ledger accounts might be kept for each type of fixed asset, e.g. *buildings* and *machinery*. The ledger account for machinery might be sub-divided as *office machinery* and *production machinery*.

Ledger accounts for *rent, business rates* and *property insurance* might be kept sep-arately or the business might instead choose to keep one ledger account to record transactions in all of these items, giving them the collective name *administrative expenses*. The decision would depend on the number of transactions in an account-ing period and on whether it was useful to have separate records.

The managers of the business have discretion to combine or subdivide ledger accounts to suit the information requirements of the business concerned.

Using the accounting equation

Before entries are made in ledger accounts, the double entry system of bookkeeping assigns to each aspect of a business transaction a *debit* or a *credit* notation, based on the analysis of the transaction using the accounting equation.

In its simplest form the accounting equation is stated as:

Assets minus **Liabilities**	equals	**Ownership interest**

To derive the debit and credit rules it is preferable to rearrange the equation so that there is no minus sign.

Assets	equals	**Liabilities** plus **Ownership interest**

There are three elements to the equation and each one of these elements may either *increase* or *decrease* as a result of a transaction or event. The six possibilities are set out in Exhibit 2.4. The double entry bookkeeping system uses this classification (which preserves the symmetry of the equation) to distinguish debit and credit entries as shown in Exhibit 2.5.

Exhibit 2.4

Combinations of increases and decreases of the main elements of transactions

Left-hand side of the equation		
Assets	Increase	Decrease
Right-hand side of the equation		
Liabilities	Decrease	Increase
Ownership interest	Decrease	Increase

Exhibit 2.5

Rules of debit and credit for ledger entries, basic accounting equation

	Debit entries in a ledger account	Credit entries in a ledger account
Left-hand side of the equation		
Asset	Increase	Decrease
Right-hand side of the equation		
Liability	Decrease	Increase
Ownership interest	Decrease	Increase

It was shown in the main body of the chapter that the ownership interest may be increased by:

- earning revenue; and
- new capital contributed by the owner;

and that the ownership interest may be decreased by:

- incurring expenses; and
- capital withdrawn by the owner.

So the 'ownership interest' section of Exhibit 2.5 may be expanded as shown in Exhibit 2.6.

Exhibit 2.6

Rules of debit and credit for ledger entries, distinguishing different aspects of ownership interest

	Debit entries in a ledger account	Credit entries in a ledger account
Left-hand side of the equation		
Asset	Increase	Decrease
Right-hand side of the equation		
Liability	Decrease	Increase
Ownership interest	Expense	Revenue
	Capital withdrawn	Capital contributed

That is all you ever have to know about the rules of bookkeeping. All the rest can be reasoned from this table. For any transaction there will be two aspects. (If you find there are more than two, the transaction needs breaking down into simpler steps.) For each aspect there will be a ledger account. Taking each aspect in turn you ask yourself: *Is this an asset, a liability, or an aspect of the ownership interest?* Then you ask yourself: *Is it an increase or a decrease?* From exhibit 2.6 you then know immediately whether to make a debit or a credit entry.

Examples of the application of the rules of debit and credit recording are given in the supplement to Chapter 5 for a service business and in the supplement to Chapter 6 for a manufacturing business. They will also be used in later chapters to explain how particular transactions are reported.

LO12, S01 ## Test your understanding

(The answer to each of the following questions is either *debit* or *credit*)

S2.1 What is the bookkeeping entry for an increase in an asset?

S2.2 What is the bookkeeping entry for a decrease in a liability?

S2.3 What is the bookkeeping entry for an increase in an expense?

S2.4 What is the bookkeeping entry for a withdrawal of owner's capital?

S2.5 What is the bookkeeping entry for an increase in revenue?

Chapter 3

Financial statements from the accounting equation

After studying this chapter you should be able to:

LO1 Explain the benefits and problems of producing annual financial statements.

LO2 Explain the purpose and structure of the balance sheet.

LO3 Explain the purpose and structure of the profit and loss account.

LO4 Explain the purpose and structure of the cash flow statement.

LO5 Comment on the usefulness to users of the financial statements prepared.

Additionally for those who choose to study the Supplement:

LO6 Apply the debit and credit form of analysis to the transactions of a short period of time, summarising them in a list which may be used for preparation of simple financial statements.

3.1 Introduction

In the previous chapter the accounting equation was developed as a representation of the relationships among key items of accounting information: assets, liabilities and the ownership interest. An understanding of the accounting equation and the various elements of the equation provides a systematic approach to analysing transactions and events, but it gives no guidance as to how the results should be communicated in a manner which will be helpful and meaningful to users. The accounting equation is used in this chapter as a basis for explaining the structure of financial statements. Ideas beyond the accounting equation are required as to what qualities are expected of financial statements.

The various financial statements produced by enterprises for the owners and other external users are derived from the accounting equation. The Statement of Principles identifies the purposes of financial reporting as producing information about the financial position, performance and financial adaptability of the enterprise. The three most familiar primary financial statements, and their respective purposes, are:

Primary financial statement	*Purpose is to report*
Balance sheet	Financial position
Profit and loss account	Performance
Cash flow statement	Financial adaptability

LO1 ## 3.2 The accounting period

In the far-away days of traders sailing out of Italian ports on three-year voyages, the accounting period was determined by the date of return of the ship, when the accounts could be prepared for the whole voyage. That rather leisurely view of the scale of time would not be tolerated in an industrial and commercial society where there is always someone demanding information. The convention is that businesses should prepare financial statements at least once in every calendar year. That convention is a requirement of law expressed in the Companies Act 1985 in the case of limited liability companies. Where companies have a Stock Exchange listing they are required to produce an interim report six months into the accounting year. Some companies voluntarily produce quarterly reports to shareholders, reflecting the practice of listed companies in the United States. For internal management accounting purposes, a business may produce reports more frequently (e.g. on a monthly or a weekly basis).

Businesses may choose their accounting date as a time convenient to their activities. Many companies choose 31 December for the year-end, but others (including many of the utility companies which were formerly owned by the government) use 31 March. Some prefer a September or October date after the peak of the summer sales has passed. Whatever the choice, companies are expected to keep the same date from one year to the next unless there is a strong reason for changing.

The use of a 12-month accounting period should not be too much of a problem where the trading cycle fits neatly into a year. If the business is seasonal, there will be a peak of production to match the seasonal peak of sales and the pattern will be repeated every year. There could be a few technical problems of deciding exactly how to close the door on 31 December and whether transactions towards the end of the year are to be included in that year or carried to the next period. These problems can be dealt with by having systematic 'cut-off' rules. There is a bigger problem for those companies whose trading cycle is much longer. It could take two years to build a section of a motorway or three years to build a bridge over a wide river estuary. Such a company will have to subdivide the work on the main contract so that some can be reported each year.

The use of the 12-month accounting period also causes problems for recognition of assets and liabilities. Waiting for the ship to arrive was much safer evidence for the Venetian traders than hoping it was still afloat or relying on reported sightings. For today's business the equivalent situation would be waiting for a property to be sold or for a large customer to pay the amount due as a debt. However, in practice the balance sheet cannot wait. Notes to the accounts give additional explanations to help users of financial statements evaluate the risk, but it is all quite tentative.

L02 ## 3.3 The balance sheet

The balance sheet reflects the accounting equation in the form:

Assets minus **Liabilities**	equals	**Ownership interest**

It is usually presented in a narrative form, reading down the page, as:

Assets
minus
Liabilities
equals
Ownership interest

The assets are subdivided into fixed assets and current assets (defined in Chapter 2), while the liabilities are subdivided into current liabilities (due within one year) and longer-term liabilities (due after one year). The ownership interest may also be subdivided to show separately the capital contributed or withdrawn and the profit of the period. Because current assets and current liabilities are closely inter-twined in the day-to-day operations of the business, they are grouped close to each other in the balance sheet (Exhibit 3.1).

Exhibit 3.1
Structure of a balance sheet

Fixed assets
plus
Current assets
minus
Current liabilities
minus
Liabilities due after one year
equals
Capital at start of year plus/minus **Capital contributed or withdrawn** plus **Profit of the period**

Exhibit 3.1 is sufficient to explain the structure of any balance sheet, however complex it may be. This format is used in the Companies Act 1985 (although with more detail) as one of the permitted formats and it is the one most commonly used by companies. Most companies will try to confine the balance sheet to a single side of A4 paper but there is not much space on one sheet of A4 paper to fit in all the assets and liabilities of a company. Consequently a great deal of use is made of notes to the accounts which explain more detail. The balance sheet shows only the main categories of assets and liabilities.

3.3.1 Example of balance sheet presentation

The following list of assets and liabilities of P. Mason's legal practice was prepared from the accounting records of transactions summarised at 30 September Year 5:

	£
Land and buildings	250,000
Office furniture	30,000
Debtors for fees	1,200
Prepayment of insurance premium	540
Cash at bank	15,280
Total assets (A)	**297,020**
Trade creditors for supplies	2,800
Long-term loan	150,000
Total liabilities (L)	**152,800**
Ownership interest (A − L)	**144,220**

Exhibit 3.2 shows how this would appear in a balance sheet.

L02 **Activity 3.1**

Before looking at Exhibit 3.2, make sure that you can explain why each item in the accounting records is an asset or a liability, as shown in the foregoing list. If you have any doubts, read Chapter 2 again before proceeding with this chapter.

Exhibit 3.2

Presenting information on assets and liabilities, in a useful format

<table>
<tr><td colspan="3" align="center">P. Mason's legal practice
Balance sheet at 30 September Year 5</td></tr>
<tr><td></td><td align="right">£</td><td align="right">£</td></tr>
<tr><td>Fixed assets</td><td></td><td></td></tr>
<tr><td>Land and buildings</td><td></td><td align="right">250,000</td></tr>
<tr><td>Office furniture</td><td></td><td align="right">30,000</td></tr>
<tr><td>Total fixed assets</td><td></td><td align="right">280,000</td></tr>
<tr><td>Current assets</td><td></td><td></td></tr>
<tr><td>Debtors for fees</td><td align="right">1,200</td><td></td></tr>
<tr><td>Prepayment of insurance premium</td><td align="right">540</td><td></td></tr>
<tr><td>Cash at bank</td><td align="right">15,280</td><td></td></tr>
<tr><td>Total current assets</td><td align="right">17,020</td><td></td></tr>
<tr><td>Current liabilities</td><td></td><td></td></tr>
<tr><td>Trade creditors</td><td align="right">2,800</td><td></td></tr>
<tr><td>Current assets less current liabilities</td><td></td><td align="right">14,220</td></tr>
<tr><td></td><td></td><td align="right">294,220</td></tr>
<tr><td>Long-term liabilities</td><td></td><td></td></tr>
<tr><td>Long-term loan</td><td></td><td align="right">150,000</td></tr>
<tr><td>Net assets</td><td></td><td align="right">144,220</td></tr>
<tr><td>Ownership interest</td><td></td><td align="right">144,220</td></tr>
</table>

3.3.2 Comment

The balance sheet in Exhibit 3.2 is more informative than the list of assets and liabilities from which it was prepared because it has been arranged in a helpful *format*. The first helpful feature is the use of *headings* (in bold) for similar items grouped together, such as fixed assets, current assets, current liabilities and long-term liabilities. The second helpful feature is the use of *subtotals* (identified by descriptions in italics and shaded) for similar items grouped together. The subtotals used in this example are those for: total fixed assets; total current assets; and current assets less current liabilities. There are no standard rules on use of subtotals. They should be chosen in a manner most appropriate to the situation.

A person using this balance sheet can see at a glance that there is no problem for the business in meeting its current liabilities from its resources of current assets. The financing of the business is split almost equally between the long-term liabilities and the ownership interest, a split which would not be regarded as excessively risky by those who lend to businesses. The fixed assets used as a basis for generating profits from one year to the next are collected together as a group, although the balance sheet alone cannot show how effectively those assets are being used. For that, a profit and loss account is needed.

L03 3.4 The profit and loss account

The profit and loss account reflects that part of the accounting equation which defines profit:

Profit	equals	Revenue minus Expenses

As with the balance sheet, it is presented in a vertical form so that it can be read down the page as a narrative (Exhibit 3.3).

Exhibit 3.3
Structure of a profit and loss account

Revenue
minus
Expenses
equals
Profit

3.4.1 Example of profit and loss account presentation

The accounting records of P. Mason's legal practice at 30 September Year 5 showed that the ownership interest could be explained as follows (using brackets to show negative items):

	£
Increases in ownership interest	
Capital contributed at start of month	140,000
Fees	8,820
Decreases in ownership interest	
Computer rental and on-line searches	(1,500)
Gas	(100)
Electricity	(200)
Telephone/fax	(1,000)
Salary of assistant	(1,800)
Ownership interest at end of month	144,220

The profit and loss account is quite simple, as shown in Exhibit 3.4.

Exhibit 3.4

Financial statement of profit and loss, in a useful format

P. Mason's legal practice Profit and loss account for the month of September		
	£	£
Revenues		
Fees		8,820
Expenses		
Computer rental and on-line searches	(1,500)	
Gas	(100)	
Electricity	(200)	
Telephone/fax	(1,000)	
Salary of assistant	(1,800)	
Total expenses		4,600
Net profit of the month		4,220

3.4.2 Comment

The profit and loss account improves on the mere list of constituent items by providing headings (shown in bold) for each main category. As this is a very simple example, only two headings and one subtotal are required. Headings and subtotals are most useful where there are groups of items of a similar nature. The resulting net profit shows how the revenues and expenses have contributed overall to increasing the ownership interest during the month.

L03 **Activity 3.2**

Taking each item of the profit and loss account in turn, explain to an imaginary friend why each item of revenue and expense is regarded as increasing or decreasing the ownership interest. If necessary, look back to the definitions of revenue and expense in Chapter 2. Make sure that you feel confident about the profit and loss account before you move on.

L04 ## 3.5 The cash flow statement

It was shown in Chapter 1 that liquidity is of interest to more than one user group, but of particular interest to creditors of the business.

Liquidity is measured by the cash and near-cash assets and the change in those assets, so a financial statement which explains cash flows should be of general interest to user groups:

Cash flow	equals	**Cash inflows to the enterprise** minus **Cash outflows from the enterprise**

The cash flow statement will appear in a vertical form:

Cash inflows
minus
Cash outflows
equals
Change in cash assets

In a business there will be different factors causing the inflows and outflows of cash. The enterprise will try to make clear what the different causes are. Sub-divisions are commonly used for operating activities, investing activities and financing activities. *Operating activities* are the actions of buying and selling goods, or manufacturing goods for resale, or providing a service to customers. *Investing activities* are the actions of buying and selling fixed assets for long-term purposes. *Financing activities* are the actions of raising and repaying the long-term finance of the business. Exhibit 3.5 sets out the basic structure of a basic cash flow statement.

Exhibit 3.5
Structure of a cash flow statement

Operating activities **Cash inflows** minus **Cash outflows**
plus
Investing activities **Cash inflows** minus **Cash outflows**
plus
Financing activities **Cash inflows** minus **Cash outflows**
equals
Change in cash assets

3.5.1 Example of cash flow presentation

The cash transactions of P. Mason's legal practice for the month of September were recorded as follows:

Accounting records

Year 5		£
Cash received		
Sept. 1	Capital contributed by P. Mason	140,000
Sept. 1	Loan from bank	150,000
Sept. 19	Fees received from clients	7,620
	Total cash received	297,620
Cash paid		
Sept. 1	Land and buildings	250,000
Sept. 5	Prepayment of insurance premium	540
Sept. 26	Supplier for office furniture	30,000
Sept. 30	Salaries	1,800
	Total cash paid	282,340
	Cash remaining at 30 September	15,280

The cash flow statement would be presented as shown in Exhibit 3.6.

Exhibit 3.6
Financial statement showing cash flows of an enterprise

P. Mason's legal practice Cash flow statement for the month of September Year 5	
Operating activities	£
Inflow from fees	7,620
Outflow to insurance premium	(540)
Outflows to salaries	(1,800)
Net inflow from operations	5,280
Investing activities	
Payment for land and building	(250,000)
Payment for office furniture	(30,000)
Net outflow for investing activities	(280,000)
Financing activities	
Capital contributed by owner	140,000
Five-year loan from bank	150,000
Net inflow from financing activities	290,000
Increase in cash at bank over period	15,280

3.5.2 Comment

The cash flows, listed at the start of section 3.5.1 in the accounting records for the legal practice, relate to three different types of activity which are brought out more clearly in the cash flow statement by the use of headings and subtotals. The headings are shown in bold and the subtotals are highlighted by italics and shading. The story emerging from the cash flow statement is that the owner put in £140,000 and the bank lent £150,000, providing a total of £290,000 in start-up finance. Of this amount, £280,000 was used during the month to pay for fixed assets. That left £10,000 which, when added to the positive cash flow from operations, explains why the cash resources increased by £15,280 over the month.

It is quite common to compare the increase in ownership claim caused by making a profit with the increase in the cash resources of a business caused by operations. In this case the profit is £4,220 (Exhibit 3.4) but the operations have added £5,280 to the cash assets of the business.

To make the comparison, Exhibit 3.7 takes the profit and loss account of Exhibit 3.4 and sets alongside it the cash flows relating to operations.

Exhibit 3.7

Comparison of profit and cash flow for the month of September

P. Mason's legal practice	Profit £	Cash flow £
Revenues		
Fees/cash received	8,820	7,620
Expenses		
Computer rental and on-line searches	(1,500)	nil
Gas	(100)	nil
Electricity	(200)	nil
Telephone/fax	(1,000)	nil
Salary of assistant	(1,800)	(1,800)
Payment for insurance premium	nil	(540)
Total expenses/total cash paid	4,600	(2,340)
Net profit of the month	4,220	
Increase in cash in the month		5,280

Exhibit 3.7 shows that the cash flow from fees was £1,200 less than the fee revenue earned because some customers had not paid at the month end. This is the amount shown in the balance sheet (Exhibit 3.2) as debtors for fees. Exhibit 3.7 also shows that expenses of rental, gas, electricity and telephone amounting to £2,800 in total had not been paid at the month end. These are shown as trade creditors for supplies in the balance sheet. The cash flow from operations is reduced by the payment for the insurance premium which does not affect the profit and loss account for the month.

Users of financial statements regard both the profit and the cash flow as interesting items of information. The profit shows the overall increase in ownership claim which contributes to the overall wealth of the business. The cash flow shows the ability of the business to survive financially through planning the timing and amount of inflows and outflows of cash.

L05 3.6 Usefulness of financial statements

Here are Leona and David, still working on Leona's flat, discussing the usefulness of financial statements.

LEONA: *Which financial statement is the most important for you?*

DAVID: *It has to be the profit and loss account. Profit creates wealth. Future profit creates future wealth. I have to make a forecast of each company's profit as part of my planning to meet our overall investment strategy. Maybe I should qualify that by adding that cash flow is also important, especially where there is high uncertainty about future prospects.*

We talk about 'quality of profits' and regard some types of profit as of higher quality than others. Cash flow support is one aspect of that quality. We have doubts about some accounting amounts which don't have a close relationship to cash. A business cannot survive if it can't pay its way.

LEONA: *Where does that leave the balance sheet?*

DAVID: *I'm not sure. It is a list of resources and claims on those resources. We are shareholders and so we have a claim on those resources but we don't think about it to any great extent because we are concentrating on the going concern aspects of the business, rather than closing down and selling the assets. The balance sheet numbers don't mean very much because they are out of date.*

LEONA: *We studied research at university which suggested that cash flow is the answer and profit and loss accounts are too difficult to understand. It was suggested that the balance sheet should show what the assets could be sold for. I don't think the ideas had caught on in practice, but they seemed to have some merits.*

DAVID: *I like to know the dynamics of the business. I like to see the movements of different aspects and the interactions. I think I would feel that cash flow alone is concentrating on only one aspect of the wealth of the business. I suppose the balance sheet is a useful check on the position which has been reached as a result of making profits for the period. One thing we do look at in the balance sheet is how much has been borrowed for use in the business. We don't like to see that become too high in comparison with the ownership interest.*

LEONA: *At least you are admitting to seeing something in the financial statements. I still have to persuade you that the auditors are important in giving you the reassurance you obviously obtain.*

L05   **Activity 3.3**

Analyse your own view of wealth and changes in wealth. Which items would you include in your personal balance sheet today? Which items would you include in your personal 'profit and loss' account for the past year? Which items would you include in your personal cash flow statement? Has your view of 'wealth' been modified as a result of reading these first three chapters? If so, how have your views changed?

3.7 Summary

Now score your view of your confidence in achieving the learning outcomes of the chapter.

1 = Very confident about knowledge, application, problem solving and evaluation.

2 = Confident about knowledge and application, less sure about problem solving and evaluation.

3 = Need to read again to be more certain of basic knowledge and application.

LO1 Explain the benefits and problems of producing annual financial statements.

1	2	3
☐	☐	☐

LO2 Explain the purpose and structure of the balance sheet.

1	2	3
☐	☐	☐

LO3 Explain the purpose and structure of the profit and loss account.

1	2	3
☐	☐	☐

LO4 Explain the purpose and structure of the cash flow statement.

1	2	3
☐	☐	☐

LO5 Comment on the usefulness to users of the financial statements prepared.

1	2	3
☐	☐	☐

Additionally for those who choose to study the Supplement:

LO6 Apply the debit and credit form of analysis to the transactions of a short period of time, summarising them in a list which may be used for preparation of simple financial statements.

1	2	3
☐	☐	☐

If your scores are all 1 or 2, try the questions in the series A, B and C. This will give you feedback on your assessment of how well you have achieved the learning outcomes. Read again any sections of the chapter where you find your knowledge and understanding are less comprehensive than you first estimated.

If your scores include some at 3, try the series A questions to find where the problems lie. Read the relevant sections again, work through any illustrative examples and case studies, then try the questions in the series B. Once you feel confident at that level of knowledge and application, move on to try some or all of the series C questions.

International perspective

The balance sheet outlined in section 3.3 follows the pattern of the accounting equation favoured by UK companies, which is:

Assets minus **Liabilities**	equals	**Ownership interest**

In some countries of continental Europe the balance sheet is arranged differently as:

Assets	**Liabilities** plus **Ownership interest**

This reflects a different stakeholder perspective in the accounting equation:

Assets	equals	**Liabilities** plus **Ownership interest**

Companies in the USA commonly stack the asset section above the liabilities and ownership interest.

Assets
Liabilities plus **Ownership interest**

The terminology may also be different. For example 'trade debtors' becomes 'accounts receivable' in the USA, while 'trade creditors' becomes 'accounts payable' and 'profit' becomes 'net income'.

Test your understanding

Skills outcomes
SO1 Application of technical skills   SO2 Problem solving and evaluation skills   SO3 Communication skills

L01, SO1 **A3.1** Explain the problems created by using an accounting period of 12 months as the basis for reporting to external users of financial statements.

L02, SO1 **A3.2** Explain how the structure of the balance sheet corresponds to the accounting equation.

L03, SO1 **A3.3** Explain how the structure of the profit and loss account represents a subsection of the accounting equation.

L04, SO1 **A3.4** Explain how the structure of the cash flow statement represents another subsection of the accounting equation.

L05, SO1 **A3.5** List three features of a balance sheet format which are particularly useful in making the format helpful to readers.

L05, SO1 **A3.6** List three features of a profit and loss account format which are particularly useful in making the format helpful to readers.

L05, SO1 **A3.7** List three features of a cash flow statement format which are particularly useful in making the format helpful to readers.

Application

L02, L03, SO1 **B3.1** John Timms is the sole owner of Sunshine Wholesale Traders, a company which buys fruit from farmers and sells it to supermarkets. All goods are collected from farms and delivered to supermarkets on the same day, so no stocks of fruit are held. The accounting records of Sunshine Traders at 30 June Year 2, relating to the year then ended, have been summarised by John Timms as follows:

	£
Fleet of delivery vehicles, after deducting depreciation	35,880
Furniture and fittings, after deducting depreciation	18,800
Debtors	34,000
Bank deposit	19,000
Trade creditors	8,300
Sales	294,500
Cost of goods sold	188,520
Wages and salaries	46,000
Transport costs	14,200
Administration costs	1,300
Depreciation of vehicles, furniture and fittings	1,100

Required
(a) Identify each item in the accounting records as either an asset, a liability, or owner-ship interest (identifying separately the expenses and revenues which contribute to the change in the ownership interest).
(b) Prepare a balance sheet at 30 June Year 2.
(c) Prepare a profit and loss statement for the year ended 30 June Year 2.

LO2, SO1 **B3.2** Prepare a balance sheet from the following list of assets and liabilities, regarding the ownership interest as the missing item.

	£
Trade creditors	43,000
Cash at bank	9,000
Stock of goods for resale	35,000
Land and buildings	95,000
Wages due to employees but not paid	2,000
Vehicles	8,000
Five-year loan from a bank	20,000

Explain how the balance sheet will change for each of the following transactions:

(a) The wages due to the employees are paid at £2,000.
(b) One-quarter of the stock of goods held for resale is destroyed by fire and there is no insurance to cover the loss.
(c) Goods for resale are bought on credit at a cost of £5,000.

Activities for study groups

Return to the annual reports your group obtained for the exercise in Chapter 1. Find the balance sheet, profit and loss account and cash flow statement. Use the outline formats contained in this chapter to identify the main areas of each of the published statements. Work together in preparing a list of features which make the formats useful to the reader. Note also any aspects of the presentation which you find unhelpful at this stage. (It may be useful to look back on this note at the end of the course as a collective check on whether your understanding and awareness of annual report items has improved.)

Using the accounting equation to analyse transactions

In the main body of the chapter the transactions of P. Mason's legal practice are set out in summary form and are then presented in financial statements. This supplement goes back one stage and looks at the transactions and events for the month of September which resulted in the summary and financial statements shown in the chapter.

The list of transactions and events is as follows:

Sept. 1   P. Mason deposits £140,000 in a bank account to commence the business under the name *P. Mason's legal practice.*

Sept. 1   P. Mason's legal practice borrows £150,000 from a finance business to help with the intended purchase of a property for use as an office. The loan is to be repaid in five years' time.

Sept. 1   A property is purchased at a cost of £75,000 for the land and £175,000 for the buildings. The full price is paid from the bank account.

Sept. 3   Office furniture is purchased from Stylecraft at a cost of £30,000. The full price is to be paid within 90 days.

Sept. 5   An insurance premium of £540 is paid in advance. The insurance cover will commence on 1 October.

Sept. 8   An applicant is interviewed for a post of legal assistant. She agrees to start work on 10 September for a salary of £24,000 per annum.

Sept. 11   Invoices are sent to some clients for work done in preparing contracts for them. The total of the invoiced amounts is £8,820. Clients are allowed up to 30 days to pay.

Sept. 19   Cheques received from clients in payment of invoices amount to £7,620.

Sept. 26   Payment is made to Stylecraft for the amount due for office furniture, £30,000.

Sept. 28   Bills are received as follows: for computer rental and on-line searches, £1,500; gas, £100; electricity, £200; and telephone/fax, £1,000.

Sept. 30   Legal assistant is paid salary of £1,800 for period to end of month.

In the Supplement to Chapter 2 a table was prepared, based on the accounting equation, showing the classification used for debit and credit bookkeeping entries. As a reminder, the form of the equation used to derive the debit and credit rules is:

Assets	equals	**Liabilities** plus **Ownership interest**

As a further reminder, the rules are set out again in Exhibit 3.8. Each of the transactions of P. Mason's legal practice for the month of September is now analysed in terms of the effect on the accounting equation and the resulting debit and credit entries which would be made in the accounting records.

Exhibit 3.8
Rules for debit and credit recording

	Debit entries in a ledger account	Credit entries in a ledger account
Left-hand side of the equation		
Asset	Increase	Decrease
Right-hand side of the equation		
Liability	Decrease	Increase
Ownership interest	Expense	Revenue
	Capital withdrawn	Capital contributed

Analysis of each transaction

Sept. 1   P. Mason deposits £140,000 in a bank account to commence the business under the name *P. Mason's legal practice*.

The business acquires an asset (cash in the bank) and an ownership interest is created through contribution of capital.

Transaction number: 1	Debit	Credit
Asset	Bank £140,000	
Ownership interest		Capital contributed £140,000

Sept. 1   P. Mason's legal practice borrows £150,000 from a finance business to help with the intended purchase of a property for use as an office. The loan is to be repaid in five years' time.

The business acquires an asset of cash and a long-term liability is created.

Transaction number: 2	Debit	Credit
Asset	Bank £150,000	
Liability		Long-term loan £150,000

Sept. 1   A property is purchased at a cost of £75,000 for the land and £175,000 for the buildings. The full price is paid from the bank account.

The business acquires an asset of land and buildings (£250,000 in total) and the asset of cash in the bank is reduced.

Transaction number: 3	Debit	Credit
Asset	Land and buildings £250,000	Bank £250,000

Sept. 3   Office furniture is purchased from Stylecraft at a cost of £30,000. The full price is to be paid within 90 days.

The business acquires an asset of furniture and also acquires a liability to pay the trade creditor, Stylecraft.

Transaction number: 4	Debit	Credit
Asset	Furniture £30,000	
Liability		Trade creditor (Stylecraft) £30,000

Sept. 5   An insurance premium of £540 is paid in advance. The insurance cover will commence on 1 October.

The business acquires an asset of prepaid insurance (the benefit of cover exists in the future) and the asset of cash at bank is reduced.

Transaction number: 5	Debit	Credit
Asset	Prepayment £540	Bank £540

Sept. 8   An applicant is interviewed for a post of legal assistant. She agrees to start work on 10 September for a salary of £24,000 per annum.

The successful outcome of the interview is an *event* and there is an expected future benefit from employing the new legal assistant. The employee will be controlled by the organisation through a contract of employment. The organisation has a commitment to pay her the agreed salary. It could be argued that the offer of employment, and acceptance of that offer, create an asset of the human resource and a liability equal to the future salary. That does not happen because the *recognition* conditions are applied and it is felt too risky to recognise an asset when there is insufficient evidence of the future benefit. Commercial prudence dictates that it is preferable to wait until the employee has done some work and pay her at the end of the month for work done during the month. The accounting process is similarly prudent and no accounting recognition takes place until the payment has occurred. Even then it is the expense of the past which is recognised, rather than the asset of benefit for the future.

Sept. 11   Invoices are sent to some clients showing fees due for work done in preparing contracts for them. The total of the invoiced amounts is £8,820. Clients are allowed up to 30 days to pay.

Earning fees is the main activity of the legal practice. Earning fees makes the owner better off and is an example of the more general activity *of increasing the ownership interest* by creating revenue. The clients have not yet paid and therefore the business has an *asset* called a debtor.

Transaction number: 6	Debit	Credit
Asset	Debtors £8,820	
Ownership interest (revenue)		Fees for work done £8,820

Sept. 19   Cheques received from clients in payment of invoices amount to £7,620.

When the customers pay, the amount due to the business from debtors will be decreased. So the asset of debtors decreases and the asset of cash in the bank increases.

Transaction number: 7	Debit	Credit
Asset	Bank £7,620	Debtors £7,620

Sept. 26   Payment is made to Stylecraft for the amount due for office furniture, £30,000.

The asset of cash in the bank decreases and the liability to Stylecraft decreases to nil.

Transaction number: 8	Debit	Credit
Asset		Bank £30,000
Liability	Trade creditor (Stylecraft) £30,000	

Sept. 28   Bills are received as follows: for computer rental and on-line searches, £1,500; gas, £100; electricity, £200; and telephone/fax £1,000 (total £2,800).

The computer rental, on-line searches, gas, electricity and telephone have been used up during the period and are all expenses which reduce the ownership interest. They are unpaid and, therefore, a liability is recorded.

Transaction number: 9	Debit	Credit
Liability		Trade creditors £2,800
Ownership interest	Expenses £2,800	

Sept. 30   Legal assistant is paid salary of £1,800 for period to end of month.

The asset of cash at bank decreases and the salary paid to the legal assistant is an expense of the month.

Transaction number: 10	Debit	Credit
Asset		Bank £1,800
Ownership interest	Expense £1,800	

Exhibit 3.9

Spreadsheet of transactions for P. Mason's legal practice, during the month of September

Date	Assets					Liabilities		Ownership interest		
	Land and buildings £	Office furniture £	Debtors £	Pre-payments £	Cash at bank £	Trade creditors £	Bank loan £	Revenue £	Expenses £	Owner's capital contributed £
1 Sept.					140,000 Dr					140,000 Cr
1 Sept.					150,000 Dr		150,000 Cr			
1 Sept.	250,000 Dr				250,000 Cr					
3 Sept.		30,000 Dr				30,000 Cr				
5 Sept.				540 Dr	540 Cr					
11 Sept.			8,820 Dr					8,820 Cr		
19 Sept.			7,620 Cr		7,620 Dr					
26 Sept.					30,000 Cr	30,000 Dr				
28 Sept.						2,800 Cr			2,800 Dr	
30 Sept.					1,800 Cr				1,800 Dr	
Total debit entries in each column										
	250,000 Dr	30,000 Dr	8,820 Dr	540 Dr	297,620 Dr	30,000 Dr	nil	nil	4,600 Dr	nil
Total credit entries in each column										
	nil	nil	7,620 Cr	nil	282,340 Cr	32,800 Cr	150,000 Cr	8,820 Cr	nil	140,000 Cr
Surplus of debits over credits (or credits over debits)										
	250,000 Dr	30,000 Dr	1,200 Dr	540 Dr	15,280 Dr	2,800 Cr	150,000 Cr	8,820 Cr	4,600 Dr	140,000 Cr

Summarising the debit and credit entries

The formal system of bringing together debit and credit entries is based on ledger accounts. These are explained in the supplement to Chapter 5. For the present it will be sufficient to use a spreadsheet (Exhibit 3.9) to show how the separate debit and credit entries analysed in this Supplement lead to the list of items used in the main part of the chapter as the basis for the financial statements presented there.

In the spreadsheet there are dates which correspond to the dates of the foregoing ten separate analyses of transactions. The debit and credit entries are shown with Dr or Cr alongside to distinguish them. For each column all the debit entries are totalled and all the credit entries are totalled separately. The surplus of debits over credits (or credits over debits) is calculated and shown in the final line. This allows a summarised list to be prepared as shown in Exhibit 3.10.

A spreadsheet is useful where there are not too many entries, but ledger accounts become essential when the volume of information increases.

Exhibit 3.10

Summary of debit and credit entries for each category of asset, liability and ownership interest

	Debit	Credit
	£	£
Assets		
Land and buildings	250,000	
Office furniture	30,000	
Debtors	1,200	
Prepayment	540	
Cash at bank	15,280	
Liabilities		
Trade creditors		2,800
Long-term loan		150,000
Ownership interest		
Revenue		8,820
Expenses	4,600	
Capital contributed		140,000
Totals	301,620	301,620

Note: The totals of each column have no particular meaning, but they should always be equal because of the symmetry of the debit and credit records, and so are useful as an arithmetic check that no item has been omitted or recorded incorrectly.

Turning the spreadsheet back to a vertical listing, using the debit column for items where the debits exceed the credits, and using the credit column for items where the credits exceed the debits, the list becomes as in Exhibit 3.10. You will see that this list is the basis of the information provided about P. Mason's legal practice in the main body of the chapter, except that the debit and credit notation was not used there.

LO6 **Activity 3.4**

The most serious problem faced by most students, once they have understood the basic approach, is that of making errors. Look back through this Supplement and think about the errors which might have been made. What type of error would be detected by finding totals in Exhibit 3.10 which were not in agreement? What type of error would not be detected in this way because the totals would be in agreement despite the error? Types of error will be dealt with in the supplement to Chapter 5.

Test your understanding

LO6, SO1 **S3.1** Analyse the debit and credit aspect of each transaction listed at (a), (b) and (c) of question **B3.2**.

LO6, SO1 **S3.2** Prepare a spreadsheet similar to that presented in Exhibit 3.9, setting out on the first line the items contained in the list of assets and liabilities of question **B3.2** and then on lines 2, 3 and 4 adding in the transactions (a), (b) and (c). Calculate the totals of each column of the spreadsheet and show that the accounting equation remains equal on both sides.

Chapter 4

Ensuring the quality of financial statements

After studying this chapter you should be able to:

L01 List and explain the qualitative characteristics desirable in financial statements.

L02 Explain the approach to measurement used in financial statements.

L03 Explain why there is more than one view on the role of prudence in accounting.

L04 Understand and explain how and why financial reporting is regulated or influenced by external authorities.

L05 Be aware of the process by which financial statements are reviewed by an investor.

4.1 Introduction

The previous chapter used the accounting equation as a basis for explaining the structure of financial statements. It showed that design of formats for financial statements is an important first step in creating an understandable story from a list of accounting data.

The objective of financial statements is to provide information about the reporting entity's financial performance and financial position, that is useful to a wide range of users for assessing the stewardship of management and for making economic decisions.[1]

A complete set of financial statements for a public limited company consists of a profit and loss account, a statement of total recognised gains and losses, a balance sheet and a cash flow statement, together with those notes and other statements and explanatory material that are specified as an integral part of the financial statements.[2]

L01   4.2 Qualitative characteristics of financial statements

To meet the needs of readers it is suggested[3] that accounting information in financial statements must have characteristics of:

- relevance;
- reliability;
- comparability; and
- understandability.

The provision of accounting information is also affected by a requirement that the information must meet the conditions of *materiality*. The ASB suggests that materiality is a test to be applied at the threshold of considering an item. If any information is not material, it does not need to be considered further.

Information is said to be *material* if it could influence users' decisions taken on the basis of the financial statements. The test to be applied is, 'Would the user make a different decision if this information were omitted or misstated?' If the information would make no difference then it is immaterial. Disclosing immaterial information may confuse the user by overloading the information. The materiality of the misstatement or omission depends on the size and nature of the item in question judged in the particular circumstances of the case.[4] It should be noted here that the application of materiality tests is very much dependent on circumstances and will vary from one accountancy practitioner to the next. Practising accountants and auditors usually guard quite jealously their private criteria for materiality but there have been those who would venture to suggest that any item which changes profit by 10 per cent or more is material while any item which changes profit by 5 per cent or less could well be immaterial, depending on the nature of the item. That leaves a rather grey area but serves as a starting point.

Furthermore, it may be the case that while an item in isolation is not in itself material, it becomes material when considered together with another related item. In this textbook the reader is not expected to make materiality decisions, but there is occasional reference to the idea of materiality in explaining various accounting practices.

The relationships between the various qualitative characteristics are summarised in Exhibit 4.1.[5] Each of these characteristics is now considered in turn.

4.2.1 Relevance and reliability

Information has the quality of *relevance* when it has the ability to influence the economic decisions of users and is provided in time to influence those decisions.[6] To be relevant, information must either help in making a prediction or help in confirming the outcome of a past prediction made by the user of the information.

Information has the quality of *reliability* when it is free from material error and deliberate or systematic bias and can be depended upon by users to represent faithfully what it either purports to represent or could reasonably be expected to represent.[7]

Information may be relevant but so unreliable that it could be misleading (for example, where a director has given a highly personal view of the value of an investment). On the other hand, it could be reliable but quite non-relevant (for example, the information that a building standing in the centre of a major shopping street was bought for 50 guineas some one hundred and fifty years ago). Relevance and reliability are twin targets which may cause some tension in deciding the most appropriate way to report accounting information. There is a trade-off between relevance and reliability when it comes to ensuring that information is delivered in a timely manner so that it is still relevant, and when it comes to deciding whether the costs of producing further information exceed the benefits.

1 Faithful representation

Faithful representation is important if accounting information is to be relevant and reliable. Faithful representation involves the words as well as the numbers in the

Exhibit 4.1
Diagram to show relationships of the qualitative characteristics of financial information

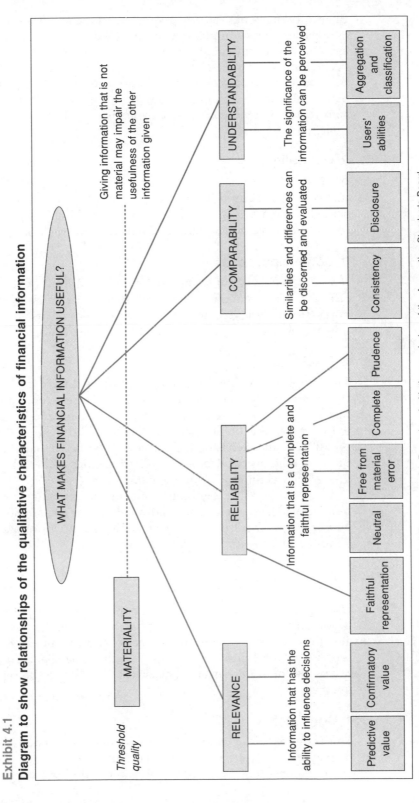

Source: ASB (1999) *Statement of Principles for Financial Reporting,* p. 34. Reproduced with the permission of the Accounting Standards Board.

financial statements and also requires that the *substance* of transactions or events is recorded. For example, if a company has sold its buildings to a bank to raise cash and then pays rent for the same buildings for the purpose of continued occupation, carrying all the risks and problems of being the owner, there could be a view that the commercial substance of that sequence of transactions is comparable to ownership, although the legal form is that there has been a sale. Information in the financial statements would show the commercial substance of the situation.[8]

2 Neutrality

Information is *neutral* if it is free from deliberate or systematic bias. Financial statements are not neutral if they include information that has been selected or presented in such a way as to influence the making of a decision or judgement in order to achieve a predetermined result or outcome.[9]

3 Completeness

It almost goes without saying that information cannot be reliable if it is not *complete*. The information in financial statements must be complete, within the bounds of materiality and cost. An omission can cause information to be false or misleading and thus to lack reliability and relevance.[10]

4 Prudence

The preparers of financial statements have to contend with uncertainty surrounding many events and circumstances. The existence of uncertainties is recognised by the disclosure of their nature and extent and by the exercise of *prudence* in the preparation of the financial statements. Prudence is the inclusion of a degree of caution in the exercise of the judgements needed in making the estimates required under conditions of uncertainty, such that gains and assets are not overstated and losses and liabilities are not understated.[11]

Decisions about recognition of income or assets and of expenses or liabilities require evidence of existence and reliability of measurement. Stronger evidence and greater reliability of measurement are required for assets and gains than for liabilities and losses.[12]

4.2.2 Comparability

Users must be able to compare the financial statements of an enterprise over time to identify trends in its financial position and performance. Users must also be able to compare the financial statements of different enterprises to evaluate their relative financial position, performance and financial adaptability. It is therefore necessary for similar events and states of affairs to be represented in a similar manner.[13]

1 Consistency

This is one aspect of comparability. Comparability requires the measurement and display of the financial effect of like transactions and other events to be carried out in a consistent way within each accounting period and from one period to the next, and also in a consistent way by different entities. However, the need for consistency should not be allowed to become an impediment to the introduction of improved accounting practices.[14] Consistency does not require absolute uniformity.

2 Disclosure of accounting policies

This is another important aspect of comparability. There must be disclosure of the *accounting policies* employed in the preparation of financial statements and also any changes in those policies and the effects of such changes.[15] The general guidance of the *Statement of Principles* is taken further in an accounting standard which requires that:

- an entity adopts the accounting policies most appropriate to its particular circumstances for the purpose of giving a true and fair view;
- the accounting policies adopted are reviewed regularly to ensure that they remain appropriate, and are changed when a new policy becomes more appropriate to the entity's particular circumstances; and
- sufficient information is disclosed in the financial statements to enable users to understand the accounting policies adopted and how they have been improved.

The annual report of a company will usually have a separate section headed 'Accounting policies'. It will be located immediately following the primary financial statements, leading into the detailed notes to the accounts. The statement of accounting policies is essential reading for any user of the annual report.

4.2.3 Understandability

It is essential that the information provided in financial statements is readily understandable by users.[16] Understandability depends on how information is aggregated, classified and presented. It also depends on the capabilities of users.[17] Users are assumed to have a reasonable knowledge of business and economic activities and accounting and a willingness to study the information with reasonable diligence. Information on complex matters should not be omitted from financial statements merely on the grounds that some users may find it difficult to understand. The ASB suggests that users who do not have a reasonable knowledge of business and economic activities and accounting will use the services of those who do have that knowledge to help them devise information from the financial statements.[18]

L01   **Activity 4.1**

> *Look back to Exhibit 4.1. Is there any aspect of that diagram which came as no surprise to you? Is there any aspect of that diagram which was a surprise to you? Having read the explanations in this section, do you hold the same surprise that you did at the outset? With the benefit of hindsight, can you explain why you were surprised or not surprised? Has this analysis caused you to modify your own objectives for what you hope to learn from the textbook?*

4.3 Measurement in financial statements

You have seen in Chapter 2, sections 2.5 and 2.8, that the recognition of assets and liability requires reliability of measurement. You have seen in Chapter 3 the methods of presentation of accounting information containing numbers that represent measurement. We now need to know more about the accounting measurement principles that establish reliability and about the disclosure of information that allows users of financial statements to understand the measurement process.

4.3.1 Accounting measurement principles

The accounting measurement principles that are most widely known in the UK are found within the Companies Act 1985:[19]

- Going concern
- Accruals
- Consistency
- Prudence

Going concern

Being a 'going concern' means staying in business for the foreseeable future. The Companies Act statement on 'going concern' is rather like a crossword clue, in being short and enigmatic. It states 'The company shall be presumed to be carrying on business as a going concern'. How does that help us understand measurement?

An accounting standard gives more guidance. It requires an entity to prepare its financial statements on a going concern basis unless the entity is being liquidated or has ceased trading, when a 'break-up' valuation may be more appropriate. On a forced sale, very little is obtained for the assets of a business. If the company is still operating but the directors are aware of conditions that cast doubts on the company's ability to continue as a going concern, they should disclose those uncertainties. They must take into account all available information about the 'foreseeable future'.

If the company is staying in business then the directors are allowed to use valuations that reflect continuity. They do not have to report 'break-up' values, which are values for immediate sale of assets. Investors are probably quite happy when the company is continuing as a going concern. They will be more concerned about the risk that it will not continue. For that reason, the directors are required to make a statement in their report to confirm that the business remains a 'going concern' for the foreseeable future. There is no readily available definition of 'foreseeable future' but the guidance given to directors and auditors points towards considering a period of 12 months from the balance sheet date.

Accruals (also called 'matching')

The Companies Act requires that all income and charges (i.e. expenses) relating to the financial year shall be taken into account, without regard to the date of receipt or payment. The word 'accrue' means 'to fall due' or 'to come as a natural result'. If, during a year, a company sells £100m of goods but collects only £80m from customers, it records sales as £100m in the profit and loss account. The cash yet to be collected from customers is reported as an asset called 'debtor' in the balance sheet. If, during the year, it uses electricity costing £50m but has only paid £40m so far, it records the expense of £50m in the profit and loss account. The unpaid electricity bill is reported as a liability called 'accruals' in the balance sheet.

The idea of 'matching' is also used in applying the idea of 'accruals'. Matching has two forms, matching losses or gains against time and matching expenses against revenue. Time matching occurs when a gain or loss is spread over the relevant period of time, such as receiving interest on a loan or paying rent on a property. Matching of revenues and expenses occurs when costs such as labour are matched against the revenue earned from providing goods or services.

Consistency

The Companies Act requires that accounting policies shall be applied consistently within the same accounts and from one period to the next. You have already seen a discussion of consistency in section 4.2.2. It is described in the *Statement of Principles* as an aspect of comparability. The disclosure of accounting policies is also discussed in section 4.2.2.

Prudence

The Companies Act does not define prudence but uses the word prudent in relation to measurement. It requires that the amount of any item shall be determined on a prudent basis, and in particular:

(a) only profits realised at the balance sheet date shall be included in the profit and loss account; and
(b) all liabilities and losses which have arisen or are likely to arise in respect of the financial year shall be taken into account, including those which only become apparent between the balance sheet date and the date on which it is signed by the board of directors.

Realisation

There is no clear statement of the conditions that will make a profit 'realised'. It is an example of an idea that is so widely used that it appears to be almost impossible to explain. If you turn to a dictionary you will find 'realise' equated to 'convert into cash'. The accounting standard FRS 18[20] confirms that it is the general view that profits shall be treated as realised when evidenced in the form of cash or other assets whose cash realisation is reasonably certain. However, the standard avoids linking realisation to 'prudence', explaining that a focus on cash does not reflect more recent developments in financial markets. Evidence of 'reasonable certainty' in such markets does not necessarily require cash. It is based on confidence in the reliable operation of the market.

L02 **Activity 4.2**

Take a piece of paper having two wide columns. Head the left-hand column 'My thoughts on measurement in accounting' and head the right-hand column 'What the textbook tells me about measurement'. Fill in both columns and then exchange your paper with a fellow student. Discuss with each other any similarities and differences in the left-hand column and relate these to your personal views and prior experience. Discuss with each other any similarities and differences in the right-hand column and evaluate the extent to which different people see textbooks differently. Finally, discuss with each other the extent to which reading this section has changed your views on measurement as a subject in accounting.

L03 ## 4.4 Views on prudence

The Companies Act makes an explicit link between prudence and realisation that reflects UK accounting practice when the Companies Act was written. The *Statement of Principles* avoids mentioning realisation and describes prudence in terms of 'exercising caution'.[21] FRS 18 acknowledges the meaning of realisation but breaks the link between realisation and prudence.[22] Because FRS 18 is relatively new, it is not possible to say whether it will change the entrenched conservatism of accounting practice which tends towards understatement on grounds of caution. Where does that leave the student of accounting who wants to understand the meaning of prudence?

The most important message for students of accounting (and for many practitioners) is contained in the ASB's *Statement of Principles*,[23] echoing the IASB's *Framework for the Preparation and Presentation of Financial Statements*.[24]

> Nor is it appropriate to use prudence as a reason for . . . deliberately understating assets or gains, or deliberately overstating liabilities or losses, because that would mean that the financial statements are not neutral and, therefore, are not reliable.

Why are there different views on understatement and overstatement, depending on the item being reported? Here is your first chance to use the accounting equation to solve a problem:

Assets minus **Liabilities**	equals	**Capital contributed/withdrawn** plus **Profit**

Profit	equals	**Revenue** minus **Expenses**

L03 **Activity 4.3**

Ask yourself what will happen to profit in the accounting equation if the amount of an asset is increased while the liabilities and the capital contributed remain the same. Then ask yourself what will happen to profit in the accounting equation if the amount of a liability is decreased while the assets and the capital contributed remain the same. Next ask yourself what will happen to profit if revenue is overstated. Finally ask yourself what will happen to profit if expenses are understated.

Assuming that capital contributed/withdrawn remains constant, overstating assets will overstate profit. Understating liabilities will overstate profit. Overstating revenue will overstate profit. Understating expenses will overstate profit.

Examples

A market trader buys £100 of stock on credit, promising to pay the supplier at the end of the day. The trader sells three-quarters of the stock at a price of £90 and takes the rest home to keep for next week's market. At the end of the day the trader has £90 in cash, one-quarter of the stock which cost £25, and owes £100 to the supplier. How much profit has the trader made? The answer is that the profit is £15 (£90 received for the sale of stock less the cost of the items sold, £75, being three-quarters of the stock purchased). The accounting equation is:

Assets minus Liabilities at the end of the period	equals	Ownership interest at the start of the period plus Capital contributed/ withdrawn plus Revenue of the period minus Expenses of the period
stock £25 + cash £90 – liability £100	equals	nil + nil + revenue £90 – expenses £75
£15	equals	£15

1 Supposing the trader 'forgets' part of the liability and thinks it is only £84 owing, rather than £100. The assets remain at stock £25 + cash £90, which equals £115. The liability is now thought to be £84 and therefore the equation becomes:

£25 + £90 – £84	equals	nil + nil + revenue £90 – expenses £75 + [?] £16 [?]
£31	equals	£31

For the equation to be satisfied there must be a total of £31 on both sides. The total of £31 is therefore written in. The recorded profit is still only £15, calculated as revenue £90 minus expenses £75, so there is a 'hole' amounting to £16 on the right-hand side of the equation. The accounting equation has to balance so the extra £16 is written in, surrounded by question marks, on the right-hand side. It is assumed on the right-hand side that the trader has either forgotten to record revenue of £16 or has recorded too much expense, so that the amount appears to represent an unexplained profit. Thus *understating a liability will overstate profit*. That favourable news might mislead a competitor or investor. It might be bad news when the Inland Revenue demands tax on profit of £31. Also there is the unpaid supplier who may not be entirely patient when offered £84 rather than £100.

2 Supposing instead that the trader 'forgets' there is some unsold stock left. The only recorded asset would be the cash at £90 and there would be a liability of £100. This gives negative net assets of (£10) and, because the accounting

equation has to balance, suggests that there is a 'forgotten' expense of £25 on the right-hand side. The equation then becomes:

£90 – £100	equals	nil + nil + £90 – £75 – [?] £25 [?]
(£10)	equals	(£10)

This would cause the Inland Revenue to ask a lot of questions as to why there was no record of stock remaining, because they know that omitting stock from the record is a well-tried means of fraudulently reducing profits and therefore reducing tax bills. *Understating an asset will understate profit.*

These two examples have illustrated the meaning of the warning that deliberate understatement or overstatement is not acceptable. The general message of prudence is: *avoid overstating profit*. In down-to-earth terms, don't raise the readers' hopes too high, only to have to tell them later that it was all in the imagination.

L04 4.5 Regulation of financial reporting

Because the external users of accounting information do not have day-to-day access to the records of the business, they rely on the integrity and judgement of management to provide suitable information of a high quality. But will the management be honest, conscientious and careful in providing information? In an ideal world there should be no problem for investors in a company because, as shareholders, they appoint the directors and may dismiss them if dissatisfied with the service provided. However, the world is not ideal. Some companies are very large and they have many shareholders whose identity changes as shares are bought and sold. Over the years it has been found that regulation is needed particularly for financial reporting by companies. This regulation is provided by parliamentary legislation, through the Companies Act 1985, and by the independent Accounting Standards Board (ASB) which sets standards higher than the minimum required by legislation. Where the company's shares are listed on the Stock Exchange, further rules are applied to the provision of accounting information. These are found in the Listing Rules issued by the Financial Services Authority. Assurance about the application of law and standards is provided by the Financial Reporting Review Panel and the external auditors.

4.5.1 Company law

The Companies Act 1985 prescribes formats of presentation of the balance sheet and profit and loss account. Companies must select one of the permitted formats. It also prescribes methods of valuation of the assets and liabilities contained in the balance sheet, broadly expecting that normally these items will be recorded at their cost at the date of acquisition, subject to diminutions in value since that date. Some other approaches to valuation are permitted, but these are carefully regulated and are subject to requirements for prudence, consistency and an expectation that the business is a going concern (i.e. will continue for some time into the future). The UK legislation places strong emphasis on the requirement to present a *true and fair* view in financial statements. This *true and fair* view will be a strong feature underlying the rest of this financial accounting text.

Although this text is primarily concerned with United Kingdom accounting practice, it is important to note from the outset that the United Kingdom is part of the European Union and its company law is subject to Directives of the European Union which seek to ensure harmonisation of legislation across the Union. Two Directives in particular (the Fourth and Seventh Directives) have had a strong influence on the Companies Act 1985 (*see* Chapter 7).

The directors are responsible for the preparation of company accounts. Exhibit 4.2 sets out the statement made by directors of one major public company regarding their responsibilities in these matters. This type of statement will be found in the annual reports of most of the large listed companies. It is regarded as an important aspect of giving reassurance to investors and others that there is a strong system of corporate governance within the company. It is also intended to clarify any misunderstandings the shareholders may have about the work of directors as distinct from the work of the auditors (*see* below).

Exhibit 4.2

Statement of directors' responsibilities as expressed in the annual report of a public limited company

---

Statement of directors' responsibilities

Company law requires the directors to prepare accounts for each financial year which give a true and fair view of the state of affairs of the company and of the group and of the profit or loss and cash flows of the group for that period. In preparing these accounts, the directors have adopted suitable accounting policies and then applied them consistently, made judgements and estimates that are reasonable and prudent, followed applicable accounting standards and adopted the going concern basis.

The directors are responsible for ensuring that the company keeps proper accounting records which disclose with reasonable accuracy at any time the financial position of the company and enable them to ensure that the accounts comply with the Companies Act 1985. They are also responsible for safeguarding the assets of the company and taking reasonable steps for the prevention and detection of fraud and other irregularities.

4.5.2 Accounting Standards Board

Traditionally, professions in the United Kingdom have been expected to regulate their own affairs and control their members. The accounting profession satisfied this expectation between 1970 and 1990 by forming the Accounting Standards Committee (ASC) and requiring members of each professional body to apply accounting standards or face disciplinary action. Over a period of years there was growing dissatisfaction with this pure self-regulatory model because the disciplinary aspects appeared to be applied only rarely and the existence of potential conflicts of self-interest was pointed to by some critics as weakening the standard-setting process. Consequently, in 1990 the purely self-regulatory approach was abandoned in favour of an independent regime having statutory backing, but retaining some self-regulatory features.

This independent regime is led by a high-level Financial Reporting Council (FRC), existing as an independent body with wide representation on its membership which guides the ASB on its work programmes and on issues of public concern. The Chairman of the FRC is appointed jointly by the Secretary of State for Trade and Industry and the Governor of the Bank of England. Funding for the FRC is drawn from three broad sectors: the accountancy profession, the financial community and the government.

The ASB is financed by the FRC. It has the task of developing, issuing and withdrawing accounting standards and is helped by an Urgent Issues Task Force (UITF) which assists in areas where conflicting interpretations have developed in relation to an existing accounting standard or Companies Act rule.

Since 1990 the ASB has published Financial Reporting Standards (FRSs) setting standards of practice which go beyond the requirements of company law in particular problem areas. In the period from 1970 to 1990 the standards set by the ASC were called Statements of Standard Accounting Practice (SSAPs). Those SSAPs which remained valid were adopted by the ASB and are gradually being replaced. SSAPs and FRSs collectively are referred to as 'accounting standards'.

4.5.3 The tax system

Businesses pay tax to the Inland Revenue (as the tax collecting agent of the government) based on the profits they make. Sole traders and partnerships pay income tax on their profits while companies pay corporation tax. There are differences in detail of the law governing these two types of taxes but broadly they both require as a starting point a calculation of profit using commercial accounting practices. The law governing taxation is quite separate from the law and regulations governing financial reporting, so in principle the preparation of financial statements is not affected by tax matters. That is very different from some other countries in the European Union where the tax law stipulates that an item must be in the financial accounting statements if it is to be considered for tax purposes. Those countries have an approach to financial reporting which is more closely driven by taxation matters.

In the United Kingdom the distinction may be blurred in practice in the case of sole traders because the Inland Revenue is the main user of the financial statements of the sole trader. Similarly, tax factors may influence partnership accounts, although here the fairness of sharing among the partners is also important. The very smallest companies, where the owners also run the business, may in practice have the same attitude to tax matters as does the sole trader or partnership. For larger companies with a wider spread of ownership, the needs of shareholders will take priority.

4.5.4 The Financial Services Authority

Under the Financial Services and Markets Act 2000, the Financial Services Authority (FSA) is a single regulator with responsibility across a wide range of financial market activity. It is required to maintain confidence in the UK financial system, to promote public understanding of the financial system, to secure protection for consumers and to reduce the scope for financial crime. The FSA is an independent, non-governmental body and receives no funds from government. It reports annually to Parliament through the Treasury.

The FSA regulates listing of companies' shares on the UK stock exchange. The work is carried out by a division called the UK Listing Authority (UKLA). When a company first has its shares listed, it must produce a prospectus, which is normally much more detailed than the annual report. The regulations covering the content of a prospectus are set by the UKLA. Once a company has achieved a listing, it must keep up with ongoing obligations under the Listing Rules, which includes providing accounting information to the market in the annual report and press releases. Details of the Listing Rules are not necessary for first-year study but if you are interested you can read them on the FSA's website: www.fsa.gov.uk.

4.5.5 The Financial Reporting Review Panel

When the Accounting Standards Board was established in 1990 it was felt to be important that there was a mechanism for enforcing accounting standards. An effective mechanism had been lacking in the previous process of setting standards. Accordingly the Financial Reporting Council established a Financial Reporting Review Panel (FRRP) which enquires into annual accounts where it appears that the requirements of the Companies Act, including the requirement that annual accounts shall show a true and fair view, might have been breached. The FRRP has the power to ask companies to revise their accounts where these are found to be defective. If companies do not voluntarily make such a revision, the FRRP may take proceedings in a court of law to require the company to revise its accounts. These powers are contained in the Companies Act 1985 and delegated to the FRRP by the Secretary of State for Trade and Industry. So far the FRRP has not found it necessary to resort to legal action, having found its powers of persuasion were sufficient.

4.5.6 Auditors

The shareholders of companies do not have a right of access to the records of the day-to-day running of the business, and so they need someone to act on their behalf to ensure that the directors are presenting a true and fair view of the company's position at a point in time and of the profits generated during a period of time. To achieve this reassurance, the shareholders appoint a firm of auditors to investigate the company's financial records and give an opinion on the truth and fairness of the financial information presented. Exhibit 4.3 sets out the wording of a typical auditors' report to the shareholders of a public company. There are some words and phrases in this report which will become more familiar as you progress through the text. These include 'historical cost convention' (Chapter 15), 'revaluation of certain fixed assets' (Chapter 12) and 'accounting policies' (introduced in Chapter 3 but mentioned again at various points).

You will note that the auditors do not look at all the pages of the annual report. The earlier part of the annual report is important to the companies in setting the scene and explaining their businesses. These earlier pages are reviewed by the auditors to ensure that anything said there is consistent with the information presented in the audited financial statements. You will also note that the auditors have their own code of practice, referred to as Auditing Standards. These are prepared by a body called the Auditing Practices Board (APB) which is formed by the principal professional accountancy bodies as part of their mechanism of self-regulation.

Exhibit 4.3
Sample auditors' report

Report of the auditors to the members of XXX plc

Respective responsibilities of directors and auditors
We have audited the financial statements on pages 22 to 57 which have been prepared using the accounting policies on pages 25 and 26.

The directors' responsibilities for preparing the Annual Report and the financial statements in accordance with applicable United Kingdom law and accounting standards are set out in the statement of directors' responsibilities.

Our responsibility is to audit the financial statements in accordance with relevant legal and regulatory requirements, United Kingdom Auditing Standards issued by the Auditing Practices Board and the Listing Rules of the Financial Services Authority.

We report to you our opinion as to whether the financial statements give a true and fair view and are properly prepared in accordance with the Companies Act 1985. We also report to you if, in our opinion, the directors' report is not consistent with the financial statements, if the Company has not kept proper accounting records, if we have not received all the information and explanations we require for our audit, or if information specified by law or the Listing Rules regarding directors' remuneration and transactions is not disclosed.

We read the other information contained in the Annual Report and consider the implications for our report if we become aware of any apparent misstatements or material inconsistencies with the financial statements. The other information comprises only the directors' report, the remuneration report, the chairman's statement, the operating and financial review and the corporate governance statement.

We review whether the corporate governance statement reflects the Company's compliance with the seven provisions of the Combined Code specified for our review by the Listing Rules, and we report if it does not. We are not required to consider whether the Board's statements on internal control cover all risks and controls, or to form an opinion on the effectiveness of the Company's corporate governance procedures or its risk and control procedures. The maintenance of the Company's website is the responsibility of the directors; the work carried out by the auditors does not involve consideration of these matters.

Basis of audit opinion
We conducted our audit in accordance with auditing standards issued by the Auditing Practices Board. An audit includes examination, on a test basis, of

---

Exhibit 4.3 continued

evidence relevant to the amounts and disclosures in the financial statements. It also includes an assessment of the significant estimates and judgements made by the directors in the preparation of the financial statements, and of whether the accounting policies are appropriate to the Company's circumstances, consistently applied and adequately disclosed.

We planned and performed our audit so as to obtain all the information and explanations which we considered necessary in order to provide us with sufficient evidence to give reasonable assurance that the financial statements are free from material misstatement, whether caused by fraud or caused by other irregularity or error. In forming our opinion we also evaluated the overall adequacy of the presentation of information in the financial statements.

Opinion
In our opinion the financial statements give a true and fair view of the state of affairs of the Company and Group at the balance sheet date and of the profit and cash flows of the Group for the year then ended and have been properly prepared in accordance with the Companies Act 1985.

What surprises some readers is the phrase 'reasonable assurance that the accounts are free from material misstatement'. The auditors are not expected to be totally certain in their opinion and they are only looking for errors or fraud which is material. The meaning of the word 'material' has proved difficult to define and it tends to be a matter left to the judgement of the auditor. The best guidance available is that an item is material if its misstatement or omission would cause the reader of the annual report (shareholder or creditor) to take a different decision or view based on the financial statements.

4.5.7 Is regulation necessary?

There are those who would argue that all this regulatory mechanism is unnecessary. They take the view that in a market-based economy, competitive forces will ensure that those providing information will meet the needs of users. It is argued that investors will not entrust their funds to a business which provides inadequate information. Banks will not lend money unless they are provided with sufficient information to answer their questions about the likelihood of receiving interest and eventual repayment of the loan. Employee morale may be lowered if a business appears non-communicative regarding its present position and past record of performance. Suppliers may not wish to give credit to a business which appears secretive or has a reputation for producing poor-quality information. Customers may be similarly doubtful.

Against that quite attractive argument for the abolition of all regulations stand some well-documented financial scandals where businesses have failed. Employees have lost their jobs, with little prospect of finding comparable employment elsewhere; suppliers have not been paid and have found themselves in financial difficulties as a result. Customers have lost a source of supply and have been unable to meet the requirements of their own customers until a new source is found. Those who have provided long-term finance for the business, as lenders and investors, have lost their investment. Investigation shows that the signs and warnings had existed for those who were sufficiently experienced to see them, but these signs and warnings did not emerge in the published accounting information for external use.

Such financial scandals may be few in number but the large-scale examples cause widespread misery and lead to calls for action. Governments experience pressure from the electorate and lobby groups; professional bodies and business interest groups decide they ought to be seen to react; and new regulations are developed which ensure that the particular problem cannot recur. All parties are then reasonably satisfied that they have done their best to protect those who need protection against the imbalance of business life, and the new practices are used until the next scandal occurs and the process starts over again.

There is no clear answer to the question 'Is regulation necessary?' Researchers have not found any strong evidence that the forces of supply and demand in the market fail to work and have suggested that the need for regulation must be justified by showing that the benefits exceed the costs. That is quite a difficult challenge but is worth keeping in mind as you explore some of the more intricate aspects of accounting regulation.

LO4
Activity 4.4

Look back through this section and, for each subheading, make a note of whether you were previously aware that such regulation existed. In each case, irrespective of your previous state of knowledge, do you now feel a greater or a lesser sense of confidence in accounting information? How strong is your confidence in published accounting information? If not 100 per cent, what further reassurance would you require?

LO5
4.6 Reviewing published financial statements

If you look at the annual report of any large listed company you will find that it has two main sections. The first part contains a variety of diagrams and photographs, a statement by the chairman, a report by the chief executive and, in many cases, an Operating and Financial Review which may extend to a considerable number of pages. Other aspects of the business, such as its corporate governance and environmental policy, may also be explained. This first part is largely unregulated in a formal sense, although there are many sources of influence on its contents, some of which will be explained in later chapters of this textbook.

The second part contains the financial statements, which are heavily regulated. As if to emphasise this change of status, the second part of the annual report will often have a different appearance, perhaps being printed on a different colour or grade of paper, or possibly having a smaller print size. Appendix I to this book contains extracts from the financial statements of a fictitious company, Safe and Sure plc, which will be used for illustration in this and subsequent chapters.

Relaxing after a hard workout at the health club, David Wilson took the opportunity to buy Leona a drink and tell her something about Safe and Sure prior to a visit to the company's headquarters to meet the finance director.

DAVID: *This is a major listed company, registered in the UK but operating around the world selling its services in disposal and recycling, cleaning and security. Its name is well known and its services command high prices because of the company's reputation gained over many years. Basically it is a very simple business to understand. It sells services by making contracts with customers and collects cash when the service is performed.*

In preparation for my visit I looked first at the performance of the period. This company promises to deliver growth of at least 20 per cent in turnover and in profit before tax so first of all I checked that the promise had been delivered. Sure enough, at the front of the annual report under 'Highlights of the year' there was a table showing turnover had increased by 22.4 per cent and profit before tax had increased by 20.4 per cent. I knew I would need to look through the profit and loss account in more detail to find out how the increases had come about, but first of all I read the operating review (written by the chief executive) and the financial review (written by the finance director). The chief executive gave more details on which areas had the greatest increase in turnover and operating profit and which areas had been disappointing. That all helps me in making my forecast of profit for next year.

The chief executive made reference to acquisitions during the year, so I knew I would also need to think whether the increase in turnover and profits was due to an improvement in sales and marketing as compared with last year or whether it reflected the inclusion of new business for the first time.

In the financial review, the finance director explained that the business tries to use as little working capital as possible (that means they try to keep down the current assets and match them as far as possible with current liabilities). I guessed I would need to look at the balance sheet to confirm that, so I headed next for the financial statements at the back of the annual report, pausing to glance at the auditors' report to make sure there was nothing highlighted by them as being amiss.

The financial statements are quite detailed and I wanted a broad picture so I noted down the main items from each in a summary format which leaves out some of the detail but which I find quite useful.

4.6.1 Profit and loss account

Safe and Sure plc
Summary profit and loss account (with comparative figures)

	Year 7 £m	Year 6 £m
Turnover	734.6	600.3
Cost of sales	(531.5)	(427.3)
Gross profit	203.1	173.0
Expenses and interest	(26.1)	(26.0)
Profit on ordinary activities before tax	177.0	147.0
Tax on profit	(62.2)	(52.4)
Profit for ordinary shareholders	114.8	94.6
Dividends	(33.7)	(27.8)
Retained profit for the year	81.1	66.8

DAVID: *It is part of my job to make forecasts of what the next reported profit of the company is likely to be (i.e. the profit of Year 8). This is March Year 8 now so there are plenty of current signs I can pick up, but I also want to think about how far Year 7 will be repeated or improve during Year 8. A few years ago I would have made a rough guess and then phoned the finance director for some guidance on whether I was in the right area. That's no longer allowed because the Financial Services Authority tightened up the rules on companies giving information to some investors which is not available to others, especially where that information could affect the share price.*

One easy way out is for me to collect the reports which come in from our stockbrokers. Their analysts have specialist knowledge of the industry and can sometimes work out what is happening in a business faster than some of the management. However, I like to form my own opinion using other sources, such as trade journals, and I read the annual report to give me the background structure for my forecast.

When I meet the finance director next week I'll have with me a spreadsheet analysing turnover and profit before tax – so far as I can find the data – by product line and for each of the countries in which the company trades. I'll also ask the following questions:

1 *Although the turnover has increased, the ratio of gross profit to turnover has decreased slightly, from 28.8 per cent in Year 6 to 27.6 per cent in Year 7. That suggests that the company has increased turnover by holding price rises to less than the increase in operating costs. Does the company expect to see a fall in demand when its prices eventually rise?*
2 *The tax charge in both years is approximately 35 per cent, higher than the rate which would be expected of United Kingdom companies. I know that this company is trading overseas. You say in your financial review that the tax charge is 30 per cent in the United Kingdom and rates on overseas profits will reduce, so am I safe in assuming that 30 per cent is a good working guide for the future in respect of this company?*
3 *With all this overseas business there must be an element of foreign exchange risk. You say in your financial review that all material foreign currency transactions are matched back into the currency of the group company undertaking the transaction. You don't hedge the translation of overseas profits back into sterling. You also say that using Year 6 exchange rates the Year 7 profit would have been £180.5 million rather than the £177.0 million reported. That seems a fairly minimal effect but are these amounts hiding any swings in major currencies where large downward movements are offset by correspondingly large upward movements?*
4 *The detail in the profit and loss account shows that the acquisitions in Year 7 contributed £13.5m to turnover. If I strip that amount out of the total turnover I'm left with an increase in respect of activities continuing from Year 6 which is just meeting the 20 per cent target you set yourselves. When the scope for acquisitions is exhausted, will you be able to sustain the 20 per cent target by organic growth alone?*

4.6.2 Balance sheet

DAVID: *Looking at the balance sheet, this is a fairly simple type of business. It is financed almost entirely by equity capital (shareholders' funds), so there are none of the risks associated with high levels of borrowings which might be found in other companies.*

Again, I have summarised and left out some of the details which aren't significant in financial terms.

Safe and Sure plc
Summarised balance sheet (with comparative amounts)

At 31 December	Year 7 £m	Year 6 £m
Fixed assets		
Goodwill	260.3	237.6
Land and buildings	29.1	26.1
Plant and equipment	42.2	37.6
Vehicles	66.2	58.2
Investments	2.8	2.0
Total fixed assets	400.6	361.5
Current assets		
Stocks	26.6	24.3
Trade debtors	128.1	117.0
Prepayments	18.8	17.7
Short-term bank deposits and cash	107.3	90.5
	280.8	249.5
Current liabilities due within one year		
Bank borrowings	(40.1)	(74.3)
Trade creditors	(23.6)	(20.4)
Dividends payable	(23.8)	(19.6)
Corporation tax	(31.5)	(26.5)
Other creditors and accruals	(110.4)	(103.7)
	(229.4)	(244.5)
Net current assets	51.4	5.0
Liabilities due after one year		
Provisions for liabilities and charges	(20.2)	(22.2)
Other long-term items	3.0	1.7
Net assets	434.8	346.0
Capital and reserves		
Share capital	19.6	19.5
Accumulated profit and loss account	415.2	326.5
Shareholders' funds	434.8	346.0

DAVID: *By far the largest fixed asset is the intangible asset of goodwill arising on acquisition. It reflects the fact that the group has had to pay a price for the future prospects of companies it has acquired. Although the company reports this in the group's balance sheet, and I like to see whether the asset is holding its value from the group's point of view, I have some reservations about the quality of the asset because I know it would vanish overnight if the group found itself in difficulties.*

The fixed assets are mainly equipment for carrying out the cleaning operations and vehicles in which to transport the equipment. I've checked in the notes to the accounts that vehicles are being depreciated over 4 to 5 years and plant and equipment over 5 to 10 years, all of which sounds about right. Also, they haven't changed the depreciation period, or the method of calculation, since last year so the amounts are comparable. Estimated useful lives for depreciation are something I watch closely. There is a great temptation for companies which have underperformed to cut back on the depreciation by deciding the useful life has extended. (Depreciation is explained more fully in Chapter 8.)

I think I might ask a few questions about working capital (the current assets minus the current liabilities of the business). Normally I like to see current assets somewhat greater than current liabilities – a ratio of 1.5 to 1 could be about right – as a cushion to ensure the liabilities are met as they fall due. However, in this company the finance director makes a point of saying that they like to utilise as little working capital as possible, so I'm wondering why it increased from £5m in Year 6 to more than £51m in Year 7. There appear to be two effects working together: current assets went up and current liabilities went down. Trade debtors increased in Year 7 in absolute terms but that isn't as bad as it looks when allowance is made for the increase in turnover. Debtors in Year 7 are 17.4 per cent of turnover, which shows some control has been achieved when it is compared with the Year 6 amount at 19.4 per cent of turnover. My questions will be:

1 *Mostly, the increase in the working capital (net current assets) appears to be due to the decrease in bank borrowing. Was this a voluntary action by the company or did the bank insist?*
2 *The second major cause of the increase in the working capital is the increase in the balance held in the bank account. Is that being held for a planned purpose and, if so, what?*
3 *The ratio of current assets to current liabilities has increased from last year. What target ratio are you aiming for?*

I always shudder when I see 'provisions' in a balance sheet. The notes to the financial statements show that these are broadly:

	£m
For treating a contaminated site	12.0
For restructuring part of the business	4.2
For tax payable some way into the future	4.0
Total	20.2

I shall want to ask whether the estimated liability in relation to the contaminated site is adequate in the light of any changes in legislation. I know the auditors will have asked this question in relation to existing legislation but I want to think also about forthcoming legislation.

I am always wary of provisions for restructuring. I shall be asking more about why the restructuring is necessary and when it will take place. I want to know that the provision is sufficient to cover the problem, but not excessive.

The provision for tax payable some way into the future is an aspect of prudence in accounting. I don't pay much attention unless the amount is very large or suddenly changes dramatically. (An explanation of deferred taxation is contained in Chapter 10.)

4.6.3 Cash flow statement

DAVID: *Cash is an important factor for any business. It is only one of the resources available but it is the key to survival. I've summarised the totals of the various main sections of the cash flow statement. 'Net cash' means the cash less the bank borrowings.*

Safe and Sure plc
Summary cash flow statement (with comparative amounts)

For the years ended 31 December	Year 7	Year 6
	£m	£m
Net cash inflow from operating activities	196.7	163.5
Dividends paid and interest paid	(27.6)	(20.9)
Taxation paid (United Kingdom and overseas)	(50.6)	(44.8)
Investing activities	(103.3)	(91.2)
Financing activities	19.3	(22.0)
Increase/(decrease) in net cash per balance sheet	34.5	(15.4)

What I'm basically looking for in the cash flow statement is how well the company is balancing various sources of finance. It generated £196.7m from operating activities and that was more than sufficient to cover all its short-term needs for paying dividends and taxes and to cover its investing activities in new fixed assets and acquisitions. There was no immediate need for any long-term financing flows with a healthy cash flow like that, although the company did raise new loan finance in the period. That brings me back to my earlier question of why they are holding so much cash.

L05 **Activity 4.5**

Read David's explanation again and compare it carefully with the financial statements. It is quite likely that you will not understand everything immediately because the purpose of this book as a whole is to help you understand published financial statements and we are, as yet, only at the end of Chapter 4. Make a note of the items you don't fully understand and keep that note safe in a file. As you progress through the rest of the book, look back to that note and tick off the points which subsequently become clear. The aim is to have a page full of ticks by the end of the book.

4.7 Summary

Now score your view of your confidence in achieving the learning outcomes of the chapter.

1 = Very confident about knowledge, application, problem solving and evaluation.

2 = Confident about knowledge and application, less sure about problem solving and evaluation.

3 = Need to read again to be more certain of basic knowledge and application.

L01 You are now able to explain the qualitative characteristics desirable in financial statements. The key qualitative characteristics are relevance, reliability, comparability and understandability.

1 2 3
☐ ☐ ☐

L02 You are now able to explain the accounting measurement principles set out in the Companies Act. These are going concern, consistency, accruals and prudence.

1 2 3
☐ ☐ ☐

LO3 You can explain the significance of understatement and overstatement of assets and liabilities and can explain why there is more than one view on the role of prudence in accounting.

1 2 3 □ □ □

LO4 You know and can explain the main external authorities that regulate or influence financial reporting.

1 2 3 □ □ □

LO5 You have read David's commentary on Safe and Sure and as a result you are aware of how an investor reviews financial statements.

1 2 3 □ □ □

If your scores are all 1 or 2, try the questions in the series A, B and C. This will give you feedback on your assessment of how well you have achieved the learning outcomes. Read again any sections of the chapter where you find your knowledge and understanding are less comprehensive than you first estimated.

If your scores include some at 3, try the series A questions to find where the problems lie. Read the relevant sections again, work through any illustrative examples and case studies, then try the questions in the series B. Once you feel confident at that level of knowledge and application, move on to try some or all of the series C questions.

There is no Supplement to this chapter because no new aspects of the accounting equation have been introduced. The work of the supplements continues at the end of Chapter 5.

International perspective

The ASB's *Statement of Principles* has many similarities to the IASB's *Framework for the Preparation and Presentation of Financial Statements*. The qualitative characteristics in particular are very similar. The accounting measurement principles of going concern, accruals and consistency are common to most accounting systems. The concept of prudence is more variable in its application, with higher caution being taken in some countries, particularly where the accounting profit determines the tax bill. In some countries it is seen as desirable to tend towards understating profit as an act of 'conservatism' (this word being used rather than prudence).

Further reading

Paterson, R. (2002) 'Whatever happened to Prudence?', *Accountancy*, January, p. 105.

Test your understanding

Skills outcomes
SO1 Application of technical skills   SO2 Problem solving and evaluation skills   SO3 Communication skills

LO1, SO1   **A4.1** Explain what is meant by:

(a) relevance;
(b) reliability;
(c) faithful representation;
(d) neutrality;
(e) prudence;
(f) completeness;

(g) comparability;

(h) understandability; and

(i) materiality.

L02, S01 **A4.2** Explain the accounting measurement principles of:

(a) going concern;

(b) accruals;

(c) consistency;

(d) the concept of prudence.

L03, S01 **A4.3** Explain why companies should avoid overstatement of assets or understatement of liabilities.

L04, S01 **A4.4** Explain the responsibilities of directors of a company towards shareholders in relation to the financial statements of a company.

L04, S01 **A4.5** Explain the impact on financial statements of:

(a) company law;

(b) the Accounting Standards Board; and

(c) the United Kingdom tax law.

L04, S01 **A4.6** Explain how the monitoring of financial statements is carried out by:

(a) the auditors; and

(b) the Financial Reporting Review Panel.

Application

L04, S01 **B4.1**

(a) What is the purpose of accounting standards in the UK?

(b) How are United Kingdom standards produced?

(c) How are United Kingdom standards enforced?

L02, S01 **B4.2** Explain any two accounting measurement principles, explaining how each affects current accounting practice.

L04, S01 **B4.3** Discuss the extent to which the regulatory bodies explained in this chapter have, or ought to have, a particular concern for the needs of the following groups of users of financial statements:

(a) shareholders;

(b) employees;

(c) customers; and

(d) suppliers.

Problem solving and evaluation

L01, S02 **C4.1** Choose one or more characteristics from the following box that you could use to discuss the accounting aspects of each of the statements 1 to 5:

- relevance
- reliability
- comparability
- understandability
- materiality
- neutrality
- completeness
- prudence
- faithful representation

1 Director: 'We do not need to tell shareholders about a loss of £2,000 on damaged stock when our operating profit for the year is £60m.'

2 Shareholder: 'I would prefer the balance sheet to tell me the current market value of land is £20m than to tell me that the historical cost is £5m, although I know that market values fluctuate.'

3 Analyst: 'If the company changes its stock valuation from average cost to FIFO, I want to hear a good reason and I want to know what last year's profit would have been on the same basis.'

4 Regulator: 'If the company reports that it has paid "*commission on overseas sales*" I don't expect to discover later that it really meant bribes to local officials.'

5 Director: 'We have made a profit on our drinks sales but a loss on food sales. In the Notes to the Accounts on segmental results I suggest we combine them as "food and drink". It will mean the annual report is less detailed for our shareholders but it will keep competitors in the dark for a while.'

LO2, S02 **C4.2** Choose one or more accounting measurement principles from the following box that you could use to discuss the accounting aspects of each of the problems 1–5.

- Going concern - Accruals - Consistency - Prudence

1 Director: 'The fixed assets of the business are reported at depreciated historical cost because we expect the company to continue in existence for the foreseeable future. The market value is much higher but that is not relevant because we don't intend to sell them.'

2 Auditor: 'We are insisting that the company raises the provision for doubtful debts from 2% to 2.5% of debtor amount. There has been recession among the customer base and the financial statements should reflect that.'

3 Analyst: 'I have great problems in tracking the depreciation policy of this company. It owns several airports. Over the past three years the expected useful life of runways has risen from 30 years to 50 years and now it is 100 years. I find it hard to believe that the technology of tarmacadam has improved so much in three years'.

4 Auditor: 'We have serious doubts about the ability of this company to renew its bank overdraft at next month's review meeting with the bank. The company ought to put shareholders on warning about the implications for the financial statements.'

5 Shareholder: 'I don't understand why the company gives a profit and loss account and a cash flow statement in the annual report. Is there any difference between profit and cash flow?'

Activities for study groups

Continuing to use the annual reports of a company that you obtained for Chapter 1, look for the evidence in each report of the existence of the directors, the auditors and the various regulatory bodies.

In your group, draw up a list of the evidence presented by companies to show that the annual report has been the subject of regulation. Discuss whether the annual report gives sufficient reassurance of its relevance and reliability to the non-expert reader.

Notes and references

1 ASB (1999) *Statement of Principles for Financial Reporting*, ch. 1, Principles section.
2 *Ibid.*, ch. 7, Principles section.
3 *Ibid.*, ch. 3, 'The qualitative characteristics of financial information'.
4 *Ibid.*, paras 3.28 to 3.32.
5 *Ibid.*, p. 34.
6 *Ibid.*, paras 3.1 to 3.6.
7 *Ibid.*, paras 3.7 and 3.8.
8 *Ibid.*, paras 3.9 to 3.14.
9 *Ibid.*, para. 3.15.
10 *Ibid.*, paras 3.16 and 3.17.
11 *Ibid.*, paras 3.18 to 3.20.
12 *Ibid.*, Appendix III, paras 21–23.
13 *Ibid.*, ch. 3 paras 3.21 and 3.22.
14 *Ibid.*, para. 3.23.
15 *Ibid.*, paras 3.24 and 3.25.
16 *Ibid.*, para. 3.26.
17 *Ibid.*, para. 3.27.
18 *Ibid.*, Appendix III, para. 25.
19 Companies Act 1985, sch. 4, paras 10–14.
20 ASB (2000) Financial Reporting Standard 18 (FRS 18) *Accounting Policies*, Accounting Standards Board, para. 28.
21 ASB (1999), para. 3.19.
22 ASB (2000) Appendix IV, paras 12 to 20.
23 ASB (1999), para. 3.20.
24 IASB. Annual volume of International Accounting Standards includes *Framework for the Preparation and Presentation of Financial Statements* (1989) (see para. 37).

Part 2

Reporting the transactions of a business

Chapter 5

Accounting information for service businesses

Learning outcomes

After studying this chapter you should be able to:

LO1 Explain how the accounting equation is applied to transactions of a service business.

LO2 Analyse the transactions of a service business during a specific period of time, using the accounting equation.

LO3 Prepare a spreadsheet analysing the transactions and show that the results of the spreadsheet are consistent with the financial statements provided by the organisation.

LO4 Explain the main aspects of the cash flow statement, profit and loss account and balance sheet of a service business.

Additionally, for those who read the Supplement:

LO5 Analyse the transactions of a service business using the rules of debit and credit bookkeeping.

LO6 Prepare, from a list of transactions of an organisation, ledger accounts and a trial balance which could be used to prepare the financial statements provided by the organisation.

5.1 Introduction

A person who starts a service business intends to offer a service based on personal skills for which other people will be willing to pay a fee. The most important asset of the service business is the person or people providing the service. Despite that, the workforce as an asset never appears in an accounting balance sheet. That is because, although it satisfies all the conditions of the *definition*, it is too difficult to measure objectively and so does not meet the conditions for *recognition*. (*See* Chapter 2 for definitions and conditions of recognition.)

The service business will have other assets which accounting is able to record: for example, the taxi driver may own a taxi; the electrician will have electrical tools; the joiner will have a workbench and joinery tools; the car mechanic will have a repair garage and equipment; the lawyer will have an office and a word-processor. The service business will also buy materials for use in any particular job and the customer will be asked to pay for these materials as well as for the labour time involved. Moreover, it will have liabilities to suppliers of goods and services used by the business itself.

There will be an owner or owners having an ownership interest in the business. The service business will make profits for the owner (and thus increase the ownership interest) by charging a price for services which is greater than the cost of labour and materials used in providing the service.

All these aspects of the service business may be analysed and recorded on the basis of the accounting equation as specified in Chapter 2. This chapter will discuss the analysis of transactions using the accounting equation and will then apply that analysis to the transactions of a doctor providing a service of medical health screening for managerial and secretarial staff.

Activity 5.1

Choose a service business and write down the main activity of that business. Then write down the types of expense you would expect to find in the profit and loss account of such a business. Write down the types of asset you would expect to find in the balance sheet. Exchange your list with a fellow student. What are the similarities and what are the differences? Keep your list safe and when you have finished the chapter compare your list with the example in the chapter. Ask yourself, at that point, whether you would be able to apply what you have learned to the business you have chosen.

LO1

5.2 Analysing transactions using the accounting equation

Three main categories of accounting elements in the accounting equation have been defined in Chapter 2: asset, liability and ownership interest. Any one of these elements may increase or decrease during a period of time but the ownership interest may conveniently be subdivided. There will be increases and decreases caused by the decision of the owner(s) to make further contributions of capital or to withdraw capital. There will be increases and decreases due to the activity of the business, with revenues increasing the ownership claim and expenses decreasing it.

Decrease in ownership interest	Increase in ownership interest
Withdrawals of capital by the owner	Contributions of capital by the owner
Expenses	Revenues

Consequently there are several aspects to consider when transactions are analysed according to the accounting equation.

The accounting equation will be used in this chapter in the form:

Assets minus **Liabilities**	equals	**Ownership interest**

When one item in the equation increases, an upward arrow will be used and when one item decreases a downward arrow will be used:

Assets ↓	denotes a decrease in an asset.

Liabilities ↑	denotes an increase in a liability.

For further emphasis, **bold** highlighting will be used for the elements of the equation which are changed as a result of the transaction or event.

Each business transaction has two aspects in terms of the accounting equation. These aspects must be considered from the viewpoint of the *business*. Exhibit 5.1 sets out a list of some common types of transaction encountered in a service business. Each transaction is then analysed using the accounting equation.

Exhibit 5.1
List of transactions for a service business

Transaction
1 Receive cash from the owner.
2 Buy a vehicle for cash.
3 Receive a bill for gas consumed.
4 Pay the gas bill in cash.
5 Buy materials for cash.
6 Buy materials on credit terms.
7 Sell services for cash.
8 Sell services on credit terms.
9 Pay wages to an employee.
10 Pay cash to the owner for personal use.

Transaction 1: Receive cash from the owner

In this transaction the business acquires an *asset* (cash) and must note the *ownership interest* created by this contribution of capital from the owner:

Assets ↑ – Liabilities	equals	**Ownership interest** ↑

The equation remains in balance because an increase to the left-hand side is exactly matched by an increase to the right-hand side.

Transaction 2: Buy a vehicle for cash

In this transaction the business *acquires* a new *asset* (the vehicle) but *gives up* another *asset* (cash):

Assets ↑↓ – Liabilities	equals	**Ownership interest**

Transaction 3: Receive a bill for gas consumed

The business becomes aware that it has a *liability* to pay for gas consumed and also knows that the *ownership interest has been reduced* by the expense of using up gas in earning revenue for the business:

Assets – **Liabilities** ↑	equals	**Ownership interest** ↓ **(expense)**

Transaction 4: Pay the gas bill in cash

The *asset* of cash is *reduced* and the *liability* to the gas supplier is *reduced*:

Assets ↓ – Liabilities ↓	equals	Ownership interest

Transaction 5: Buy materials for cash

When the materials are acquired they will create an asset of stock, for future use. The *asset* of stock will therefore *increase* and the *asset* of cash will *decrease*:

Assets ↓↑ – Liabilities	equals	Ownership interest

Transaction 6: Buy materials on credit terms

Again, materials are acquired which cause an *increase* in the *asset* of stock. Obtaining goods on credit means that there is a *liability* created for amounts owing to the supplier:

Assets ↑ – Liabilities ↑	equals	Ownership interest

Transaction 7: Sell services for cash

The cash received from the customer causes an *increase in the asset* of cash, while the act of selling services *increases the ownership interest* through earning revenue:

Assets ↑ – Liabilities	equals	**Ownership interest ↑ (revenue)**

Transaction 8: Sell services on credit terms

The sale of services creates an *increase in the ownership interest* through earning revenue, but also creates an *increase in the asset* of debtors:

Assets ↑ – Liabilities	equals	**Ownership interest ↑ (revenue)**

Transaction 9: Pay wages to an employee

The *asset* of cash *decreases* when the wage is paid and there is a *decrease in the ownership interest* because the business has used up the service provided by the employee (an expense has been incurred):

Assets ↓ – Liabilities	equals	**Ownership interest ↓ (expense)**

This is a transaction which often causes problems to those new to accounting. They would like to argue that paying wages creates an asset, rather than an expense, because there is an expected future benefit to be gained from the services of the employee. The answer to that argument is that, while there is no disputing the expected future benefit from the services of most employees, the wages paid are for work *already done* and so there can be no future expectations about that particular week's or month's work. The question of whether the workforce as a whole should be recognised as an asset of the business is one of the unresolved problems of accounting.

Transaction 10: Pay cash to the owner for personal use

The asset of cash decreases and the ownership interest decreases because the owner has made a voluntary withdrawal of capital:

Assets ↓ – Liabilities	equals	Ownership interest ↓ (voluntary withdrawal)

L01

Activity 5.2

Write down the transactions of Exhibit 5.1 in a different order and put the piece of paper away for two days. Then take it out and practise the analysis of each transaction without looking at the answers in the book. If your answers are all correct, is it the result of memory or of genuine understanding? If your answers are not entirely correct, can you decide where the problem lies? It is very important that you can analyse transactions correctly using the accounting equation. It is also important that you use your powers of reasoning and not your powers of memory. You cannot possibly memorise the accounting treatment of every transaction you will meet.

L02

5.3 Illustration of accounting for a service business

We now move on to an example which considers the private medical practice of Dr Lee. At the start of October Dr Lee commenced a new medical practice offering a general health screening service to managerial and secretarial staff at a standard fee of £500 per examination. Where patients make personal arrangements they will be asked to pay cash on the day of the examination. If the patient's employer has agreed to pay for the screening, Dr Lee will send an invoice to the employer, requiring payment within 30 days.

In Exhibit 5.2 there is a list of transactions for Dr Lee's medical practice during the month of October. Try to work out the effect on the accounting equation of each transaction listed. Do this before you read the rest of this section. Then compare your answers and your reasoning with that in the rest of this section. Being able to reason correctly at this stage will reduce the likelihood of error later.

Oct. 1   When Dr Lee provides the practice with cash in a bank account to allow the business to start, the business *acquires an asset of cash at bank* and the transaction creates an *ownership interest* by Dr Lee in the assets of the business. This means that the business now has the use of £50,000, but, if the business ceases immediately, that £50,000 must be returned to Dr Lee. The accounting equation is satisfied because an increase in an asset is matched by an increase in the ownership interest:

Assets ↑ – Liabilities	equals	Ownership interest ↑

Exhibit 5.2

Transactions of Dr Lee's medical practice for the month of October

Date	Business transactions of the entity (Nature of the entity: medical practice)	Amount
		£
Oct. 1	Dr Lee provides the practice with cash to allow business to start.	50,000
Oct. 2	The entity acquires medical equipment for cash.	30,000
Oct. 2	One month's rent is paid in advance for consulting rooms.	1,900
Oct. 2	Office furniture is purchased on two months' credit from Office Supplies Company.	6,500
Oct. 7	The practice purchases medical supplies on credit from P. Jones and receives an invoice.	1,200
Oct. 8	Dr Lee pays the medical receptionist for one week's work, 2 to 8 October.	300
Oct. 10	Four patients are examined, each paying £500 cash.	2,000
Oct. 11	The business pays P. Jones in cash for the goods it acquired on credit.	1,200
Oct. 14	The business pays an electricity bill in cash.	100
Oct. 15	Dr Lee pays the medical receptionist for one week's work, 9 to 15 October.	300
Oct. 17	Three patients are examined, their employer (Mrs West) being sent an invoice requesting payment of £500 for each.	1,500
Oct. 22	Dr Lee pays the medical receptionist for one week's work, 16 to 22 October.	300
Oct. 23	The employer (Mrs West) pays in cash for the examination of three patients.	1,500
Oct. 24	Four patients are examined, their employer (Mr East) being sent an invoice requesting payment of £500 for each.	2,000
Oct. 28	Dr Lee draws cash from the business for personal use	1,000
Oct. 29	Dr Lee pays the medical receptionist for one week's work, 23 to 29 October.	300
Oct. 31	The medical equipment and office furniture is estimated by Dr Lee to have fallen in value over the month.	250
Oct. 31	Dr Lee checks the stock of medical supplies and finds that items costing £350 have been used during the month.	350

Oct. 2   The medical practice now becomes the business entity so far as accounting is concerned (although it is fairly clear that Dr Lee is making all the decisions as the manager of the business as well as being the owner). The entity *acquires an asset* of medical equipment in exchange *for an equal amount of an asset* of cash. The accounting equation is satisfied because the increase in one asset is exactly equal to the decrease in another.

Assets ↑↓ – Liabilities	equals	Ownership interest

Oct. 2   The medical practice pays one month's rent in advance. At the moment of paying the rent, an asset is acquired representing the benefit to be gained from the use of the consulting rooms for the month ahead. However, this benefit only lasts for a short time and will have expired at the end of the accounting period (which has been chosen as one month for the purpose of this example). Once the benefit of an asset has expired, the business becomes worse off and the ownership interest decreases. That decrease is called an expense of the business. To save the time and trouble of recording such transactions as assets and then re-naming them as expenses at the end of the accounting period, the short-cut is taken of calling them expenses from the outset. There needs to be a check on such items at the end of the accounting period to ensure that there is no part of the benefit remaining which could still be an asset.

    In terms of the accounting equation there is a *decrease in the ownership interest due to an expense of the business*. There is a corresponding *decrease in the asset* of cash.

Assets ↓ – Liabilities	equals	**Ownership interest ↓ (expense)**

Oct. 2   The entity *acquires an asset* of office furniture. It does not pay cash on this occasion, having been given two months to pay. Looking over the rest of the transactions for October it is clear that there has been no payment by the end of the month. At the moment of taking delivery of the asset, the business incurs a liability to the supplier, Office Supplies Company. The accounting equation is satisfied because the *increase in an asset* is exactly equal to *the increase in a liability*.

Assets ↑ – **Liabilities** ↑	equals	Ownership interest

Oct. 7   The practice purchases medical supplies on credit from P. Jones and receives an invoice. This is very similar to the previous transaction. There *is acquisition of an asset* and *creation of a liability* to a supplier. The liability is recognised when the practice accepts delivery of the goods because that is the moment of accepting legal liability. For convenience, accounting procedures normally use the arrival of the invoice as the occasion for recording the liability but, even if the invoice failed to arrive, the liability must be recognised in relation to accepting the goods.

Assets ↑ – Liabilities ↑	equals	Ownership interest

Oct. 8 The medical receptionist has worked for one week and is paid for the work done. The amount paid in wages is an expense of the business which *decreases the ownership interest* because the benefit of that work has been used up in providing support for the medical practice. There is a *decrease in the asset* of cash.

Assets ↓ – Liabilities	equals	Ownership interest ↓ (expense)

Oct. 10 The medical practice now begins to carry out the activities which increase the wealth of the owner by earning revenue. The patients pay cash, so there is an *increase in the asset* of cash, and the owner becomes better off so there is an *increase in the ownership interest*.

Assets ↑ – Liabilities	equals	Ownership interest ↑ (revenue)

Oct. 11 The business pays P. Jones in cash for the goods it acquired on credit. Payment of cash *decreases the asset* of cash and *decreases the liability* to the supplier. Because the supplier is paid in full, the liability is extinguished.

Assets ↓ – Liabilities ↓	equals	Ownership interest

Oct. 14 The business pays an electricity bill in full. The business has enjoyed the use of the electricity but there is no benefit remaining. This is an *expense of the business* which causes a *decrease in the ownership interest*. There is a *decrease in the asset* of cash.

Assets ↓ – Liabilities	equals	Ownership interest ↓ (expense)

Oct. 15 The payment to the medical receptionist is similar in effect to the payment made on 8 October, causing a further *expense* which *decreases the ownership interest* and causes a *decrease in the asset* of cash.

Assets ↓ – Liabilities	equals	Ownership interest ↓ (expense)

Oct. 17 There is an increase in the *ownership interest* which arises from the operations of the business and so is termed *revenue*. On this occasion there is *acquisition of an asset* of a debtor, showing that an amount of money is owed by the employer of these patients.

Assets ↑ – Liabilities	equals	Ownership interest ↑ (revenue)

Oct. 22   The payment to the medical receptionist causes a further *expense* and a *decrease in the asset* of cash.

Assets ↓ – Liabilities	equals	Ownership interest ↓ (expense)

Oct. 23   The cash received from the employer of the three patients examined on 17 October causes an *increase in the asset* of cash and a *decrease in the asset* of the debtor. Because the amount is paid in full, the asset of the debtor is reduced to nil.

Assets ↑↓ – Liabilities	equals	Ownership interest

Oct. 24   Again the business carries out the activities intended to make the owner better off. The accounting effect is similar to that of 17 October, with *an increase in the ownership interest* and an *increase in the asset* of cash.

Assets ↑ – Liabilities	equals	Ownership interest ↑ (revenue)

Oct. 28   The owner of a sole trader business does not take a salary or wage as an employee would, but nevertheless needs cash for personal purposes. Taking cash for personal use is called taking 'drawings' and is recorded in terms of the accounting equation as a *decrease in the ownership interest* and a *decrease in the asset* of cash.

Assets ↓ – Liabilities	equals	Ownership interest ↓ (drawings)

Oct. 29   Paying wages causes an *expense* and a *decrease in the asset* of cash.

Assets ↓ – Liabilities	equals	Ownership interest ↓ (expense)

Oct. 31   The medical equipment and the office furniture are fixed assets of the business. They are expected to have some years' useful life in the business but they will eventually be used up. In accounting, the term 'depreciation' is applied to this gradual using up and there are various ways of deciding how much of the fixed asset has been 'used up' in any period. (Chapter 8 gives more information on depreciation.) For this example the owner's estimate of depreciation is sufficient. There is a *decrease in the fixed assets* which is not matched by an increase in any other asset and so there is a *decrease in the ownership interest* due to the operations of the business. Depreciation is an *expense* of the business.

Assets ↓ – Liabilities	equals	Ownership interest ↓ (expense)

Oct. 31   Dr Lee checks the stock of medical supplies and finds that items costing £350 have been used during the month. When these medical supplies

Exhibit 5.3
Spreadsheet analysing transactions into the elements of the accounting equation

Date	Business transactions of the entity (nature of the entity: medical practice)	Assets				Liabilities	Ownership interest		
		Cash and bank £	Debtors £	Stock £	Fixed assets £	Liabilities £	Capital contributed or withdrawn £	Revenue + £	Expenses − £
Oct. 1	Dr Lee provides the practice with cash to allow business to start	50,000					50,000		
Oct. 2	The entity acquires medical equipment for cash	(30,000)			30,000				
Oct. 2	One month's rent is paid in advance for consulting rooms	(1,900)							1,900
Oct. 2	Office furniture is purchased on two months' credit from Office Supplies Company				6,500	6,500			
Oct. 7	The practice purchases medical supplies on credit from P. Jones and receives an invoice			1,200		1,200			
Oct. 8	Dr Lee pays the medical receptionist for one week's work, 2 to 8 October	(300)							300
Oct. 10	Four patients are examined, each paying £500 cash	2,000						2,000	
Oct. 11	The business pays P. Jones in cash for the goods it acquired on credit	(1,200)				(1,200)			
Oct. 14	The business pays an electricity bill in cash	(100)							100
Oct. 15	Dr Lee pays the medical receptionist for one week's work, 9 to 15 October	(300)							300
Oct. 17	Three patients are examined, their employer (Mrs West) being sent an invoice requesting payment of £500 for each		1,500					1,500	
Oct. 22	Dr Lee pays the medical receptionist for one week's work, 16 to 22 October	(300)							300
Oct. 23	The employer (Mrs West) pays in cash for the examination of three patients	1,500	(1,500)						
Oct. 24	Four patients are examined, their employer (Mr East) being sent an invoice requesting apyment of £500 for each		2,000					2,000	
Oct. 28	Dr Lee draws cash from the business for personal use	(1,000)					(1,000)		
Oct. 29	Dr Lee pays the medical receptionist for one week's work, 23 to 29 October	(300)							300
Oct. 31	The medical equipment and office furniture is estimated by Dr Lee to have fallen in value over the month				(250)				250
Oct. 31	Dr Lee checks the stock of medical supplies and finds that items costing £350 have been used during the month			(350)					350
	Totals	18,100	2,000	850	36,250	6,500	49,000	5,500	3,800

57,200   50,700

were received on 7 October, they were all treated as an asset of the business. It appears now that the asset has been reduced from £1,200 to £850 and that the items used up have caused a decrease of £350 in the ownership interest. This decrease is the expense of medical supplies which will appear in the profit and loss account of the month. The two aspects of this event are therefore a *decrease in the ownership interest* and a *decrease in the asset* of stock of medical supplies.

Assets ↓ – Liabilities	equals	Ownership interest ↓ (expense)

This analysis has been set out in some detail to show that each transaction must first of all be considered, in order to establish the nature of the two aspects of the transaction, before any attempt is made to deal with the monetary amounts. The next section uses the analysis based on the accounting equation to produce a spreadsheet which can be totalled to give a summary picture of the transactions of the month in terms of the accounting equation.

L03   5.4   A process for summarising the transactions: a spreadsheet

In Exhibit 5.3 the transactions are repeated in the left-hand column but the relevant money amounts are shown in columns which correspond to the assets, liabilities and ownership interest, using brackets to show a negative amount. (It would be equally acceptable to use a minus sign but minus signs tend to disappear or be confused with unintentional blobs on the paper, so brackets are frequently used in accounting in order to ensure clarity.)

Taking the first line as an example, the analysis of the transaction showed that there was an increase in the asset of cash and an increase in the ownership interest. Thus the amount of £50,000 is written in the spreadsheet column for cash and again in the spreadsheet column for ownership interest. In the second line, the asset of cash decreases by £30,000 and the asset of medical equipment increases by £30,000. A similar pattern follows down the spreadsheet for each transaction.

It may be seen that where there are more than a few transactions during the month, a spreadsheet of the type shown in Exhibit 5.3 would need to be much larger and use more columns.

At the foot of the spreadsheet in Exhibit 5.3 there is a total for each column. Those totals from Exhibit 5.3 are used in Exhibit 5.4, which represents the accounting equation, to show the state of the accounting equation at the end of the month. It may be used to explain to Dr Lee how the ownership interest has changed over the month. The owner contributed £50,000 at the start of the month and has a claim of £50,700 at the end of the month. The ownership interest was increased by earning revenue of £5,500 but reduced by incurring expenses of £3,800 and withdrawing £1,000 for personal use.

Exhibit 5.4
Summary of transactions analysed into the elements of the accounting equation

Assets	minus	Liabilities	=	Ownership interest at start of period	plus	Capital contributed/ withdrawn	plus	Revenue	minus	Expenses
£57,200	–	£6,500		nil	+	£49,000	+	£5,500	–	£3,800
	£50,700					£50,700				

L04 · 5.5 Financial statements as a means of communication

This chapter has established the approach taken in accounting towards analysing and classifying transactions in such a way that Dr Lee as the owner of a business knows how much better off or worse off he or she has become during a period. There is sufficient information contained in Exhibit 5.3 and it is possible to write an interpretation based on Exhibit 5.4. However, this presentation is not particularly informative or easy on the eye.

The process of communication requires some attention to a clear style of presentation. Accounting practice has evolved the cash flow statement, the profit and loss account and the balance sheet to give the owner a more informative presentation of the information contained in Exhibits 5.3 and 5.4.

Chapter 3 set out the structure of the financial statements of a business. These ideas are now applied to Dr Lee's medical practice. Don't worry too much about how the information is transferred from Exhibit 5.3 to these financial statements, but look back to the table and satisfy yourself that you can find the corresponding pieces of information.

5.5.1 Cash flow statement

Medical Practice of Dr Lee
Cash flow statement for the month of October Year XX

	£
Operating activities	
Inflow from fees	3,500
Outflow: rent paid	(1,900)
payment to supplier (P. Jones)	(1,200)
wages	(1,200)
electricity	(100)
Net outflow from operations	(900)
Investing activities	
Payment for equipment	(30,000)
Net outflow for investing activities	(30,000)

Financing activities	£
Capital contributed by owner	50,000
Capital withdrawn as drawings	(1,000)
Net inflow from financing activities	49,000
Increase in cash at bank over period	18,100

Comment: All the amounts for this statement are taken from the 'Cash at bank' column of Exhibit 5.3 but are regrouped for the three headings of operating activities, investing activities and financing activities. The statement shows that the business had a net outflow of cash of £900 due to operations and an outflow of cash amounting to £30,000 due to purchase of medical equipment. The owner contributed £50,000 at the start of the month but took drawings of £1,000 at the end, resulting in a net inflow of £49,000 from financing. The overall effect was an increase in cash over the period amounting to £18,100.

5.5.2 Statement of profit or loss

Medical Practice of Dr Lee
Profit and loss account for the month of October Year XX

	£	£
Fees charged		5,500
Medical supplies used	350	
Wages	1,200	
Rent	1,900	
Electricity	100	
Depreciation	250	
		3,800
Profit		1,700

Comment: The total fees charged constitute the total revenue of the period as may be seen in the column in Exhibit 5.3 headed 'revenue'. The expenses of the period amount to £3,800 and are taken from the final column of Exhibit 5.3. The difference between revenue and expenses is the profit of £1,700. This is the amount by which the ownership interest has increased to make the owner of the business better off.

Some students ask at this point why the owner's drawings are not included in the profit and loss account. One answer is that it has always been done that way. The answer usually given by textbooks is that making drawings of cash has nothing to do with the operations of the business. It is a voluntary action taken by the owner, who is also the manager, balancing the owner's personal need for cash against the needs of the business for cash to ensure continued smooth running. That answer is usually sufficient unless a student has been reading ahead and has found that when the owners of a company take cash in the form of dividends, that information does appear in the profit and loss account. The difference between the two situations lies in the additional discretion available to the owner/manager of a sole trader or partnership business. In a limited liability company the shareholders are dependent on the recommendations of directors regarding the best use of the company's cash.

L04 | **Activity 5.3**

The medical practice of Dr Lee has made a profit of £1,700 over the month but the cash flow caused by operations is an outflow of £900. How can a business make a profit and yet see an outflow of cash caused by operations? This question is asked all too often in reality. You can provide the answer by comparing the cash flow due to operating activities and the calculation of net profit. If you are not sure how to make the comparison, look back to Chapter 3 where the financial statements of P. Mason's legal practice were analysed (Exhibit 3.7).

5.5.3 Balance sheet

Medical Practice of Dr Lee
Balance sheet at 31 October Year XX

Accounting equation		£	£
	Fixed assets		
	Medical equipment at cost		30,000
	Office furniture		6,500
			36,500
	Depreciation		(250)
FA	Depreciated cost of fixed assets		36,250
	Current assets		
	Medical supplies	850	
	Debtors	2,000	
	Cash at bank	18,100	
		20,950	
	Current liabilities		
	Trade creditors	(6,500)	
CA – CL	Current assets less current liabilities		14,450
A – L	Net assets		50,700
	Capital at start		50,000
	add: profit		1,700
	less: drawings		(1,000)
OI	**Total ownership interest**		50,700

Comment: The balance sheet follows the pattern of the accounting equation, as shown at the left-hand side. The fixed assets (FA) are presented first of all, showing the resources available to the business over a longer period of time. The depreciation is deducted to leave an amount remaining which is probably best described as the 'depreciated cost' but is often labelled 'net book value' or 'written down value'. Chapter 8 contains more information on the procedures for measuring and recording depreciation and the limitations of using the word 'value' in relation to those procedures.

The next section contains the current assets (CA) which are expected to be converted into cash within a 12-month period. The medical supplies shown are those which have not yet been used and therefore remain as a benefit for the next month.

Debtors are those customers who are expected to pay in the near future. The other current asset is the cash held at the bank, which is very accessible in the short term.

The only liability is the amount of £6,500 owing to the Office Supplies Company, due for payment at the start of December. This is a current liability because it is due for payment within 12 months.

It is felt to be helpful in the balance sheet to set out subtotals which may guide the reader. These have been shaded in the balance sheet. The total of fixed assets is interesting as the long-term asset base used to generate profits. The difference between the current assets and the current liabilities is sometimes called the *working capital*. At the moment the current assets look rather high in relation to the need to cover current liabilities. This is because the amount of cash held is quite high in relation to the apparent needs of the business. It is possible that Dr Lee has plans to use the cash for business purposes quite soon but, in the absence of such plans, Dr Lee ought to consider investing it to earn interest or else withdrawing it for other uses.

The amount for total assets less total liabilities (A − L) is usually called the *net assets* of the business. (The word 'net' means 'after taking something away' – in this case, after taking away the liabilities.) There is not much to say here except to note that it equals the ownership interest as would be expected from the accounting equation. The ownership interest has increased over the period through making a profit of £1,700 but decreased by £1,000 through making drawings, so that the resulting increase is £700 overall.

L04 | **Activity 5.4**

Compare the financial statements of Dr Lee's medical practice with the information collected in the spreadsheet of Exhibit 5.3. Take a pencil and, very lightly, place a tick against each amount in the financial statements and a tick against each amount in the spreadsheet, as you match them together. If you are able to work backwards in this way from the financial statements to the spreadsheet then you will be well on the way to understanding how the financial statements are related to the original list of transactions.

5.6 Summary

Now score your view of your confidence in achieving the learning outcomes of the chapter.

1 = Very confident about knowledge, application, problem solving and evaluation.

2 = Confident about knowledge and application, less sure about problem solving and evaluation.

3 = Need to read again to be more certain of basic knowledge and application.

L01 You can now explain how the accounting equation is applied to transactions of a service business.   1 2 3 ☐ ☐ ☐

L02 You can analyse the transactions of a service business during a specific period of time, using the accounting equation.   1 2 3 ☐ ☐ ☐

LO3 You can prepare a spreadsheet analysing the transactions and show that the results of the spreadsheet are consistent with the financial statements provided by the organisation.

1	2	3
☐	☐	☐

LO4 You can explain the main aspects of the cash flow statement, profit and loss account and balance sheet of a service business.

1	2	3
☐	☐	☐

LO5 If you wish to be able to analyse the transactions of a service business using the rules of debit and credit bookkeeping, you should now read the Supplement.

1	2	3
☐	☐	☐

LO6 You will also learn from the Supplement how to prepare, from a list of transactions of an organisation, ledger accounts and a trial balance which could be used to prepare the financial statements provided by the organisation.

1	2	3
☐	☐	☐

If your scores are all 1 or 2, try the questions in the series A and B. This will give you feedback on your assessment of how well you have achieved the learning outcomes. Read again any sections of the chapter where you find your knowledge and understanding are less comprehensive than you first estimated.

If your scores include some at 3, try the series A questions to find where the problems lie. Read the relevant sections again, work through any illustrative examples and case studies, then try the questions in the series B.

International perspective

The rules for debit and credit bookkeeping are used in all countries which apply the double entry system. However some countries have more rules in their company law about the structure of the ledger accounts. In France, for example, there is a Chart of Accounts which creates a national system for numbering ledger accounts.

Test your understanding

Skills outcomes
SO1 Application of technical skills   SO2 Problem solving and evaluation skills   SO3 Communication skills

LO2, SO1 **A5.1** The following list of transactions relates to a television repair business during the first month of business. Explain how each transaction affects the accounting equation:

Transaction
(a) Owner puts cash into the business.
(b) Buy a vehicle for cash.
(c) Receive a bill for electricity consumed.
(d) Purchase stationery for office use, paying cash.
(e) Pay the electricity bill in cash.
(f)   Pay rental for a computer, used to keep customer records.
(g) Buy spare parts for cash, to use in repairs.
(h) Buy spare parts on credit terms.

(i) Pay garage service bills for van, using cash.

(j) Fill van with petrol, using credit account at local garage, to be paid at the start of next month.

(k) Carry out repairs for cash.

(l) Carry out repairs on credit terms.

(m) Pay wages to an employee.

(n) Owner takes cash for personal use.

L04, S01   **A5.2** Which of the items in the list of transactions in question **A5.1** will have an effect on a profit and loss account?

L04, S01   **A5.3** Which of the items in the list of transactions in question **A5.1** will have an effect on a cash flow statement?

L04, S01   **A5.4** Which of the items in the list of transactions in question **A5.1** will have an effect on a balance sheet?

L02, S01   **A5.5** Analyse each of the following transactions to show the two aspects of the transaction:

Apr. 1   Jane Gate commenced her dental practice on 1 April by depositing £60,000 in a business bank account.

Apr. 1   Rent for a surgery was paid, £800, for the month of April.

Apr. 2   Dental equipment was purchased for £35,000, paying in cash.

Apr. 3   Dental supplies were purchased for £5,000, taking 30 days' credit from a supplier.

Apr. 4   Fees of £1,200 were collected in cash from patients and paid into the bank account.

Apr. 15   Dental assistant was paid wages for two weeks, £700.

Apr. 20   Jane Gate withdrew £500 cash for personal use.

Apr. 21   Fees of £2,400 were collected in cash from patients and paid into the bank.

Apr. 29   Dental assistant was paid wages for two weeks, £700.

Apr. 29   Invoices were sent to patients who are allowed 20 days' credit, for work done during April amounting to £1,900.

Apr. 30   Telephone bill for April was paid, £80.

Apr. 30   Dental supplies unused were counted and found to be worth £3,500, measured at cost price.

Application

L03, S01   **B5.1**

(a) Using the list of transactions at question **A5.5** of Test your understanding *above*, prepare a spreadsheet similar to that presented in Exhibit 5.3.

(b) Show that the spreadsheet totals satisfy the accounting equation.

L04, S01   **B5.2** Using the totals from the columns of the spreadsheet of question **B5.1**, prepare for the dental practice in the month of April:

(a) a cash flow statement;

(b) a balance sheet; and

(c) a profit and loss account.

There are no questions in the C series for this chapter. These skills are tested in specific situations in Chapters 8 to 12.

Recording transactions in ledger accounts: a service business

In the Supplement to Chapter 2 it was shown that the rules for debit and credit book-keeping may be summarised in terms of the elements of the accounting equation as shown in Exhibit 5.5.

Exhibit 5.5
Rules for debit and credit entries in ledger accounts

	Debit entries in a ledger account	Credit entries in a ledger account
Left-hand side of the equation		
Asset	Increase	Decrease
Right-hand side of the equation		
Liability	Decrease	Increase
Ownership interest	Expense	Revenue
	Capital withdrawn	Capital contributed

In the Supplement to Chapter 3 a spreadsheet was used to show that a series of transactions could be analysed and summarised in tabular form. That spreadsheet format is becoming increasingly used as the basis for computer-based recording of transactions but the more conventional approach to analysing transactions is to collect them together in ledger accounts. This supplement takes the transactions of Chapter 5 and analyses them in debit and credit form in order to produce a trial balance as a basis for the preparation of financial statements.

In Exhibit 5.1 some common transactions of a service business were listed and then analysed using the accounting equation. They will now be analysed in terms of where the debit and credit entries would be made in a ledger account. Test yourself by trying out the answer before you look at the answer in Exhibit 5.6 below. Once you are satisfied that you could produce the correct answer for the transactions in Exhibit 5.1, you are ready to deal with Dr Lee's medical practice.

Exhibit 5.6

Analysis of service business transactions (from Exhibit 5.1) to identify two aspects of each

Transaction	Aspects of the transaction	Debit entry in	Credit entry in
Receive cash from the owner	Acquisition of an asset (cash)	Cash	
	Acceptance of ownership interest		Ownership interest
Buy a vehicle for cash	Acquisition of an asset (vehicle)	Vehicle	
	Reduction in an asset (cash)		Cash
Receive a bill for gas consumed	Incur an expense (gas consumed)	Gas expense	
	Incur a liability (to the gas supplier)		Supplier
Pay the gas bill in cash	Decrease a liability (to the gas supplier)	Supplier	
	Reduction in an asset (cash)		Cash
Buy materials for cash	Increase in an asset (stock of materials)	Stock	
	Decrease in an asset (cash)		Cash
Buy materials on credit	Acquisition of an asset (stock of materials)	Stock	
	Incur a liability (to the supplier)		Supplier
Sell services for cash	Acquisition of an asset (cash)	Cash	
	Earn revenue		Sales
Sell services on credit	Acquisition of an asset (debtors)	Debtors	
	Earn revenue		Sales
Pay wages to an employee	Incur an expense (cost of wages)	Wages expense	
	Decrease in asset (cash)		Cash
Pay cash to the owner for personal use	Reduction in the ownership interest	Ownership interest	
	Reduction in an asset (cash)		Cash

Illustration: Dr Lee's medical practice

The first transaction in Exhibit 5.2 reads:

'Oct. 1   Dr Lee provides the practice with cash, £50,000.'

The two aspects of this transaction were identified as:

1   Acquisition of an asset (cash)
2   Increasing the ownership interest (voluntary contribution).

The bookkeeping system requires two ledger accounts in which to record this transaction. One ledger account is called **Cash** and the other is called **Ownership interest**. There will be a *debit* entry of £50,000 in the **Cash** ledger account showing that the business has acquired an asset of £50,000 cash. There will be a *credit* entry of £50,000 in the **Ownership interest** ledger account showing that the business acknowledges the claim of the owner for eventual return of the amount contributed.

The second transaction in Exhibit 5.2 reads:

'Oct. 2   The entity acquires medical equipment for cash, £30,000.'

The two aspects of this transaction were identified as:

1   Acquisition of an asset (medical equipment)
2   Decrease of an asset (cash).

The bookkeeping system requires two ledger accounts in which to record this transaction. One ledger account is called **Medical equipment** and the other is called **Cash**.

There will be a *debit* entry of £30,000 in the **Medical equipment** ledger account showing that the business has acquired an asset of £30,000 medical equipment.

There will be a *credit* entry of £30,000 in the **Cash** ledger account showing that the business has reduced its asset of cash by £30,000 to pay for the medical equipment.

L05   Analysing the debit and credit entries for each transaction

Exhibit 5.7 takes the information contained in Exhibit 5.2 and analyses it under debit and credit headings showing the ledger accounts in which each entry will be made.

Ledger accounts required to record these transactions are:

L1	Cash	L8	Stock of medical supplies
L2	Ownership interest	L9	P. Jones
L3	Medical equipment and office furniture	L10	Electricity
L4	Office Supplies Company	L11	Mrs West
L5	Rent	L12	Mr East
L6	Wages	L13	Depreciation
L7	Patients' fees	L14	Expense of medical supplies

Exhibit 5.7

Analysis of debit and credit aspect of each transaction of the medical practice

Date	Business transactions of medical practice	Amount	Debit	Credit
		£		
Oct. 1	Dr Lee provides the practice with cash to allow business to start.	50,000	Cash	Owner
Oct. 2	The entity acquires medical equipment for cash.	30,000	Equipment	Cash
Oct. 2	One month's rent is paid in advance for consulting rooms.	1,900	Rent	Cash
Oct. 2	Office furniture is purchased on two months' credit from Office Supplies Company.	6,500	Furniture	Office supplies
Oct. 7	The practice purchases medical supplies on credit from P. Jones and receives an invoice.	1,200	Stock	P. Jones
Oct. 8	Dr Lee pays the medical receptionist for one week's work, 2 to 8 October.	300	Wages	Cash
Oct. 10	Four patients are examined, each paying £500 cash.	2,000	Cash	Patients' fees
Oct. 11	The business pays P. Jones in cash for the goods it acquired on credit.	1,200	P. Jones	Cash
Oct. 14	The business pays an electricity bill in cash.	100	Electricity	Cash
Oct. 15	Dr Lee pays the medical receptionist for one week's work, 9 to 15 October.	300	Wages	Cash
Oct. 17	Three patients are examined, their employer (Mrs West) being sent an invoice requesting payment of £500 for each.	1,500	Mrs West	Fees
Oct. 22	Dr Lee pays the medical receptionist for one week's work, 16 to 22 October.	300	Wages	Cash
Oct. 23	The employer (Mrs West) pays in cash for the examination of three patients.	1,500	Cash	Mrs West
Oct. 24	Four patients are examined, their employer (Mr East) being sent an invoice requesting payment of £500 for each.	2,000	Mr East	Fees
Oct. 28	Dr Lee draws cash from the business for personal use.	1,000	Owner	Cash
Oct. 29	Dr Lee pays the medical receptionist for one week's work, 23 to 29 October.	300	Wages	Cash
Oct. 31	The medical equipment and office furniture is estimated by Dr Lee to have fallen in value over the month.	250	Depreciation	Equipment and furniture
Oct. 31	Dr Lee checks the stock of medical supplies and finds that items costing £350 have been used during the month.	350	Medical supplies expense	Stock

Form of ledger accounts

There is no single standard form of ledger account rulings in which to record debit and credit transactions. Historically, ledger accounts were recorded in what were called 'T' accounts where all the debit entries were on the left-hand side and all the credit entries on the right-hand side. This was designed to minimise arithmetic errors by avoiding subtractions in systems which were dealt with manually.

Form of a 'T' ledger account

Page number and name of the account

Debit entries   **Credit entries**

Date	Particulars	Page	£	p	Date	Particulars	Page	£	p

This type of layout requires a wide page if it is to be read clearly. In recent years ledger accounts have more frequently been prepared in a 'three-column' ruling which keeps a running total. This textbook will use the three-column ruling throughout. You will see by comparison of the column headings that the different types of rulings use the same information. If you have an opportunity to look at business ledgers you will probably come across yet more varieties, but they will all require the inclusion of this basic set of information.

Three-column ruling

Date	Particulars	Page	Debit	Credit	Balance
			£ p	£ p	£ p

Features are:

- The left-hand column will show the date of the transaction.
- The 'particulars' column will show essential narrative, usually confined to the name of the ledger account which records the other aspect of the transaction.
- The 'page' column will show the ledger account page number of the ledger account where the other aspect of the transaction is recorded.
- The amount of the transaction will be entered in the debit or credit column as appropriate.
- The 'balance' column will keep a running total by treating all debit entries as positive and all credit entries as negative. A credit balance will be shown in brackets as a reminder that it is negative. Some ledger systems print the letters 'dr' or 'cr' against the balance.

Illustration

The first transaction of Exhibit 5.7 may now be shown in the appropriate ledger accounts. It will require a *debit* entry in a cash account to indicate an increase in the asset of cash and a *credit* entry in the ownership interest account to indicate an increase in the owner's claim.

L1 Cash

Date	Particulars	Page	Debit	Credit	Balance
			£	£	£
Oct. 1	Ownership interest	L2	50,000		50,000

L2 Ownership interest

Date	Particulars	Page	Debit	Credit	Balance
			£	£	£
Oct. 1	Cash	L1		50,000	(50,000)

L06 Ledger accounts for Dr Lee's medical practice

The full ledger account record for the transactions in Exhibit 5.7 is now set out. Leona Rees comments on each ledger account, showing how she interprets ledger accounts in her work of auditing and accounting.

L1 Cash

Date	Particulars	Page	Debit	Credit	Balance
			£	£	£
Oct. 1	Ownership interest	L2	50,000		50,000
Oct. 2	Medical equipment	L3		30,000	20,000
Oct. 2	Rent	L5		1,900	18,100
Oct. 8	Wages	L6		300	17,800
Oct. 10	Patients' fees	L7	2,000		19,800
Oct. 11	P. Jones	L9		1,200	18,600
Oct. 14	Electricity	L10		100	18,500
Oct. 15	Wages	L6		300	18,200
Oct. 22	Wages	L6		300	17,900
Oct. 23	Mrs West	L11	1,500		19,400
Oct. 28	Ownership interest taken as drawings	L2		1,000	18,400
Oct. 29	Wages	L6		300	18,100

LEONA's comment: *The amount of £50,000 put into the business at the start is quickly eaten into by spending cash on medical equipment and paying rent in advance. Further items such as paying a supplier, paying the electricity account and the assistant's wages took the cash balance down further but it remained quite high throughout the month. With the benefit of hindsight the owner might not have needed to put so much cash into the business at the outset. Up to £18,000 could have been invested on a short-term basis to earn interest, either for the business or for Dr Lee.*

L2 Ownership interest

Date	Particulars	Page	Debit	Credit	Balance
			£	£	£
Oct. 1	Cash contributed	L1		50,000	(50,000)
Oct. 28	Cash drawn	L1	1,000		(49,000)

LEONA's comment: *The ownership interest is created when the owner contributes cash or resources to the business. In this case it was cash. The sole trader in business may withdraw cash for personal use at any time – it is called owner's drawings – but the desirability of that action depends on how useful cash is to the owner when compared to how useful it might have been if left in the business. The owner of this business has a claim remaining equal to £49,000 after making the drawing.*

L3 Medical equipment and office furniture

Date	Particulars	Page	Debit	Credit	Balance
			£	£	£
Oct. 2	Cash	L1	30,000		30,000
Oct. 2	Office Supplies Company	L4	6,500		36,500
Oct. 31	Depreciation	L13		250	36,250

LEONA's comment: *This ledger account is particularly useful as a reminder that some very valuable assets are owned by the business. Having a record in the ledger account encourages the owner to think about continuing care for the medical equipment and office furniture and also to review their value against the amount recorded. If Dr Lee intended to have a large number of fixed asset items it is possible to have a separate ledger account for each, but that seems a long-distant prospect at the moment.*

Depreciation is a way of showing that the original cost of the asset has to be spread over its useful life. If the estimate of depreciation is correct, this ledger account should reduce to nil on the day the equipment and furniture ceases to be of use. In reality, things usually are not quite so straightforward. (Depreciation of fixed assets is dealt with in more detail in Chapter 8.)

L4 Office Supplies Company

Date	Particulars	Page	Debit	Credit	Balance
			£	£	£
Oct. 2	Office furniture	L3		6,500	(6,500)

LEONA's comment: *When the office furniture was purchased from the Office Supplies Company, an invoice was received from that company showing the amount due. That invoice was used to make the credit entry on 2 October showing that the business had a liability. The liability remained owing at 31 October, but that is acceptable because the supplier allowed 2 months' credit.*

L5 Rent

Date	Particulars	Page	Debit	Credit	Balance
			£	£	£
Oct. 2	Cash	L1	1,900		1,900

LEONA's comment: *This payment in advance starts by being an asset and gradually turns into an expense as the benefit is used up. For bookkeeping purposes, a debit entry records both an asset and an expense so it is only at the end of the month that some care is needed in thinking about the nature of the debit balance. In this case it is clear that the benefit is used up but there could be a situation where part of the benefit remained to be reported as an asset.*

L6 Wages

Date	Particulars	Page	Debit	Credit	Balance
			£	£	£
Oct. 8	Cash	L1	300		300
Oct. 15	Cash	L1	300		600
Oct. 22	Cash	L1	300		900
Oct. 29	Cash	L1	300		1,200

LEONA's comment: *This is a straightforward account in which to accumulate all wages expenses. A very enthusiastic accountant would estimate the liability for the final two days of the month and add these on, but there is a very useful idea in accounting called 'materiality' which, broadly interpreted, means the extra information provided would not justify the extra amount of work involved.*

L7 Patients' fees

Date	Particulars	Page	Debit	Credit	Balance
			£	£	£
Oct. 10	Cash	L1		2,000	(2,000)
Oct. 17	Credit: Mrs West (as employer)	L11		1,500	(3,500)
Oct. 24	Credit: Mr East (as employer)	L12		2,000	(5,500)

LEONA's comment: *This is a revenue account so credit entries are expected. The balance column shows the total patients' fees earned in the month were £5,500. This could be described as 'turnover' or 'sales' but both of those words sound rather out of place when a professional service is being described.*

L8 Stock of medical supplies

Date	Particulars	Page	Debit	Credit	Balance
			£	£	£
Oct. 7	P. Jones	L9	1,200		1,200
Oct. 31	Expense of medical supplies	L14		350	850

LEONA's comment: *This is an asset account so when the medical supplies were acquired on credit from P. Jones the entire amount was recorded as an asset. These medical supplies will be quite small items and it would not be appropriate for Dr Lee to have to count every cotton wool swab, hypodermic needle or sample bottle used in each examination. It is sufficient for accounting purposes to count up what is left at the end of the period (we call it 'taking stock') and assume that the difference represents the amount used during the period. As an auditor, I might start to ask questions about possible errors, fraud or theft if the amounts of supplies used did not look sensible when compared with the number of examinations carried out on patients.*

L9 P. Jones

Date	Particulars	Page	Debit	Credit	Balance
			£	£	£
Oct. 7	Stock of medical supplies	L8		1,200	(1,200)
Oct. 11	Cash	L1	1,200		nil

LEONA's comment: *When the medical supplies were delivered to Dr Lee, the business took on a liability to pay P. Jones. That liability was recorded by a credit entry in the ledger account for P. Jones and was extinguished on 11 October when the medical practice paid £1,200 to P. Jones.*

L10 Electricity

Date	Particulars	Page	Debit	Credit	Balance
			£	£	£
Oct. 14	Cash	L1	100		100

LEONA's comment: *This is a very straightforward expense account. The balance on this account will show the total expense of electricity consumed during the period.*

L11 Mrs West

Date	Particulars	Page	Debit	Credit	Balance
			£	£	£
Oct. 17	Patients' fees	L7	1,500		1,500
Oct. 23	Cash	L1		1,500	nil

L12 Mr East

Date	Particulars	Page	Debit	Credit	Balance
			£	£	£
Oct. 24	Patients' fees	L7	2,000		2,000

LEONA's comment: *The credit sale to the employees of Mrs West and Mr East made them debtors of the business and so there is a debit entry. By the end of October Mr East had not paid, so remains a debtor, denoted by a debit balance. Mrs West has paid during October and a nil balance is the result.*

L13 Depreciation

Date	Particulars	Page	Debit	Credit	Balance
			£	£	£
Oct. 31	Medical equipment and office furniture	L3	250		250

LEONA's comment: *This is another expense account showing an item which has decreased the ownership interest through a decrease in the recorded amount of some assets. This is where accounting begins to look slightly complicated because no cash has changed hands. Recording depreciation is the accounting way of expressing caution as to the expected future benefits from an asset. These will be eroded as the asset is used up. Depreciation is a way of acknowledging that erosion.*

L14 Expense of medical supplies

Date	Particulars	Page	Debit	Credit	Balance
			£	£	£
Oct. 31	Stock of medical supplies	L8	350		350

LEONA's comment: *This account continues the story from L8 where the stock of medical supplies was found to have dwindled through use in examining patients. It is assumed that the difference between the amount purchased and the amount held at the end of the month represents the expense of using the asset during the month.*

Checking the accuracy of double entry records

At periodic intervals it may be considered necessary for a number of reasons to check the accuracy of the entries made in ledger accounts. For instance, the omission of an entry on the debit side of a customer's ledger account for goods sold on credit terms could result in a failure to issue reminders for payment of an amount owed to the business.

There are methods in double entry bookkeeping of discovering these and other errors. One such method is the use of the *trial balance*.

If a debit entry and a credit entry have been made in the appropriate ledger accounts for each business transaction, then the total money amount of all the debit entries will equal the total money amount of all the credit entries. If a debit entry has been made without a corresponding credit entry (or vice versa), then the totals will not agree.

In the ledger accounts shown in this example, the balances have been kept as running totals. It would be possible to add up all the debit and all the credit entries in each ledger account but the same arithmetic proof will be obtained by listing all the debit balances and all the credit balances. It was explained earlier in this supplement that brackets are used in the ledger accounts to show credit balances. The list of balances on all the ledger accounts for Dr Lee's medical practice is set out in Exhibit 5.8.

Exhibit 5.8

Trial balance at 31 October for Dr Lee's medical practice

Ledger account title	Debit	Credit
	£	£
L1 Cash	18,100	
L2 Ownership interest		49,000
L3 Medical equipment and office furniture	36,250	
L4 Office Supplies Company		6,500
L5 Rent	1,900	
L6 Wages	1,200	
L7 Patients' fees		5,500
L8 Stock of medical supplies	850	
L9 P. Jones		nil
L10 Electricity	100	
L11 Mrs West	nil	
L12 Mr East	2,000	
L13 Depreciation	250	
L14 Expense of medical supplies	350	
Totals	61,000	61,000

Error detection using the trial balance

The calculation of the totals of each column of the trial balance is a useful precaution which will reveal some, but not all, of the errors it is possible to make in a debit and credit recording system. Think first about the errors you might make and then check against the following list:

Errors which will be detected by unequal totals in the trial balance

- Omitting one aspect of a transaction (e.g. a debit entry but no credit entry).
- Writing incorrect amounts in one entry (e.g. debit £290 but credit £209).
- Writing both entries in one column (e.g. two debits, no credit).
- Incorrect calculation of ledger account balance.

Errors which will leave the trial balance totals equal

- Total omission of a transaction.
- Errors in both debit and credit entry of the same magnitude.
- Entering the correct amount in the wrong ledger account (e.g. debit for wages entered as debit for heat and light).

Preparing the financial statements

The main part of this chapter set out the balance sheet and profit and loss account of Dr Lee's medical practice for the month of October. If you compare the amounts in the trial balance with the amounts in the financial statements you will see they are the same. The normal practice in accounting is to use the trial balance to prepare the balance sheet and profit and loss account.

In this case it would be a little easier to use the trial balance for this purpose if it were arranged so that all the balance sheet items are together and all the profit and loss account items are together. This is done in Exhibit 5.9.

Exhibit 5.9
Rearranging the trial balance into balance sheet items and profit and loss account items

Ledger account title	£	£
L3 Medical equipment and office furniture	36,250	
L8 Stock of medical supplies	850	
L12 Mr East	2,000	
L11 Mrs West	nil	
L1 Cash at bank	18,100	
L4 Office Supplies Company		6,500
L9 P. Jones		nil
L2 Ownership interest		49,000
Subtotal	57,200	55,500
Difference: profit of the month		1,700
L7 Patients' fees		5,500
L14 Expense of medical supplies	350	
L6 Wages	1,200	
L5 Rent	1,900	
L10 Electricity	100	
L13 Depreciation	250	
Subtotal	3,800	5,500
Difference: profit of the month	1,700	
Total of ledger balances in each column	61,000	61,000

This form of trial balance will be used in later chapters as the starting point for the preparation of financial statements.

By way of providing further help in preparing the profit and loss account and balance sheet, subtotals are calculated for each part of the trial balance in Exhibit 5.9. The difference between the subtotals in each section gives the profit amount. That is because the exhibit has been subdivided according to two equations, each of which leads to profit:

Assets	*minus*	Liabilities	*minus*	Capital contributed/ withdrawn	*equals*	Profit

	Revenue	*minus*	Expenses	*equals*	Profit	

L05, L06, S01 — ## Test your understanding

S5.1 Prepare ledger accounts for the transactions of Jane Gate's dental practice, listed in question **A5.5**.

S5.2 Which of the following errors would be detected at the point of listing a trial balance?

(a) The bookkeeper enters a cash sale as a debit of £49 in the cash book and as a credit of £94 in the sales account.
(b) The bookkeeper omits a cash sale of £23 from the cash book and from the sales accounts.
(c) The bookkeeper enters cash received of £50 from Peter Jones as a debit in the cash book but enters the credit of £50 in the ledger account of Roger Jones.
(d) The bookkeeper enters a cash sale as a credit of £40 in the cash book and as a debit of £40 in the sales account.

Chapter 6

Accounting information for trading businesses

After studying this chapter you should be able to:

LO1 Explain the application of the accounting equation to transactions involving the buying and selling of trading stock.

LO2 Explain the application of the accounting equation to transactions involving the manufacture and sale of products.

LO3 Analyse transactions of a trading or manufacturing business during a specific period of time, using the accounting equation.

LO4 Prepare a spreadsheet analysing the transactions, and show that the results of the spreadsheet analysis are consistent with financial statements provided by the organisation.

LO5 Explain the main aspects of the cash flow statement, profit and loss account and balance sheet of a trading or a manufacturing business.

Additionally, for those who choose to study the Supplement:

LO6 Analyse the transactions of a trading or a manufacturing business using the rules of debit and credit bookkeeping.

LO7 Prepare, from a list of transactions of an organisation, ledger accounts and a trial balance which could be used to confirm the financial statements provided by the organisation.

6.1 Introduction

Chapter 5 has shown in detail the application of the accounting equation to the analysis of transactions in service businesses. The same approach applies in the case of trading businesses, but with one significant addition. Businesses which engage in trading have either purchased or manufactured a product with the intention of selling that product to customers. It is the purchase or manufacture of a product and the act of selling the product which must be analysed carefully in terms of the accounting equation. This chapter first analyses the transactions and events occurring when goods are purchased for resale and sold to a customer. Secondly, it analyses the transactions and events occurring when goods are manufactured and then sold to a customer. Finally, there is a worked example which takes one month's transactions of a trading business and shows the resulting financial statements.

LO1 6.2 Goods purchased for resale

A trading business which buys goods for resale (e.g. a wholesaler buying goods from a manufacturer for distribution to retailers) makes a profit by selling the goods at a price which is higher than the price paid. The difference between the selling price and the purchase price is called the *gross profit* of the business. The gross profit must be sufficient to cover all the costs of running the business (e.g. administration, marketing and distribution costs) and leave a net profit which will increase the ownership interest in the business.

6.2.1 Analysis of transactions

Consider the transactions of a trading company set out in Exhibit 6.1, relating to buying and selling goods.

Exhibit 6.1

Transactions of a trading company

		£
Apr. 1	Purchase goods from manufacturer, 100 items at £2 each, paying in cash, and store in warehouse.	200
Apr. 4	Remove 70 items from warehouse to meet a customer's request. Those 70 items cost £2 each on 1 April. They are delivered to the customer, who accepts the delivery.	140
Apr. 4	The customer pays in cash. Selling price is £2.50 per item.	175

What is the profit on the sale of 70 items? Each one cost £2.00 and is sold for £2.50, so there is a profit of 50 pence per item or £35 for 70 items. In accounting, that calculation might be set out as follows:

	£
Sale of goods (70 items)	175
Cost of goods sold (70 items)	(140)
Gross profit	35

There is an asset of unsold goods (30 items) which cost £2 each or £60 in total. Since that item is an asset, it will appear in the balance sheet.

That is a statement of the gross profit and of the monetary amount of the asset of unsold goods, using common sense and intuition to arrive at an answer. Now look at how a systematic analysis is undertaken in accounting.

6.2.2 Analysis of transactions and events

Apr. 1	Purchase goods from manufacturer, 100 items at £2 each, paying in cash, and store in warehouse	£200

This transaction has two aspects in terms of the accounting equation. It *increases the asset of stock of goods* and it *decreases the asset of cash*. One asset increases, another decreases by an equal amount and there is no effect on the ownership interest.

Assets ↑↓ – Liabilities	equals	Ownership interest

Apr. 4	Remove 70 items from warehouse to meet customer's request. Those 70 items cost £2 each on 1 April. They are delivered to the customer, who accepts the delivery.	£140

This is an event which is not a transaction. The goods which are in the store are removed to a more convenient place for sale to the customer. In this case they are removed to a delivery van and transported to the customer. The moment of delivery to, and acceptance by, the customer is the event which transforms the goods from an asset to an expense. By that event, ownership is transferred to the customer, who either pays cash immediately or agrees to pay in the future. The expense is called *cost of goods sold*.

It should be noted at this point that the acts of physical removal and transport are events which financial accounting does not record, because at that point there is not sufficient evidence for recognition that a sale has taken place. In management accounting you will find that quite a different attitude is taken to events which involve moving goods from one location to another. In management accounting, such movements are recorded in order to help the managerial process of control.

In terms of the accounting equation there is a *decrease in the asset of stock* because it is no longer owned by the business and there can be no future benefit from the item. The benefit has occurred on this day, creating a sale by the act of delivery and acceptance.

If an asset has decreased then the *ownership interest* must also have *decreased through an expense*. The expense is called cost of goods sold.

Assets ↓ – Liabilities	equals	Ownership interest ↓ (expense: cost of goods sold)

Apr. 4	The customer pays in cash. Selling price is £2.50 per item.	£175

The final transaction is the payment of cash by the customer. In timing, it will occur almost simultaneously with the delivery and acceptance of the goods. In accounting it is nevertheless analysed separately. The business receives *an increase in the asset of cash* and *the ownership interest is increased* by an act which has earned revenue for the business.

Assets ↑ – Liabilities	equals	Ownership interest ↑ (revenue)

L01 **Activity 6.1**

Return to Exhibit 6.1 and change the cost price to £3 and the selling price to £3.50. Calculate the profit if the customer receives (a) 70 items, (b) 80 items, (c) 90 items and (d) 100 items. How many items remain in stock in each of these four cases? What can you say about the pattern of profit which appears from the four calculations you have carried out? Now write down the effect on the accounting equation for each of these four separate situations. Doing this will help you to test your own understanding before you proceed further.

6.2.3 Spreadsheet summarising the transactions

It is possible to bring the analysis together in a spreadsheet similar to that used in Chapter 5, but containing column headings which are appropriate to the assets involved in these transactions. Exhibit 6.2 shows the spreadsheet. Exhibit 6.3 summarises the impact of the accounting equation, showing that the assets remaining at the end of the period, £35 in total, equal the sum of the opening capital at the start (nil in this case) plus revenue £175 minus expenses £140.

Exhibit 6.2

Spreadsheet analysing transactions and events into elements of the accounting equation

Date	Transaction or event	Assets		Ownership interest	
		Cash	Stock	Revenue +	Expense −
		£	£	£	£
Apr. 1	Purchase goods from manufacturer, paying in cash, 100 items at £2 each, and place in warehouse.	(200)	200		
Apr. 4	Remove 70 items from warehouse to meet customer's request. Those 70 items cost £2 each on Apr. 1. They are delivered to the customer, who accepts the delivery.		(140)		140
Apr. 4	The customer pays in cash. Selling price is £2.50 per item.	175		175	
	Totals at end of period	(25)	60	175	140

└── 35 ──┘

Exhibit 6.3

Summary of transactions analysed into the elements of the accounting equation

Assets	minus	Liabilities	=	Ownership interest at start of period	plus	Capital contributed/ withdrawn	plus	Revenue	minus	Expenses
£35	−	nil	=	nil	+	nil	+	£175	−	£140

L02 6.3 Manufacturing goods for resale

The manufacture of goods for resale requires the purchase of raw materials which are used in production of the finished goods. There are several stages here where the business may hold an asset of one type or another. Any unused raw materials will represent a benefit for the future and therefore be treated as an asset.

Any finished goods which are not sold will also represent a benefit for the future and therefore be treated as an asset. Less obvious than these two items is the expected future benefit of partly completed goods that may be in the production process at the accounting date. That is also regarded as an asset, called work-in-progress. If the manufacturing process is rapid, then at any date there will be relatively little work-in-progress. If the manufacturing process is slow, there could be significant amounts of work-in-progress at an accounting date.

6.3.1 Analysis of transactions

Consider the transactions of a manufacturing company which are set out in Exhibit 6.4. The company buys breakfast trays and customises them to designs requested by catering outlets.

Exhibit 6.4
Transactions of a manufacturing company

		£
July 1	Purchase raw materials from supplier, 100 trays at £2 each, paying in cash, and place in raw materials store.	200
July 3	Remove 80 trays from raw materials store to meet production department's request (cost £2 each).	160
July 4	Carry out labour work and use production facilities to convert raw materials into finished goods. Additional costs incurred for labour and use of facilities were £1.50 per tray processed.	120
July 5	Finished goods are transferred to finished goods store. The job has cost £3.50 per tray in total (80 trays × £3.50 = £280).	280
July 10	60 trays, which cost £3.50 each to manufacture, are delivered to a customer.	210
July 10	The customer pays a price of £5 cash per tray immediately on delivery.	300

What is the profit on the sale of 60 trays? Each one cost £3.50 to manufacture and is sold for £5.00 so there is a profit of £1.50 per item or £90 for 60 items.

The business retains a stock of 20 unsold finished trays which cost £3.50 each to manufacture (a cost of £70 in total) and a stock of unused raw materials (20 basic trays costing £2 each which is a total cost of £40).

That is a statement of the position using common sense and intuition to arrive at an answer. Now look at how a systematic analysis is undertaken in accounting.

6.3.2 Analysis of transactions and events

July 1	Purchase raw materials from supplier, 100 trays at £2 each, paying in cash, and place in raw materials store.	£200

The business experiences an *increase in the asset of stock of raw materials* and a *decrease in the asset of cash*. In terms of the accounting equation there is an increase in one asset matched by a decrease in another and there is no effect on the ownership interest.

Assets ↑↓ – Liabilities	equals	Ownership interest

July 3	Remove 80 trays from raw materials store to meet production department's request (cost £2 each).	£160

Next, some of the raw materials are removed for use in production. This is an event, rather than a transaction, but is recorded because it creates a possible asset of work-in-progress. The *asset of work-in-progress increases* and the *asset of raw materials decreases*. There is no effect on the ownership claim.

Assets ↑↓ – Liabilities	equals	Ownership interest

July 4	Carry out labour work and use production facilities to convert raw materials into finished goods. Additional costs incurred for labour and use of facilities were £1.50 per tray processed.	£120

The next stage is that some work is done to convert the raw materials into the product desired by customers. The work involves labour cost and other costs of using the production facilities. (You will find in management accounting that the other costs of using production facilities are usually described as *production overheads*.) This payment for labour and use of production facilities is adding to the value of the basic tray and so is adding to the value of the asset of work-in-progress (which will eventually become the asset of finished goods). So there is an *increase in the asset of work-in-progress* and a *decrease in the asset of cash*. There is no effect on the ownership interest.

Assets ↑↓ – Liabilities	equals	Ownership interest

July 5	Finished goods are transferred to finished goods store. The job has cost £3.50 per tray in total (80 trays × £3.50 = £280).	£280

When the work-in-progress is complete, it becomes finished goods and is transferred to the store. The *asset of work-in-progress decreases* and the *asset of finished goods increases*. A measure of the value of the asset is the cost of making it which, in this case, is £3.50 per item or £280 for 80 items. Again, there is no effect on the ownership interest.

Assets ↑↓ – Liabilities	equals	Ownership interest

July 10	60 trays, which cost £3.50 each to manufacture, are delivered to a customer.	£210

The customer now requests 60 trays and these are delivered from the store to the customer. At the moment of acceptance by the customer, the 60 trays cease to be an asset of the business. There is a *decrease in an asset* and a *decrease in the ownership interest* which is recorded as an *expense of cost of goods sold*.

Assets ↓ – Liabilities	equals	**Ownership interest** ↓ **(expense: cost of goods sold)**

The owner's disappointment is momentary because the act of acceptance by the customer results in immediate payment being received from the customer (or in some cases a promise of future payment).

July 10	The customer pays a price of £5 cash per tray immediately on delivery.	£300

When the customer pays immediately for the goods, there is an *increase in the asset of cash* and a *corresponding increase in the ownership interest*, recorded as revenue of the business.

Assets ↑ – Liabilities	equals	**Ownership interest** ↑ **(revenue)**

L02

Activity 6.2

Return to Exhibit 6.4. Without looking to the rest of the section, write down the effect of each transaction on the accounting equation. At what point in the sequence of events in Exhibit 6.4 is the ownership interest affected? Why is it not affected before that point in the sequence? How would the ownership interest have been affected if, on 5 July, there had been a fire as the goods were being transferred to the finished goods store and one-quarter of the finished trays were destroyed?

6.3.3 Spreadsheet summarising the transactions

Exhibit 6.5 brings the analysis together in a spreadsheet similar to that used in Exhibit 6.2, showing the effect of each transaction separately and also the overall effect on the accounting equation. Exhibit 6.6 sets out the accounting equation at the end of the period and shows that the assets remaining at the end of the period are equal to the ownership interest at the start (which is taken as nil in this example) plus the profit of the period.

Once you have understood the analysis up to this point, you are ready to embark on the financial statements of a trading business.

Exhibit 6.5

Spreadsheet analysing transactions and events into elements of the accounting equation

Date	Transaction or event	Assets				Ownership interest	
		Cash at bank	Raw materials stock	Work-in-progress	Finished goods	Revenue	Expenses
						+	−
		£	£	£	£	£	£
July 1	Purchase raw materials from supplier, paying in cash, 100 trays at £2 each, and place in raw materials store.	(200)	200				
July 3	Remove 80 trays from raw materials store to meet production department's request (cost £2 each).		(160)	160			
July 4	Carry out labour work and use production facilities to convert raw materials into finished goods. Additional costs incurred for labour and use of facilities were £1.50 per tray processed.	(120)		120			
July 5	Finished goods are transferred to finished goods store. The job has cost £3.50 per tray in total (80 trays × £3.50 = £280).			(280)	280		
July 10	60 trays, which cost £3.50 each to manufacture, are delivered to a customer.				(210)		210
July 10	The customer pays a price of £5 cash per tray immediately on delivery.	300				300	
	Totals at the end of the period.	(20)	40	nil	70	300	210

└─────── 90 ───────┘

Exhibit 6.6

Summary of transactions analysed into the elements of the accounting equation

Assets	minus	Liabilities	=	Ownership interest at start of period	plus	Capital contributed/ withdrawn	plus	Revenue	minus	Expenses
£90	−	nil	=	nil	+	nil	+	£300	−	£210

L03 ## 6.4 Illustration of accounting for a trading business

This example considers the business of M. Carter, wholesale trader. At the start of May, M. Carter commenced a trading business as a wholesaler, buying goods from manufacturers and storing them in a warehouse from which customers could be supplied. All the customers are small shopkeepers who need the services of the wholesaler because they are not sufficiently powerful in purchasing power to negotiate terms directly with the manufacturers.

In Exhibit 6.7 there is a list of transactions for M. Carter's wholesaling business during the month of May. In section 6.4.1 each transaction is analysed using the accounting equation.

Exhibit 6.7

Transactions of the business of M. Carter, wholesaler, for the month of May

Date	Business transactions and events (nature of the entity: wholesale trader)	Amount £
May 1	The owner pays cash into a bank account for the business.	50,000
May 2	The business acquires buildings for cash.	30,000
May 4	The business acquires equipment for cash.	6,000
May 6	The business purchases a stock of goods for cash.	6,500
May 7	The business purchases a stock of goods on credit from R. Busby and receives an invoice.	5,000
May 11	The business pays R. Busby in cash for the goods it acquired on credit.	5,000
May 14	The business pays an electricity bill in cash.	100
May 17	Items costing £3,500 are removed from the store because sales have been agreed with customers for this date.	3,500
May 17	The business sells items costing £2,000 to customers for a cash price of £4,000.	4,000
May 17	The business sells items costing £1,500 on credit to R. Welsby and sends an invoice for the price of £3,000.	3,000
May 24	R. Welsby pays in cash for the goods obtained on credit.	3,000
May 28	The owner draws cash from the business for personal use.	1,000
May 30	The business pays wages to an employee for the month, in cash.	2,000
May 31	The business discovers that its equipment has fallen in value over the month.	250

L03 **Activity 6.3**

Before reading section 6.4.1, analyse each transaction in Exhibit 6.7 using the accounting equation. (If necessary look back to Chapter 5 for a similar pattern of analysis.) Then compare your answer against the detail of section 6.4.1. If there is any item where you have a different answer, consult your lecturer, tutor or other expert before proceeding with the rest of the chapter.

6.4.1 Explanation of the analysis of each transaction

May 1   When M. Carter provides the business with cash in a bank account to allow the company to proceed, the business *acquires an asset of cash* and the transaction *creates an ownership interest* for M. Carter on the assets of the business. Using the symbols of the accounting equation:

Assets ↑ – Liabilities	equals	**Ownership interest** ↑ **(contribution of capital)**

May 2   The wholesale business now becomes the business entity so far as accounting is concerned (although M. Carter may still be making the decisions as an owner/manager of the business). The entity acquires an asset of buildings in exchange for an asset of cash. There is an *increase in one asset* and a *decrease in another asset*. There is no impact on the ownership interest.

Assets ↑↓ – Liabilities	equals	Ownership interest

May 4   The entity acquires an asset of equipment in exchange for an asset of cash. There is an *increase in one asset* and a *decrease in another asset*. There is no impact on the ownership interest.

Assets ↑↓ – Liabilities	equals	Ownership interest

May 6   The entity acquires an asset of stock of goods in exchange for an asset of cash. There is an *increase in one asset* and a *decrease in another asset*. There is no impact on the ownership interest.

Assets ↑↓ – Liabilities	equals	Ownership interest

May 7   The entity again acquires an asset of stock of goods but this time it is related to the acquisition of a liability to R. Busby. There is an *increase in an asset* and an *increase in a liability*. There is no impact on the ownership interest.

Assets ↑ – **Liabilities** ↑	equals	Ownership interest

May 11 When payment is made to R. Busby there is a *decrease in the asset* of cash and a *decrease in the liability* to R. Busby.

Assets ↓ – Liabilities ↓	equals	Ownership interest

May 14 When the electricity bill is paid, the benefit of using the electricity has been consumed. There is a *decrease in the asset of cash* and a *decrease in the ownership interest*, reported as an expense.

Assets ↓ – Liabilities	equals	Ownership interest ↓ (expense)

May 17 At the moment of acceptance by the customer, the goods cease to be an asset of the business. The *ownership interest decreases* (recorded as an expense of cost of goods sold) and the *asset of stock decreases*.

Assets ↓ – Liabilities	equals	Ownership interest ↓ (cost of goods sold)

May 17 The owner's wealth is then immediately restored or enhanced because some customers pay cash for the goods. There is an *increase in the asset of cash* and a corresponding *increase in the ownership interest*, recorded as revenue of the business. The information about cost of goods sold has been dealt with in the previous equation.

Assets ↑ – Liabilities	equals	Ownership interest ↑ (revenue)

May 17 The owner's wealth is similarly restored by a promise from the customer, to pay at a future date. This creates the asset of a debtor which, in accounting, is regarded as acceptable in the overall measure of shareholder wealth. There is an *increase in the asset of debtor* and a corresponding *increase in the ownership interest*, recorded as revenue of the business. The information about cost of goods sold has been dealt with in the earlier equation.

Assets ↑ – Liabilities	equals	Ownership interest ↑ (revenue)

May 24 R. Welsby is the debtor of the business. When a debtor makes payment to the business there is an *increase in the asset of cash* and a *decrease in the asset of debtor*. There is no effect on the ownership interest.

Assets ↑↓ – Liabilities	equals	Ownership interest

May 28 As was explained in Chapter 5, the owner of a sole trader business does not take a salary or wage as an employee would, but needs cash for personal purposes. Taking cash for personal use is called 'drawings' and is recorded in terms of the accounting equation as a *decrease in the ownership interest* and a *decrease in the asset of cash*.

Assets ↓ – Liabilities	equals	Ownership interest ↓ (withdrawal of capital)

May 30 Paying wages is similar in effect to paying the electricity bill. The benefit of the employee's work has been consumed. There is a *decrease in the asset of cash* and a *decrease in the ownership interest*, reported as an expense.

Assets ↓ – Liabilities	equals	Ownership interest ↓ (expense)

May 31 All fixed assets will eventually be used up by the business, after several years of useful life. Depreciation is a recognition of the *decrease in the asset* and the *decrease in the ownership interest*, reported as an expense. (There is more on depreciation in Chapter 8.)

Assets ↓ – Liabilities	equals	Ownership interest ↓ (expense)

L04 6.5 A process for summarising the transactions: a spreadsheet

In Exhibit 6.8 the transactions of Exhibit 6.7 are repeated at the left-hand side and are analysed into columns headed for assets, liabilities and ownership interest using brackets to show a negative amount. It would be equally acceptable to use a minus sign but minus signs tend to disappear or be confused with unintentional blobs on the paper, so brackets are frequently used in accounting in order to ensure clarity.

At the foot of the spreadsheet in Exhibit 6.8 there is a total for each column. Those totals are used in Exhibit 6.9 to show the state of the accounting equation at the end of the month. It may be used to explain to M. Carter how the ownership interest has changed over the month. The owner contributed £50,000 at the start of the month and has a claim of £50,150 at the end of the month. The ownership interest was increased by earning revenue of £7,000 but reduced by incurring expenses of £5,850 and withdrawing £1,000 for personal use.

Exhibit 6.8

Spreadsheet analysing transactions into the elements of the accounting equation

Date	Business transactions	Assets			Liabilities	Ownership interest		
		Cash at bank	Stock of goods	Fixed assets and debtors	Creditors	Capital contributed/withdrawn	Revenue +	Expenses −
		£	£	£	£	£	£	£
May 1	The owner provides the business with cash.	50,000				50,000		
May 2	The business acquires buildings for cash.	(30,000)		30,000				
May 4	The business acquires equipment for cash.	(6,000)		6,000				
May 6	The business purchases a stock of goods for cash.	(6,500)	6,500					
May 7	The business purchases a stock of goods on credit from R. Busby and receives an invoice.		5,000		5,000			
May 11	The business pays R. Busby in cash for the goods it acquired on credit.	(5,000)			(5,000)			
May 14	The business pays an electricity bill in cash.	(100)						100
May 17	Some of the goods purchased for resale (items costing £3,500) are removed from the store because sales have been agreed with customers for this date.		(3,500)					3,500
May 17	The business sells some of the purchased goods for cash.	4,000					4,000	
May 17	The business sells the remaining purchased goods on credit to R. Welsby and sends an invoice.			3,000			3,000	
May 24	R. Welsby pays in cash for the goods obtained on credit.	3,000		(3,000)				
May 28	The owner draws cash from the business for personal use.	(1,000)				(1,000)		
May 30	The business pays wages to an employee for the past month, in cash.	(2,000)						2,000
May 31	The business discovers that its equipment has fallen in value over the month.			(250)				250
	Totals at the end of the period	6,400	8,000	35,750	nil	49,000	7,000	5,850

— 50,150 —

Exhibit 6.9
Summary of transactions analysed into the elements of the accounting equation

Assets	minus	Liabilities	=	Capital contributed/ withdrawn	plus	Revenue	minus	Expenses
£50,150	–	nil	=	£49,000	+	£7,000	–	£5,850
└──── £50,150 ────┘				└───────── £50,150 ─────────┘				

How has the ownership interest changed over the month? The owner contributed £50,000 at the start of the month and has a claim of £50,150 at the end of the month. The ownership interest was increased by earning revenue of £7,000 but reduced by incurring expenses of £5,580 and withdrawing £1,000 for personal use.

L05   6.6 Financial statements of M. Carter, wholesaler

The transactions in Exhibit 6.8 may be summarised in financial statements for use by interested parties. The first user will be the owner, M. Carter, but others such as the Inland Revenue may ask for a copy. If the owner seeks to raise additional finance by borrowing from a bank, the bank manager may ask for a copy of the financial statements.

There are no regulations regarding the format of financial statements for a sole trader, but it is good practice to try to match, as far as possible, the more onerous requirements imposed on limited liability companies. The financial statements presented in this section follow the general formats set out in Chapter 3.

6.6.1 Statement of cash flows

M. Carter, wholesaler
Cash flow statement for the month of May Year XX

	£
Operating activities	
Cash from customers	7,000
Outflow: payment for goods	(6,500)
payment to supplier (R. Busby)	(5,000)
wages	(2,000)
electricity	(100)
Net outflow from operations	(6,600)
Investing activities	
Payment for buildings	(30,000)
Payment for equipment	(6,000)
Net outflow for investing activities	(36,000)
Financing activities	
Capital contributed by owner	50,000
Capital withdrawn as drawings	(1,000)
Net inflow from financing activities	49,000
Increase in cash at bank over period	6,400

Comment: The operating activities caused a drain on cash with a net effect that £6,600 flowed out of the business. A further £36,000 cash flow was used for investing activities. The owner contributed £50,000 at the start of the month but withdrew £1,000 at the end of the month. Cash in the bank increased by £6,400 over the month.

6.6.2 Statement of profit or loss

M. Carter, wholesaler
Profit and loss account for the month of May Year XX

	£	£
Sales		7,000
Cost of goods sold		3,500
Gross profit		3,500
Other expenses		
Wages	2,000	
Electricity	100	
Depreciation	250	
		2,350
Net profit		1,150

Comment: This profit and loss account differs slightly from that presented for the service business in Chapter 5. It has a subtotal for gross profit. The difference between sales and the cost of purchasing or manufacturing the goods sold is regarded as an important indicator of the success of the business in its particular product line. The gross profit is sometimes referred to as the 'margin' or 'gross margin' and is a piece of information which is much explored by professional investors and analysts.

Making a subtotal for gross profit means that the final line needs a different label and so is called 'net profit'. The word 'net' means 'after taking everything away', so in this case the net profit is equal to sales minus all expenses of the operations of the business.

L05 | **Activity 6.4**

The business of M. Carter, wholesaler, has made a profit of £1,150 from operations during the month but the cash flow due to operating activities has been negative to the extent of £6,600. Make a comparison of the cash flow from operating activities and the profit from operations. From your comparison, explain how a business can make a profit and yet see its cash drain away. Then make some recommendations about reducing the outflow of cash without affecting profit.

6.6.3 Statement of financial position: the balance sheet

M. Carter, wholesaler
Balance sheet at 31 May Year XX

Accounting equation		£
	Fixed assets	
	Buildings	30,000
	Equipment	6,000
		36,000
	Depreciation	(250)
FA	Depreciated cost of fixed assets	35,750
	Current assets	
	Stocks	8,000
	Cash at bank	6,400
CA		14,400
A – L	Net assets	50,150
	Ownership interest	
	Capital at start	50,000
	add: profit	1,150
	less: drawings	(1,000)
OI	Total ownership interest	50,150

Comment: There are no liabilities at the end of the month and so the net assets are the same as the total of fixed assets and current assets. That somewhat artificial situation arises from keeping the example fairly simple and manageable. The depreciation has been recorded for the equipment but many businesses would also depreciate buildings. The useful life of a building is much longer than

that of equipment and so the depreciation for any single month would be a neg-
ligible amount in relation to other information for the period. The amount of £35,750
has been described here as depreciated cost but could also be called the 'net book
value' or the 'written down value'.

The balance sheet is a statement of position and, on its own, is of limited usefulness. Companies which publish accounting information will present the previous year's amounts alongside the current year's data so that comparisons may
be made. Some companies provide, in addition, five-year or ten-year summaries
which allow comparison over a longer period.

6.7 Summary

Now score your view of your confidence in achieving the learning outcomes of
the chapter.

1 = Very confident about knowledge, application, problem solving and evaluation.

2 = Confident about knowledge and application, less sure about problem solving and
evaluation.

3 = Need to read again to be more certain of basic knowledge and application.

LO1 You can now explain the application of the accounting equation to
transactions involving the buying and selling of trading stock.
    1 2 3 ☐ ☐ ☐

LO2 You can now explain the application of the accounting equation to
transactions involving the manufacture and sale of products.
    1 2 3 ☐ ☐ ☐

LO3 You are now able to analyse transactions of a trading or manufacturing business during a specific period of time, using the
accounting equation.
    1 2 3 ☐ ☐ ☐

LO4 You are now able to prepare a spreadsheet analysing the transactions, and show that the results of the spreadsheet analysis are consistent with financial statements provided by the organisation.
    1 2 3 ☐ ☐ ☐

LO5 You can explain the main aspects of the cash flow statement, profit
and loss account and balance sheet of a trading or a manufacturing business.
    1 2 3 ☐ ☐ ☐

Additionally, for those who choose to study the Supplement:

LO6 You should now work through the Supplement if you wish to analyse the transactions of a trading or a manufacturing business
using the rules of debit and credit bookkeeping.
    1 2 3 ☐ ☐ ☐

LO7 You will also discover from the Supplement how to prepare, from
a list of transactions of an organisation, ledger accounts and a trial
balance which could be used to confirm the financial statements
provided by the organisation.
    1 2 3 ☐ ☐ ☐

If your scores are all 1 or 2, try the questions in the series A and B. This will give you
feedback on your assessment of how well you have achieved the learning outcomes. Read

again any sections of the chapter where you find your knowledge and understanding are less comprehensive than you first estimated.

If your scores include some at 3, try the series A questions to find where the problems lie. Read the relevant sections again, work through any illustrative examples and case studies, then try the questions in the series B.

Test your understanding

Skills outcomes
S01 Application of technical skills   **S02** Problem solving and evaluation skills   **S03** Communication skills

L01, S01   **A6.1** On 1 May the Sea Traders Company purchased 200 spare parts for fishing boats, costing £20 each. On 5 May, 60 of these spare parts were sold to a customer at a price of £25 each. The customer paid in cash immediately.

(a) Calculate the profit made on this transaction.
(b) Explain the impact of each transaction on the accounting equation.

L04, S01   **A6.2** Summarise the transactions of question **A6.1** in a spreadsheet and show that the totals of the spreadsheet satisfy the accounting equation.

L02, S01   **A6.3** The following transactions relate to Toy Manufacturers Company during the month of June.

Date	Business transactions	£
June 1	Purchase toy components from supplier, 100 items at £3 each, paying in cash, and place in raw materials store.	300
June 3	Remove 70 components from raw materials store to meet production department's request (cost £3 each).	210
June 5	Carry out labour work and use production facilities to convert components into finished goods. Additional costs incurred for labour and use of facilities were £2.50 per toy processed.	175
June 6	Finished goods are transferred to finished goods store. Each toy has cost £5.50 in total (70 toys × £5.50 = £385).	385
June 11	50 toys, which cost £5.50 each to manufacture, are delivered to a customer.	275
June 14	The customer pays a price of £8 cash per toy immediately on delivery.	400

(a) Calculate the profit on sale.
(b) Explain the effect of each transaction on the accounting equation.
(c) Prepare a spreadsheet summarising the transactions.

L03, S01   **A6.4** The following list of transactions relates to the business of Peter Gold, furniture supplier, during the month of April. Analyse each transaction to show the two aspects of the transaction.

Date	Business transactions and events (nature of the entity: wholesale trader)	Amount £
Apr. 1	The owner pays cash into a bank account for the business.	60,000
Apr. 2	The business acquires buildings for cash.	20,000
Apr. 4	The business acquires equipment for cash.	12,000
Apr. 6	The business purchases a stock of goods for cash.	8,500
Apr. 7	The business purchases a stock of goods on credit from R. Green and receives an invoice.	7,000
Apr. 11	The business pays R. Green in cash for the goods it acquired on credit.	7,000
Apr. 14	The business pays a gas bill in cash.	400
Apr. 17	Items costing £5,500 are removed from the store because sales have been agreed with customers for this date.	5,500
Apr. 17	The business sells some of the goods removed from store for cash of £6,000.	6,000
Apr. 17	The business sells the remainder of the goods removed from store on credit to P. Weatherall and sends an invoice.	4,200
Apr. 24	P. Weatherall pays in cash for the goods obtained on credit.	4,200
Apr. 28	The owner draws cash from the business for personal use.	2,700
Apr. 29	The business pays wages to employees for the past month, in cash.	2,800
Apr. 30	The business discovers that its equipment has fallen in value over the month.	550

Application

L04, S01 **B6.1**

(a) Using the list of transactions at question **A6.4** of Test your understanding, *above*, prepare a spreadsheet similar to that presented in Exhibit 6.8.

(b) Show the resulting impact on the accounting equation and demonstrate that it remains in balance.

L05, S01 **B6.2** Using the total from the columns of the spreadsheet of question **B6.1(a)**, prepare for the business in the month of April:

(a) a cash flow statement;

(b) a balance sheet; and

(c) a profit and loss account.

There are no questions in the C series for this chapter. These skills are tested in specific situations in Chapters 8 to 12.

Recording transactions in ledger accounts: a trading business

The supplement starts with a reminder of the rules of debit and credit bookkeeping, set out in Exhibit 6.10.

Exhibit 6.10
Rules of debit and credit

	Debit entries in a ledger account	Credit entries in a ledger account
Left-hand side of the equation		
Asset	Increase	Decrease
Right-hand side of the equation		
Liability	Decrease	Increase
Ownership interest	Expense	Revenue
	Capital withdrawn	Capital contributed

Activity 6.5

It might be a useful test of your understanding of the chapter if you try to write down the debit and credit entries before looking at Exhibit 6.11. If you find your answers don't agree with that exhibit then you should go back to the analysis contained in the chapter and think about the various aspects of the accounting equation. Debit and credit entries do nothing more than follow the analysis based on the accounting equation so you should not have a problem if you have followed the analysis.

Exhibit 6.1 presented a short list of transactions for a trading company, relating to the purchase and sale of goods. That list of transactions is repeated in Exhibit 6.11 but showing in the final two columns the ledger accounts in which debit and credit entries would be made. Compare Exhibit 6.11 with Exhibit 6.2 to see that the analysis of transactions and the analysis of debit and credit entries follow similar patterns.

Exhibit 6.11
Transactions of a trading company: debit and credit entries

		£	Debit	Credit
Apr. 1	Purchase goods from manufacturer, 100 items at £2 each, paying in cash, and store in warehouse.	200	Stock	Cash
Apr. 4	Remove 70 items from warehouse to meet a customer's request. Those 70 items cost £2 each on 1 April. They are delivered to the customer who accepts the delivery.	140	Cost of goods sold	Stock
Apr. 4	The customer pays in cash. Selling price is £2.50 per item.	175	Cash	Revenue

Exhibit 6.4 presented a short list of transactions for a manufacturing company. These are repeated in Exhibit 6.12 with the ledger accounts for debit and credit entries being shown in the final two columns. Again, you should try this first and then check your answer against Exhibit 6.12.

Exhibit 6.12
Transactions of a manufacturing company: debit and credit entries

		£	Debit	Credit
July 1	Purchase raw materials from supplier, 100 trays at £2 each, paying in cash, and place in raw materials store.	200	Raw materials stock	Cash
July 3	Remove 80 trays from raw materials store to meet production department's request (cost £2 each).	160	Work-in-progress	Raw materials stock
July 4	Carry out labour work and use production facilities to convert raw materials into finished goods. Additional costs incurred for labour and use of facilities were £1.50 per tray processed.	120	Work-in-progress	Cash
July 5	Finished goods are transferred to finished goods store. The job has cost £3.50 per tray in total (80 trays × £3.50 = £280).	280	Finished goods	Work-in-progress
July 10	60 trays, which cost £3.50 each to manufacture, are delivered to a customer.	210	Cost of goods sold	Finished goods
July 10	The customer pays a price of £5 cash per tray immediately on delivery.	300	Cash	Revenue

L06, L07 M. Carter, wholesaler: analysing the debit and credit entries

Exhibit 6.13 takes the information contained in Exhibit 6.8 and analyses it under debit and credit headings showing the ledger accounts in which each entry will be made. Ledger accounts required to record these transactions are:

L1	Cash	L2	Owner	L3	Buildings	L4	Equipment
L5	Stock of goods	L6	R. Busby	L7	Electricity	L8	Wages
L9	Cost of goods sold	L10	Sales	L11	R. Welsby	L12	Depreciation

The full ledger account records for the transactions in Exhibit 6.13 are set out. Leona Rees has commented on each one, to show how she interprets them when she is carrying out work of audit or investigation.

Exhibit 6.13

Analysis of transactions for M. Carter, wholesaler

Date	Business transactions	Amount	Debit	Credit
		£		
May 1	The owner provides the business with cash.	50,000	Cash	Owner
May 2	The business acquires buildings for cash.	30,000	Buildings	Cash
May 4	The business acquires equipment for cash.	6,000	Equipment	Cash
May 6	The business purchases a stock of goods for cash.	6,500	Stock	Cash
May 7	The business purchases a stock of goods on credit from R. Busby and receives an invoice.	5,000	Stock	R. Busby
May 11	The business pays R. Busby in cash for the goods it acquired on credit.	5,000	R. Busby	Cash
May 14	The business pays an electricity bill in cash.	100	Electricity	Cash
May 17	Items costing £3,500 are removed from the store because sales have been agreed with customers for this date.	3,500	Cost of goods sold	Stock
May 17	The business sells goods for cash.	4,000	Cash	Sales
May 17	The business sells goods on credit to R. Welsby and sends an invoice.	3,000	R. Welsby	Sales
May 24	R. Welsby pays in cash for the goods obtained on credit.	3,000	Cash	R. Welsby

Exhibit 6.13 continued

Date	Business transactions	Amount	Debit	Credit
May 28	The owner draws cash from the business for personal use.	1,000	Owner	Cash
May 30	The business pays wages to an employee for the past month, in cash.	2,000	Wages	Cash
May 31	The business discovers that its equipment has fallen in value over the month.	250	Depreciation	Equipment

L1 Cash

Date	Particulars	Page	Debit	Credit	Balance
			£	£	£
May 1	Owner's capital	L2	50,000		50,000
May 2	Buildings	L3		30,000	20,000
May 4	Equipment	L4		6,000	14,000
May 6	Stock of goods	L5		6,500	7,500
May 11	R. Busby	L6		5,000	2,500
May 14	Electricity	L7		100	2,400
May 17	Sales	L10	4,000		6,400
May 24	R. Welsby	L11	3,000		9,400
May 28	Ownership interest drawn out	L2		1,000	8,400
May 30	Wages	L8		2,000	6,400

LEONA's comment: *The amount of £50,000 put into the business at the start is quickly swallowed up by spending cash on buildings, equipment, buying a stock of goods and paying the supplier who gave credit. Paying the electricity account £100 took the cash balance down to £2,400 and it was only the sale of some goods which allowed the business to continue. If the sale of goods had not taken place, the owner might have needed to put more cash into the business at that point, or else ask the bank manager to make a loan to the business. With the benefit of hindsight, the owner might have waited a few days before paying R. Busby for goods supplied. It's not a good idea to delay paying the electricity bill in case there is a disconnection, and failing to pay wages usually means the employee does not return. It might have helped cash flow to have bought the buildings and equipment using a loan, but borrowing money has a cost in interest payments and perhaps the owner prefers not to start with a high level of borrowing.*

L2 Ownership interest

Date	Particulars	Page	Debit	Credit	Balance
			£	£	£
May 1	Cash contributed	L1		50,000	(50,000)
May 28	Cash drawn	L1	1,000		(49,000)

LEONA's comment: *The ownership interest is created when the owner contributes cash or resources to the business. In this case, it was cash. The sole trader in business may withdraw cash for personal use at any time – it is called owner's drawings – but the desirability of that action depends on how useful it is to the owner when compared to how useful it might have been if left in the business. The owner of this business has a claim remaining equal to £49,000 after making the drawing.*

L3 Buildings

Date	Particulars	Page	Debit	Credit	Balance
			£	£	£
May 2	Cash	L1	30,000		30,000

LEONA's comment: *This ledger account is particularly useful as a reminder that a very valuable asset is owned by the business. Having a record in the ledger account encourages the owner to think about continuing care for the buildings and also to review their value against the amount recorded.*

L4 Equipment

Date	Particulars	Page	Debit	Credit	Balance
			£	£	£
May 4	Cash	L1	6,000		6,000
May 31	Depreciation	L12		250	5,750

LEONA's comment: *The equipment cost £6,000 but is being gradually used up over its life in the business. Depreciation is a way of showing that the original cost of the asset has to be spread over its useful life. If the estimate of depreciation is correct, this ledger account should reduce to nil on the day the equipment ceases to be of use. In reality things usually are not quite so straightforward.* (Depreciation of fixed assets is dealt with in more detail in Chapter 8.)

L5 Stock of goods

Date	Particulars	Page	Debit	Credit	Balance
			£	£	£
May 6	Cash	L1	6,500		6,500
May 7	R. Busby	L6	5,000		11,500
May 17	Cost of goods sold	L9		3,500	8,000

LEONA's comment: *The balance on this ledger account at any point in time should equal the cost price of the goods held in the warehouse. So at the end of May, if the owner goes to the warehouse and carries out a stock check, there should be goods to a total cost of £8,000. Checking the presence of a stock of unsold goods which agrees with the ledger account is an important part of my work as an auditor. If they don't agree, I start to ask a lot of questions.*

L6 R. Busby

Date	Particulars	Page	Debit	Credit	Balance
			£	£	£
May 7	Stock of goods	L5		5,000	(5,000)
May 11	Cash	L1	5,000		nil

LEONA's comment: *When the goods were purchased from R. Busby, the supplier, an invoice was received from that supplier showing the amount due. That invoice was used to make the credit entry on May 7 showing that the business had a liability. The liability was extinguished on May 11 by a payment to R. Busby, so at the end of May the business owes that supplier nothing.*

L7 Electricity

Date	Particulars	Page	Debit	Credit	Balance
			£	£	£
May 14	Cash	L1	100		100

LEONA's comment: *This is a very straightforward expense account. The balance on this account will show the total expense of electricity consumed during the period.*

L8 Wages

Date	Particulars	Page	Debit	Credit	Balance
			£	£	£
May 30	Cash	L1	2,000		2,000

LEONA's comment: *Another very straightforward account in which to accumulate all wages expenses.*

L9 Cost of goods sold

Date	Particulars	Page	Debit	Credit	Balance
			£	£	£
May 17	Stock of goods	L5	3,500		3,500

LEONA's comment: *This is an expense account showing the cost of the goods sold during the month. The total sales are shown in ledger account L10 as £7,000 and the cost of goods sold is shown here as £3,500, so there is a profit ('margin') of 50 per cent on sales before taking into account the expenses of electricity, wages and depreciation. As an auditor I have considerable interest in the profit margin on sales. It tells me a great deal about the business.*

L10 Sales

Date	Particulars	Page	Debit	Credit	Balance
			£	£	£
May 17	Cash	L1		4,000	(4,000)
May 17	R. Welsby	L11		3,000	(7,000)

LEONA's comment: *This is a revenue account, so credit entries are expected. The balance column shows the total sales of the month were £7,000.*

L11 R. Welsby

Date	Particulars	Page	Debit	Credit	Balance
			£	£	£
May 17	Sales	L10	3,000		3,000
May 24	Cash	L1		3,000	nil

LEONA's comment: *The credit sale to R. Welsby made him a debtor of the business and so the first entry is a debit entry. When R. Welsby paid this extinguished the debt, so that by the end of the month R. Welsby owed nothing to the business.*

L12 Depreciation

Date	Particulars	Page	Debit	Credit	Balance
			£	£	£
May 31	Equipment	L4	250		250

Leona's comment: *This is another expense account showing an item which has decreased the ownership interest through a decrease in the recorded amount of an asset. This is where accounting begins to look slightly complicated because no cash has changed hands. Recording depreciation is the accounting way of expressing caution as to the expected future benefits from the asset. These will be eroded as the asset is used up. Depreciation is a way of acknowledging that erosion.*

L07 Checking the accuracy of double entry records

In Chapter 5, the process of listing all ledger account balances in a trial balance was explained.

The trial balance for the accounting records of M. Carter, wholesaler, at 31 May Year 1, is as shown in Exhibit 6.14. This is a basic list summarising the transactions of the month. If you compare it with the financial statements in the main part of the chapter you will see that all the amounts correspond.

Exhibit 6.14

Trial balance at 31 May for M. Carter, wholesaler

Ledger account title	£	£
L1 Cash	6,400	
L2 Ownership interest		49,000
L3 Buildings	30,000	
L4 Equipment	5,750	
L5 Stock of goods	8,000	
L6 R. Busby		nil
L7 Electricity	100	
L8 Wages	2,000	
L9 Cost of goods sold	3,500	
L10 Sales		7,000
L11 R. Welsby	nil	
L12 Depreciation	250	
Totals	56,000	56,000

As was the case in the Supplement to Chapter 5, it is rather easier to use the trial balance if it is arranged so that all the balance sheet items are together and all the profit and loss account items are together. This is done in Exhibit 6.15. The shaded lines are not part of the trial balance but take advantage of the various forms of the accounting equation to calculate profit in two different ways. In the first part of the table:

Profit	equals	Assets – Liabilities – Owner's capital at the start and any changes during the period

In the second part of the table:

Profit	equals	Revenue – Expenses

Exhibit 6.15
Rearranging the trial balance into balance sheet items and profit and loss account items

Ledger account title		£	£
L3	Buildings	30,000	
L4	Equipment	5,750	
L5	Stock of goods	8,000	
L11	R. Welsby	nil	
L1	Cash	6,400	
L6	R. Busby		nil
L2	Ownership interest		49,000
Subtotal X		50,150	49,000
Difference: profit of the month 50,150 – 49,000			1,150
L10	Sales		7,000
L9	Cost of goods sold	3,500	
L7	Electricity	100	
L8	Wages	2,000	
L12	Depreciation	250	
Subtotal Y		5,850	7,000
Difference: profit of the month 7,000 – 5,850		1,150	
Total of ledger balances in each column X + Y		56,000	56,000

The form of trial balance shown in Exhibit 6.15 will be used in later chapters as the starting point for the preparation of financial statements.

L06, L07, S01 Test your understanding

S6.1 Prepare ledger accounts for the transactions of Peter Gold, furniture supplier, listed in question **A6.4**.

Part 3

Recognition in financial statements

Chapter 7

Published financial statements

After reading this chapter you should be able to:

LO1 Explain the key international influences that affect accounting practice in the UK.

LO2 Explain the structure of company reporting as set out in the *Statement of Principles*.

LO3 Explain the main contents of (a) the balance sheet, (b) the profit and loss account and (c) the cash flow statement as presented by larger companies.

LO4 Define 'parent company' and 'subsidiary company' and explain how a group is structured.

LO5 Explain the main features of group financial statements.

LO6 Explain the nature of, and reason for, other forms of communication beyond the annual report.

7.1 Introduction

It was explained in Chapters 1 and 4 that in the case of sole traders and partnerships the groups of persons who have an interest in the financial statements are limited to the owners themselves, the Inland Revenue and organisations such as banks which are asked to provide finance for the company. For limited liability companies the list of potential users widens and the access to internal information becomes restricted. Even the owners of a limited liability company (the shareholders) are not permitted access to the day-to-day records of the company and are treated as being outsiders of (external to) the company they own. The quality and amount of information communicated to these users who are external to the company becomes a matter which is too important to be left entirely to the discretion of the directors running the company.

Chapter 4 outlined the various regulatory authorities which exist to establish the quality and quantity of information to be published by limited liability companies. There are over one million limited liability companies in the United Kingdom, although only a few thousand are listed on the Stock Exchange and of these only 500 have their shares bought and sold regularly. The number of such companies, and their importance to the economy in terms of the funds invested in them, means it is appropriate to take them as the benchmark for current practice in external reporting. The practices applied by limited companies set a good example as a starting point for those companies which are not limited liability companies.

In this chapter, and in Chapters 8 to 12, we refer only to companies because the aim of this textbook is to provide an understanding of the accounting information published by companies. The more general word *enterprise* could be substituted throughout most of what is said in these chapters because the principles and practice described here have a wider application, although modifications may be necessary when the needs of the users and the purposes of the enterprise are different from those relevant to a limited liability company.

L01   7.2 International influences

Although UK companies produce financial reports within UK company law and UK accounting standards, there is a strong and growing international influence on regulation. In particular the practice of accounting in the UK reflects its membership of the European Union and its role in helping to develop International Financial Reporting Standards (IFRS).

7.2.1 Impact of the European Union

The United Kingdom is a member of the European Union (EU) and is required to develop its laws so as to harmonise with those of other countries in the EU. This process of harmonisation starts when a *Directive* is issued by the European Commission, setting out the basic rules which should be followed in each Member State's national laws. For limited liability companies two such Directives have been particularly important, the Fourth Directive and the Seventh Directive. Together they form the basis of the Companies Act 1985, which was issued in 1985 and amended by a further Act in 1989. One important aspect of Directives is that they specify *formats* for the financial statements which ensure that all companies produce documents that are similar in appearance and which present items in a systematic order. The idea of having standard formats was not a familiar concept in the United Kingdom before the Directives became effective in the 1980s, but has now been accepted and makes it easier for the reader to find the starting point in reading. In later chapters we will see that having standard formats does not solve all the problems of comparability and understandability.

L01   Activity 7.1

From your study of law, or from general interest reading, make a list of other areas of activity in which the UK law is harmonised with that of other countries in the European Union.

7.2.2 International Financial Reporting Standards

The International Accounting Standards Board (IASB) is an independent body that sets International Financial Reporting Standards (IFRS). It was formed in 2000 as the successor to the International Accounting Standard Committee (IASC) which had been setting International Accounting Standards (IAS) since 1973. These IAS have been adopted by the IASB and will gradually be revised as IFRS. Collectively they are described here as 'IASB Standards'. The IASB's objective is to bring about convergence of national accounting standards and international accounting standards to high-quality solutions. This will help participants in the world's capital markets and other users to make economic decisions.

There are many similarities between the UK accounting standards and the IASB Standards. There are also some differences where the UK standard setter believes a particular approach is justified, or where historical developments have a strong influence. The UK Accounting Standards Board works on projects with the IASB, as do other countries' standard setting bodies, all seeking to develop international convergence.

7.2.3 Convergence in Europe

It is the intention of the European Commission that, by 2005, all listed companies in the European Union will use IASB Standards in preparing their financial statements. This is intended to cause convergence ('bringing together') of accounting practices, and so improve the movement of capital across the stock markets of the European Union. The Commission, which prepares and implements the legislation of the European Parliament, has established procedures for giving European approval to each of the IASB Standards. It will take advice from EFRAG (the European Financial Reporting Advisory Group), a team of experts that includes a UK member.

L02 | 7.3 The Statement of Principles

The Accounting Standards Board (ASB) has issued, as part of its *Statement of Principles*, chapter 7 dealing with the presentation of financial information.[1] Repeating the objective stated in its first chapter, which is the provision of financial information that is useful to a wide range of users, the ASB analyses the way in which information should be presented in order to meet that objective.

It refers to four primary financial statements:

- the balance sheet;
- the profit and loss account;
- the statement of total recognised gains and losses (explained in Chapter 12 of this book);
- the cash flow statement;

and emphasises that these must be read with their related notes of explanation.[2] It also lists features of financial statements and gives guidance on how to make the best of those features.

7.3.1 Categories of financial information

The primary financial statements are the core of a much wider range of sources of financial information which users may obtain about a company. The relative position of the primary financial statements is shown in Exhibit 7.1.

L02 | Activity 7.2

Write down three items of accompanying information about a company which you feel would be useful in the annual report of a company. Exchange lists with other members of the class and establish the similarities and differences across the group. To what extent would one general set of financial statements with notes and accompanying information meet your collective expectations?

Exhibit 7.1

Categories of financial information

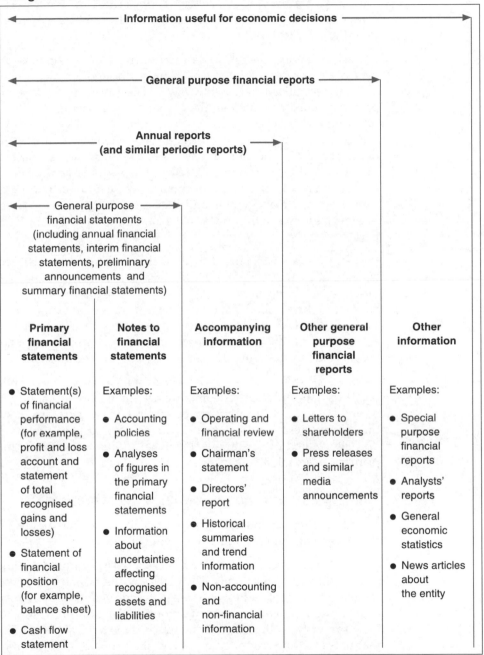

Source: ASB (1999) *Statement of Principles for Financial Reporting*, Accounting Standards Board, Introduction.
Reproduced with the permission of the Accounting Standards Board.

7.3.2 The primary financial statements

The ASB's *Statement of Principles* identifies three different purposes for financial statements. These are to report on financial performance, financial position and financial adaptability.[3]

Financial performance comprises the return an entity obtains on the resources it controls. It is reported by means of the profit and loss account and the statement of total recognised gains and losses. The profit and loss account has already been explained as matching the revenue of a period with the expenses incurred in earning that revenue. In the statement of total recognised gains and losses the profit of the period is added to other items which may have increased or decreased the ownership interest (such as increases or decreases in the value of assets held by the company, where the assets have not been sold).

Statements of financial performance are seen as providing an account of the stewardship of management and also as helping readers to check the accuracy of previous estimates they may have made about the expected outcome of the period.

Financial position is reported in the balance sheet. It reports economic resources controlled by the company, its financial structure, its liquidity and its financial viability. Such information helps users to estimate the amount, timing and probability of future cash flows by defining the asset life or the maturity date of debt. The balance sheet is not a statement of the value of the company because there are limitations in the measurement process and also because not all items which are of value to the company are included in the balance sheet.

Financial adaptability refers to the ability of the company to respond to unexpected needs or opportunities.[4] A company has financial adaptability if it can raise new capital at short notice, or if it can obtain cash from sale of assets without disrupting the continuing operations, or if it can achieve a rapid improvement in the cash flows generated by operations. Financial adaptability may be indicated by all the primary financial statements in different ways.

7.3.3 Notes and accompanying information

The annual report contains the primary financial statements, notes to the financial statements and accompanying information.

Notes to the financial statements are essential in amplifying and explaining the primary financial statements. The notes and the primary financial statements form an integrated whole. Many of these notes are required by regulations such as the Companies Act 1985 or relevant accounting standards. The wording of the notes is as important as the numbers if ambiguity is to be avoided. The ASB also warns that notes to the accounts are not the place to correct or justify a misrepresentation in the primary financial statements. That potential misrepresentation should be dealt with by amending the financial statement to eliminate the problem.

Accompanying information is any other information additional to the primary financial statements and notes. It could be information which is highly relevant but of lower reliability than the financial statements and notes. It could be information which will only interest a particular group of users. Such accompanying information may not be subject to the audit process which is compulsory for the primary financial statements and notes. The view of the ASB is that such accompanying information may be very important, one example being the Operating and Financial Review now presented by many large companies as management's explanation of the information given in the financial statements (*see* Chapter 14). Accompanying information may include disclosures of a voluntary or evolutionary nature.

Many annual reports include *highlights* pages showing amounts, ratios and other calculations that distil a great deal of information into a few key items. The ASB agrees that highlights can be useful but warns against focusing attention exclusively on one or two measures. You cannot read about financial statements for long without meeting the phrase 'the bottom line'. That refers to the line in the profit and loss account which reports the profit attributable to ordinary shareholders. It is sometimes referred to as *earnings for ordinary shareholders*. When this amount is divided by the number of shares which have been issued by the company it becomes the *earnings per share*. Investors, financial journalists and brokers' analysts have traditionally paid great attention to the earnings per share. The ASB would prefer to discourage this narrow focus and encourage instead a 'building block' approach where the company produces information in such a way that the user of the annual statement can create useful arrangements and combinations of information.

Companies also produce accompanying information for specialised needs. Regulated industries (such as gas, electricity, telecommunications and water) provide supplementary information about their regulated activities. Some companies give non-financial performance indicators (such as speed of answering customer enquiries, or level of customer satisfaction). Graphs, charts, diagrams and even photographs are all ways of providing accompanying information which adds to users' understanding of a document.

LO3a 7.4 Balance sheet

The Companies Act 1985 permits two different formats of balance sheet, each conforming to the accounting equation but permitting different layouts on the page. It was explained in Chapter 2 that there are different national preferences for layout and these are reflected in the two permitted formats:

Format 1 uses the accounting equation to create a vertical format:

Assets
minus
Liabilities
equals
Ownership interest

Format 2 uses the accounting equation to create a horizontal format:

		Ownership interest
Assets	equal	plus
		Liabilities

Format 2 is included for the benefit of those Continental European countries where the horizontal format is preferred. Format 1 is the preference of most UK companies and will be used in this textbook.

7.4.1 Balance sheet format 1: list of contents

The Companies Act sets out the format as a list of items. The list attaches letters A to K to the main headings and uses roman numerals for subheadings of items which are important but slightly less important than the main headings. The headings labelled by letters A to K and the subheadings labelled by roman numerals must be shown in the main body of the balance sheet. There are further lists of detailed items which must be reported but which may be contained in additional pages of notes to the balance sheet. These lists are given arabic numerals to identify them. There is a general rule that where an item under any heading is not relevant to the company, or is of zero amount, it need not be disclosed. So if a company does not mention one of the items in the format, it has to be presumed that the particular item is not relevant to that company.

The full format is set out in the Supplement to this chapter. The headings and subheadings are summarised in Exhibit 7.2.

7.4.2 Comment

You will see that the list in Exhibit 7.2 contains the elements of the accounting equation in putting together assets, liabilities and ownership interest. Fixed assets are separate from current assets. Current liabilities (due in less than one year) are separate from other liabilities (due in more than one year). Some of the items under the headings A to J may look rather strange at this stage (particularly A, D, I and J). Don't worry about that at present. If they are appropriate to first-level study they will be explained at some point in this text. If they are not explained, then they are relatively rare in occurrence and the time taken to explain them will outweigh the benefits you would gain from understanding.

The ownership interest is shown at heading K as *capital and reserves*. The word *capital* here means the claim which owners have because of the number of shares they own and the word *reserves* means the claim which owners have because the company has created new wealth for them over the years. Various labels are used to describe the nature of that new wealth and how it is created. Some of the new wealth is created because new investors pay more than a specified amount for the shares. Paying more is referred to as *paying a premium*, so this kind of ownership interest is labelled the *share premium*. Some of the new wealth is created because the fixed assets held by the company increase in value and that new valuation is

Exhibit 7.2
Balance sheet: format 1 – Headings and subheadings

A   **Called-up share capital not paid**

B   **Fixed assets**
   I   *Intangible assets*
   II   *Tangible assets*
   III *Investments*

C   **Current assets**
   I   *Stocks*
   II   *Debtors*
   III *Investments*
   IV *Cash at bank and in hand*

D   **Prepayments and accrued income**

E   **Creditors: amounts falling due within one year**

F   **Net current assets (liabilities)**

G   **Total assets less current liabilities**

H   **Creditors: amounts falling due after more than one year**

I   **Provisions for liabilities and charges**

J   **Accruals and deferred income**

K   **Capital and reserves**
   I   *Called-up share capital*
   II   *Share premium account*
   III *Revaluation reserve*
   IV *Other reserves*
   V   *Profit and loss account*

recorded. This kind of ownership interest is labelled the *revaluation reserve*. Some of the new wealth is created by making profits through operating activities. This kind of ownership interest is labelled the *profit and loss account* reserve. There are various other explanations of wealth creation which are collected under the label *other reserves*.

The format prescribed by the Companies Act does not show how the accounting equation is to be presented because it does not indicate places for subtotals and totals. Companies have to decide for themselves how to apply the accounting equation to the presentation of the list of items in the format. The remainder of this chapter explores the published financial statements of a hypothetical listed company which operates in a service industry. Buildings and vehicles are its main fixed assets. It sells recycling and cleaning services to customers based on the high reputation of the company's products and name.

L03 **Activity 7.3**

Read again the format for the balance sheet. How many of the items there came as no surprise to you? How many looked unfamiliar? Make a note of these and check that you find out about them in later chapters.

7.4.3 Illustration of balance sheet presentation

The following illustration sets out the balance sheet of Safe and Sure plc for Year 7 with comparative amounts alongside for the previous year. The balance sheet is followed by a comment on matters of particular interest.

Safe and Sure plc
Consolidated balance sheet at 31 December

		Notes	Year 7 £m	Year 6 £m
Fixed assets	Intangible assets	1	260.3	237.6
	Tangible assets	2	137.5	121.9
	Investments	3	2.8	2.0
			400.6	361.5
Current assets	Stocks	4	26.6	24.3
	Debtors	5	146.9	134.7
	Short-term deposits and cash		107.3	90.5
			280.8	249.5
Current liabilities due within one year	Creditors	6	(189.3)	(170.2)
	Bank and other borrowings	7	(40.1)	(74.3)
			(229.4)	(244.5)
	Net current assets		51.4	5.0
Deferred assets	Taxation recoverable	8	5.9	4.9
	Total assets less current liabilities		457.9	371.4
Liabilities due after one year	Creditors	9	(2.7)	(2.6)
	Bank and other borrowings	10	(0.2)	(0.6)
	Provisions for liabilities and charges	11	(20.2)	(22.2)
	Net assets		434.8	346.0
Capital and reserves	Called-up share capital	12	19.6	19.5
	Share premium account	13	8.5	5.5
	Revaluation reserve	14	4.6	4.6
	Other reserves	15	9.1	7.2
	Profit and loss account	16	393.0	309.2
	Shareholders' funds		434.8	346.0

7.4.4 Discussion

The first feature to note is the title, *Consolidated balance sheet*. Companies which are listed on the Stock Exchange are generally using one name as an umbrella for a group of several companies linked together under one parent. It is thought to be more useful to the shareholders of the parent company to see all the assets controlled by that company within the single financial statement. The word *control* is important here. The parent company owns the other companies, but they, in turn, own their separate assets. The parent company controls the use of those assets indirectly by controlling the companies it owns. The balance sheet as presented here represents a group where the parent company owns 100 per cent of all the other companies in the group (called its subsidiary undertakings). A similar consolidated balance sheet would be produced if the parent owned less than 100 per cent, provided it had the same element of control. The only additional item would be a 'minority interest' in the ownership claim.

The second feature of the balance sheet as presented is that there are two columns of figures. Companies are required to present the figures for the previous year, in order to provide a basis for comparison.

The balance sheet follows the accounting equation and this company has helpfully set out in the left-hand margin the main elements of the equation. It has expanded the equation by adding *deferred assets*. You should not feel intimidated by seeing new titles when you can work out what they mean. You already know what assets are, and you know that *deferred* means *delayed until later*. So deferred assets are those whose benefit is delayed beyond the period expected for a current asset, but not quite so long as to make them part of the fixed assets held on a long-term basis.

Intangible assets means assets which may not be touched – they have no physical existence. Examples are the goodwill of a business or the reputation of a branded product.

Tangible fixed assets is another phrase which you are seeing here for the first time, but again you can work out the meaning. You know from Chapter 2 what *fixed assets* are and you know that tangible means *something that may be touched*. So you would not be surprised to find that note 2 to the accounts gives more detail on land and buildings, plant, equipment, vehicles and office equipment.

Investments here means shares in other companies which are not subsidiary undertakings within the group.

Current assets comprise stocks, debtors and cash. These are the items having arabic numerals in the prescribed formats. Such items may be shown by way of a note rather than on the face of the balance sheet. They are set out in order of increasing liquidity, stocks being the least readily convertible into cash, debtors being closer to collection of cash and the cash itself being the most liquid asset. The notes to the accounts contain more detailed information. Take as an example note 4, relating to stocks. It appears as follows:

Note 4		Year 7	Year 6
		£m	£m
Stocks	Raw materials	6.2	5.4
	Work-in-progress	1.9	1.0
	Finished products	18.5	17.9
		26.6	24.3

The notes are shown in full in Appendix I at the end of this book. There is a note relating to debtors, mainly relating to trade debtors. *Creditors due within one year* has a similar type of note to the balance sheet.

The *deferred asset* is an amount of tax which has been paid already but may be reclaimed in 18 months' time.

The *liabilities due after one year* include long-term borrowings, which are quite low in amount compared with those of many other companies of this size. The provisions relate to future obligations caused by: treating a contaminated site; reorganisation of part of the business; and future tax payable.

That stage of the balance sheet concludes with the net assets, defined as all assets minus all liabilities. It is not an item of the Companies Act format, but is used by most companies as the point which creates a pause in the balance sheet before moving on to the ownership interest.

For a company the *ownership interest* is specified in company law as comprising the claim created through the shares owned by the various shareholders and the claim representing additional reserves of wealth accumulated since the company began. That wealth is accumulated by making profits year after year. The claim is reduced when the owners take dividends from the company. (Further information on the reporting of share capital, reserves and dividends is contained in Chapter 12.)

The ownership interest is the part of the balance sheet which causes greatest confusion to most readers. It is purely a statement of a legal claim on the assets after all liabilities have been satisfied. The word *reserves* has no other significance. There is nothing to see, touch, count or hold. To add to the potential confusion, company law delights in finding names for various different kinds of ownership interest. If you are the kind of person who takes a broad-brush view of life you won't worry too much about share premium account, revaluation reserve, other reserves, and profit and loss account reserve. They are all part of accounting terminology which becomes important to a company lawyer when there is a dispute over how much dividend may be declared, but are less important to the investor who says 'How much is my total claim?'

L03b 7.5 Profit and loss account

The Companies Act 1985 provides four formats for profit and loss accounts but the version most frequently observed in the United Kingdom is format 1. This will be used for illustration throughout this textbook.

7.5.1 Profit and loss account format 1: list of contents

Format 1 is set out in Exhibit 7.3, as follows:

Exhibit 7.3
Profit and loss account: format 1

1 Turnover
2 Cost of sales
3 Gross profit
4 Distribution costs
5 Administrative expenses
6 Other operating income
7 Income from shares in group undertakings
8 Income from participating interests (excluding group undertakings)
9 Income from other fixed asset investments
10 Other interest received and similar income

Exhibit 7.3 continued

11	Amounts written off investments
12	Interest payable and similar charges
13	Tax on profit or loss of ordinary activities
14	Profit or loss on ordinary activities after taxation
15	Extraordinary income
16	Extraordinary charges
17	Extraordinary profit or loss
18	Tax on extraordinary profit or loss
19	Other taxes not shown under the above items
20	Profit or loss for the financial year

7.5.2 Illustration of profit and loss account presentation

The published profit and loss accounts of most major companies are very similar to the illustration set out here for Safe and Sure plc.

Safe and Sure plc
Consolidated profit and loss account for the years ended 31 December

	Notes	Year 7 £m	Year 6 £m
Turnover			
Continuing operations		701.1	589.3
Acquisitions		13.5	
		714.6	
Discontinued operations		20.0	11.0
Turnover	17	734.6	600.3
Cost of sales	18	(531.5)	(427.3)
Gross profit		203.1	173.0
Distribution expenses		(2.2)	(2.5)
Administrative expenses	19	(26.2)	(26.5)
Operating profit			
Continuing operations		192.5	154.0
Acquisitions		2.7	
		195.2	
Discontinued operations		(20.5)	(10.0)
Profit on ordinary activities before interest		174.7	144.0
Interest receivable (net)	20	2.3	3.0
Profit on ordinary activities before tax	21	177.0	147.0
Tax on profit on ordinary activities	22	(62.2)	(52.4)
Profit attributable to ordinary shareholders		114.8	94.6
Dividends		(33.7)	(27.8)
Retained profit for the year		81.1	66.8
Earnings per share (pence)	23	11.74	9.71

7.5.3 Discussion

The first point to note is the heading. This is a consolidated profit and loss account bringing together the results of the activities of all the companies in the group during the year. The individual companies will also produce their own separate profit and loss accounts and these are added together to produce the consolidated picture. Where one company in the group sells items to another in the group, the sale and purchase are matched against each other on consolidation so that the results reported reflect only sales to persons outside the group.

The second point to note is that the profit and loss account as presented by the company is more informative than the list contained in Exhibit 7.3 might suggest. That is partly because the company has used subtotals to break up the flow and make it digestible for the reader. It is also partly due to the work of the Accounting Standards Board (ASB) in its Financial Reporting Standard (FRS 3), *Reporting Financial Performance*.[5] In particular the ASB requires companies to report separately the results of activities which were acquired or discontinued during the year. This is intended to help the reader who wishes to make a projection of the likely profits of the following year and needs to know what amount of profit relates to continuing activities. So the turnover is subdivided into amounts for continuing operations, acquisitions during the year and discontinued operations. Operating profit is similarly subdivided. In the notes to the accounts, the items between these two points (cost of sales, gross profit, distribution expenses and administrative expenses) are also subdivided between continuing operations, acquisitions and discontinued operations.

Working down the profit and loss account, it has already been explained that *turnover* is another word used to identify revenue. Turnover represents sales to third parties outside the group of companies. The cost of sales is the total of the costs of materials, labour and overheads which relate closely to earning the sales. The gross profit is sometimes referred to as the gross margin and is monitored closely by those who use the financial statements to make a judgement on the operations of the company. Within any industry the gross profit as a percentage of sales is expected to be within known limits. If that percentage is low then the company is either underpricing its goods or else taking the market price but failing to control costs. If the percentage is high, then the company is perhaps a market leader which can command higher prices for its output because of its high reputation. However, it might also be seen by customers and competitors as charging too much for its goods or services.

The next item in the profit and loss account is distribution expenses, which would include the costs of delivering goods to customers. For this company the distribution costs are low because it provides services by contract and does not carry out much distribution work. For many users the trends in an amount are more interesting than the actual amount. They might ask why the amount has decreased. On the other hand, it is not a particularly significant component of the overall picture and the users might show little interest. They would pay more attention to the administrative expenses, a collective term for all those costs which have to be incurred in order to keep the business running but which are less closely related to the direct activity of creating sales. The directors' salaries, head office costs and general maintenance of buildings and facilities are the kinds of details brought together under this heading. Directors' salaries are always a matter of some fascination and companies are expected to give considerable detail in the notes to the accounts about how much each director is paid and what other benefits are provided.

The profit on ordinary activities before interest is the end of the first stage of the profit and loss account, where the story of the business operations is complete. The rest of the profit and loss account is concerned with the cost of financing the company. Interest is paid and received, usually brought together in one net amount which shows, in this case, an excess of interest received over interest paid. That suggests a fairly cash-rich company with relatively low levels of borrowing. Next comes the corporation tax, which all companies must pay as a percentage of the profit before tax. The percentage is a standard percentage applied to the profit calculated according to the tax rules. Because the tax rules are not identical to the accounting rules, the percentage appears to vary when the reader looks at the profit and loss account. Helpful companies will explain the tax charge in the Operating and Financial Review, as well as providing more detailed notes to the accounts on the tax charge.

Finally the shareholders see their reward in the form of a dividend which returns to them some of the wealth created by the company during the period. Most companies try to increase the dividend each year, or at least to keep it constant. They also have to look at the relationship between what is paid out and what is retained for reinvestment in the business. Dividend policy is a complex issue facing the financial managers of a company. Accounting merely records the decisions taken by management.

LO3c 7.6 Cash flow statement

The presentation of cash flow statements by companies is regulated by FRS 1, *Cash Flow Statements*.[6] One of the useful features of the FRS series of accounting standards is that they contain a section headed *Explanation*. For the student this often provides more information than the main standard section itself. The need for a cash flow statement is expressed in terms of providing information about liquidity, viability and financial adaptability. There is a warning that it must be looked at together with the balance sheet showing the position of various assets and liabilities. Various classifications are felt by the ASB to be helpful. These are: operating activities; returns on investment and servicing of finance; taxation capital expenditure and financial investments; acquisitions and disposals; equity dividends paid; management of liquid resources; financing activities and cash movement. Safe and Sure uses these classifications. They are more detailed than the three headings used in Chapter 3, section 3.5, for the legal practice of P. Mason. That example had three categories: operating activities, investing activities and financing activities. These follow the International Accounting Standard IAS 7. The UK standard has developed more detail within the three headings.

7.6.1 Illustration of cash flow statement presentation

Safe and Sure plc
Consolidated cash flow statement for the years ended 31 December

		Notes	Year 7 £m	Year 6 £m
Operating activities	Net cash flow from operating activities	24	196.7	163.5
Returns on investments and servicing of finance	Interest received		5.0	5.9
	Interest paid		(3.1)	(2.4)
	Net cash outflow from returns on investments and servicing of finance		1.9	3.5
Taxation	UK corporation tax paid		(20.1)	(18.3)
	Overseas tax paid		(30.5)	(26.5)
	Total tax paid		(50.6)	(44.8)
Capital expenditure and financial investments	Purchase of tangible fixed assets		(60.0)	(47.5)
	Sale of tangible fixed assets		12.0	10.1
	Net capital expenditure		(48.0)	(37.4)
Acquisitions and disposals	Purchase of companies and businesses	25	(27.7)	(90.1)
	Sale of a company		3.1	–
	Net payment for acquisitions		(24.6)	(90.1)
Equity dividends paid	Dividends paid to shareholders		(29.5)	(24.4)
Management of liquid resources	Net movement in short-term deposits		(30.7)	36.3
	Net loan movement (excluding overdraft)	26	16.2	(24.0)
	Net cash movement on liquid resources		(14.5)	12.3
Financing activities	Issue of ordinary share capital	27	3.1	2.0
Cash movement	Increase/decrease in cash and deposits repayable on demand, net of bank overdrafts	28	34.5	(15.4)

Note 24: Cash flow from operating activities
Reconciliation of operating profit to net cash flow from operating activities

	Year 7	Year 6
	£m	£m
Operating profit	174.7	144.0
Depreciation charge	33.2	30.1
Increase in stocks*	(1.9)	(1.1)
Increase in debtors*	(7.4)	(5.3)
Decrease in creditors*	(0.4)	(3.6)
Net cash inflow from continuing activities	198.2	164.1
Cash outflow in respect of discontinued item	(1.5)	(0.6)
Net cash inflow from operating activities	196.7	163.5

[*Note: It is not possible to reconcile these amounts with the balance sheet information because of the effect of acquisitions during the year.]

7.6.2 Discussion

The first line of the cash flow statement is *net cash flow from operating activities*, highlighted by the company as an important feature. Note 24 to the accounts explains why this is not the same as operating profit. When a company makes a profit it earns revenue which is greater than the expenses. Some of the revenue is collected as cash but some will be collected later when the credit customers pay. When expenses are incurred, some are paid for immediately but others relate to goods and services taken from suppliers. Note 24 to the accounts is set out above and shows that cash is generated by profits but is used when stock levels increase and when debtors increase. Allowing stocks to increase will use up cash because more has to be paid for them. Allowing debtors to increase means they are not paying the cash so fast and therefore the cash is not coming in. That will diminish cash flow. Allowing creditors to decrease is a further way of diminishing cash flow because it means they are being paid faster.

There is one other line in note 24 which gives pause for thought. That is the second line *depreciation charge*. Depreciation is a measure of how much a fixed asset has been used up. It is an amount which is deducted from profits as a measure of using up the cost of the fixed asset in the accounting period. It does not of itself generate cash, but it stops the owners removing so much cash from the company that they are unable to replace a fixed asset at the end of its useful life. Since it is not a cash item it has to be added back to the reported profit. By way of illustration, suppose a company pays £100 for goods and sells them for £150. It has generated £50 cash. In the profit and loss account £10 is deducted for depreciation, so the reported profit becomes £40. The reconciliation of profit to cash flow from operations will be written as:

	£
Operating profit	40
add Depreciation	10
Cash inflow from operating activities	50

There is more about depreciation in Chapter 8 and more about cash flow in Chapter 14.

The cash flow statement then assumes that cash inflows from operations are augmented or depleted by the interest received and paid. Interest received is a return on loans to others, while interest paid is the cost of servicing loans received by this company. The government takes its share of the cash flow in a taxation payment and the company looks at what is left over for long-term investment. Next are shown the capital expenditure, cash paid for acquisitions and the cash paid as dividend to the company's shareholders. The cash inflow from operating activities may be insufficient to cover all the investment requirements for capital expenditure and acquisitions, so more finance has to be raised from external sources. On the one hand the company may use relatively short-term sources of loans and may put surplus cash on short-term deposit. This is described as management of liquid resources. For long-term financing needs the company may raise finance from external sources, such as an issue of ordinary share capital, in advance of its investment needs. It then keeps the additional cash on short-term deposits until needed. These are the kinds of stories which should emerge from the well-presented cash flow statement.

For the particular cash flow statement presented here, the broad story is that the company generated sufficient cash from its operations to cover all servicing of finance, to pay the tax due, meet its investment needs and pay dividends. Despite that positive amount, the company has increased its loans by £16.2m and marginally increased its share capital by £3.1m, so that a total of £34.5m has been added to cash and deposits repayable on demand.

The company explained its cash flow management as follows in the Operating and Financial Review: 'The group's businesses are structured to use as little fixed and working capital as is consistent with the profit and earnings growth objective in order to produce a high cash flow.'

 DAVID WILSON comments on cash flow in the company:

Cash is an important factor for any business. It is only one of the resources available but it is the key to survival.

What I'm basically looking for in the cash flow statement is how well the company is balancing various sources of finance. It generated £196.7m from operating activities. The servicing of investment cost £3.1m in loan interest but the company earned £5.0m in loan interest received. The result was to add £1.9m to the cash flow generated from operations. The total of £198.6m was more than sufficient to pay taxes of £50.6m and to cover its investing activities in new fixed assets costing £48m and acquisitions costing £24.6m. That left £75.4m from which to pay dividend of £29.5m. The amount remaining after paying dividend was £45.9m. There was no immediate need for any long-term financing flows with a healthy cash flow like that. In management of liquid resources a sum of £30.7m cash was paid into short-term deposits and perhaps surprisingly there was an increase of £16.2m in short-term loans. There was an amount of £3.1m raised in cash through an issue of shares to the employee's share option scheme. Overall the cash increased by £34.5m. That brings me back to my earlier question of why they are holding so much cash and short-term deposits.

The company in this example has told me that it carries out its financial management by recognising that the tax bill has to be paid first of all. Then it plans its investment in fixed assets and its programme of disposals. Once the investment has been decided the company aims to pay a dividend which will satisfy the expectations of investors. Surplus cash after that is available for acquisition of other companies and, because this company is always looking for good opportunities to expand, it will borrow ahead of time so that it is in a position to move quickly when a target presents itself. The company does not agree with the ASB's requirement to separate out the bank deposits which had more than three months to run when they were made. The deposits are placed largely for six months, so that many have less than six months to run at the balance sheet date. It is all very accessible cash and the company sees it all as one pool.

In the Operating and Financial Review the finance director explains the company's view of cash flow as follows:

> 'A net cash flow of £196.7m was generated from operating activities. That was boosted by other amounts of cash from interest received. After paying interest and tax, the group had £148.0m remaining. Fixed assets required £48m (after allowing for the proceeds of selling some of our vehicle fleet in the routine replacement programme). That left £100m from which £24.6m was required to pay for acquisitions. The remaining £75.4m covered dividends of £29.5m leaving £45.9m. We raised £3.1m in ordinary share capital to give a net inflow of liquid funds in the year of £49.0m. Out of that amount, short-term deposits have increased by £14.5m, leaving an increase in cash of £34.5m.'

You can see there are lots of different ways of interpreting the information in the cash flow statement. What is important is that the information is available. There is a requirement in FRS 1 for the company to link this figure of £34.5m to the balance sheet items. That is done in note 29 to the accounts.

Note 29: Cash flow and net liquid funds
Reconciliation of cash flow for the year to the balance sheet items

	Year 7 £m	Year 6 £m
Balance sheet items		
Short-term deposits and cash	107.3	*90.5*
Short-term borrowings	(40.1)	*(74.3)*
Long-term borrowings	(0.2)	*(0.6)*
Net liquid funds	67.0	*15.6*
Cash flow per cash flow statement	34.5	
Exchange adjustments	2.4	
Increase in other liquid resources	14.5	
	51.4	
Add net liquid funds at start of period	15.6	
Net liquid funds at end of period	67.0	

The revised financial reporting standard is quite helpful in requiring companies to produce this reconciliation. The earlier version of FRS 1 did not require such detail and so not all companies complied. Understanding the nature and composition of cash balances and how they are managed is an important element of understanding management strategy in action.

L04 | 7.7 Group structure of companies

Most major companies in the United Kingdom operate using a group structure. Within a group there is a *parent* company which controls *subsidiary* companies undertaking various different aspects of the operations of the business. It would in theory be possible to have all the operations located within one company but in practice, because company law draws very tight boundaries around a single company, there is some safety for the organisation in having different parts of the business packaged separately. If something goes seriously wrong with one subsidiary company, that company may be allowed to fail without irreparable damage to the total group. This approach has not always worked out in practice because very often the banks which lend money to a subsidiary will request guarantees from other companies in the group. So if one subsidiary fails in a spectacular way, it may drag the rest of the group with it.

Other reasons for retaining separate subsidiaries include: employee loyalty, product reputation, taxation legislation and overseas operations. When a new company is taken into the group, a sense of pride in the formerly independent company may be retained by continuing to use the traditional company name. The company name may be linked to a reputation for a high-quality product so that it is desirable to perpetuate the benefit of that reputation. Tax legislation applies to individual companies and not to the group as a whole. Efficient use of the tax rules may require different types of business to operate in different companies. Operations located in other countries will come under the legal systems of those countries and may be required to have a separate legal identity.

For accounting purposes the group as a whole is the *economic entity* for which financial statements are prepared. An entity should prepare and publish financial statements if there is a legitimate demand for the information that its financial statements would provide and it is a cohesive economic unit.[7] The process of combining all the financial statements of the companies within a group is called *consolidation*. This chapter will explain sufficient aspects of the preparation of consolidated financial statements to allow an understanding of annual reports of groups of companies. The full complexities of consolidation and the wider aspects of group accounting may be found in advanced textbooks.

Definition

Consolidated financial statements recognise the parent's control of its subsidiaries. Consolidation is a process that aggregates the total assets, liabilities and results of the parent and its subsidiaries (the group). This ensures that the effects on the parent's financial performance and financial position of its interests in its subsidiaries are fully reflected in the financial statements.[8]

The smallest group consists of two companies. A group is created when one company (the *parent undertaking*) acquires a *controlling interest* in the share capital of another (the *subsidiary undertaking*). There is no upper limit to the number of companies which may form a group.

7.7.1 Defining a group

The legislation does not define a group as such. A group comprises a parent under-taking and its subsidiary undertakings. The legislation concentrates on the *subsidiary undertaking*, defining it as one in which the parent:

(a) has a majority of the voting rights; or
(b) is a member and can appoint or remove a majority of the board of directors; or
(c) is a member and controls alone a majority of the voting rights by agreement with other members; or
(d) has the right to exercise a dominant influence through the memorandum and articles or a control contract; or
(e) has a participating interest and either
    (i) actually exercises a dominant influence over it, or
    (ii) manages both on a unified basis.[9]

This definition looks rather daunting at first glance but closer reading shows it to be an example of how a definition has to grow to keep pace with the ingenuity of those who try to find a way round it. The most commonly used part of the definition is clause (a), concentrating on clear control through voting power. A right to appoint or remove the majority of the directors is also a strong contrac-tual indication of control. A definition based on these visible types of control was sufficient for many years until the expansionary period of the early and mid-1980s indicated creativity in establishing control by less direct means.

The definition quoted above, contained in the 1985 Act, is in fact a 1989 amendment closing various loopholes. It uses a very broad form of wording in some places. The meaning of the phrase 'exercises a dominant influence' is left to be defined by the accounting standard setters. The relevant standard takes the view that the actual exercise of dominant influence is evidenced by its effect in practice.[10] Normal commercial relationships (such as those between customer and supplier) do not in themselves provide evidence of dominant influence.

The legislation also leaves it to the standard setters to define the meaning of the phrase 'managed on a unified basis'. This may be observed where the whole of the operations of the undertakings are integrated and they are managed as a single unit.[11]

7.7.2 The importance of control

Control describes the highest degree of influence that an investor can have over its investee. If an investor (the parent) controls its investee (the subsidiary), it has the ability to direct the investee's operating and financial policies with a view to gaining economic benefit from its activities. The parent becomes fully account-able for the risks and rewards arising from its subsidiary's activities and obtains access to any benefits generated by the subsidiary's activities.[12]

Whatever the percentage holding, the concept of control is the guiding prin-ciple which allows the consolidated balance sheet to report *all* the assets and *all* the liabilities of the combined companies. The consolidated profit and loss account reports *all* the profit generated by those assets and liabilities.

7.7.3 The parent company's balance sheet

The parent company will continue to produce its own balance sheet, showing as an asset the cost of the investment in the subsidiary, but this information is not regarded as being particularly useful. The investment in the subsidiary is reported by the parent company as a single-line item but the consolidated balance sheet shows all the assets and all the liabilities of the group under each separate heading. The group balance sheet is more useful to readers. In previous chapters, where the financial statements of Safe and Sure plc have been discussed, the group accounts have been used.

7.7.4 Acquisition or merger?

The general term *business combination* may be applied to any transaction whereby one company becomes a subsidiary of another. The most common form of business combination is an *acquisition* where one party is clearly the dominant entity and the other is seen to be under new control. In rare cases there may be a *merger* in which the shareholders of the combining entities come together in a spirit of equal partnership for mutual sharing of risks and benefits. The existence of a true merger allows special accounting treatment. In particular the profits of both parties for the full year of a merger may be added together in the consolidated financial statements despite the merger taking place part-way through the year. True mergers are very rare in the United Kingdom and in the rest of this chapter we concentrate on acquisitions.

L04

> ### Activity 7.4
>
> *Check your understanding of the terms: parent, subsidiary, control, acquisition, merger. Write down a definition of each and then look back through this section to test your definition against that in the text.*

L05 # 7.8 Group financial statements

This section explains how the acquisition of a subsidiary affects the balance sheet of the parent company. It shows how the group's balance sheet and profit and loss account are created. It also explains the nature of goodwill arising on acquisition and it outlines the nature and treatment of associated companies.

7.8.1 The parent company's balance sheet

When an acquisition takes place, the parent company acquires shares in the subsidiary in exchange for cash or for shares in the parent. The parent company will offer cash if it has adequate cash resources to make the offer and it appears that those selling the shares would prefer to take cash for investment elsewhere. The parent company will offer its own shares in exchange where it may not have sufficient cash resources available or where it thinks it can persuade those selling their shares in the target company of the desirability of acquiring shares in the new parent. Many deals offer a mixture of shares and cash.

For a cash purchase the effect on the parent company's balance sheet, in terms of the accounting equation, is:

Assets ↑↓   –   Liabilities   =   Ownership interest

> Decrease in asset of cash
> Increase in asset of
> investment in subsidiary

For a share exchange, the effect on the parent company's balance sheet is to increase the assets and increase the ownership interest. In terms of the accounting equation:

Assets ↑   –   Liabilities   =   **Ownership interest** ↑

> Increase in asset of
> investment in subsidiary

> Increase by new shares
> issued

7.8.2 The group's consolidated balance sheet

In the group's consolidated balance sheet the parent company's assets and liabilities are added to the assets and liabilities of the subsidiary companies. The assets and liabilities of the subsidiary take the place of the parent company's investment in the subsidiary. Exhibit 7.4 shows the net assets of P and S separately. The arrows indicate the net assets of S moving in to take the place of P's investment in S. Removing the investment in S from the balance sheet of P and replacing it with the net assets of S leads to the group's consolidated balance sheet. Exhibit 7.5(a) shows the resulting amalgamation. The assets and liabilities in Exhibit 7.5(a) are then rearranged under each asset and liability category to result in Exhibit 7.5(b).

Exhibit 7.4
Separate net assets of parent and subsidiary

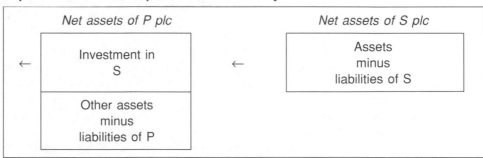

Exhibit 7.5
Completing the process of consolidation

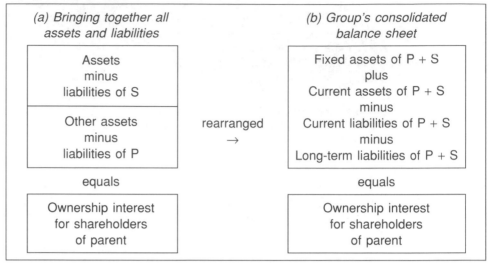

7.8.3 The group profit and loss account

Investors and their advisers may wish to use the profit and loss account of the group to make predictions of the future profitability of the group. To be able to do this, they must know how much of the current year's profit relates to continuing operations and how much relates to changes during the year. The illustration of the profit and loss account of Safe and Sure plc in section 7.5.2 shows how the consolidated profit and loss account is subdivided into continuing activities, acquisitions and discontinued activities, down as far as the operating profit line.

One rule of acquisition accounting is that, where a subsidiary is acquired partway through the year, only the profits earned after the date of acquisition may be included in the group profit and loss account. The analyst seeking to make a forecast for the year ahead will have to scale up the reported profit from acquisitions to a full 12-month contribution.

The clarity of information presented on profits and losses of acquisitions and disposals is due to the accounting standard FRS 3 *Reporting Financial Performance*. It is an example of the determination of the Accounting Standards Board to create a 'building block' type of financial statement where information is clearly presented but users may rearrange it to suit the particular picture they are seeking to build.

Groups are not required to present separately the parent company's profit and loss account. It is not felt to be particularly interesting to users as, generally, the parent company's main income comprises the dividends received from its investments in subsidiaries. Usually it is the subsidiaries which carry out the operations generating profit. It is far more interesting to know about the underlying operating profits which allow those dividends to be paid to the parent.

L05

Activity 7.5

P plc pays cash of £6m for an investment in net assets of S Ltd having a net book value of £6m. Explain how this transaction will affect the balance sheet of P plc as the parent company and explain how it will affect the group balance sheet of P Group plc, whose only subsidiary is S Ltd.

7.8.4 Goodwill on acquisition

In the illustration presented in Exhibits 7.4 and 7.5 the net assets of the subsidiary were shown as being of the same magnitude as the amount of the investment in the subsidiary so that the substitution of the former for the latter was a neat replacement process. That situation is unlikely to apply in real life because the price paid for an investment will rarely depend solely on the net assets being acquired. The purchaser will be looking to the future expectations from the investment and the seller will be seeking a reward for all that has been built into the business which cannot readily be quantified in terms of tangible assets. The future expectations will rest upon the reputation of the product or service, the quality of the customers, the skills of the workforce and the state of the order book, amongst many other things. The price negotiated for the business will include some recognition of all these qualities under the global heading of *goodwill*.

In these circumstances the price paid for the investment in the subsidiary will be greater than the amount of the net assets of the subsidiary. When the consolidation into the group balance sheet is attempted, a space will appear. Exhibit 7.6 shows the separate net assets of P plc and S plc. The amount of the cost of the investment in S is greater than the net assets of S plc. Exhibit 7.7 shows the resulting consolidation. The space shaded is equal to the difference between the amount of the investment in S and the net assets of S. This space is, in arithmetic terms, nothing more than a *difference on consolidation* but has traditionally been called *goodwill* because it is explained in terms of paying for something more than the underlying net assets.

Exhibit 7.6

Net assets of the separate companies P plc and S plc

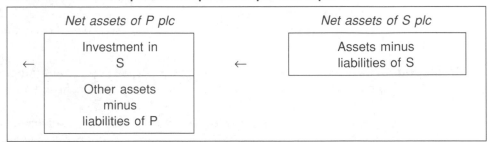

Exhibit 7.7
Group net assets of the P group

Group net assets

Assets minus
liabilities of S

Difference on consolidation

Other assets
minus
liabilities of P

Definition

Goodwill arising on acquisition is calculated as the difference between the fair value of the price paid for the subsidiary and the fair value of the net assets acquired. Fair value is the amount at which the item could be traded at arm's length between willing parties.

The existence of the difference on consolidation is an inescapable consequence of the process of combining the balance sheets of parent and subsidiary. For many years it caused one of the most difficult problems facing the accounting standard setters. The questions asked were: 'How should this consolidation difference be reported in the balance sheets of succeeding years?' and 'Is it an asset?'

In 1998 the UK accepted the international view that purchased goodwill confers on the group an expected future benefit as a result of a past transaction and is therefore an intangible fixed asset which should appear in the group balance sheet with all the other assets. It will gradually amortise over its useful life, reducing the amount of the asset and reducing the ownership interest through the expense of amortisation.

The effect on the group balance sheet may be expressed in terms of the accounting equation:

Assets ↓	–	Liabilities	=	**Ownership interest** ↓

Amortise goodwill over specified period of years				Record expense of amortisation in profit and loss account each year

Definition

Amortisation is the process of allocating the cost of an intangible asset, as an expense in the profit and loss account, over the useful life of the asset.

Some companies have said that although they agree that acquisition goodwill is an asset, they do not agree that it should be amortised. They say that the asset holds its value. They prefer an *impairment test* which asks, 'Can the business expect to recover the carrying value of the intangible asset, through either using it or selling it?' If the answer is 'no' then the asset is *impaired* and its value must be reduced. If the answer is 'yes' then the asset value should remain in the balance sheet. The ASB and the IASB permit impairment tests, with the procedures being specified in some detail. UK companies that do not carry out an impairment test must amortise over no more than 20 years. A similar rule is applied by the IASB. It has been the practice of companies in the USA to amortise goodwill over a maximum of 40 years but changes introduced in 2001 allow US companies to move to impairment tests.

| Definition | *Impairment* means 'damaged' or 'spoiled'. Where the carrying value of goodwill cannot be recovered through sale or use, it is said to be 'impaired'. The asset value in the balance sheet must be reduced. |

L05 **Activity 7.6**

P pays cash of £8m for an investment in net assets of S Ltd having a net book value of £6m. Explain how this transaction will affect the balance sheet of P plc as the parent company and explain how it will affect the group balance sheet of P Group plc, whose only subsidiary is S Ltd.

7.8.5 Associated companies

Where company P holds less than a controlling interest in company A, it may nevertheless have a significant influence over company A. Such significant influence would involve the power to participate in the financial and operating policy decisions of company A. Significant influence is presumed to exist when one company or a group of companies holds 20 per cent or more of the ordinary shareholders' voting rights of another company, unless the facts indicate that significant influence is not possible.

Where significant influence over a company exists, that company is called an *associated company*. The group must show in its balance sheet the group's share of the net assets of the associated company as a single line item, and must show in the profit and loss account the group's share of the profits or losses of the associated company.

This treatment of an investment in an associated company is called *equity accounting* because it reports the group's share of the investment in the ownership interest (also referred to as the equity).

Accounting for investments in associated companies was the first subject dealt with by accounting standards in the United Kingdom.[13] It was revised in 1997[14] because it had become apparent over the years that some groups had given a boost to their reported profit by holding 20 per cent of the share capital of a company in which the power to influence financial and operating policies was not really significant. It had also appeared that the percentage holding was sometimes rapidly reduced to 19 per cent where the associated company started to make losses, so that there was no adverse impact on the group profit and loss account. The main purpose of the revised standard was to take account of changes in legislation since the first standard was published.

For investments which do not meet the conditions of being reported as associated companies, the accounting treatment is to record the investment in the associate at cost in the balance sheet and to record in the profit and loss account of the group only the dividend income received from the associate.

7.9 Beyond the annual report

Beyond the annual report there are questions such as:

- How frequently should a company communicate with shareholders and other stakeholders?
- Does the present company law place too high a burden on small companies?
- What help already exists for small and medium-sized companies?
- How do larger companies avoid information overload for their shareholders?
- Can users have confidence in additional information provided beyond the annual report?

This section outlines developments on each issue.

7.9.1 Other forms of communication

This chapter has made repeated reference to the annual report of a company, but, in reality, companies communicate with shareholders and other users more than once in the accounting year. A company which has a Stock Exchange listing is required to produce a half-yearly report, sometimes referred to as an *interim report*. That will be less detailed than the annual report but will include summaries of the financial statements.

When the year-end results and half-yearly results are ready for publication, a *preliminary announcement* of key information is made in a manner set out by the Stock Exchange. The preliminary announcement is usually accompanied by meetings with professional investors and brokers' analysts at which key personnel in the company (usually the chairman, chief executive and finance director) will make speeches and answer questions.

When a major company wants to raise significant amounts of finance through selling shares on the Stock Market, it issues a *prospectus*. The contents of the prospectus are regulated by the UK Listing Authority, backed up on some items by the Companies Act 1985.

All these sources are of interest to those who want to know a company thoroughly. They are all available in the public domain, although some are not as easy to obtain as others. They provide potential research material for the enthusiastic student of accounting practices.

7.9.2 Company Law Review

A major inquiry into proposals for modernising company law led to a final report in 2001 which made recommendations to government. Changes in company law are usually slow, so it may be some time before these are achieved. However it is useful to be aware of the direction proposed for good practice. Furthermore some of the ideas could be developed as 'good practice' ahead of legislation.

At the heart of the Review was the idea 'think small first'. This reflected a concern that company law has grown by being written for the larger company and then 'slimmed down' for the smaller company. This has tended to leave too great a burden on small companies. Focusing first on the small company should reduce the risk of excessive burden. The Review concluded that the law allows financial reporting to be a slow process. Companies could make their preliminary announcement of results available on a website after release to the share market. The annual report could also be made available on a website without having to wait for paper versions to be published.

7.9.3 Small and medium-sized companies

The amount of detail in the information presented by companies depends on their size. The Companies Act 1985 defines small and medium-sized companies. The definitions are based on turnover, balance sheet totals and average number of employees. The amounts for turnover and balance sheet totals are altered from time to time by Statutory Instrument to keep pace with inflation, so it is perhaps easiest to take as a 'rule of thumb' the employee limits of 50 for a small company and 250 for a medium-sized company. For these companies there are substantial exemptions from requirements to publish information (although they must still provide details to shareholders if asked to do so). Consequently, the example discussed in this chapter is relevant only to the larger public companies. Since these are the companies which lead their industries and lead the stock market, they will continue to be the subject of explanation in subsequent chapters.

During the 1980s, concerns were expressed about the 'burden' of regulation for small companies. This burden was seen as falling from all directions, including tax laws, employment laws, product protection laws, health and safety laws and accounting regulation. The government of the time committed itself to reducing this burden. One consequence was that the Accounting Standards Board introduced a Financial Reporting Standard for Smaller Entities (FRSSE). This condenses into one standard the essential aspects of all the separate accounting standards for larger companies. It reduces disclosure requirements but maintains standards for measurement. Small companies may choose either to apply the FRSSE in full or to comply with the full range of separate standards.

The Companies Act 1985 permits small companies to file 'abridged' financial statements with the Registrar of Companies. The word 'abridged' can be explained as 'cutting down the detail' but views have been expressed that this has gone too far and that abridged financial statements do not provide useful information about small companies.

7.9.4 Avoiding information overload

Even the very largest companies may take advantage of the rule which allows them to publish summary financial statements. These are usually very much shorter than the full annual report and are offered to shareholders as an alternative to the full report. There is a short form of the balance sheet, profit and loss account and cash flow statement, no notes to the accounts but usually an accompanying commentary by the company directors. Shareholders are reminded of the existence of the full report and invited to ask for a copy if desired.

The Company Law Review report of 2001 recommended that summary financial statements should continue to be available as an option for companies in communicating with shareholders. The option should be extended to all sizes of company but the summary should include a narrative discussion as well as financial statements. The precise details would be set out by the Accounting Standards Board. The 'abridged financial statements' currently allowed for small companies would disappear as they are felt to be relatively uninformative.

7.9.5 'Pro forma' financial statements

'Pro forma' financial statements represent a recent development in company reporting that is causing some confusion among users of accounting information, and some concern among the regulators. When companies first announce their profits of the financial year, or the results of an interim period, they do so through an 'earnings announcement' at the Stock Exchange. This is accompanied by a press release which may draw investors' attention to a particular component of the financial statements. According to the dictionary, the phrase 'pro forma' means 'as a matter of form'. The underlying accounting meaning is 'outside the normal reporting regulations'. It usually involves selective editing from a larger body of information that has been prepared under accounting rules. The risk is that the selective information may not, by itself, represent a true and fair view. This does not necessarily mean that the information is bad or misleading, but it does mean that the investor is deprived of the full protection of regulation.

7.10 Summary

Now score your view of your confidence in achieving the learning outcomes of the chapter.

1 = Very confident about knowledge, application, problem solving and evaluation.

2 = Confident about knowledge and application, less sure about problem solving and evaluation.

3 = Need to read again to be more certain of basic knowledge and application.

L01 You can now explain the key international influences that affect accounting practice in the UK, with particular knowledge of the application of EU Directives and the role of the IASB.

   1 2 3
   ☐ ☐ ☐

L02 You can explain the structure of company reporting as set out in the *Statement of Principles*, with an understanding of the layers of information that accompany the primary financial statements in the annual report.

   1 2 3
   ☐ ☐ ☐

L03 You can now explain the main contents of (a) the balance sheet, (b) the profit and loss account and (c) the cash flow statement as presented by larger companies.

   1 2 3
   ☐ ☐ ☐

LO4 You are able to define 'parent company' and 'subsidiary company' and explain how a group is structured.

1	2	3
☐	☐	☐

LO5 You can explain the main features of group financial statements, particularly the meaning of acquisition goodwill, the nature of amortisation and the meaning of impairment.

1	2	3
☐	☐	☐

LO6 You can explain the nature of, and reasons for, other forms of communication beyond the annual report. You are also aware of some of the directions expected in future amendments to company law.

1	2	3
☐	☐	☐

If your scores are all 1 or 2, try the questions in the series A, B and C. This will give you feedback on your assessment of how well you have achieved the learning outcomes. Read again any sections of the chapter where you find your knowledge and understanding are less comprehensive than you first estimated.

If your scores include some at 3, try the series A questions to find where the problems lie. Read the relevant sections again, work through any illustrative examples and case studies, then try the questions in the series B. Once you feel confident at that level of knowledge and application, move on to try some or all of the series C questions.

There is no bookkeeping supplement to this chapter. The bookkeeping supplements continue in Chapters 8 to 12. The Supplement to this chapter sets out the balance sheet format most commonly used by UK companies.

International perspective

The presentation of the financial statements of Safe and Sure in this chapter is typical of most UK listed companies. The balance sheet of a French or German company would have the same sequence of assets and liabilities but usually on opposite pages of the annual report. The balance sheet of a US company would show the assets in a different sequence. The target of *harmonisation* with IASB Standards by 2005 will not necessarily lead to *uniformity* of presentation. It should ensure comparability of measurement but will leave scope for national variation within the agreed framework.

Further reading

ASB (1999) *Statement of Principles for Financial Reporting*, ch. 7, 'Presentation of Financial Information', Accounting Standards Board.

ASB (1992, amended 1993) FRS 3, *Reporting Financial Performance*. Read in particular the Explanation section, paras 35 to 48 (dealing with components of financial performance and continuing or discontinued operations).

ASB (1996) FRS 1, *Cash Flow Statements*. Read in particular Appendix III on the development of the FRS.

Useful websites

Company Law Review: *www.dti.gov.uk*
Financial Services Authority: *www.fsa.gov.uk*
Accounting Standards Board: *www.asb.org.uk*
London Stock Exchange: *www.londonstockex.co.uk*

Test your understanding

L01, S01 **A7.1** What is a Directive?

L01, S01 **A7.2** What is the role of the IASB?

L02, S01 **A7.3** Name the primary financial statements and explain the purpose of each.

L02, S01 **A7.4** The following technical terms appear in this chapter. Check that you know the meaning of each. (If you can't find them again in the text, there is a glossary at the end of the book).

(a) articulation	(k) gross margin
(b) capital	(l) gross profit
(c) deferred asset	(m) net
(d) depreciation	(n) net assets
(e) directors	(o) primary financial statements
(f) earnings for ordinary shareholders	(p) reserves
(g) earnings per share	(q) revaluation reserve
(h) external users (of financial statements)	(r) share premium
(i) financial adaptability	(s) tangible fixed assets
(j) gross	(t) turnover

L03, S01 **A7.5** How do companies report:

(a) financial performance;
(b) financial position; and
(c) financial adaptability?

L03, S01 **A7.6** What are the main headings to be found in most company balance sheets?

L03, S01 **A7.7** What is the reason for the order of items under heading C: current assets?

L03, S01 **A7.8** What are the main headings to be found in most company profit and loss accounts?

L03, S01 **A7.9** What are the main sections of a cash flow statement prepared according to FRS 1?

L03, S01 **A7.10** Why does depreciation appear as a line item in the reconciliation of operating profit with cash flow?

L03, S01 **A7.11** Apart from the annual report, what other documents do companies use to communicate financial statement information to investors, creditors and other users of financial statements?

L04, S01 **A7.12** Define the terms:

(a) group;
(b) parent company; and
(c) subsidiary undertaking.

L04, S01 **A7.13** Explain why groups of companies are formed.

L05, S01 **A7.14** Explain the purpose of consolidated financial statements.

L05, S01   **A7.15** Explain, using the accounting equation, the effect on the parent company's balance sheet of a cash payment for an investment in a subsidiary company.

L05, S01   **A7.16** Explain, using the accounting equation, the effect on the parent company's balance sheet of a share issue in exchange for shares in the subsidiary company.

L05, S01   **A7.17** Explain what is meant by *goodwill on acquisition*.

L05, S01   **A7.18** What is an associated company?

Application

To answer these questions fully you may wish to consult chapter 6 of the *Statement of Principles*.

L02, S01, S03   **B7.1** Write a letter to the financial controller of a company advising on the factors which a company should take into consideration when deciding how to arrange information in financial statements.

L03, S01, S03   **B7.2** Write a note for financial analysts explaining how the profit and loss account, as presented under FRS 3, provides a useful indication of the financial performance of a company.

L03, S01   **B7.3** What features are likely to make a balance sheet helpful to users?

L03, S01   **B7.4** Could a cash flow statement be presented as the only financial statement reported by a company?

Problem solving and evaluation

L02, L03, S01, S02, S03   **C7.1** A listed company is of the view that shareholders might welcome a statement of highlights and supplementary information as a leaflet to be inserted in the annual report. Give advice on the principles to be followed in making such information useful to users.

Activities for study groups

Continuing to use the annual reports of companies which you obtained for Chapters 1 and 4, find the financial statements (balance sheet, profit and loss account and cash flow statement) and the notes to the accounts.

1 Compare the financial statements with the formats and presentations shown in this chapter, and note any differences which you observe. Look at the notes to the accounts for items which are required by the regulations but are included in the notes rather than the main financial statements.

2 Find the Operating and Financial Review (sometimes named the finance director's review) and compare the cash flow discussion there with the FRS 1 presentation. Form a view on how readily the discussion may be related to the financial statement.

3 In your group, take the list of qualitative characteristics listed at section 4.2 of Chapter 4 and use the financial statements as a means of illustrating how the company has met those characteristics. If you have a set of different annual reports, each member of the group should take the role of a finance director pointing out the qualitative characteristics of their own company's financial statements. The group together should then decide on a ranking with a view to nominating one of the annual reports for an award of 'Communicator of the Year'.

Notes and references

1 ASB (1999) *Statement of Principles for Financial Reporting*, ch. 7, 'Presentation of financial information', Accounting Standards Board.
2 *Ibid.*, para. 7.4.
3 *Ibid.*, ch. 1, Principles section and paras 1.13–1.16.
4 *Ibid.*, paras 1.19–1.21.
5 ASB (1992, amended 1993) Financial Reporting Standard (FRS 3), *Reporting Financial Performance*, Accounting Standards Board.
6 ASB (1996) Financial Reporting Standard (FRS 1), *Cash Flow Statements*, Accounting Standards Board (revised from 1991 version).
7 ASB (1999), ch. 2, 'The reporting entity', Principles section.
8 *Ibid.*, ch. 8, para. 8.2.
9 Companies Act 1985, s. 258.
10 ASB (1992) Financial Reporting Standard (FRS 2), *Accounting for Subsidiary Undertakings*, paras 69–73, Accounting Standards Board.
11 *Ibid.*, para. 12.
12 ASB (1999), ch. 2, para. 2.9.
13 ASC (1971, amended 1974, revised 1982, amended 1990) Statement of Standard Accounting Practice (SSAP 1), *Accounting for Associated Companies*, Accounting Standards Board.
14 ASB (1997) Financial Reporting Standard (FRS 9), *Associates and Joint Ventures*, Accounting Standards Board.

Balance sheet format 1, as prescribed by the Companies Act 1985

A   Called-up share capital not paid

B   Fixed assets
    I   *Intangible assets*
          1   Development costs
          2   Concessions, patents, licences, trade marks and similar rights and assets
          3   Goodwill
          4   Payments on account
    II   *Tangible assets*
          1   Land and buildings
          2   Plant and machinery
          3   Fixtures, fittings, tools and equipment
          4   Payments on account and assets in course of construction
    III   *Investments*
          1   Shares in group undertakings
          2   Loans to group undertakings
          3   Participating interests (excluding group undertakings)
          4   Loans to undertakings in which the company has a participating interest
          5   Other investments other than loans
          6   Other loans
          7   Own shares

C   Current assets
    I   *Stocks*
          1   Raw materials and consumables
          2   Work-in-progress
          3   Finished goods and goods for resale
          4   Payments on account
    II   *Debtors*
          1   Trade debtors
          2   Amounts owed by group undertakings
          3   Amounts owed by undertakings in which the company has a participating interest
          4   Other debtors
          5   Called-up share capital not paid
          6   Prepayments and accrued income
    III   *Investments*
          1   Shares in group undertakings
          2   Own shares
          3   Other investments
    IV   *Cash at bank and in hand*

D   **Prepayments and accrued income**

E   **Creditors: amounts falling due within one year**
   1 Debenture loans
   2 Bank loans and overdrafts
   3 Payments received on account
   4 Trade creditors
   5 Bills of exchange payable
   6 Amounts owed to group undertakings
   7 Amounts owed to undertakings in which the company has a participating interest
   8 Other creditors including taxation and social security
   9 Accruals and deferred income

F   **Net current assets (liabilities)**

G   **Total assets less current liabilities**

H   **Creditors: amounts falling due after more than one year**
   1 Debenture loans
   2 Bank loans and overdrafts
   3 Payments received on account
   4 Trade creditors
   5 Bills of exchange payable
   6 Amounts owed to group undertakings
   7 Amounts owed to undertakings in which the company has a participating interest
   8 Other creditors including taxation and social security
   9 Accruals and deferred income

I   **Provisions for liabilities and charges**
   1 Pensions and similar obligations
   2 Taxation, including deferred taxation
   3 Other provisions

J   **Accruals and deferred income**

   Minority interests*

K   **Capital and reserves**
   I   *Called-up share capital*
   II   *Share premium account*
   III   *Revaluation reserve*
   IV   *Other reserves*
         1 Capital redemption reserve
         2 Reserve for own shares
         3 Reserves provided by the articles of association
         4 Other reserves
   V   *Profit and loss account*

   Minority interests*

Note: Where minority interests are relevant, they are to be treated as having a letter attached. Companies may choose one of the two permitted locations.

Chapter 8

Fixed assets

After studying this chapter you should be able to:

LO1   Define a fixed asset and apply the definition.

LO2   Explain the recognition conditions that are applied to tangible fixed assets, intangible fixed assets and fixed asset investments.

LO3   Explain users' needs for information about fixed assets.

LO4   Describe and explain the fixed asset information provided in annual reports of companies.

LO5   Evaluate the usefulness of published information about fixed assets.

LO6   Explain the nature of depreciation.

LO7   Calculate depreciation, record the effect on the accounting equation and report the result in financial statements.

Additionally, for those who choose to study the Supplement:

LO8   Record fixed assets and depreciation in ledger accounts.

8.1 Introduction

If you have progressed through Chapters 1 to 7 you are now familiar with the accounting equation and the analysis of transactions or events using that equation. You know what is meant by the terms asset, liability, revenue, expense and ownership interest. You are aware of the structure of the primary financial statements and the way in which they seek to provide information which is relevant and reliable.

This chapter starts a new phase of the text which will help you to develop a critical awareness of some of the component items in the financial statements. Chapters 8 to 12 progress through the main sections of the balance sheet. Inevitably, they also cover relevant aspects of the profit and loss account and the cash flow statement because of the *articulation* of financial statements (explained in Chapter 7).

It is important at this stage not to become so enthusiastic for the intricacies of accounting procedures as to lose sight of the importance of user needs, which were set out in Chapter 1. That chapter set out, in section 1.2, the structure of most conceptual frameworks, which provides a sequence for each of Chapters 8 to 12, as follows:

● What are the rules for defining and recognising these items?
● What are the information needs of users in respect of the particular items?
● What information is currently provided by companies to meet these needs?
● Does the information show the desirable qualitative characteristics of financial statements?
● What are the rules for measuring, and processes for recording, these items?

That analysis is applied to fixed assets in this chapter.

L01　8.2 Definitions

The following definition of assets was provided in Chapter 2.

Definition　*Assets* are rights or other access to future economic benefits controlled by an entity as a result of past transactions or events.

The Accounting Standards Board has produced more detailed definitions of tangible and intangible fixed assets.

Definition　*Tangible fixed assets* are assets that have physical substance and are held for use in the production or supply of goods or services, for rental to others, or for administrative purposes on a continuing basis in the reporting entity's activities (FRS 15, para. 2).[1]

Definition　*Intangible fixed assets* are non-financial fixed assets that do not have physical substance but are identifiable and are controlled by the entity through custody or legal rights (FRS 10, para. 2).[2]

These definitions are taken from two separate sources and it is unfortunate that there is no general definition of a fixed asset. The Accounting Standards Board has spent many years in discussion over the subjects of accounting for tangible and intangible fixed assets because both are complex matters.

8.2.1 Examples of fixed assets

The following is a sample of the fixed assets found in company balance sheets.

Tangible fixed assets

- Land and buildings owned by the enterprise
- Buildings leased by the enterprise
- Plant and equipment (owned or leased)
- Vehicles (owned or leased)
- Office equipment
- Assets under construction
- Telecommunications network
- Airport runways
- Water pipes and sewers
- Oil and mineral reserves.

Intangible fixed assets

- Newspaper titles and publishing rights
- Patents
- Trade marks
- Goodwill purchased
- Brand names purchased.

Investments

- Long-term investments in subsidiary companies
- Long-term investments in other companies.

That sample was taken from only 10 annual reports of leading companies. Looking at more companies would soon extend the list considerably. The potential variety and the likelihood of encountering something new is one reason why definitions are essential.

8.2.2 Cost of a fixed asset

There is one issue which is not as straightforward as it seems. That is the question of measuring the cost of a fixed asset. When a toffee manufacturer buys a new toffee-shaping machine, the purchase price will be known from the supplier's invoice and the manufacturer's catalogue, but should the costs of delivery and installation be added to the amount recorded as the asset cost? When an insurance company buys a new head office, the purchase price will be shown in the contract, but should the legal costs be added to the amount recorded as the asset cost? When a new head office building is under development and interest is being paid on the funds borrowed to finance the development, should the interest paid on the borrowed funds be added to the cost of the development as part of the asset value?

The answer in all three cases is 'yes', although the third example causes greatest discussion and debate. The general principle is that the cost of a fixed asset is the purchase price or the amount spent on its production together with any other expenditure incurred in bringing the fixed asset to working condition for its intended use at its intended location.

Definition

> The *cost* of a fixed asset is the purchase price or the amount spent on its production together with any costs directly attributable to bringing the fixed asset to working condition for its intended use at its intended location.

8.2.3 Repairs and improvements

There are sometimes problems in deciding whether a payment for a repair to a fixed asset should be treated as an expense of the business or an asset. The key lies in the words of the definition and the phrase *expected future benefits*. If the payment relates to some act which merely preserves the existing life of the asset and the existing expectations of benefit from the asset, then the payment is treated as a *repair* and reported as an expense. The asset of cash decreases and there is a decrease in the ownership interest caused by the expense.

If the payment relates to some act which significantly extends the useful life of the asset, or increases the expectations of benefit from the asset, then the payment is treated as an *improvement* and reported as an asset. It may be reported as a separate asset, but more usually the amount will be added to the cost or value recorded for the asset which has been improved. The asset of cash decreases and is replaced by an asset of improvements. There is no effect on the ownership interest.

The following are examples of improvements and repairs.

Improvements

- Extensions to a building which increase the operating capacity of the business.
- A new roof which gives a building an extra 10 years of life.
- A new engine for a delivery van which is more powerful than the existing engine and allows faster delivery in hilly districts.
- Renewing the fittings and interior decoration of a hotel to attract international visitors instead of the traditional local customers.

Repairs

- A new roof, required because of storm damage, which will keep the building weatherproof for the remainder of its expected life.
- A new engine for a delivery van which replaces an existing damaged engine.
- Redecorating inside a building to preserve the existing standards of cleanliness and appearance.

L01 | **Activity 8.1**

Imagine you are the owner of a big hotel in the centre of town. Make a list of the items you would expect to include in your business balance sheet as fixed assets. Make a list of the types of repair which would be classed as 'improvements'. Use the definition of a fixed asset to show that your list includes items which are correctly classified.

L02 | ## 8.3 Recognition

This section outlines the recognition issues faced in reporting tangible fixed assets, intangible fixed assets and fixed asset investments.

8.3.1 Tangible fixed assets

Tangible fixed assets are those items which can be touched, seen or heard and meet the conditions set out in the definition of a fixed asset. *Recognition* by reporting in the balance sheet presents no problem where the future benefit can be identified and the cost of the asset can be measured. The evidence of cost is usually a purchase invoice. Some tangible fixed assets are recorded at a valuation made subsequent to the purchase. Revaluations are discussed in Chapter 12.

As the list in the previous section indicates, there is considerable variety in tangible fixed assets. The common feature is that they all have a limited life expectancy. They may wear out, be used up, go out of fashion, break down or be sold for scrap. Whatever the reason, the effect is the same and the effect is called *depreciation*. Users have many questions to ask about tangible fixed assets, such as: 'What kinds of tangible fixed assets are in use?', 'How old are they?',

'How has the company measured the depreciation?', 'Where is the depreciation recorded?'

Answering those questions will take up most of the remainder of this chapter.

8.3.2 Intangible fixed assets

An intangible fixed asset is an item which meets the definition of a fixed asset but has no physical substance. It cannot be touched, seen or heard. The evidence of its existence is the benefit flowing from it. For many years, items such as patents, trade marks and licences to manufacture products have been bought and sold between companies. The purchase has been recorded as a fixed asset and depreciated over the expected life of the patent, trade mark or licence. The expected life is decided by law (for patents and trade marks) or by legal contract (for licences). The depreciation of intangible fixed assets is usually referred to as *amortisation* (in which you may recognise the French word *mort* meaning *death*).

The intangible fixed asset which has attracted most accounting-related comment in recent years has been the brand name of a company's product. When a company works over many years to develop the reputation of its product, that reputation creates an expected future benefit for the company and meets the *definition* of an asset as set out in Chapter 2. However, the generally held view is that it should not be recognised in the balance sheet because it fails the *recognition* test of Chapter 2. The conventional argument is that there is no measurable *cost* of the reputation gained by the brand name and the *value* cannot be measured with reliability.

That is the generally held view which was challenged in the mid-1980s by a number of leading companies. Some had bought other companies which had developed brand names. The new owners argued that they were buying the other company purely because of the quality of the brand name and they wanted to show that brand name in the new balance sheet. They had a reasonable argument because they had paid a price in the market and could show the cost of the brand name acquired. Other companies who had developed their own brand names did not want to be left behind and so paid expert valuers to calculate a value for their home-grown brands. A new professional specialism of brand valuation gained prominence and the experts claimed they could measure the value of a home-grown brand with reliability.

The companies which reported brand names in the balance sheet argued that the brand had a long life and did not require amortisation. This argument gave them the advantage of expanding the balance sheet without the disadvantage of amortisation appearing in the profit and loss account.

The Accounting Standards Board has issued a standard, FRS 10, which includes accounting for intangible assets. Brand names should appear in a balance sheet only where there is a readily ascertainable market value. Amortisation is a requirement.

L02 **Activity 8.2**

A company which has manufactured a well-known brand of brown bread for many years has decided that the brand name is so well known that it should appear in the balance sheet. Write down two arguments in favour of this, to be made by the company's finance director, and two arguments against which will appear in a newspaper article.

8.3.3 Investments as fixed assets

Investments exist in many different forms but the essential feature is an ability to generate future economic benefits so that the wealth of the owner increases. This increase in wealth may arise because the value of the investment increases, or may arise because the investment creates income for the owner in the form of a distribution such as interest paid or dividends. Companies may hold investments for a variety of reasons. A fixed asset investment is one which is held for long-term purposes, such as shares in another company which has close trading links with the investing company.

The number of shares held may be such as to give direct control of the investment or may be of a lesser amount which indicates a long-term relationship, without direct control, in a similar line of business.

Fixed asset investments may be held so that resources are available to meet a long-term obligation, such as the payment of pensions. Such fixed assets are normally found in the balance sheets of insurance companies or pension funds, rather than in the balance sheet of the company employing staff.

The features which make investments different as fixed assets are the importance of the increase in value of the investment itself and the fact that they are not used in the production or service process. Both features require a different kind of accounting treatment from that given to other fixed assets. Those special treatments are advanced accounting matters and will not be dealt with in any detail in this text. What you should look for in accounts is the existence of fixed asset investments and the information provided about them. The questions users will ask are: 'How well is this investment keeping up its value?' and 'How important is the income from this investment to the overall profit of the company?'

L03 | 8.4 Users' needs for information

L03 | **Activity 8.3**

Before you read this section, make a list of the information about fixed assets which would be useful to you if you wished to learn more about a specific company. Then read the section and compare it with your list. How far-thinking are you in respect of accounting information?

Analysts who write reports for professional and private investors have a particular interest in the fixed assets because these are the base from which profits are generated. They want to know what types of assets are held, how old they are and what plans the company has for future investment in fixed assets.

The analysts also want to know about the impact of the depreciation charge on the profit of the year. They are aware that detailed aspects of calculations of depreciation may vary from one year to the next and this may affect the comparability of the profit amounts.

To estimate the remaining life of the assets, analysts compare the accumulated depreciation with the total cost (or value) of the fixed assets. If the accumulated depreciation is relatively low, then the fixed assets are relatively new. Other companies in the industry will be used for comparison. The analysts also compare the depreciation charge for the year with the total cost (or value) of the assets and expect to see a similar relationship from one year to the next. A sudden change will cause them to ask more questions about a change in the basis of calculation.

L04 8.5 Information provided in the financial statements

In Chapter 7 the balance sheet of Safe and Sure plc was presented. The balance sheet showed a single line of information on tangible fixed assets. This section shows how that single line becomes understandable when read in conjunction with the notes to the accounts, the statement of accounting policy and the finance director's review.

8.5.1 Balance sheet

		Notes	Year 7 £m	Year 6 £m
Fixed assets	Tangible assets	2	137.5	121.9

8.5.2 Notes to the balance sheet

In the notes to the balance sheet there is considerably more information:

Note 2
Tangible fixed assets

	Land and buildings £m	Plant and equipment £m	Vehicles £m	Total £m
Cost or valuation				
At 1 January Year 7	28.3	96.4	104.8	229.5
Additions at cost	3.9	18.5	37.8	60.2
On acquisitions	0.3	1.0	0.7	2.0
Disposals	(0.6)	(3.1)	(24.7)	(28.4)
At 31 December Year 7	31.9	112.8	118.6	263.3
Aggregate depreciation				
At 1 January Year 7	2.2	58.8	46.6	107.6
Depreciation for the year	0.5	13.5	19.2	33.2
On acquisitions	0.1	0.7	0.6	1.4
Disposals	(0.2)	(2.8)	(13.4)	(16.4)
At 31 December Year 7	2.6	70.2	53.0	125.8
Net book value at 31 December Year 7	29.3	42.6	65.6	137.5
Net book value at 31 December Year 6	26.1	37.6	58.2	121.9

Analysis of land and buildings at cost or valuation

	Year 7 £m	Year 6 £m
At cost	10.4	7.1
At valuation	21.5	21.2
	31.9	28.3

From Year 5 freehold and long leasehold properties are revalued on a rolling basis, each property being valued at least every five years by an external qualified surveyor. Interim valuations within the five-year cycle are carried out on properties where there is an indication that the value has changed significantly due to market conditions. Valuations were made on the basis of the market value for existing use. The book values of the properties were adjusted to the revaluations and the resultant net surplus was credited to the revaluation reserve.

Analysis of net book value of land and buildings

	Year 7 £m	Year 6 £m
Freehold	24.5	21.0
Leasehold:		
Over 50 years unexpired	2.1	2.4
Under 50 years unexpired	2.7	2.7
	29.3	26.1

If the revalued assets were stated on the historical cost basis the amounts would be:

	Year 7 £m	Year 6 £m
Land and buildings at cost	15.7	14.5
Aggregate depreciation	(2.2)	(1.9)
	13.5	12.6

It is clear from the extensive nature of note 2 to the balance sheet that tangible fixed assets are regarded as important by those who regulate the information. All of the information contained in note 2 is required by the Companies Act 1985 and the accounting standard FRS 15, *Tangible Fixed Assets.*

8.5.3 Statement of accounting policy

In addition the company is required, by the accounting standard FRS 18, *Accounting Policies*, to make a statement of accounting policy. For this company the wording of the accounting policy statement is as follows:

Freehold and leasehold property
Freehold and leasehold land and buildings are stated either at cost or at their revalued amounts less depreciation. Full revaluations are made at five-year intervals with interim valuations in the intervening years.
[*Note: Further detail on revaluations is provided by Safe & Sure plc, but not reproduced here.*]
    Provision for depreciation of freehold land and buildings is made at the annual rate of 1% of cost or the revalued amounts. Leasehold land and buildings are amortised in equal annual instalments over the periods of the leases subject to a minimum annual provision of 1% of cost or the revalued amounts. When properties are sold the difference between sales proceeds and net book value is dealt with in the profit and loss account.

Other tangible fixed assets

Other tangible fixed assets are stated at cost less depreciation. Provision for depreciation is made mainly in equal annual instalments over the estimated useful lives of the assets as follows:

4 to 5 years   vehicles
5 to 10 years   plant, machinery and equipment

8.5.4 Operating and financial review

There is also a comment in the finance director's report, as a contribution to the operating and financial review:

> The major items of capital expenditure are vehicles, equipment used on customers' premises and office equipment, particularly computers. Disposals during the year were mainly of vehicles being replaced on a rolling programme.

L04, L05

Activity 8.4

Find the annual report of a company of your choice. This may be through access to the website, or by requesting a printed copy of the annual report through the website **www.ft.com**, *or by using the free annual reports offer on the London Stock Exchange page of the Financial Times.*

In the annual report find the information that corresponds to the extracts from Safe & Sure given in section 8.5. What are the similarities and differences? What do you learn about the fixed asset base of your chosen company?

L05   # 8.6 Usefulness of published information

Here is David Wilson to explain how useful he sees the information provided by companies about their tangible fixed assets. If you look back to Chapter 4 you will see that he was about to visit the company and had made a preliminary list of questions. He has now made the visit and has a better understanding of what is reported in the balance sheet. He talks to Leona in a break at a workout session.

DAVID: *I told you that in making my review before visiting the company I looked closely at the type of tangible fixed assets held and the estimated useful life. I also checked that the depreciation period and method of calculation had not changed from previous years.*

As I was making a site visit I took the opportunity to look at the various fixed assets. This is a group of companies, expanding by acquisition of other companies, and each acquisition brings in more land and buildings. Some of these assets are recorded at valuation every five years rather than original cost. That is quite a common practice and I have confidence in the firm of valuers used.

Plant and equipment has an aggregate depreciation of £70.2m which is 62 per cent of the cost of the assets at £112.8m. It seems to me that must be saying that the plant and equipment is more than half-way through its expected life. The finance director wasn't too enthusiastic about this interpretation. He pointed out that when another company is acquired the fixed assets may be quite old and have to be brought into the group balance sheet, but once they are in group control there is a strict policy of evaluation and replacement. He views the depreciation policy as being at the prudent end of the spectrum, so the realistic life remaining might be marginally over half, but discretion and the fast-moving nature of the industry requires an element of caution. He called in the plant manager who showed me the replacement schedules for plant and equipment for the next three years. It certainly reassured me that risk of obsolescence is probably not a serious worry. I also met the vehicle fleet supervisor who showed me similar replacement schedules for the vehicles.

I saw how the vehicle fleet is managed so that every vehicle is idle for the minimum time. Each vehicle is assigned to a group of cleaning operatives, whose shifts are scheduled so that the vehicle's use is maximised. Plant and equipment are the responsibility of area managers who have to look after security, maintenance and efficiency of usage. I thought it was all really quite impressive.

The depreciation charge for the plant and equipment in Year 7 is £13.5m which is 12 per cent of the cost of £112.8m and suggests an expected life of just over 8 years is being applied. That is within the range of 5 to 10 years stated as the company's accounting policy. I think the wording '5 to 10 years' is too vague. Using five years would double the depreciation charge compared with ten. I tried to pin down the finance director so that I can get a good figure for my forecast but all he would say was that there is no reason to suppose there are any unusual features in the amount in the accounts. The depreciation charge for vehicles is £19.2m which is 16 per cent of the cost of £118.6m. That suggests an expected life of just over 6 years is being applied. I asked the finance director how that squared with the accounting policy statement of estimated useful lives of 4 to 5 years for vehicles. He did seem to sigh a little at that point but was quite patient in explaining that there are some fully depreciated vehicles still in use (because they are quite prudent in their estimates of depreciation) and so the depreciation charge is not the 20 per cent to 25 per cent I was looking for. I'll need to think about that one but I might move my estimate for next year closer to 20 per cent.

You asked me how this company's information measures up to the qualitative characteristics (set out in Chapter 4). Relevance I would rate highly, because there is plenty of information in the notes which I can use to ask questions about the effective use of fixed assets and the impact on profit and loss account through the depreciation charge. Reliability, faithful representation and neutrality are qualities I leave to the auditors. Prudence is something which seems to come out strongly in conversation with the finance director. The detailed schedule of assets which I saw suggests that completeness is not a problem. Comparability is fine because there are amounts for the previous year and the standard format allows me to make comparison with other companies in the industry. Understandability is perhaps more of a problem than I thought. Those fully depreciated assets caught me out.

LEONA: *Well, I have now heard you admit that there is some value in having auditors. Shall I tell you how much you have missed? You could have asked more searching questions about the way in which they measure the cost of plant and equipment. Does it include delivery charges and installation costs? You could have asked whether a technical expert inside the company estimates and reviews the asset lives used, or whether the finance director makes a guess. Did you ask whether they are perhaps verging on being over-prudent so that surprises come later when the depreciation charge is less than expected? You could have asked how the interim valuations are carried out. These are all questions we ask as auditors so that you may treat the information as being reliable and a faithful representation.*

Hopefully you now have a feeling for the information provided by companies on tangible fixed assets and how it is used by the professional investor. The nature and recording of depreciation is now explained.

L06   8.7 Depreciation: an explanation of its nature

L06   Activity 8.5

Before you read this section, write down what you think 'depreciation' means. Then read the section and compare it with your initial views. Depreciation is a very subjective matter and there are different views of its purpose, so your answer may be interesting even if it does not match the text. You should consult your lecturer, tutor or other expert in the area to understand why your perceptions may be different.

Definition   *Depreciation* is defined as the measure of the cost or revalued amount of the economic benefits of the tangible fixed asset that have been consumed during the period. Consumption includes the wearing out, using up or other reduction in the useful economic life of a tangible fixed asset whether arising from use, effluxion of time or obsolescence through either changes in technology or demand for the goods and services produced by the asset. (FRS 15, para. 2.)

The fixed asset may be an item of plant or equipment which is wearing out through being used. It may be a payment made by a company for the right to become a tenant of a property. That payment purchases a lease which reduces in value through the passage of time. The fixed asset may be a computer system which becomes out of date in a very short space of time because of obsolescence. It may be a machine which produces goods for which demand falls because of changing market conditions.

The definition shows that depreciation is a device used in accounting to spread the cost of a fixed asset over its useful life. The process of spreading cost over more than one accounting period is called *allocation*.

In terms of the accounting equation, the useful life of the fixed asset is being reduced and this will reduce the ownership interest.

	Assets		Liabilities		**Ownership interest**
Year		−		=	
1	↓				↓
2	↓				↓
3	↓				↓
etc.					

As the asset becomes older, the depreciation of one year is added to the depreciation of previous years. This is called the *accumulated depreciation*. The accumulated depreciation at the end of any year is equal to the accumulated depreciation at the start of the year plus the depreciation charge for that year.

Deducting the accumulated depreciation from the original cost leaves the *net book value*. The net book value could also be described as the *cost remaining* as a benefit for future years.

Showing the effect of depreciation by use of arrows and the accounting equation is relatively easy. Deciding on the amount of depreciation each year is much more difficult because there are so many different views of how to calculate the *amount* of asset used up in each period.

8.7.1 Calculation of depreciation

Calculation of depreciation requires three pieces of information:

1 the cost of the fixed asset;
2 the estimated useful life; and
3 the estimated residual value (the value remaining at the end of the useful life).

The total depreciation of the fixed asset is equal to the cost of the fixed asset minus the estimated residual value. The purpose of the depreciation calculation is to spread the total depreciation over the estimated useful life.

The first point at which differences of opinion arise is in the estimation of the useful life and residual value. These are matters of judgement which vary from one person to the next.

Unfortunately the differences do not stop at those estimates. There is also no agreement on the arithmetical approach to spreading the total depreciation over the useful life. Some people are of the opinion that a fixed asset is used evenly over time and that the depreciation should reflect the benefit gained from its use. Others argue that the fixed asset declines in value most in the early years and so the depreciation charge should be greater in earlier years.

8.7.2 Straight-line method

Those who are of the opinion that a fixed asset is used evenly over time apply a method of calculation called straight-line depreciation. The formula is:

$$\frac{\text{Cost} - \text{Expected residual value}}{\text{Expected life}}$$

To illustrate the use of the formula, take a fixed asset which has a cost of £1,000 and an expected life of five years. The expected residual value is nil. The calculation of the annual depreciation charge is:

$$\frac{£1,000 - \text{nil}}{5} = £200 \text{ per annum}$$

The depreciation rate is sometimes expressed as a percentage of the original cost. In this case the company would state its depreciation policy as follows:

'Accounting policy:
Depreciation is charged on a straight-line basis at a rate of 20% of cost per annum.'

The phrase 'straight line' is used because a graph of the net book value of the asset at the end of each year produces a straight line. Exhibit 8.1 sets out the five-year pattern of depreciation and net book value for the example used above. Exhibit 8.2 shows a graph of the net book value at the end of each year. The graph starts at the cost figure of £1,000 when the asset is new (Year 0) and reduces by £200 each year until it is zero at the end of Year 5.

Exhibit 8.1

Pattern of depreciation and net book value over the life of an asset

End of year	Depreciation of the year (a) £	Total depreciation (b) £	Net book value of the asset (£1,000 – b) £
1	200	200	800
2	200	400	600
3	200	600	400
4	200	800	200
5	200	1,000	nil

Exhibit 8.2

Graph of net book value over Years 1 to 5, for the straight-line method of depreciation

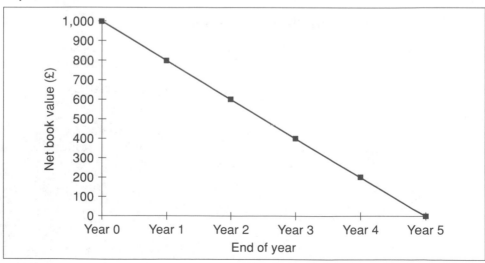

8.7.3 Reducing balance method

Those who believe that the asset depreciates most in earlier years would calculate the depreciation using the formula:

Fixed percentage × Net book value at the start of the year

Take the example of the asset costing £1,000. The fixed percentage applied for the reducing balance method might be as high as 50 per cent. The calculations would be as shown in the table in Exhibit 8.3.

Exhibit 8.3
Calculation of reducing balance depreciation

Year	Net book value at start of year (a) £	Annual depreciation (b) = 50% of (a) £	Net book value at end of year (a – b) £
1	1,000	500	500
2	500	250	250
3	250	125	125
4	125	63	62
5	62	31	31

You will see from the table in Exhibit 8.3 that under the reducing balance method there is always a small balance remaining. In this example, the rate of 50 per cent is used to bring the net book value to a relatively small amount. The formula for calculating the exact rate requires a knowledge of compound interest and may be found at the end of the Supplement to this chapter. For those whose main interest is in understanding and interpreting accounts it is not necessary to know the formula, but it is useful to be aware that a very much higher percentage rate is required on the reducing balance method as compared with the straight-line method. As a useful guide, the reducing balance rate must be at least twice the rate of the straight-line calculation if the major part of the asset is to be depreciated over its useful life.

A graph of the net book value at the end of each year under the reducing-balance method is shown in Exhibit 8.4. The steep slope at the start shows that the net book value declines rapidly in the early part of the asset's life and then less steeply towards the end when most of the benefit of the asset has been used up.

Exhibit 8.4

Graph of net book value over Years 1 to 5, for the reducing-balance method of depreciation

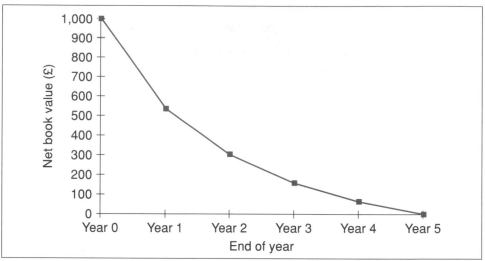

8.7.4 Which method to choose?

The choice of depreciation method should be based on the expected pattern of usage of the asset. If the usage is evenly spread then the straight-line method is appropriate. If the usage is heaviest in early years then the reducing-balance method is the best representation of the economic activity. In practice it is found that most UK companies use straight-line depreciation. In some other countries, particularly those where tax rules and accounting laws are closely linked, the reducing-balance method is commonly observed. So it appears that there are different international practices that may reflect different conditions in the respective countries. David and Leona discuss the problem.

DAVID: *The choice of depreciation method may have a significant impact on reported profit. Companies that are actively investing in fixed assets will do so in the expectation of increased profits. However it may take some time for such profits to emerge. If, in the meantime, there is a relatively high charge to profit and loss account through reducing balance depreciation, profits may fall in the short term. In contrast the use of straight-line depreciation will have a less dramatic impact on reported profit immediately following the new investment, so the company avoids a dip in profits.*

LEONA: *I can't accept that as a valid argument to give to the auditor. I ask the company what the pattern of usage is. If the company tells me that the asset produces benefit evenly over its useful life, I can accept straight-line depreciation. If, on the other hand, I hear that the asset is more productive in its early years of life, I expect to see reducing balance depreciation.*

DAVID: *Well let me try your social conscience. I came across a case of a UK company that had been taken over by a German parent company. The UK company had always used straight-line depreciation and was making small profits each year. The parent company had always used reducing balance depreciation and so changed the accounting method of the UK subsidiary. Small profits turned into large losses and the parent company said that there would have to be a reduction in the workforce to cut costs. The employee represent- atives said that nothing had changed except that the accountants had redefined the game. They blamed the accountants for the resulting job losses and increased unemployment.*

LEONA: *My role is confined to giving an opinion on the accounting information. If a particular accounting process is detrimental to the public interest then it is the job of government to legislate.*

L05 | **Activity 8.6**

Consider the discussion between David and Leona. Do you share the concern of the employee representatives as described by David? Do you agree with Leona that the economic impact of accounting information is not a problem for the auditor? What is your view on the social responsibility attached to financial reporting?

8.7.5 Retaining cash in the business

Suppose that the policy of the owner is to take all the available profits as draw- ings for personal use. Take a company that has fee income of £100,000 and pays wages and other costs of £58,000. If the company did not recognise the expense of depreciation the owner's drawings could be as high as £62,000. Suppose now that depreciation of fixed assets is calculated as £10,000. The net profit after depre- ciation becomes £52,000. The owner can still see £62,000 in the bank account but knows that £10,000 of that represents using up fixed assets. Leaving the £10,000 in the bank will allow the business to save cash for asset replacement. The owner should withdraw no more than £52,000.

It is often said that depreciation limits the amount of profits available for cash drawings by the owner and encourages saving for asset replacement. However there is nothing to stop the business spending the £10,000 on some purpose other than replacement of fixed assets. We can only say that cash withheld from share- holders **may** be used to replace assets at the end of the asset life.

L07 | ## 8.8 Reporting fixed assets and depreciation in financial statements

This section moves step by step through the recording process. First, it looks at a situation of straight-line depreciation with no residual value expected for the asset. Then it takes in the additional complication of an expected residual value.

8.8.1 Straight-line depreciation, no residual value

When a retail company wants new premises, it must either buy a shop or rent one. Renting is referred to as *leasing*. When the rent agreement is signed, the tenant may pay an agreed price for the privilege of having the lease. This is called the *capital cost* of the lease. It is paid in addition to the annual rental payment. The initial payment for purchase of the lease provides a benefit of occupation for the entire period of the lease and so is a fixed asset. Because the lease has a known life, it must be depreciated.

On 1 January Year 2 Electrical Instruments purchased a three-year lease of a shop for a payment of £60,000. Using the straight-line method of depreciation the amount of depreciation each year will be calculated on a straight-line basis as £20,000 (one-third of the cost of the lease). The profit and loss account will report this amount as an expense in each of the three years of the lease. The balance sheet will show on one line the original cost of £60,000 and, on a second line, the accumulated depreciation to be subtracted at the end of each year.

The financial statements over the period of three years will show the following information relating to this lease:

Profit and loss account (extract)			
Year ended 31 December	*Year 2*	*Year 3*	*Year 4*
	£000s	*£000s*	*£000s*
Depreciation expense	(20)	(20)	(20)

Balance sheet (extract)			
At 31 December	*Year 2*	*Year 3*	*Year 4*
	£000s	*£000s*	*£000s*
Lease at cost	60	60	60
Less accumulated depreciation	20	40	60
Net book value	40	20	nil

8.8.2 Straight-line depreciation with a residual value

In the case of Electrical Instruments the lease had no residual value. Take now the example of The Removals Company which commences business on 1 January Year 2 by paying cash for a van costing £60,000. It is estimated to have a useful life of three years and at the end of that time is expected to have a residual value of £6,000. On 31 December Year 2 the owner calculates annual depreciation of the van as £18,000, using the formula:

$$\frac{Cost - Expected\ residual\ value}{Expected\ life}$$

During each year of operating the van, the company collected £120,000 in cash from customers and paid £58,000 in cash for drivers' wages, fuel and other running costs.

These transactions and events may be summarised using the accounting equation and a spreadsheet similar to that used in Chapter 5 (Exhibit 5.3). In Exhibit 8.5 there is a spreadsheet for the first year of the use of the van by the company. The assets section of the spreadsheet has three columns, one of which is for cash but two of which are for the van. The two columns for the van keep a separate record of the original cost and the accumulated depreciation. The original cost is the positive part of the asset but the accumulated depreciation is the negative part of the asset. Taking the accumulated depreciation from the original cost leaves the net book value. That is the amount of cost not yet amortised which acts as a measure of the benefit remaining in the asset for the future. In Exhibit 8.6 the information collected together by Exhibit 8.5 is presented in the form of a balance sheet and a profit and loss account.

Exhibit 8.5
Spreadsheet analysing transactions and events of The Removals Company into the elements of the accounting equation

	Transaction or event	Assets			Ownership interest	
		Van at cost	Accumulated depreciation of van	Cash	Capital contributed or withdrawn	Profit = revenue minus (expenses)
Year 2		£	£	£	£	£
1 Jan.	Owner contributes cash			60,000	60,000	
1 Jan.	Purchase furniture van	60,000		(60,000)		
All year	Collected cash from customers			120,000		120,000
All year	Paid for wages, fuel, etc.			(58,000)		(58,000)
31 Dec.	Calculate annual depreciation		(18,000)			(18,000)
	Totals	60,000	(18,000)	62,000	60,000	44,000

———— 104,000 ————   ———— 104,000 ————

Exhibit 8.6

The Removals Company: Balance sheet at end of Year 2 and Profit and loss account for Year 2

The Removals Company
Balance sheet at 31 December Year 2

	£
Fixed assets	
Furniture van at cost	60,000
Accumulated depreciation	(18,000)
Net book value	42,000
Current assets	
Cash	62,000
Total assets	104,000
Ownership interest	
Ownership interest at the start of the year	nil
Capital contributed during the year	60,000
Profit of the year	44,000
	104,000

The Removals Company
Profit and loss account
for the year ended 31 December Year 2

	£	£
Revenue		
Fees for removal work		120,000
Expenses		
Wages, fuel and other running costs	(58,000)	
Depreciation	(18,000)	
		(76,000)
Net profit		44,000

8.8.3 Continuing to use the fixed asset

So far, the accounting entries have related to the first year of the business so that there was no need to ask any questions about the position at the start of the period. To show the full impact of the progressive depreciation of the asset, the spreadsheet and financial statements are now presented for Year 3. Exhibit 8.7 sets out the spreadsheet and Exhibit 8.8 sets out the financial statements. It is assumed that for Year 3 the amounts of cash collected from customers and the amounts paid in cash for running costs are the same as for Year 2. No further capital is contributed by the owner and no new vans are acquired.

The first line of the spreadsheet in Exhibit 8.7 shows the position at the start of the year. The asset columns show the amounts as they were at the end of the previous year. The ownership interest shows the amount resulting at the end of the previous year, as seen in the Year 2 balance sheet. The columns for revenue and expenses are empty at the start of the year, awaiting the transactions and events of Year 3.

Exhibit 8.7
Spreadsheet analysis of transactions of The Removals Company, Year 3

	Transaction or event	Assets			Ownership interest		
		Van at cost	Accumulated depreciation of van	Cash	Ownership interest at start of year	Capital contributed or withdrawn	Profit = revenue minus (expenses)
Year 3		£	£	£	£	£	£
1 Jan.	Amounts brought forward at start of year	60,000	(18,000)	62,000	104,000		
All year	Collected cash from customers			120,000			120,000
All year	Paid for wages, fuel, etc.			(58,000)			(58,000)
31 Dec.	Calculate annual depreciation		(18,000)				(18,000)
	Totals	60,000	(36,000)	124,000	104,000		44,000

———— 148,000 ————   ———— 148,000 ————

8.8.4 Disposing of the fixed asset

During Year 4 the amounts of cash received from customers and cash paid for running costs are the same as they were in Year 3. Exhibit 8.9 sets out the spreadsheet for the transactions and events.

Exhibit 8.8

The Removals Company: Balance sheet at end of Year 3 and Profit and loss
account for Year 3

The Removals Company
Balance sheet at 31 December Year 3

	£
Fixed assets	
Furniture van at cost	60,000
Accumulated depreciation	(36,000)
Net book value	24,000
Current assets	
Cash	124,000
Total assets	148,000
Ownership interest	
Ownership interest at the start of the year	104,000
Profit of the year	44,000
	148,000

The Removals Company
Profit and loss account
for the year ended 31 December Year 3

	£	£
Revenue		
Fees for removal work		120,000
Expenses		
Wages, fuel and other running costs	(58,000)	
Depreciation	(18,000)	
		(76,000)
Net profit		44,000

Now suppose that the van is sold for £6,000 in cash on the final day of December
Year 4. That is the amount to be expected if the residual value was estimated
correctly at the outset. The spreadsheet contained in Exhibit 8.9 requires further
attention, the additional accounting impact of the sale being seen in Exhibit 8.10.
    The disposal of the van must be analysed in stages:

1 Collecting cash;
2 Transferring ownership of the vehicle;
3 Removing the vehicle from the accounting records.

When the vehicle is removed from the record, two columns must be reduced to
zero. These are the *van at cost* column and the *accumulated depreciation* column.
The van at cost column shows the original cost of £60,000 and the accumulated
depreciation shows the amount of £54,000 which has to be deducted to show the

Exhibit 8.9
Spreadsheet analysis of transactions of The Removals Company, Year 4

	Transaction or event	Assets			Ownership interest		
		Van at cost	Accumulated depreciation of van	Cash	Ownership interest at start of year	Capital contributed or withdrawn	Profit = revenue minus (expenses)
Year 4		£	£	£	£	£	£
1 Jan.	Amounts brought forward at start of year	60,000	(36,000)	124,000	148,000		
All year	Collected cash from customers			120,000			120,000
All year	Paid for wages, fuel, etc.			(58,000)			(58,000)
31 Dec.	Calculate annual depreciation		(18,000)				(18,000)
	Totals	60,000	(54,000)	186,000	148,000		44,000

└──────── 192,000 ────────┘ └──────── 192,000 ────────┘

amount of the net book value. The asset of cash increases by £6,000. In terms of the accounting equation:

Assets		Liabilities		Ownership interest
	£	−	=	
Increase in cash	6,000	no change		no change
Decrease van:				
At cost	60,000			
Accumulated depreciation	(54,000)			
	6,000			

The resulting balance sheet and profit and loss account are shown in Exhibit 8.11.

Exhibit 8.10
Spreadsheet analysis of transactions of The Removals Company, Year 4, including sale of fixed asset

	Transaction or event	Assets			Ownership interest		
		Van at cost	Accumulated depreciation of van	Cash	Ownership interest at start of year	Capital contributed or withdrawn	Profit = revenue minus (expenses)
Year 4		£	£	£	£	£	£
1 Jan.	Amounts brought forward at start of year	60,000	(36,000)	124,000	148,000		
All year	Collected cash from customers			120,000			120,000
All year	Paid for wages, fuel, etc.			(58,000)			(58,000)
31 Dec.	Calculate annual depreciation		(18,000)				(18,000)
31 Dec.	Van disposal	(60,000)	54,000	6,000			
	Totals	nil	nil	192,000	148,000		44,000

└────── 192,000 ──────┘ └────── 192,000 ──────┘

8.8.5 Selling for a price which is not equal to the net book value

The previous illustration was based on selling the van for £6,000, an amount equal to the net book value. Suppose instead it was sold for £9,000. That could be regarded as a pleasant surprise for the owner of the company. It could alternatively be regarded as evidence that the residual value was wrongly estimated at the start and that the depreciation has been wrongly calculated over the years. The second of these explanations may be closer to the truth but no one likes going back in time to change what has already gone. The practical answer is usually to admit that there was a miscalculation of depreciation but to bring all the difference into the profit and loss account in the year of disposal.

This is a failure to apply the matching concept in a strict manner but is a judgement taken on grounds of *relevance* and *materiality*. It is argued that, in most cases,

Exhibit 8.11

The Removals Company: Balance sheet at end of Year 4 and Profit and loss account for Year 4

The Removals Company
Balance sheet at 31 December Year 4

	£
Fixed assets	nil
Current assets	
Cash	192,000
Total assets	192,000
Ownership interest	
Ownership interest at the start of the year	148,000
Profit of the year	44,000
	192,000

The Removals Company
Profit and loss account
for the year ended 31 December Year 4

	£	£
Revenue		
Fees for removal work		120,000
Expenses		
Wages, fuel and other running costs	(58,000)	
Depreciation	(18,000)	
		(76,000)
Net profit		44,000

there would be no relevance to the needs of users in recalculating depreciation of previous years and producing amended financial statements. It is also argued that the amounts involved would not be material to the decision-making needs of users. In the relatively unusual case where the difference would be material, and therefore relevant, the enterprise would be expected to give readers some information about the impact on previous financial statements.

Assets		–	Liabilities	=	**Ownership interest**
	£				
Increase cash	**9,000**				
Decrease van:			no change		**Increase by £3,000**
At cost	**60,000**				
Accumulated depreciation	**(54,000)**				
	6,000				

The increase in ownership interest is £3,000, which is the difference between the amount of the cash collected and the net book value of the van sold. This amount of £3,000 results from overestimating depreciation of previous years and is usually reported as a deduction from the depreciation charge of the year. The profit and loss account would appear as shown in Exhibit 8.12 where bold printing highlights the difference when compared with the profit and loss account in Exhibit 8.11.

Exhibit 8.12
Profit and loss account for Year 4 when proceeds of sale exceed net book value of fixed asset

The Removals Company		
Profit and loss account		
for the year ended 31 December Year 4		
	£	£
Revenue		
Fees for removal work		120,000
Expenses		
Wages, fuel and other running costs	(58,000)	
Depreciation (18,000 – 3,000)	**(15,000)**	
		(73,000)
Net profit		47,000

8.8.6 A table of depreciation expense

To test your understanding of the impact of depreciation you may wish to use a table of the type shown in Exhibit 8.13. It shows that, whatever the proceeds of sale of the asset, the total expense in the profit and loss account will always be the same but the amount of expense each year will vary. If the original estimate of residual value is too high then the depreciation charge each year will be too low and the expense of the year of disposal will be higher than expected. If the original estimate of residual value is too low then the depreciation charge each year will be too high and the expense of the year of disposal will be lower than expected.

Section (b) of Exhibit 8.13 shows the ideal matching which would have been preferred from the outset if the eventual outcome had been known at that time. If you compare the two tables (a) and (b) you will see that:

● total depreciation over the three years is the same in both cases;
● total net profit after depreciation over the three years is the same in both cases;
● annual depreciation in Years 1 and 2 is lower in table (b);
● net profit after depreciation in Years 1 and 2 is higher in table (b);
● net book value of the asset at the end of Years 1 and 2 is higher in table (b);
● the depreciation charge in Year 3 is higher in table (b);
● the net profit after depreciation in Year 3 is lower in table (b).

Exhibit 8.13
Table of depreciation charge

(a) A van cost £60,000, was estimated to have a useful life of three years and a residual value of £6,000. It was sold for £9,000 on the last day of Year 3. Net profit before depreciation is £62,000.

Year	Net profit before depreciation	Depreciation expense of the year	Net profit after depreciation	Cost less accumulated depreciation	Net book value
	£	£	£	£	£
1	62,000	18,000	44,000	60,000 – 18,000	42,000
2	62,000	18,000	44,000	60,000 – 36,000	24,000
3	62,000	15,000	47,000	60,000 – 54,000	6,000
Total depreciation charge	51,000				
Total reported net profit			135,000		

Proceeds of sale exceed net book value by £3,000. This means there was overdepreciation amounting to £3,000 in previous years. The overdepreciation is deducted from the full depreciation expense of £18,000 leaving £15,000 as the expense of the year.

(b) A van cost £60,000, was estimated to have a useful life of three years and a residual value of £9,000. The annual depreciation was calculated as £17,000. The van was sold for £9,000 on the last day of Year 3. Net profit before depreciation is £62,000.

Year	Net profit before depreciation	Depreciation expense of the year	Net profit after depreciation	Cost less accumulated depreciation	Net book value
	£	£	£	£	£
1	62,000	17,000	45,000	60,000 – 17,000	43,000
2	62,000	17,000	45,000	60,000 – 34,000	26,000
3	62,000	17,000	45,000	60,000 – 51,000	9,000
Total depreciation	51,000				
Total reported net profit			135,000		

Net book value equals proceeds of sale so the depreciation charge of Year 3 is the same as that of previous years.

This is an example of what is referred to in accounting as an *allocation problem*. The expense is the same in total but is allocated differently to different years. As a result, there are different amounts in the profit and loss account for each year but the total profit over the longer period is the same.

8.8.7 Impairment

An asset is impaired when the business will not be able to recover the amount shown in the balance sheet, either through use or through sale. If the enterprise believes that impairment may have taken place, it must carry out an 'impairment review'. This requires comparison of the net book value with the cash-generating ability of the asset. Accounting standards have been published but there remain international differences on the precise method of estimating cash-generating ability (the details are beyond a first-level text).

The impairment test may be applied to intangible fixed assets such as goodwill, in order to justify non-amortisation. If no impairment is detected it may be argued that the asset has maintained its value and so amortisation is not necessary. If there has been impairment of the historical cost net book value, then the loss in asset value becomes an expense for the profit and loss account. The enterprise may choose to report this as an exceptional item.

8.9 Summary

Now score your view of your confidence in achieving the learning outcomes of the chapter.

1 = Very confident about knowledge, application, problem solving and evaluation.

2 = Confident about knowledge and application, less sure about problem solving and evaluation.

3 = Need to read again to be more certain of basic knowledge and application.

L01 You have learned a definition of fixed assets and you have seen examples of fixed assets that meet that definition, such as the information in Safe and Sure plc.

L02 You have seen that recognition is not a problem in relation to tangible fixed assets but can lead to debate in relation to intangible fixed assets.

L03 You have read a description of users' needs for information about fixed assets and you have seen how Safe and Sure meets some of these needs.

L04 You have seen the financial statements of Safe and Sure and have read the explanation of the content.

L05 You have read the discussions between David and Leona and should have taken an opportunity to visit company websites to find more annual reports so that you can practise evaluation similar to that of David.

LO6 You can now explain the nature of depreciation and the methods of straight-line and reducing balance.

    1   2   3
    ☐ ☐ ☐

LO7 You have seen worked examples of the calculation and recording of depreciation, applying the accounting equation to spreadsheet recording.

    1   2   3
    ☐ ☐ ☐

LO8 If you wish to develop skills of recording in ledger accounts, you should now read the Supplement to the chapter.

    1   2   3
    ☐ ☐ ☐

If your scores are all 1 or 2, try the questions in the series A, B and C. This will give you feedback on your assessment of how well you have achieved the learning outcomes. Read again any sections of the chapter where you find your knowledge and understanding are less comprehensive than you first estimated.

If your scores include some at 3, try the series A questions to find where the problems lie. Read the relevant sections again, work through any illustrative examples and case studies, then try the questions in the series B. Once you feel confident at that level of knowledge and application, move on to try some or all of the series C questions.

International perspective

The separate recording of asset at cost and accumulated depreciation is accounting information provided in many countries. The UK practice at a general level is consistent with the IASB standard. Country-specific factors may lead to differences in matters of detail such as the choice of depreciation method or the expected life of fixed assets. In some countries, the depreciation expense in the accounting profit and loss account must match that used for the purposes of calculating taxable profit. This may encourage the use of the reducing balance method, giving a higher expense (and so a lower profit) in the early years of the asset's life. In the UK there are separate rules in tax law for calculating depreciation, and so this has no effect on accounting profit.

Further reading

ASB (1997) FRS 10, *Goodwill and Intangible Assets*, Accounting Standards Board.

ASB (1999) FRS 15, *Measurement of Tangible Fixed Assets*, Accounting Standards Board. Appendix IV explains the development of the FRS.

ASB (2000) FRS 18, *Accounting Policies*, Accounting Standards Board.

Test your understanding

L01, S01   **A8.1** State the definition of a fixed asset and explain why each sentence is required.

L02, S01   **A8.2** Explain the categories:

(a) tangible fixed assets;
(b) intangible fixed assets; and
(c) fixed asset investments;
and give an example of each.

L03, S01   **A8.3** What do users of financial statements particularly want to know about fixed assets?

L04, S01   **A8.4** What type of information would you expect to find about fixed assets in the financial statements and notes of a major UK listed company?

L06, S01   **A8.5** State the definition of depreciation.

L07, S01   **A8.6** What information is needed to calculate annual depreciation?

L07, S01   **A8.7** What is meant by *accumulated depreciation* (sometimes called *aggregate depreciation*)?

L07, S01   **A8.8** What is the formula for calculating straight-line depreciation?

L07, S01   **A8.9** How is reducing balance depreciation calculated?

L07, S01   **A8.10** Why does the net book value of a fixed asset not always equal the proceeds of sale?

L06, S01   **A8.11** Why is depreciation said to cause an *allocation problem* in accounting?

L05, S01   **A8.12** How should the cost of a fixed asset be calculated?

L06, S01   **A8.13** What are the matters of judgement relating to fixed assets which users of financial statements should think about carefully when evaluating financial statements?

L07, S01   **A8.14** What is meant by *impairment*?

Application

L07, S01   **B8.1** On reviewing the financial statements of a company, the company's accountant discovers that expenditure of £8,000 on repair to factory equipment has been incorrectly recorded as a part of the cost of the machinery. What will be the effect on the profit and loss account and balance sheet when the error is corrected?

L07, S01   **B8.2** On 1 January Year 1, Angela's Employment Agency was formed. The owner contributed £300,000 in cash which was immediately used to purchase a building. It is estimated to have a 20-year life and a residual value of £200,000. During Year 1 the agency collects £80,000 in fee income and pays £60,000 in wages and other costs. Record the transactions and events of Year 1 in an accounting equation spreadsheet. (See Exhibit 8.5 for an illustration.) Prepare the balance sheet at the end of Year 1 and the profit and loss account for Year 1.

L07, S01 **B8.3** Assume that fee income and costs are the same in Year 2 as in Year 1. Record the transactions and events of Year 2 in an accounting equation spreadsheet. Prepare the balance sheet at the end of Year 2 and the profit and loss account for Year 2.

L07, S01 **B8.4** Angela's Employment Agency sells the building for £285,000 on the final day of December Year 3. Record the transactions and events of Year 3 in an accounting equation spreadsheet. (See Exhibit 8.9 for an illustration.) Assume depreciation is calculated in full for Year 3.

L07, S01 **B8.5** Explain how the accounting equation spreadsheet of your answer to question **B8.4** would alter if the building had been sold for £250,000.

L07, S01 **B8.6** On 1 January Year 1, Company A purchased a bus costing £70,000. It was estimated to have a useful life of three years and a residual value of £4,000. It was sold for £8,000 on the last day of Year 3.

On 1 January Year 1, Company B purchased a bus also costing £70,000. It was estimated to have a useful life of three years and a residual value of £7,000. It was sold for £8,000 on the last day of Year 3.

Both companies have a net profit of £50,000 before depreciation. Calculate the depreciation charge and net profit of each company for each of the three years. Show that over the three years the total depreciation charge for each company is the same. (See Exhibit 8.13 for an example.)

Problem solving and evaluation

L06, L07, **C8.1** The Biscuit Manufacturing Company commenced business on 1 January Year 1 with
S01, S02, S03 capital of £22,000 contributed by the owner. It immediately paid cash for a biscuit machine costing £22,000. It was estimated to have a useful life of four years and at the end of that time was expected to have a residual value of £2,000. During each year of operation of the machine, the company collected £40,000 in cash from sale of biscuits and paid £17,000 in cash for wages, ingredients and running costs.

Required
(a) Prepare spreadsheets for each of the four years analysing the transactions and events of the company.
(b) Prepare a balance sheet at the end of Year 3 and a profit and loss account for that year.
(c) Explain to a non-accountant how to read and understand the balance sheet and profit and loss account you have prepared.

L06, L07, **C8.2** The biscuit machine in question **C8.1** was sold at the end of Year 4 for a price of
S01, S02, S03 £3,000.

Required
(a) Prepare the spreadsheet for Year 4 analysing the transactions and events of the year.
(b) Prepare the balance sheet at the end of Year 4 and the profit and loss account for Year 4.
(c) Explain to a non-accountant the accounting problems of finding that the asset was sold for £3,000 when the original expectation was £2,000.

L07, S01, S02 **C8.3** The Souvenir Company purchased, on 1 January Year 1, a machine producing embossed souvenir badges. The machine cost £16,000 and was estimated to have a five-year life with a residual value of £1,000.

Required
(a) Prepare a table of depreciation charges and net book value over the five-year life using straight-line depreciation.
(b) Make a guess at the percentage rate to be used in the reducing balance calculation, and prepare a table of depreciation charges and net book value over the five years using reducing balance depreciation.
(c) Using the straight-line method of depreciation, demonstrate the effect on the accounting equation of selling the asset at the end of Year 5 for a price of £2,500.
(d) Using the straight-line method of depreciation, demonstrate the effect on the accounting equation of disposing of the asset at the end of Year 5 for a zero scrap value.

Activities for study groups

Turn to the annual report of a listed company which you have used for activities in previous chapters. Find every item of information about fixed assets. (Start with the financial statements and notes but look also at the operating and financial review, chief executive's review and other non-regulated information about the company.)

As a group, imagine you are the team of fund managers in a fund management company. You are holding a briefing meeting at which each person explains to the others some feature of the companies in which your fund invests. Today's subject is *fixed assets*. Each person should make a short presentation to the rest of the team covering:

1 the nature and significance of fixed assets in the company;
2 the asset lives stated in the accounting policies for depreciation purposes;
3 the asset lives estimated by you from calculations of annual depreciation as a percentage of asset cost;
4 the remaining useful life of assets as indicated by comparing accumulated depreciation with asset cost;
5 the company's plans for future investment in fixed assets.

Notes and references

1 ASB (1999) FRS 15, *Measurement of Tangible Fixed Assets*, Accounting Standards Board.
2 ASB (1997) FRS 10, *Goodwill and Intangible Assets*, Accounting Standards Board.

Recording fixed assets and depreciation

The rules for debit and credit entries in a ledger account should by now be familiar but are set out again in Exhibit 8.14 for convenience. If you still feel unsure about any aspect of Exhibit 8.14 you should revisit the supplements of earlier chapters before attempting this one.

Exhibit 8.14
Rules for debit and credit entries in ledger accounts

	Debit entries in a ledger account	Credit entries in a ledger account
Left-hand side of the equation		
Asset	Increase	Decrease
Right-hand side of the equation		
Liability	Decrease	Increase
Ownership interest	Expense	Revenue
	Capital withdrawn	Capital contributed

In this supplement you will concentrate primarily on the ledger accounts for the fixed assets. It takes The Removals Company of the main chapter as the example for illustration.

Information to be recorded

The Removals Company commences business on 1 January Year 2 by paying cash for a van costing £60,000. The cash was contributed by the owner. The van is estimated to have a useful life of three years and at the end of that time is expected to have a residual value of £6,000. On 31 December Year 2 the owner calculates annual depreciation of the van as £18,000, using the formula:

$$\frac{Cost - Expected\ residual\ value}{Expected\ life}$$

During each year of operating the van, the company collected £120,000 in cash from customers and paid £58,000 in cash for drivers' wages, fuel and other running costs.

The transactions of Year 2 have been analysed in Exhibit 8.5 for their impact on the accounting equation. That same list may be used to set out the debit and credit bookkeeping entries, as shown in Exhibit 8.15.

Exhibit 8.15
Analysis of transactions for The Removals Company, Year 2

Date	Transaction or event	Amount	Dr	Cr
Year 2		£		
1 Jan.	Owner contributes cash	60,000	Cash	Ownership interest
1 Jan.	Purchase furniture van	60,000	Van at cost	Cash
All year	Collected cash from customers	120,000	Cash	Sales
All year	Paid for running costs	58,000	Running costs	Cash
31 Dec.	Calculate annual depreciation	18,000	Depreciation expense	Accumulated depreciation

Ledger accounts required to record transactions of Year 2 are as follows:

L1 Ownership interest	L4 Accumulated depreciation of van
L2 Cash	L5 Sales
L3 Van at cost	L6 Running costs
	L7 Depreciation of the year

L1 Ownership interest

Date	Particulars	Page	Debit	Credit	Balance
Year 2			£	£	£
Jan. 1	Cash	L2		60,000	(60,000)

LEONA's comment: *This ledger account shows the opening contribution to the start of the business which establishes the ownership interest.*

L2 Cash

Date	Particulars	Page	Debit	Credit	Balance
Year 2			£	£	£
Jan. 1	Ownership interest	L1	60,000		60,000
Jan. 1	Van	L3		60,000	nil
Jan.–Dec.	Sales	L5	120,000		120,000
Jan.–Dec.	Running costs	L6		58,000	62,000

LEONA's comment: *For convenience in this illustration all the sales and running costs have been brought together in one amount for the year. In reality there would be a large number of separate transactions recorded throughout the year. The balance at the end of the year shows that there is £62,000 remaining in the bank account.*

L3 Van at cost

Date	Particulars	Page	Debit	Credit	Balance
Year 2			£	£	£
Jan. 1	Cash	L2	60,000		60,000

LEONA's comment: *The van is recorded by a debit entry and this entry remains in the ledger account for as long as the van is in use by the company. A separate ledger account is maintained for the cost of the asset because it is regarded as a useful piece of information for purposes of financial statements.*

L4 Accumulated depreciation of van

Date	Particulars	Page	Debit	Credit	Balance
Year 2			£	£	£
Dec. 31	Depreciation for the year	L7		18,000	(18,000)

LEONA's comment: *The accumulated depreciation account completes the story about the van. It has an original cost of £60,000 and an accumulated depreciation at the end of Year 2 equal to £18,000. The accumulated depreciation account will always show a credit balance because it is the negative part of the asset. Deducting accumulated depreciation from cost gives a net book value of £42,000.*

L5 Sales

Date	Particulars	Page	Debit	Credit	Balance
Year 2			£	£	£
Jan.–Dec.	Cash	L2		120,000	(120,000)

LEONA's comment: *For convenience all the sales transactions of the year have been brought together in one single amount, but in reality there would be many pages of separate transactions.*

L6 Running costs

Date	Particulars	Page	Debit	Credit	Balance
Year 2			£	£	£
Jan.–Dec.	Cash	L2	58,000		58,000

LEONA's comment: *As with the sales transactions of the year, all running costs have been brought together in one single amount, but in reality there will be several pages of separate transactions recorded over the year.*

L7 Depreciation of the year

Date	Particulars	Page	Debit	Credit	Balance
Year 2			£	£	£
Dec. 31	Accumulated depreciation	L4	18,000		18,000

LEONA's comment: *The depreciation of the year is a debit entry because it is an expense. The process of depreciation is continuous but that is not convenient for ledger account recording, so companies prefer a single calculation at the end of the year.*

At this point a trial balance may be prepared, as explained in the Supplement to Chapter 5, and shown in Exhibit 8.16.

Exhibit 8.16
Trial balance at the end of Year 2 for The Removals Company

Ledger account title	£	£
L1 Ownership interest		60,000
L2 Cash	62,000	
L3 Van at cost	60,000	
L4 Accumulated depreciation of van		18,000
L5 Sales		120,000
L6 Running costs	58,000	
L7 Depreciation	18,000	
Totals	198,000	198,000

Closing at the end of Year 2 and starting the ledger accounts for Year 3

At the end of the year the balances on asset and liability accounts are *carried forward* to the next year. The phrase 'carried forward' means that they are allowed to remain in the ledger account at the start of the new year. The balances on revenue and expense accounts are treated differently. After the trial balance has been prepared and checked, the amounts on each revenue account and expense account are *transferred to a profit and loss account*. Transferring a balance requires an entry of the opposite type to the balance being transferred. A debit entry is made to transfer a credit balance. A credit entry is made to transfer a debit balance. Matching but opposite entries are made in the profit and loss account. This is called 'closing' the expense or revenue account.

L5 Sales

Date	Particulars	Page	Debit	Credit	Balance
Year 2			£	£	£
Jan.–Dec.	Cash	L2		120,000	(120,000)
Dec. 31	Transfer to profit and loss account	L8	120,000		nil

LEONA's comment: *The ledger account for sales shows a credit balance of £120,000 for the total transactions of the year. This is transferred to the profit and loss account by making a debit entry of similar amount, so that the balance of the sales account is reduced to nil.*

L6 Running costs

Date	Particulars	Page	Debit	Credit	Balance
Year 2			£	£	£
Jan.–Dec.	Cash	L2	58,000		58,000
Dec. 31	Transfer to profit and loss account	L8		58,000	nil

LEONA's comment: *The ledger account for running costs shows a debit balance of £58,000 for the total transactions of the year. This is transferred to the profit and loss account by making a credit entry of similar amount, so that the balance of the running costs account is reduced to nil.*

L7 Depreciation of the year

Date	Particulars	Page	Debit	Credit	Balance
Year 2			£	£	£
Dec. 31	Accumulated depreciation	L4	18,000		18,000
Dec. 31	Transfer to profit and loss account	L8		18,000	nil

LEONA's comment: *The ledger account for depreciation expense shows a debit balance of £18,000 for the depreciation charge of the year. This is transferred to the profit and loss account by making a credit entry of similar amount, so that the balance of the depreciation expense account of the year is reduced to nil.*

L8 Profit and loss account

Date	Particulars	Page	Debit	Credit	Balance
Year 2			£	£	£
Dec. 31	Sales	L5		120,000	(120,000)
Dec. 31	Running costs	L6	58,000		(62,000)
Dec. 31	Depreciation of the year	L7	18,000		(44,000)

LEONA's comment: *The profit and loss account in ledger form shows all items of revenue in the credit column and all items of expense in the debit column. The balance in the third column shows, at the end of the ledger account, the profit of £44,000 for the year. There is one final entry to be made, and that is to transfer the £44,000 balance of the profit and loss account to the ownership interest account. That requires a debit entry in the profit and loss account to remove the credit balance.*

L8 Profit and loss account

Date	Particulars	Page	Debit	Credit	Balance
Year 2			£	£	£
Dec. 31	Sales	L5		120,000	(120,000)
Dec. 31	Running costs	L6	58,000		(62,000)
Dec. 31	Depreciation	L7	18,000		(44,000)
Dec. 31	Transfer to ownership interest	L1	44,000		nil

L1 Ownership interest

Date	Particulars	Page	Debit	Credit	Balance
Year 2			£	£	£
Jan. 1	Cash	L2		60,000	(60,000)
Dec. 31	Transfer from profit and loss account	L8		44,000	(104,000)

LEONA's comment: *The transfer from the profit and loss account is shown as a credit entry in the ledger account for the ownership interest. That credit entry matches the debit entry, removing the balance from the ledger account. As a check on the common sense of the credit entry, go back to the table at the start of this Supplement (Exhibit 8.14), which shows that a credit entry records an increase in the ownership interest. In the ledger account the credit entry of £44,000 increases the ownership interest from £60,000 to £104,000.*

Subsequent years

The profit and loss accounts for Year 3 and Year 4 are identical to that for Year 2. The cash account flows on in a pattern similar to that of Year 2. These ledger accounts are therefore not repeated here for Years 3 and 4. Attention is concentrated on the asset at cost and the accumulated depreciation.

L3 Van at cost

Date	Particulars	Page	Debit	Credit	Balance
Year 2			£	£	£
Jan. 1	Cash	L2	60,000		60,000
Year 3	Balance	b/fwd			60,000
Year 4	Balance	b/fwd			60,000

LEONA's comment: *The asset continues in use from one year to the next and so the ledger account remains open with the balance of £60,000 remaining. At the start of each new year the balance on each asset account is brought forward (repeated) from the previous line to show clearly that this is the amount for the start of the new accounting year. Because this is merely a matter of convenience in tidying up at the start of the year, the abbreviation 'b/fwd' (for 'brought forward') is entered in the 'page' column to show that there are no debit or credit entries for transactions on this line.*

L4 Accumulated depreciation

Date	Particulars	Page	Debit	Credit	Balance
Year 2			£	£	£
Dec. 31	Depreciation charge for the year	L7		18,000	(18,000)
Year 3					
Dec. 31	Depreciation charge for the year	L7		18,000	(36,000)
Year 4					
Dec. 31	Depreciation charge for the year	L7		18,000	(54,000)

LEONA's comment: *The accumulated depreciation account is now showing more clearly what the word 'accumulated' means. Each year it is building in a further amount of £18,000 annual depreciation to build up the total shown in the 'balance' column. After three years the accumulated depreciation has built up to £54,000.*

L7 Depreciation of the year: Year 3

Date	Particulars	Page	Debit	Credit	Balance
Year 2			£	£	£
Dec. 31	Accumulated depreciation	L4	18,000		18,000
Dec. 31	Transfer to profit and loss account	L8		18,000	nil

L7 Depreciation of the year: Year 4

Date	Particulars	Page	Debit	Credit	Balance
Year 2			£	£	£
Dec. 31	Accumulated depreciation	L4	18,000		18,000
Dec. 31	Transfer to profit and loss account	L8		18,000	nil

LEONA's comment: *The depreciation of the year is a profit and loss account item and so is transferred to the profit and loss account each year in Years 3 and 4 in the manner explained earlier for Year 2.*

Disposal of the asset

At the end of Year 4 the asset is sold for a cash price of £6,000 which is the amount expected initially as the residual value. To remove the asset requires entries in the 'Van at cost' account (L3), the 'Accumulated depreciation' account (L4) and the 'Cash' account (L2). The corresponding debit and credit entries are recorded in a 'Fixed asset disposal' account (L9).

Exhibit 8.17 shows the breakdown of the sale transaction into the removal of the asset at cost, the removal of the accumulated depreciation, and the collection of cash. The entry required to remove a balance on a ledger account is the opposite to the amount of the balance. So in the 'Van at cost' account (L3) a credit entry of £60,000 is required to remove a debit balance of £60,000. In the 'Accumulated depreciation' account (L4) a debit entry is required to remove a credit balance of £54,000. In the 'Cash' account (L2) there is a debit entry of £60,000 to show that the asset of cash has increased. In each case the 'Disposal' account (L9) collects the matching debit or credit.

Exhibit 8.17
Analysis of debit and credit aspects of sale of a fixed asset

Date	Transaction or event	Amount	Dr	Cr
Year 4		£		
Dec. 31	Removal of asset at cost	60,000	Disposal	Van at cost
Dec. 31	Accumulated depreciation	54,000	Accumulated depn	Disposal
Dec. 31	Cash	6,000	Cash	Disposal

L3 Van at cost

Date	Particulars	Page	Debit	Credit	Balance
Year 2			£	£	£
Jan. 1	Cash	L2	60,000		60,000
Year 3	Balance	b/fwd			60,000
Year 4	Balance	b/fwd			60,000
Dec. 31	Disposal	L9		60,000	nil

L4 Accumulated depreciation

Date	Particulars	Page	Debit	Credit	Balance
Year 2			£	£	£
Dec. 31	Depreciation charge for the year	L7		18,000	(18,000)
Year 3					
Dec. 31	Depreciation charge for the year	L7		18,000	(36,000)
Year 4					
Dec. 31	Depreciation charge for the year	L7		18,000	(54,000)
Dec. 31	Disposal	L9	54,000		nil

L9 Fixed asset disposal account

Date	Particulars	Page	Debit	Credit	Balance
Year 2			£	£	£
Dec. 31	Van at cost	L3	60,000		60,000
Dec. 31	Accumulated depreciation	L4		54,000	6,000
Dec. 31	Cash	L2		6,000	nil

LEONA's comment: *The disposal account is a very convenient way of bringing together all the information about the disposal of the van. The first two lines show the full cost and accumulated depreciation. The balance column, on the second line, shows that the difference between these two items is the net book value of £6,000. Collecting cash of £6,000 is seen to match exactly the net book value, which means that there is no depreciation adjustment on disposal.*

Sale for an amount greater than the net book value

In the main text of this chapter there is a discussion of the consequences of selling the van for £9,000 cash rather than the £6,000 expected. There would be no problem in recording that in the bookkeeping system. Everything explained in the previous section would be unchanged except for the amount of the cash received. The Disposal account would now be recorded as:

L9 Fixed asset disposal account

Date	Particulars	Page	Debit	Credit	Balance
Year 2			£	£	£
Dec. 31	Van at cost	L3	60,000		60,000
Dec. 31	Accumulated depreciation	L4		54,000	6,000
Dec. 31	Cash	L2		9,000	(3,000)
Dec. 31	Transfer to profit and loss account, overdepreciation of earlier years	L8	3,000		nil

The profit and loss account for Year 4 would be recorded as:

L8 Profit and loss account

Date	Particulars	Page	Debit	Credit	Balance
Year 2			£	£	£
Dec. 31	Sales	L5		120,000	(120,000)
Dec. 31	Running costs	L6	58,000		(62,000)
Dec. 31	Depreciation of the year	L7	18,000		(44,000)
Dec. 31	Overdepreciation of earlier years	L9		3,000	(47,000)

LEONA's comment: *This profit and loss account in ledger form matches the profit and loss account presented at Exhibit 8.12 in the main text as a financial statement, although you will see that the latter is much more informative.*

Formula for calculating percentage rate for reducing balance depreciation

The rate of depreciation to be applied under the reducing balance method of depreciation may be calculated by the formula:

$$\text{rate} = (1 - \sqrt[n]{(R/C)}) \times 100\%$$

where: n = the number of years of useful life
R = the estimated residual value
C = the cost of the asset.

For the example given in the main chapter:

$n = 5$ years
$C = £1,000$
$R = £30$ (The residual value must be of reasonable magnitude. To use an amount of nil for the residual value would result in a rate of 100%).

$$\text{rate} = (1 - \sqrt[5]{(30/1,000)}) \times 100\%$$

To prove that the rate is 50 per cent you will need a scientific calculator or a suitable computer package. You may know how to calculate a fifth root using logarithms. Otherwise, if you have a very basic calculator it may be easier to use trial-and-error methods.

L08, S01, S03 | **Test your understanding**

S8.1 Prepare ledger accounts to report the transactions and events of questions **C8.1** and **C8.2**. Write a short commentary on each ledger account which would enable a non-accountant to understand their purpose and content.

Chapter 9

Current assets

After studying this chapter you should be able to:

L01 Define a current asset and apply the definition.

L02 Explain the operation of the working capital cycle.

L03 Explain the factors affecting recognition of stock, debtors and investments.

L04 Explain how the information presented in a company's balance sheet and notes, in relation to current assets, meets the needs of users.

L05 Explain the different approaches to measurement of stocks and cost of goods sold.

L06 Analyse provisions for doubtful debts using a spreadsheet.

L07 Analyse prepayments using a spreadsheet.

L08 Explain the term 'revenue' and the application of principles of revenue recognition.

Additionally, for those who choose to study the Supplement:

L09 Record debtors and prepayments in ledger accounts.

9.1 Introduction

This chapter will continue the progress through the balance sheet which we began in Chapter 8. As in that chapter, the approach will be:

● What are the rules for defining and recognising these items?
● What are the information needs of users in respect of the particular items?
● What information is currently provided by companies to meet these needs?
● Does the information show the desirable qualitative characteristics of financial statements?
● What are the rules for measuring, and processes for recording, these items?

L01 ## 9.2 Definitions

The definition of an asset was provided in Chapter 2. The definition of a current asset, as stated in the Companies Act 1985, says very little beyond confirming that a current asset is something which is not a fixed asset:

Definition *Assets* are rights or other access to future economic benefits controlled by an entity as a result of past transactions or events.[1]

Definition A *current asset* is an asset that is not intended for use on a continuing basis in the company's activities.[2]

The following list is a sample of the current assets found in most company balance sheets:

- raw materials
- work-in-progress
- finished goods

- trade debtors
- amounts owed by other companies in a group
- prepayments and accrued income

- investments held as current assets

- short-term bank deposits
- bank current account (also called 'cash at bank')
- cash in hand.

L01 **Activity 9.1**

Using the definition provided, explain why each item in the foregoing list may be classed as a current asset. Could a plot of land ever be treated as a current asset?

Since the definition provided by the Companies Act is disappointingly brief, it may be helpful to create a definition, based on these familiar examples of current assets, which gives more positive indications of the common features of current assets. Current assets are items which have been acquired with the intention of sale, or conversion into cash, within a short space of time, usually less than 12 months. The period of 12 months is suggested because that is the length of the trading cycle experienced by many businesses (covering all the seasons of one year), and because it is the reporting period most commonly used by most enterprises for reporting to external users of financial statements.

Definition A *current asset* is an asset that has been acquired with the intention of sale, or conversion into cash, within a relatively short space of time, usually less than 12 months. It is not intended for use on a continuing basis in the company's activities.

L02 ## 9.3 The working capital cycle

Working capital is the amount of long-term finance the business has to provide in order to keep current assets working for the business. Some short-term finance for current assets is provided by the suppliers who give credit by allowing time to pay, but that is not usually sufficient. Some short-term finance for current assets is provided by short-term bank loans but, in most cases, there still remains an excess of current assets over current liabilities.

The working capital cycle of a business is the sequence of transactions and events, involving current assets and current liabilities, through which the business makes a profit.

Exhibit 9.1 shows how the working capital cycle begins when suppliers allow the business to obtain goods on credit terms, but do not insist on immediate payment. While they are waiting for payment they are called *creditors*. The goods obtained by the business are used in production, held for resale or used in providing a service. While the goods acquired are held by the business they are called the *stock* of the business. Any products manufactured from these goods and held for resale are also part of the stock of the business. (In some countries, particularly the United States, the stock is more commonly referred to as *inventory*.) The resulting product or service is sold to customers who may pay immediately in cash, or may be allowed time to pay. If they are allowed time to pay they become *debtors* of the business. Debtors eventually pay and the business obtains cash. *Cash* is a general term used to cover money held in the bank, and money held in notes and coins on the business premises. Cash held in the bank will be in an account such as a current account which allows immediate access. Finally the cash may be used to pay the suppliers who, as creditors, have been waiting patiently for payment.

Stock, debtors and cash are all current assets of the business and will be dealt with in this chapter. Creditors who have supplied goods to the business are current liabilities and will be dealt with in the next chapter.

Exhibit 9.1
The working capital cycle for a manufacturing or service business

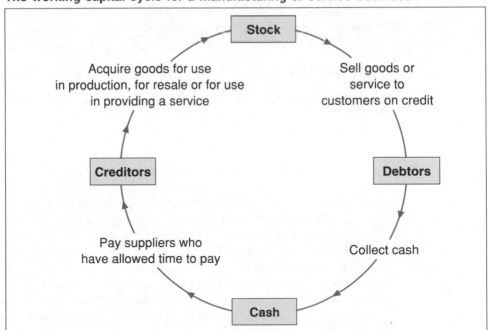

Working capital is calculated as *current assets minus current liabilities*. If the working capital is low, then the business has a close match between current assets and current liabilities but may risk not being able to pay its liabilities as they fall due. Not all the current assets are instantly available in cash (particularly the stocks of unsold goods), and an impatient supplier or bank manager may cause difficulties if cash is not available when payment of a liability is due. On the other hand, if current assets are very much greater than current liabilities, then the business has a large amount of finance tied up in the current assets when perhaps that finance would be better employed in the acquisition of more fixed assets to expand the profit-making capacity of the operations.

Definition   *Working capital* is the amount which a business must provide to finance the current assets of a business, to the extent that these are not covered by current liabilities. It is calculated by deducting current liabilities from current assets.

L03 ## 9.4 Recognition

The general conditions for recognition were set out in Chapter 2. An item that meets the definition of an asset should be recognised if there is sufficient evidence that the new asset has been created and the item can be measured at a monetary amount with sufficient reliability. There is no doubt that stocks, debtors, investments and cash are commonly recognised in a balance sheet but it is useful to be aware of the element of doubt which may be attached to the expectation of economic benefit which creates the asset and to the reliability of measurement. That awareness is essential to understanding the level of uncertainty which surrounds reported financial statements.

9.4.1 Stocks

There are three main categories of stocks: raw materials, work-in-progress and finished goods. Consider these in reverse order.

Finished goods

The future economic benefit expected from finished goods is that they will be sold to customers for a price which exceeds the cost of purchase or manufacture. That makes a profit which increases the ownership interest. However, until the sale is agreed with the customer, this expected benefit is uncertain and the qualitative characteristic of *prudence* (explained in Chapter 4) dictates that it is safer not to anticipate that the profit will arise. The value of the stock of finished goods is therefore measured at the *cost* of purchase or manufacture. In most cases that is a reliable measure because it is based on recorded costs and is not anticipating an uncertain selling price. Sometimes there may be a disappointment where goods are manufactured and then it is found there is a lack of demand. Where there is strong doubt about the expected selling price, such that it might be less than the cost of purchase or manufacture, the asset of finished goods stock is valued at the net realisable value. This is defined as the estimated proceeds from sale of the items in question, less all costs to be incurred in marketing, selling and distributing these items.

The accounting policy note of most companies confirms this prudent approach. You will see in a later section of this chapter that Safe and Sure plc recognises stocks in its balance sheet at the lower of cost and net realisable value.

Work-in-progress

During the course of production the asset of finished goods is gradually being created. The expected future benefit of that activity is gradually building up as the work moves towards completion. A business could wait until the asset is totally finished, before recognising the asset in the balance sheet. That would satisfy the qualitative characteristic of *prudence*, supported by the characteristic of *reliability*, but would run into problems with the characteristic of *relevance*. Where work-in-progress is a substantial aspect of the operations of the business, users need to know how much work-in-progress there is, whether it is increasing or decreasing, and what risks are attached. The risks attached to work-in-progress are often greater than those attached to finished goods because there is the risk of non-completion to add to all the risks faced when the goods are completed and awaiting sale. There is a reliable measurement, in the cost of work completed at the date of the balance sheet, but careful checking is required by the managers of the business to ensure that this is a reliable measure.

A particularly important type of work-in-progress is the long-term contract such as may be found in the engineering and building industries. A company building a bridge over three years will want to tell the shareholders about the progress being made in creating profit. Each year a portion of the total contract price will be reported as turnover and costs of the period will be matched against that turnover to calculate profit. The value of the work completed will be recognised in the balance sheet, sometimes called *work-in-progress* but more commonly recognised as an eventual *amount due from the customer*, within the category of debtors. Reporting long-term contracts is a rather specialised aspect of accounting, the detail of which is beyond a first-level textbook. The reporting of profit on long-term contracts is reviewed later in this chapter in the section on *revenue recognition*.

Raw materials

The approach to recognition is the same as that for finished goods. Raw materials are expected to create a benefit by being used in the manufacture of goods for sale. On grounds of prudence the profit is not anticipated and the raw materials are recognised at the lower of cost and net realisable value.

Definition   Stocks of raw materials, work-in-progress and finished goods are *recognised* at the lower of cost or net realisable value. The comparison of cost and net realisable value is carried out for each separate item of stock or groups of similar items.[3]

9.4.2 Debtors and prepayments

Debtors are those persons who owe money to a business. Usually the largest amount shown under this heading relates to customers buying goods on credit. These are the trade debtors. Additionally, the business may have lent money to another enterprise to help that enterprise in its activities. There may be loans to employees to cover removal and relocation expenses or advances on salaries. The business may be due to receive a refund of overpaid tax.

Trade debtors meet the recognition conditions because there is an expectation of benefit when the customer pays. The profit on the sale of the goods is known because the customer has taken the goods or service and agreed the price. Trade debtors are therefore measured at the selling price of the goods and the profit is recognised in the profit and loss account. There is a risk that the customer will not pay, but the view taken is that the risk of non-payment should be seen quite separately from the risk of not making a profit on a sale. The risk of non-payment is dealt with by reducing the reported value of the asset using an estimate for doubtful debts. That process is explained later in the chapter.

Prepayments are amounts of expenses paid in advance. Insurance premiums, rent of buildings, lease charges on a vehicle, road fund licences for the delivery vans and lorries, are all examples of items which have to be paid for in advance. At the balance sheet date some part of the future benefit may remain. This is recognised as the prepayment. Take the example of an insurance premium of £240 paid on 1 October to cover a 12-month period. At the company's year-end of 31 December, three months' benefit has expired but nine months' benefit remains. The balance sheet therefore reports a prepayment of £180.

9.4.3 Investments

Investments held as current assets are usually highly marketable and readily convertible into cash. The expectation of future economic benefit is therefore usually sufficient to meet the conditions of recognition. Measurement is more of a problem. There are two possible measures. One is the cost of the investment and the other is the market value. Recognising the investment at cost is prudent and reliable, but not as relevant as the current market value which is the amount of cash that could be released by sale of the investment. There is no agreed answer to this problem at the present time, although the issue has been debated in the standard-setting context. Most businesses report current asset investments at cost but a smaller number use the market value. Using the market value is called *marking to market*. It is a departure from the normal practice of recording assets at original cost but is justified in terms of the requirement of company law that financial statements should show a *true and fair view* (*see* Chapter 4). It is seen in companies whose business involves dealing in investments.

9.4.4 Cash

Recognising cash is no problem either in the expectation of benefit or in the measurement of the asset. The amount is known either by counting cash in hand or by looking at a statement from the bank which is holding the business bank account. The expectation of benefit lies in making use of the cash in future to buy fixed assets or to contribute to the working capital cycle so that the business earns a profit. In the meantime, cash which is surplus to immediate requirements should be deposited in such a way that it is earning interest. Where a company has substantial cash balances there should be indications in the profit and loss account that investment income has been earned, to provide a benefit to the business.

L04

Activity 9.2

This section has covered in some detail the characteristics of various groups of current assets. Before reading the next section, write down what information you would expect to see, in respect of these groups of assets, in the balance sheet and notes to the accounts. Then read the section and consider similarities to, or differences from, the views given there.

L04

9.5 Users' needs for information

Investors have an interest in knowing that current assets are not overstated. If the assets are overstated the profit of the business will be overstated (see the explanation in Chapter 4, using the accounting equation). They will want to know particularly whether there has been allowance for stocks of goods which may not lead to sales and whether there has been allowance for customers who may not be able to pay the debts shown as due to the business. They may also want the reassurance that the auditors have established the existence of all the current assets, particularly ensuring that a very portable asset such as cash is where it ought to be in the ownership of the company.

The needs of users do not stop with the investors. The trade creditors who supply goods and services to the business are strongly reliant on the working capital cycle for their eventual payment. Employees look for their salaries and wages from the cash generated during the working capital cycle. They want to know that the cash will be there on the day it is required, rather than being tied up in stocks or debtors awaiting release as cash. Tax collecting authorities, such as the Inland Revenue and the Customs and Excise, have definite dates on which payments are required. All these persons have an interest in the working capital of the business and how it is managed. The concern of creditors and employees is primarily with the flow of cash and its availability on the day required. That information will not appear in the balance sheet but there will be some indications of flow in the cash flow statement (outlined in Chapter 3).

L04

9.6 Information provided in the financial statements

In Chapter 7 the balance sheet of Safe and Sure plc contained three lines relating to current assets:

	Notes	Year 2 £m	Year 1 £m
Current assets			
Stocks	4	26.6	24.3
Debtors	5	146.9	134.7
Short-term deposits and cash		107.3	90.5
		280.8	249.5

There is more information provided in the notes to the balance sheet.

9.6.1 Details in notes

There are two relevant notes, of which note 4 deals with stocks and note 5 with debtors:

Note 4		Year 2 £m	Year 1 £m
Stocks	Raw materials	6.2	5.4
	Work-in-progress	1.9	1.0
	Finished products	18.5	17.9
		26.6	24.3

This company is a service company so it is not surprising that stocks do not figure prominently in the overall collection of current assets. It is perhaps more surprising that there are stocks of finished products, but reading the description of the business shows that there is a Products Division which manufactures special cleaning chemicals under the company name.

The note on debtors shows that the main category is trade debtors:

Note 5		Year 2 £m	Year 1 £m
Debtors	Trade debtors	128.1	117.0
	Other debtors	10.9	9.8
	Prepayments and accrued income	7.9	7.9
		146.9	134.7

There is no indication of the nature of 'other debtors'. It could indicate employees who have received loans or advances of salaries. It could indicate a loan to a company which has trading links with the group but is not a full subsidiary. Prepayments are expenses paid in advance of gaining the benefit, as explained in the previous section of this chapter.

9.6.2 Accounting policy

It will be shown later in this chapter that the valuation of stocks is a matter of potential variation from one person to the next, so it is important to know that the company has followed an acceptable policy in its valuation of stock. The accounting policy note provides that confirmation. For the moment you will have to accept that this form of wording represents standard practice, but each phrase will be explained later in the chapter.

Definition

> *Accounting policy:* Stocks and work-in-progress are stated at the lower of cost and net realisable value, using the first-in-first-out principle. Cost includes all direct expenditure and related overheads incurred to the date of the balance sheet.

9.6.3 Operating and financial review

The finance director commented as follows in his review:

> 'The group's businesses are structured to utilise as little fixed and working capital as is consistent with the profit and earnings growth objective in order to produce a high cash flow.'

The focus on working capital is perhaps an indication of the importance seen in explaining how the company manages its current assets and current liabilities. It also shows that for this business the high cash flow is planned and is not an accident of events.

9.6.4 Analyst's view

DAVID WILSON comments: *This is a service business and so holds stocks of goods to be used in the service process. The note to the balance sheet does not actually say what the stocks are, so I asked when I made my visit. They tell me the raw materials are stocks of cleaning materials and chemicals for processes such as disinfecting. My main concern is to be assured that there is nothing in the stock which could carry a risk of losing value through obsolescence or deterioration. There is not much problem of that with cleaning materials. The finished goods took me by surprise until I found out that there is a Products Division. It was actually the cleaning products that I knew best from years ago but I thought they had moved entirely into service contracts.*

In any event, stocks are not all that important for this company. The debtors' amount is much larger. I know they have a relatively low risk of bad debts because most customers pay in advance for their contracts.

When I started as an analyst I worked alongside someone who had twenty years' experience. He told me that he had always used what he called 'the 10 per cent test' when looking at stocks and debtors in a balance sheet. He worked out what effect a 10 per cent error in the stock or debtors would have on the profit before tax. In this case a 10 per cent error in stock would be £2.7m. The profit before tax is £177m. A difference of £2.7m on £177m is 1.5 per cent. An error of 1.5 per cent in profit would not have a significant impact on the view of most investors. So in this company stock is not a matter which needs time taken for questions. On the other hand, a 10 per cent error in debtors would be £14.7m. That is 8.3 per cent of profit before tax. So debtors are worth more attention. If this were a company I didn't know, I would ask about the quality of the asset and the type of customer who is given credit. In fact I do know the answer here. The finance director told me that when I met him. The debtors are largely public sector bodies such as local authorities and hospitals who insist on paying after the work has been done to their satisfaction. There could be a risk of non-payment because of shoddy work but there is little risk of non-payment through default.

The final point to note in relation to current assets is that this company is a cash-generating business. I looked at the cash flow statement (see Chapter 4) and the group builds up cash balances, buys another company, and then generates even more cash. I suppose that can't go on for ever but there are no signs of problems at present.

LEONA: I told you I would be looking for admissions of how much you rely on the auditor without knowing it. Your '10 per cent test' is a very rough-and-ready example of the ratio analysis we carry out on a systematic basis as part of our analytical review of the financial statements. Maybe one day I'll tell you more about that. We have quite a long list of ratios which we calculate. We also look at interrelationships between ratios and relative changes in one compared with another.

It is also an application of what we call 'materiality'. When we see an asset, such as debtors in this case, where an error in estimation of the asset value could cause a serious impact on profit, we identify that as a matter for special attention. We would probably spend more time on debtors than on stock in our audit of this company but we would target the risk-related aspects of what is reported about each asset. For debtors it is the risk of non-payment through either disputed debts or lack of funds. For stock it is the risk of obsolescence or similar loss which is not covered by insurance.

Have you decided on how the company's information on current assets meets the list of desirable qualitative characteristics?

DAVID: You're trying to get me to admit that I need the auditors. Reliability is in the auditors' hands as far as the numbers go, but I place a lot of reliance on my assessment of the qualities of senior management when I meet them. You can't audit that kind of feeling. It's all a matter of chemistry. Also, the main current asset is debtors and I know they are reliable because the finance director told me what class of customer was involved. I didn't need the auditors for that. Relevance probably scores about eight out of ten because there aren't any complications here with unusual types of stocks. Faithful representation and neutrality are something I leave to the auditors for now but I'll be asking questions next year if the information in the financial statements turns out not to be neutral. Prudence, I know, is built into all aspects of accounting which uses historical cost measures. That sometimes works against relevance. Completeness is not a problem for current assets. The company is unlikely to leave anything out. They are more likely to include too much. I do expect the auditor to check that the assets are there. Comparability is a matter of presentation. This company has a five-year summary elsewhere in the annual report and gives the previous year's amounts in the financial statements. As for understandability, I like to think that I can see my way around figures for stocks, debtors and cash. I usually get the answers I want when I phone the financial controller.

LEONA: But don't you see that by admitting that you have to ask more questions to help you understand the amounts, there must be some further explanations which the company could give in the annual report so that your understanding may be shared by others?

DAVID: *My fund manager colleagues would say that only the professional investors have the expertise. Even if more information were reported by companies, only the professionals would know how to use it.*

L05–8 ## 9.7 Measurement and recording

The basic measurement rule applying to all current assets is that they should be measured at the lower of cost and net realisable value. The exception is debtors which are measured at selling price because the related profit is earned when the sale is made and not when the credit customer chooses to pay.

The next three sections look at issues of measurement and recording, in relation to stocks, debtors and current asset investments, which are essential to an understanding of how much variability and uncertainty lies behind the apparent confidence of the numbers reported in financial statements.

L05 ## 9.8 Stocks of raw materials and finished goods

The analysis of transactions involving stocks of raw materials, work-in-progress and finished goods has been explained in detail in Chapter 6 and will not be repeated here. This section examines the problems created by the general rule that stocks must be valued at the lower of cost and net realisable value. This rule is a consequence of the prudence concept, based on not anticipating a sale until the goods are delivered to the customer.

Net realisable value means *the proceeds of selling an item, after deducting the costs of sale.* For example, damaged stock is sold at auction for £10,000. The auctioneer charges selling commission of 20 per cent which is £2,000. The amount received by the seller is £8,000, called *the net realisable value.*

The section covers first of all the accounting equation in relation to the rule. It then looks at the meaning of cost and the allocation of overhead costs. Various specific models to deal with changing input prices are then discussed and the section concludes with the rules to be applied in financial reporting.

Definition *Net realisable value* is calculated as the proceeds of sale of an item minus the costs of selling.

9.8.1 Lower of cost and net realisable value

Consider the example of a container of coffee beans purchased by a coffee manufacturer at a cost of £1,000. The beans are held for three months up to the balance sheet date. During that time there is a fall in the world price of coffee beans and the container of coffee beans would sell for only £800 in the market.

When the asset is acquired, the impact on the accounting equation is an increase of £1,000 in the asset of stock and a decrease of £1,000 in the asset of cash.

| Assets ↑↓ | – | Liabilities | = | Ownership interest |

+ £1,000 stock
– £1,000 cash

At the end of the year the asset is found to be worth £800 and the ownership interest is reduced because the asset has fallen in value. The asset is reduced by £200 and an expense of loss of stock value is reported in the profit and loss account.

| Assets ↓ | – | Liabilities | = | Ownership interest ↓ |

– £200 stock   – £200 expense

If a business fails to report a fall in the value of the asset of stock, the profit of the period will be overstated.

Where there are separate categories of stock the rule of 'lower of cost and net realisable value' must be applied to each category separately. Suppose, for example, there is a stock of paper at a cost of £2,000 with a net realisable value of £2,300 and a stock of pens with a cost of £1,800 and a net realisable value of £1,400. The lower amount must be taken in each case, giving a stock value of £3,400 (calculated as £2,000 plus £1,400).

9.8.2 Meaning of cost

The cost of any item of stock or work-in-progress is specified as the expenditure which has to be incurred in the normal course of business in bringing the product or service to its present location and condition.[4] This expenditure will include not only the cost of purchase but also costs of converting raw materials into finished goods or services.

Costs of purchase include the price charged by the supplier, plus transport and handling costs, plus import duties, and less discounts and subsidies.[5] Costs of conversion include items readily identifiable with the product, such as labour, expenses and subcontractors' costs directly related to the product. They also include production overheads and any other overheads directly related to bringing the product or service to its present condition and location. Production overheads are items such as depreciation of machines, service costs, rental paid for a factory, wages paid to supervisory and support staff, costs of stores control and insurance of production facilities.

Example

Take the example of a business which purchases 10 wooden furniture units for conversion to a customer's specification for installation in a hotel. The units cost £200 each and the labour cost of converting them is £100 each. Production overheads for the period are fixed at £3,500. Two units remain unsold at the end of the period. These two units will be recorded in the balance sheet at £1,300, calculated as £650 each (materials cost of £200 plus labour cost of £100 plus a share of the production overheads at £350 per item).

That was easy because there were 10 identical units to take equal shares of the production overheads. But suppose they had all been different and required different amounts of labour? Would it have been fair to share the overheads equally? Probably not. The problems of sharing out production overhead costs create a chapter in themselves and are revisited in Chapter 18 on management accounting. You need to be aware, in reading published accounting information, that there is considerable scope for discretion to be exercised by management in the allocation of overheads between completed goods and goods held in stock. The general risk of overstatement of assets applies here. If the asset is overstated by having too much production overheads allocated, the profit of the period is also overstated because it is not bearing the share of production overheads which it should.

9.8.3 Costs when input prices are changing

One very tiresome problem faced by the accounts department in its record keeping is that suppliers change their prices from time to time. Goods held in store may have arrived at different times and at different unit prices. How does the accounts department decide on the unit price to be charged to each job when all the materials look the same once they are taken into store?

In some cases it may be possible to label the materials as they arrive so that they can be identified with the appropriate unit price. That is a very time-consuming process and would only be used for high-value low-volume items of materials. In other cases a convenient method is needed which gives an answer that is useful and approximately close to the true price of the units used. Some possibilities are shown in Exhibit 9.2 using three options – first-in-first-out (FIFO), last-in-first-out (LIFO) and average cost. In each case, Exhibit 9.2 takes a very simple approach, not complicated by having inventory at the start of the period. In real life the calculations can be even more tricky.

Exhibit 9.2
Pricing the issue of goods to production

There are three parts to this illustration. Part (a) contains a table setting out the data to be used in the calculation. Part (b) defines the three bases of calculation. Part (c) uses the data from part (a) to illustrate each of the three bases.

(a) data

Date	Received	Unit price	Price paid	Issued to production
	Units	£	£	Units
1 June	100	20	2,000	–
20 June	50	22	1,100	–
24 June	–	–	–	60
28 June	–	–	–	70
Total	150		3,100	130

Exhibit 9.2 continued

(b) bases of calculation
First-in-first-out (FIFO)
Assume that the goods which arrived first are issued first.

Last-in-first-out (LIFO)
Assume that the goods which arrived last are issued first.

Average cost
Assume that all goods are issued at the average price of the stock held.

(c) calculations

Basis	Date	Quantity and unit price	Issued to production	Held in stock	Total
			£	£	£
FIFO					
	24 June	60 units at £20	1,200		
	28 June	40 units at £20			
		30 units at £22	1,460		
	30 June	20 units at £22		440	
Total			2,660	440	*3,100*
LIFO					
	24 June	50 units at £22			
		10 units at £20	1,300		
	28 June	70 units at £20	1,400		
	30 June	20 units at £20		400	
Total			2,700	400	*3,100*
Average					
	24 June	60 units at *£20.67	1,240		
	28 June	70 units at *£20.67	1,447		
	30 June	20 units at *£20.67		413	
Total			2,687	413	*3,100*

Note: *Weighted average [(100 × 20) + (50 × 22)]/150 = £20.67.

9.8.4 Approximation when dates are not recorded

In business there may not be time to keep the detailed records shown in the calculations in Exhibit 9.2. In such cases the sales volume is known in total but the dates of sales are not recorded. The calculation then uses the best approximation available, which usually means working through the costs from the oldest date, for FIFO, or the most recent date, for LIFO, without attempting to match the various batches bought and sold during the year.

9.8.5 Choice of FIFO, LIFO or average cost

Look at table (c) of Exhibit 9.2 and compare it with table (a) of that exhibit. You will see from table (a) that the total amount spent on materials during the month was £3,100. You will see from table (c) that the total of the cost of goods issued to production, plus the cost of unsold goods, is always £3,100 irrespective of which approach is taken. All that differs is the allocation between goods used in production and goods remaining unsold. Cost can never be gained or lost in total because of a particular allocation process, provided the process is used consistently over time. The FIFO approach suffers the disadvantage of matching outdated costs against current revenue. The LIFO approach improves on FIFO by matching the most recent costs against revenue, but at the expense of an inventory value which becomes increasingly out of date. The average cost lies between the two and becomes more intricate to recalculate as more items come into inventory. In practice, the choice for internal reporting in management accounting is a matter of finding the best method for the purpose.

There is an effect on profit of the year which may influence management choice. When prices are rising and stock volumes are steady or increasing, FIFO gives a lower cost of sales and so a higher profit than LIFO. If there were no regulations, companies that wished to show high profits (perhaps to impress the stock market) might prefer FIFO. Companies that wished to show lower profits (perhaps to reduce tax bills) might prefer LIFO.

In financial reporting for external purposes the subject becomes more complicated by the intervention of statute law, accounting standards and the fiscal authorities. The Companies Act 1985 allows the use of LIFO[6] but the Inland Revenue will not accept it for tax purposes (because it generally shows a lower profit than FIFO and therefore a company paying tax on LIFO profit would pay less tax). The accounting standard says that methods such as LIFO 'are not usually appropriate'.[7]

L05 | **Activity 9.3**

Look back to Exhibit 9.2 and write your own table of data for goods received, unit price, price paid and goods issued to production. Create calculations of cost of goods sold, using the various models in Exhibit 9.2 (FIFO, LIFO and average stock). Check that the value of goods issued to production, plus the value of goods held in stock, will always add up to the same answer in total.

9.9 Debtors

The measurement of debtors requires attention to bad and doubtful debts. A debt is described as a *bad debt* when there is no further hope of the customer paying the amount owed. This might be due to the customer being declared bankrupt or else disappearing without trace. If the customer is known to be in difficulties or there is some dispute over the amount owed, the debt is described as a *doubtful debt*. The company still hopes to recover the cash owed but realistically has some doubt. Evidence of doubtful debts may be seen in slow payment, partial payments, the need for several reminders or even rumours in the business community. A company will usually analyse the age of its debts to help identify those which may be doubtful.

Example

At the end of Year 1 the Garden Pond Company has a balance sheet comprising £2,000 debtors, £7,000 other assets and £9,000 ownership interest that consists of £1,800 ownership interest at the start of the period and £7,200 profit of the period. On the balance sheet date the manager of the company reviews the debtors list and decides that debts amounting to £200 are doubtful because there are rumours of a customer not paying other suppliers in the trade. The balance sheet at the end of Year 1 is amended to show that the asset is of lower value than was thought and the ownership interest has consequently diminished.

Exhibit 9.3 shows the spreadsheet for analysis set out to reflect the accounting equation. The new column is the one headed *provision for doubtful debts*. This is included in the assets section because it tells the user more about the asset of debtors, although it is the negative part of the asset. It causes some confusion to those who meet it for the first time because anything called a provision is usually reported under the heading of liabilities. However, on grounds of usefulness to readers and relevance to the provision of information about the asset, the provision for doubtful debts has special treatment in being included as a negative aspect within the asset section of the balance sheet.

It is quite a difficult matter for a company to be prudent in expressing doubt about a debtor while still pursuing the non-payer with a view to collection of the debt. To remove the debt from the record would be to admit defeat. Even to show a separate provision among the liability headings might lead other customers to think, 'Why not me also?' Some companies therefore do not disclose a separate provision for doubtful debts in a company's balance sheet. They deduct the provision from the full debtors' list and report only the resulting net amount.

Exhibit 9.3

Spreadsheet to analyse the effect of provision for doubtful debts at the end of Year 1, using the accounting equation

Date	Transaction or event	Assets			Ownership interest	
Year 1		Debtors	Provision for doubtful debts	Other assets	Ownership interest at start	Profit of the period
		£	£	£	£	£
Dec. 31	Balance sheet first draft	2,000		7,000	1,800	7,200
Dec. 31	Recognition of doubtful debts		(200)			(200)
Dec. 31	Revised balance sheet	2,000	(200)	7,000	1,800	7,000

The balance sheet after incorporating a provision for the doubtful debt would appear as in Exhibit 9.4.

There is no single method of calculating the provision for doubtful debts. Some companies consider separately the amount owed by each customer. To economise on time, most companies use previous experience to estimate a percentage of total debtors. A mixture of approaches could be used, with known problems being identified separately and a general percentage being applied to the rest.

Exhibit 9.4

Balance sheet of Garden Pond Company showing the presentation of information on doubtful debts

Garden Pond Company
Balance sheet at 31 December Year 1

	£	£
Other assets		7,000
Debtors	2,000	
Less: provision for doubtful debts	(200)	
		1,800
		8,800
Ownership interest at the start of the year		1,800
Profit of the year		7,000
		8,800

9.9.1 Change in a provision

During Year 2 matters take an upward turn and in July the customer who was showing signs of financial distress manages to pay the amount of £200 owed. The effect on the accounting equation is that the asset of cash is increased and the asset of debtor is reduced by £200. The provision for doubtful debts is now no longer required and could be transferred back to the profit and loss account, but in practice it tends to be left for tidying up at the end of the year.

The business continues and at the end of Year 2 the debtors amount to £2,500. A review of the list of debtors causes considerable doubt regarding an amount of £350. It is decided to create a new provision of £350. The old provision of £200 related to last year's debtors and is no longer required.

Exhibit 9.5 shows the spreadsheet at the end of Year 2, before and after recording the new provision for doubtful debts. It is assumed that the other assets have grown to £10,000 and there is a profit of £3,500 before amending the provision for doubtful debts.

The profit and loss account could show two separate entries, one being £200 increase in ownership interest and the other being £350 decrease in ownership interest. It is rather cumbersome in that form and most enterprises would report as an expense, in the profit and loss account, the single line:

Increase in provision for doubtful debts   £150

Exhibit 9.5

Spreadsheet to analyse the effect of provision for doubtful debts at the end of Year 2, using the accounting equation

Date	Transaction or event	Assets			Ownership interest	
Year 2		Debtors	Provision for doubtful debts	Other assets	Ownership interest at start	Profit of the period
		£	£	£	£	£
Dec. 31	Balance sheet first draft	2,500	(200)	10,000	8,800	3,500
Dec. 31	Elimination of provision no longer required		200			200
Dec. 31	Creation of new provision		(350)			(350)
Dec. 31	Revised balance sheet	2,500	(350)	10,000	8,800	3,350

LO7 9.10 Prepayments

Prepayments arise when an item of expense is paid in advance of the benefit being received. A common example is the payment of an insurance premium. The payment is made in advance for the year ahead and the benefit is gradually used up as the year goes along. The balance sheet recognises the unexpired portion of the insurance premium as an asset, while the profit and loss account reports the amount consumed during the period.

Example

On 1 October Year 1 a company paid £1,200 for one year's vehicle insurance. At the balance sheet date of 31 December there have been three months' benefit used up and there is a nine-month benefit yet to come. The transactions relating to insurance would be reported as in Exhibit 9.6.

Exhibit 9.6
Spreadsheet recording prepayment of insurance at the balance sheet date

Date	Transaction or event	Assets		Ownership interest
Year 2		Cash £	Prepayment £	Expense £
Oct. 1	Payment of premium	(1,200)		(1,200)
Dec. 31	Identification of asset remaining as prepayment		900	900
		(1,200)	900	(300)

The effect of identifying the asset is to reduce the expense of the period from £1,200 to £300 and to hold the remaining £900 as a benefit for the next accounting period. In Year 2 the amount of £900 will be transferred from the prepayment column to the expense column, so that the decrease in the ownership interest is reported in the period in which it occurs.

LO8 9.11 Revenue recognition

The sale of goods and services creates *revenue* for the business. Sometimes that revenue is referred to as *sales* or *turnover*. The term revenue may also be applied to rents received from letting out property, or interest received on investments made. In the conceptual frameworks of various countries, different views are held of the exact meaning and extent of the word *revenue*. The International Accounting Standards Committee defines revenue in terms of equity (ownership interest).

Definition
> *Revenue* is defined as the gross inflow of economic benefits during the period arising in the course of the ordinary activities of an enterprise when those inflows result in increases in equity, other than increases relating to contributions from equity participants.[8]

The main problem in recognition of revenue lies in the timing. Assets are recognised at a point in time but revenue is created over a period of time. What are the rules for deciding on the time period for which revenue should be reported? One suggestion has been that the *critical event* is the important factor.[9,10] When goods are produced or services are carried out, there is one part of the process which is critical to providing sufficient reassurance that the revenue has been earned by the efforts of the enterprise. For the sale of goods the point of delivery to the customer is the usual critical event which determines the date of revenue recognition. For a contract of service, the critical event is the production of the service.

9.11.1 Contract revenue

Where the service extends over more than one time period, the revenue may be split over the time periods involved. That may happen in a civil engineering or a building contract. In each year of the contract a portion of the revenue will be matched against costs of the period so as to report a portion of profit.

Take the example of a two-year bridge-building contract. The contract price is £60m. Two-thirds of the work has been completed in Year 1 and it is expected that the remainder will be completed in Year 2. The costs incurred in Year 1 are £34m and the costs expected for Year 2 are £17m.

The profit and loss account of the business for Year 1 will report, in respect of this contract, turnover of £40m less costs of £34m giving profit of £6m. This gives a fair representation of the profit earned by the activity of the year (as two-thirds of the total). An independent expert, in this case an engineer, would confirm that the work had been completed satisfactorily to date. The effect on the accounting equation would be:

Reporting turnover of £40m in Year 1 will increase the ownership interest by £40m. A matching asset will be reported, representing the customer's obligation to pay for the bridge when it is completed. This is not strictly a debtor because the legal liability to pay only comes into force when the bridge is completed according to the conditions of the contract. However, the customer's obligation is thought to be very similar in substance to a debtor and so it is reported in the debtors' section of the balance sheet as an *amount recoverable on a contract*. The expenses of £34m are reported in the usual way and a profit of £6m results. All being well, the profit and loss account of Year 2 will report the remaining £20m of revenue minus £17m of expenses, leaving a profit of £3m. Over the two years the total profit of £9m will be reported.

Users of accounting information need to pay particular attention to contract revenue in a business and ask some careful questions. Has prudence been exercised in deciding what portion of revenue to report? Is there a risk that the future costs will escalate and there will be an overall loss? They should look carefully at the provisions section of the balance sheet (*see* Chapter 11).

Where the customer has paid money in advance as an instalment towards the final contract price, the effect on the accounting equation is to increase the asset of cash and create a liability towards the customer. This liability is the obligation for the business to repay the customer if the contract is not completed on time or on specification. Although it might be expected that the liability towards the customer would appear in the current liabilities section of the balance sheet, that may not in fact be the case. The accounting standard which deals with stocks and long-term contracts requires the liability in respect of payments made in advance to be deducted from the amount recoverable on contract in the balance sheet. That may mean that, at first glance at the balance sheet, the reader does not realise the true size of the contract being undertaken for the customer. There is no guarantee that any better information will be found anywhere else in the financial statements, because turnover is aggregated for all activities. For the analyst as an expert user, long-term contracts require a great deal of careful questioning if the underlying details are to be understood.

9.11.2 A continuing debate

There are problems in revenue recognition that continue to be debated. Consider three examples. In the first, a film production company sells a programme to a television company which agrees to pay royalties every time the programme is broadcast. In the second, a farmer sells a cow to a neighbour in return for five sheep. In the third, a mobile phone company charges customers a start-up fee that is 24 times the monthly rental and service charge. There is no specific accounting standard to cover any of these situations. One approach to each is to ask, 'Has the revenue been earned?' The companies would all answer 'yes, we have completed our side of the transaction'. So perhaps revenue should be recognised in all three cases. Another approach is to ask, 'Are there any risks related to recognising revenue?' The answer is 'yes – the programme may never be broadcast; we are not sure about the exchange values between cows and sheep; and the telephone company may not be able to provide the service for the long period implied by the high initial charge'. So perhaps the revenue should not be reported until the risks are diminished. Both views are being applied, with the result that there has been some lack of clarity and comparability as new types of business have emerged. It is necessary to pay careful attention to the accounting policy on revenue recognition.

9.12 Summary

Now score your view of your confidence in achieving the learning outcomes of the chapter.

1 = Very confident about knowledge, application, problem solving and evaluation.

2 = Confident about knowledge and application, less sure about problem solving and evaluation.

3 = Need to read again to be more certain of basic knowledge and application.

L01 You have learned the definition of 'current asset' and have applied that definition to identify current assets for presentation in a balance sheet.

1	2	3
☐	☐	☐

L02 You have read about the working capital cycle and can explain the need for all elements to contribute to the effectiveness of the cycle.

1	2	3
☐	☐	☐

L03 You are now able to explain the factors affecting recognition of stock, debtors and investments.

1	2	3
☐	☐	☐

L04 You have used the example of Safe and Sure to help you understand how the information presented in a company's balance sheet and notes, in relation to current assets, meets the needs of users.

1	2	3
☐	☐	☐

L05 You are now able to use numerical illustrations to explain the different approaches to measurement of stocks and cost of goods sold.

1	2	3
☐	☐	☐

L06 You are able to analyse provisions for doubtful debts using a spreadsheet, and explain the purpose of the provision.

1	2	3
☐	☐	☐

L07 You are able to analyse prepayments using a spreadsheet.

1	2	3
☐	☐	☐

L08 You are able to explain the term 'revenue' and the application of principles of revenue recognition in recognising revenue on contracts. You can also explain why some problems of revenue recognition are still under debate.

1	2	3
☐	☐	☐

L09 If you wish to be able to record debtors and prepayments in ledger accounts you should now work through the Supplement.

1	2	3
☐	☐	☐

If your scores are all 1 or 2, try the questions in the series A, B and C. This will give you feedback on your assessment of how well you have achieved the learning outcomes. Read again any sections of the chapter where you find your knowledge and understanding are less comprehensive than you first estimated.

If your scores include some at 3, try the series A questions to find where the problems lie. Read the relevant sections again, work through any illustrative examples and case studies, then try the questions in the series B. Once you feel confident at that level of knowledge and application, move on to try some or all of the series C questions.

International perspective

Some countries follow US practice in using the term 'accounts receivable' to describe trade debtors and 'accounts payable' to describe trade creditors. The US term 'inventories' may be used to describe stocks of raw materials and finished goods.

There are variations in the measurement of the value of unsold stocks. You have seen in section 9.8.5 the comparison of FIFO and LIFO methods of valuing stocks in times of changing prices. Companies in the UK commonly use the FIFO approach. The LIFO approach is not accepted by the Inland Revenue for tax purposes. Companies in the USA commonly use the LIFO approach. In some countries of continental Europe the average cost method is favoured. The diversity of practice makes it difficult for the IASB to produce an agreed international standard. Previous attempts to harmonise on the FIFO approach has met resistance but the IASB would still prefer to have one agreed approach worldwide.

S01 Test your understanding

Skills outcomes
S01 Application of technical skills   S02 Problem solving and evaluation skills   S03 Communication skills

L01, S01 **A9.1** What is the definition of a current asset?

L02, S01 **A9.2** What is the working capital cycle?

L03, S01 **A9.3** What are the features of raw materials, work-in-progress and finished goods which justify their recognition in a balance sheet?

L04, S01 **A9.4** What information do users need about current assets?

L05, S01 **A9.5** What is meant by FIFO, LIFO and the average cost method of pricing issues of goods?

L06, S01 **A9.6** How is a provision for doubtful debts decided upon?

L07, S01 **A9.7** What is a prepayment?

L08, S01 **A9.8** What is meant by *revenue recognition*?

L08, S01 **A9.9** Why are there problems with revenue recognition?

L05, S01 **A9.10** The Sycamore Company has trading stock which includes the following four items:

Description	Purchase cost £	Selling price £	Cost of selling £
Engine	6,500	8,250	350
Chassis	2,000	1,800	200
Frame	4,800	4,900	300

What amount should be reported as trading stock in respect of these three items?

L05, S01 **A9.11** On reviewing the company's financial statements, the company accountant discovers that items of year-end stock which cost £18,000 have been omitted from the record. What will be the effect on the profit and loss account and the balance sheet when this omission is rectified?

L06, S01 **A9.12** On reviewing the financial statements, the company accountant discovers that an amount of £154,000 owed by a customer will be irrecoverable because the customer has fled the country. What will be the effect on the profit and loss account and the balance sheet when this event is recognised?

Application

L05, S01 **B9.1** During its first month of operations, a business made purchases and sales as shown in the table below:

Date	Number of units purchased	Unit cost	Number of units sold
Jan. 5	100	£1.00	
Jan. 10			50
Jan. 15	200	£1.10	
Jan. 17			150
Jan. 24	300	£1.15	
Jan. 30			200

All sales were made at £2 each.

Required
Calculate the profit for the month and the stock value held at the end of the month using:

(a) the FIFO approach to the issue of units for sale, where:
  (i) the calculation is carried out at the date of sale; and
  (ii) the calculation is carried out at the end of the month without regard for the date of sale; and
(b) the LIFO approach to the issue of units for sale, where:
  (i) the calculation is carried out at the date of sale; and
  (ii) the calculation is carried out at the end of the month without regard for the date of sale; and
(c) the average-cost approach to the issue of units for sale, making the calculation at the end of the month without regard for the date of sale.

L05, S01 **B9.2** A company has a stock of goods consisting of four different groups of items. The cost and net realisable value of each group is shown in the table below.

Group of items	Cost £	Net realisable value £
A	1,000	1,400
B	1,000	800
C	2,100	1,900
D	3,000	3,100

Required
Calculate the amount to be shown as the value of the company's stock.

L06, S01 **B9.3** At the end of Year 3 the Bed Company has a balance sheet comprising £3,000 debtors, £8,000 other assets and £11,000 ownership interest, consisting of £2,000 ownership interest at the start of the period and £9,000 profit of the period. On the balance sheet date the manager of the company reviews the debtors list and decides that debts amounting to £450 are doubtful because the customers have not replied to repeated requests for payment.

Required
(a) Prepare an accounting equation spreadsheet to show the effect of the provision. (*See* Exhibit 9.3 for an illustration.)
(b) Show the balance sheet information. (*See* Exhibit 9.4 for an illustration.)

L06, S01 **B9.4** The Bed Company continues trading during Year 4. The balance sheet at the end of Year 4, in its first draft, showed debtors as £4,850 and the provision for doubtful debts unchanged from Year 3 at £450. Enquiry showed that during Year 4 some of the debtors at the end of Year 3 had been confirmed as bad. They amounted to £250 but nothing had yet been recorded. The management wish to make the provision £550 at the end of Year 4. Other assets amount to £12,000, ownership interest at the start of Year 4 is £10,550 and the profit is £5,750.

Required

Prepare an accounting equation spreadsheet to show the effect of the bad debt being recognised and of the decision to make a provision at the end of Year 4. (*See* Exhibit 9.5 for an illustration.)

L07, S01 **B9.5** On 1 December Year 1 a company paid £2,400 as an insurance premium to give accident cover for the 12 months ahead. The accounting year-end is 31 December.

Required

Prepare an accounting equation spreadsheet to show the effect of the prepayment in the year ended 31 December Year 1.

Problem solving and evaluation

L05, S02 **C9.1** A fire destroyed a company's detailed stock records and much of the merchandise held in stock. The company accountant was able to discover that stock at the beginning of the period was £40,000, purchases up to the date of the fire were £250,000, and sales up to the date of the fire were £400,000. In past periods, the company has earned a gross profit of 35 per cent of sales.

Required

Calculate the cost of the stock destroyed by the fire.

L06, S02 **C9.2** It is the policy of Seaton Ltd to make provision for doubtful debts at a rate of 10 per cent per annum on all debtor balances at the end of the year, after deducting any known bad debts at the same date. The following table sets out the total debtors as shown by the accounting records and known bad debts to be deducted from that total. There is no provision at 31 December Year 0.

Year-end	Debtor balances	Known bad debts
	£	£
31 Dec. Year 1	30,000	2,000
31 Dec. Year 2	35,000	3,000
31 Dec. Year 3	32,000	1,500
31 Dec. Year 4	29,000	1,000

Required

(a) Calculate the total expense in the profit and loss account in respect of bad and doubtful debts.

(b) Set out the balance sheet information in respect of debtors and provision for doubtful debts at each year-end.

Activities for study groups

Turn to the annual report of a listed company which you have used for activities in previous chapters. Find every item of information about current assets. (Start with the financial statements and notes but look also at the operating and financial review, chief executive's review and other non-regulated information about the company.)

As a group, imagine you are the team of fund managers in a fund management company. You are holding a briefing meeting at which each person explains to the others some feature of the companies in which your fund invests. Today's subject is current assets. Each person should make a short presentation to the rest of the team covering:

1 The nature and significance of current assets in the company.
2 The effect on profit of a 10 per cent error in estimation of any one of the major categories of current asset.
3 The company's comments, if any, on its present investment in working capital and its future intentions.
4 The risks which might attach to the stocks of the company.
5 The liquidity of the company.
6 The trends in current assets since last year (or over five years if a comparative table is provided).
7 The ratio of current assets to current liabilities.

Notes and references

1 ASB (1999) *Statement of Principles for Financial Reporting*, ch. 4, 'The elements of financial statements', para. 4.6.
2 Companies Act 1985, s. 262(1).
3 ASC (1988) SSAP 9, *Stocks and Long-Term Contracts*, para. 26, Accounting Standards Committee.
4 *Ibid.*, para. 17.
5 *Ibid.*, para. 18.
6 Companies Act 1985, sch. 4, s. 27.
7 ASC (1988) SSAP 9, App. 1, para. 12.
8 IASC (1993) IAS 18, *Revenue*, para. 7, International Accounting Standards Committee.
9 J. H. Myers (1959) 'The critical event and recognition of net profit', *Accounting Review*, **34**, pp. 528–32.
10 ASB (1999) *Statement of Principles for Financial Reporting*, ch. 5, paras 5.33–5.36.

Bookkeeping entries for (a) bad and doubtful debts; and (b) prepayments

The debit and credit recording aspects of stocks of raw materials and finished goods were explained in the Supplement to Chapter 6. That leaves, for this supplement, the recording of bad and doubtful debts as a new area where potential care is needed. Prepayments are also illustrated here.

Provision for doubtful debts

The following ledger accounts illustrate the recording of the transactions analysed in section 9.9. Look back to that section for the description and analysis of the transactions. The debit and credit analysis is shown in Exhibit 9.7. So that you will not be confused by additional information, the ledger accounts presented here show only sufficient information to illustrate the recording of transactions relating to doubtful debts. Leona comments on the main features.

Exhibit 9.7
Analysis of debit and credit aspect of each transaction and event

Date		Debit	Credit
Year 1			
End of year	Manager identifies doubtful debts £200	Profit and loss account £200	Provision for doubtful debts £200
Year 2			
July	Customer who was doubtful pays £200 in full	Cash £200	Debtors £200
End of year	Manager identifies new provision required £350	Profit and loss account £350	Provision for doubtful debts £350
End of year	Former provision no longer required	Provision for doubtful debts £200	Profit and loss account £200

The ledger accounts required are as follows:

L1   Debtors
L2   Provision for doubtful debts
L3   Cash
L4   Profit and loss account

Also required to complete the double entry, but not shown here as a ledger account, is ledger account L5 Ownership interest.

The full list of transactions for the year would be too cumbersome to deal with here, so dots are used to show that the ledger account requires more information for completeness.

L1 Debtors

Date	Particulars	Page	Debit	Credit	Balance
Year 1			£	£	£
	...			...	...
Dec. 31	Balance at end of year				2,000
Year 2					
	...			...	...
July	Cash from customer	L3		200	...
	...			...	...
Dec. 31	Balance at end of year				2,500

LEONA: *The ledger account for debtors has no entries relating to doubtful debts. That is important because although there may be doubts from the viewpoint of the business, the customer still has a duty to pay and should be encouraged by all the usual means. Keeping the full record of amounts due is an important part of ensuring that all assets of the business are looked after.*

L2 Provision for doubtful debts

Date	Particulars	Page	Debit	Credit	Balance
Year 1			£	£	£
Dec. 31	Profit and loss account – new provision	L4		200	(200)
Year 2					
Dec. 31	Profit and loss account – old provision	L4	200		nil
Dec. 31	Profit and loss account – new provision	L4		350	(350)

LEONA: *The provision for doubtful debts is a credit balance because it is the negative part of an asset. It keeps a separate record of doubt about the full value of the asset. A credit entry in the ledger account increases the amount of the provision and a debit entry decreases the amount of the provision.*

L3 Cash

Date	Particulars	Page	Debit	Credit	Balance
Year 2			£	£	£
	...		...		...
July	Cash from debtor	L1	200		
	...		...		...

LEONA: *Receiving cash from the doubtful customer looks like any other transaction receiving cash. It is important that the cash is collected and the debt is removed by receiving the full amount due.*

L4 Profit and loss account

Date	Particulars	Page	Debit	Credit	Balance
Year 1			£	£	£
	...		...		...
Dec. 31	Balance before provision for doubtful debts				(7,200)
Dec. 31	Provision for doubtful debts	L2	200		(7,000)
Dec. 31	Transfer to ownership interest	L5	7,000		nil
Year 2					
	...		...		...
Dec. 31	Balance before provision for doubtful debts				(3,500)
Dec. 31	Removal of provision no longer required	L2		200	(3,700)
Dec. 31	New provision for doubtful debts	L2	350		(3,350)
Dec. 31	Transfer to ownership interest	L5	3,350		nil

LEONA: *In Year 1 of this example the provision is established for the first time so there is one debit entry to establish an expense which decreases the profit (as a part of the ownership interest). In Year 2 of this example the old provision is removed and a new provision created. The overall effect is that the provision increases by £150. Some people would take a short-cut and make one entry of £150 to increase the provision from £200 to £350 but I am not keen on short-cuts. They sometimes lead to disaster. Separate entries make me think carefully about the effect of each.*

Recording a doubtful debt which turns bad

Suppose that in July of Year 2 it was found that the doubtful debt turned totally bad because the customer was declared bankrupt. The effect on the accounting equation is that the asset of debtor is removed. That would normally reduce the ownership interest but on this occasion the impact on ownership interest was anticipated at the end of Year 1 and so the provision for doubtful debts is now used to match the decrease in the asset. The analysis of the transaction would be:

Date	Transaction or event	Debit	Credit
Year 2			
July	Doubtful debt becomes bad	Provision for doubtful debts £200	Debtors £200

The consequence of using the provision for doubtful debts is that there is no impact on the profit and loss account of Year 2 of a bad debt which was known to be likely at the end of Year 1. However, when the provision for doubtful debts is reviewed at the end of Year 2 there is no reversal of the £200 because that has already been used during the year. The charge of £350 for Year 2 relates solely to the provision for doubt in respect of debtors owing money at the end of Year 2.

Prepayments

The prepayment transaction analysed in the chapter was as follows. On 1 October of Year 1 a company paid £1,200 for one year's vehicle insurance. At the balance sheet date of 31 December there have been three months' benefit used up and there is a nine-month benefit yet to come. (See Exhibit 9.8.)

Exhibit 9.8
Analysis of prepayment of insurance, Year 1

Date	Transaction or event	Debit	Credit
Year 2			
Oct. 1	Payment of premium £1,200	Expense (insurance)	Cash
Dec. 31	Identification of asset remaining as a prepayment £900	Asset (prepayment)	Expense (insurance)

Ledger accounts required to record the prepayment are:

L6 Expense of insurance
L7 Prepayment

Not shown, but necessary for completion of the debit and credit record, are:

L3   Cash
L4   Profit and loss account

L6 Expense of insurance

Date	Particulars	Page	Debit	Credit	Balance
Year 1			£	£	£
Oct. 31	Cash	L3	1,200		1,200
Dec. 31	Prepayment	L7		(900)	300
Dec. 31	Transfer to profit and loss account	L4		(300)	nil

LEONA: *Although it is known in October that there will be a balance remaining at the end of the year, it is usually regarded as more convenient to debit the entire payment as an expense of the period initially. The expense is reviewed at the end of the year and £900 is found to be an asset which benefits the future. It is transferred to the asset account for prepayments, leaving only the expense of £300 relating to this period, which is transferred to the profit and loss account.*

L7 Prepayment

Date	Particulars	Page	Debit	Credit	Balance
Year 1			£	£	£
Oct. 31	Insurance expense prepaid	L6	900		900

LEONA: *The prepayment account is an asset account and therefore the balance remains in the account until the benefit asset is used up. During Year 2 the benefit will disappear and the asset will become an expense. The bookkeeping treatment will be to credit the prepayment account and debit the insurance expense account.*

L09, S01 Test your understanding

S9.1 Record the transactions of question **B9.3** in ledger accounts for L1 Debtors, L2 Provision for doubtful debts, L3 Cash and L4 Profit and loss account.

S9.2 Record the transactions of question **B9.4** in ledger accounts for L1 Debtors, L2 Provision for doubtful debts, L3 Cash and L4 Profit and loss account.

S9.3 Record the transactions of question **B9.5** in ledger accounts for L6 Expense of insurance and L7 Prepayment.

Chapter 10

Liabilities due within one year

Contents

After studying this chapter you should be able to:

LO1 Define a liability and explain the distinguishing feature of liabilities due within one year.

LO2 Explain the conditions for recognition of liabilities.

LO3 Explain how the information presented in a company's balance sheet and notes, in relation to liabilities, meets the needs of users.

LO4 Explain the features of current liabilities and the approach to measurement and recording.

LO5 Explain the terms 'accruals' and 'matching concept' and show how they are applied to expenses of the period.

LO6 Explain how liabilities for taxation arise in companies.

Additionally, for those who choose to study the Supplement:

LO7 Prepare the ledger accounts to record accruals.

10.1 Introduction

The theme running through this textbook is the accounting equation:

Assets minus **Liabilities**	equals	**Ownership interest**

It was explained in Chapter 2 that the ownership interest is the residual amount found by deducting all liabilities of the company from total assets. Chapters 8 and 9 have taken you through aspects of fixed assets and current assets which are particularly significant to users of financial statements. Chapters 10 and 11 complete the left-hand side of the equation by providing a similar overview of liabilities due within one year and liabilities due after one year.

This chapter follows the approach established in Chapters 8 and 9:

● What are the rules for defining and recognising these items?
● What are the information needs of users in respect of the particular items?
● What information is currently provided by companies to meet these needs?
● Does the information show the desirable qualitative characteristics of financial statements?
● What are the rules for measuring, and processes for recording, these items?

LO1 ## 10.2 Definitions

The definition of a liability was provided in Chapter 2:

Definition *Liabilities* are defined as the obligations of an entity to transfer economic benefits as a result of past transactions or events.[1]

Everyday usage refers to *current liabilities* and *long-term liabilities*, which were explained in Chapter 2. Those titles, although they do not appear in the legislation, will be used in this chapter and the next as convenient short labels:

Definitions

Long-term liabilities are those liabilities expected to extend beyond one year from the balance sheet date.

Current liabilities are those liabilities expected to be repaid within one year of the balance sheet date.

These distinctions are required by the Companies Act 1985 when companies report information in the balance sheet. The supplement to Chapter 7 sets out the full specification of one of the balance sheet formats. There is no single heading for liabilities as a group but there are four main headings which are regarded as part of the liabilities section of the balance sheet. These are:

E   Creditors: amounts falling due within one year
H   Creditors: amounts falling due after more than one year
I   Provisions for liabilities and charges
J   Accruals and deferred income.

If you look at the supplement to Chapter 7 you will see that accruals and deferred income are listed at heading J but also appear at item E9. This allows some flexibility for the preparers of financial statements. We will use that flexibility in this chapter by dealing with accruals separately from deferred income. Sections H and I of the formats are dealt with in Chapter 11, together with the deferred income of section J.

L01 | **Activity 10.1**

Look back to Chapter 2 and Exhibit 2.3, which analyses some common types of liability. Set up on a blank sheet a similar table with four columns and headings for: type of liability; obligation; transfer of economic benefits; and past transaction or event. Then close the textbook and write down any ten liabilities you have come across during your study. Fill in all the columns as a check that, at this stage, you really understand what creates a liability.

L02 | ## 10.3 Recognition

The general conditions for recognition were set out in Chapter 2. An item that meets the definition of a liability should be recognised if there is sufficient evidence that the liability has been created and that the item has a cost or value that can be measured with sufficient reliability. In practice, recognition problems related to liabilities centre on ensuring that none is omitted which ought to be included. This is in contrast to the case of assets where there is a need, in practice, to guard against over-enthusiastic inclusion of items which do not meet the recognition conditions.

10.3.1 Risk of understatement of liabilities

The risk related to liabilities is therefore the risk of understatement. This is explained in Chapter 4 under the heading of *prudence*. The risk of understatement of liabilities is that it will result in overstatement of the ownership interest.

In recent years the standard-setting bodies have devoted quite strenuous efforts to discouraging companies from keeping liabilities (and related assets) off the balance sheet. This problem is called *off-balance sheet finance* and will be explained in Chapter 15.

10.3.2 Non-recognition: contingent liabilities

There are some obligations of the company which fail the recognition test because there is significant uncertainty about future events that may cause benefits to flow from the company. The uncertainty may be about the occurrence of the event or about the measurement of the consequences. These are called *contingent liabilities* because they are contingent upon (depend upon) some future event happening. Examples are:

- A company is involved in legal action where a customer is seeking damages for illness allegedly caused by the company's product. If the customer is successful, there will be more claims. The company does not believe that the customer will succeed.
- A parent company has given guarantees to a bank that it will meet the overdraft and loans of a subsidiary company if that company defaults on repayment. At the present time there is no reason to suppose that any default will take place.
- A company is under investigation by the Director General of Fair Trading for possible price-fixing within the industry in contravention of an order prohibiting restrictive practices. If there is found to be a restrictive practice, a penalty may be imposed.
- The company has acquired a subsidiary in Australia where the tax authorities have raised an action for tax due on a disputed transaction which occurred before the subsidiary was acquired. The action is being defended strenuously.

In each of these examples, the company is convinced that it will not have a liability at the end of the day, but the users of the financial statements may wish to have some indication of the upper bounds of the liability if the company's optimism proves unfounded. There may, however, be a problem for the company in publishing an estimate of the amount of the possible liability because it may be seen as admitting liability and furthermore may require disclosure of commercially sensitive confidential information.

Where a contingent liability is identified, the obligation is not recognised in the balance sheet but it may be important that users of the financial statements are aware of the problem. There will therefore be a note to the balance sheet reporting the circumstances of the contingent liability and sometimes giving an indication of the amount involved. Because of the confidentiality aspect, companies tend to give little information about the financial effect of a contingent liability, but some will try to set the outer limits of the liability.

Definition

> A *contingent liability* is:
> either:
> (a) a possible obligation that arises from past events and whose existence will be confirmed only by the occurrence of one or more uncertain future events not wholly within the entity's control;
> or:
> (b) a present obligation that arises from past events but is not recognised because:
> either: (i) it is not probable that a transfer of economic benefits will be required to settle the obligation;
> or: (ii) the amount of the obligation cannot be measured with sufficient reliability.[2]

It is a requirement of the relevant accounting standard and of company law that the company should disclose a brief description of the nature of the contingent liability and, where practicable:

(a) an estimate of its financial effect;
(b) an indication of the uncertainties relating to the amount or timing of any outflow; and
(c) the possibility of any reimbursement.[3]

Rules about measurement are given in detail in the accounting standard. The detail is not necessary for an introductory course.

L02 **Activity 10.2**

> *Consider the four examples of contingent liability given at the start of this section. Based on the definition, explain why each is a contingent liability.*

L03 ## 10.4 Users' needs for information

There are two aspects of information in relation to liabilities. The first relates to the amount owed (sometimes called the *principal sum* or the *capital amount*) and the second relates to the cost of servicing the loan (usually the payment of *interest*).

In respect of current liabilities, other than a bank overdraft or bank loans repayable within the year, it is unlikely that interest will be payable, and so generally there will be no information about interest charges. The shareholders in the company will be concerned that there are adequate current assets to meet the current liabilities as they fall due. Those who supply goods and services will want to be reassured that payment will be made on the due date.

Owners of a company need to know how much the company owes to other parties because the owners are at the end of the queue when it comes to sharing out the assets of the company if it closes down. Many of those who supply goods and services are what is known as unsecured creditors, which means they come at the end of the list of creditors. They will also have an interest in the balance of long-term and current liabilities.

L03   10.5 Information provided in the financial statements

The balance sheet of Safe and Sure plc, set out in Chapter 7, contains the following information in relation to current liabilities:

		Notes	Year 7 £m	Year 6 £m
Current liabilities				
due within	Creditors	6	(189.3)	(170.2)
one year	Bank and other borrowings	7	(40.1)	(74.3)
			(229.4)	(244.5)

Notes to the balance sheet explain more about the balance sheet items. Note 6 takes advantage of the rule which allows items with arabic numbering in the Companies Act format to appear as a note to the balance sheet:

Note 6		Year 7 £m	Year 6 £m
Creditors due	Deferred consideration on acquisition	1.1	4.3
within one year	Trade creditors	23.6	20.4
	Dividends payable	23.8	19.6
	Corporation tax	31.5	26.5
	Other tax and social security payable	24.5	21.2
	Other creditors	30.7	23.8
	Accruals and deferred income	54.1	54.4
		189.3	170.2

Note 7 gives information on the extent to which loans due for repayment within one year are secured on assets and also confirms that the interest charges incurred on these loans are payable at commercial rates:

Note 7		Year 7 £m	Year 6 £m
Bank and other	*Bank loans and overdrafts due*		
borrowings due	*within one year or on demand:*		
within one year	Secured	0.4	0.4
	Unsecured	39.7	73.9
		40.1	74.3

Interest on bank loans and overdrafts, and on other loans due within one year, which are denominated in a number of currencies, is payable at normal commercial rates appropriate to the country where the borrowing is made. Bank loans amounting to £0.4m (Year 6: £0.4m) are secured on certain assets of the group.

The report of the finance director provides further insight into the currency spread of the bank borrowings:

Foreign currency: £35.2m of foreign currency bank borrowings have been incurred to fund overseas acquisition. The main borrowings were £26.8m in US dollars and £8.4m in Japanese yen. The borrowings are mainly from banks on a short-term basis, with a maturity of up to one year, and we have fixed the interest rate on $20m of the US dollar loans through to November, Year 7, at an overall cost of 4.46 per cent.

All material foreign currency transactions are matched back into the currency of the group company undertaking the transaction.

David Wilson has already commented in Chapters 4 and 7 on some aspects of the liabilities in the financial statements of Safe and Sure plc. Here he is explaining to Leona, in the coffee bar at the health club, his views on current liabilities in particular.

DAVID: *Creditors due within one year are up compared with the previous year but the increase is mainly due to tax payable. That is the price of successful growth of cash flows and profits, so there are no particular questions to ask there.*

Then I start to think about the limits of risk. There is £40m due for repayment to the bank within the year. Will the company have any problem finding this amount? With £107m in short-term deposits and £147m collectable from debtors, it seems unlikely. The entire current liabilities are £229m, all of which could be met from the deposits and debtors.

There is another risk that £40m shown as owing to the banks may be the wrong measure of the liability if exchange rates move against the company. Whenever I see foreign borrowings I want to know more about the currency of borrowings. You know from your economics class the theory of interest rates and currency exchange rates. It backs up my rule of thumb that borrowing in currencies which are weak means paying high rates of interest. Borrowing in currencies which are strong will mean paying lower rates of interest but runs a greater risk of having to use up additional pounds sterling to repay the loan if the foreign currency strengthens more. Information about the currency mix of loans is something I can probably get from the company if I need it. In this case, the finance director's report is sufficiently informative for my purposes. In past years, before finance directors started providing explanations in the annual report, we were asking these questions at face-to-face meetings.

LEONA: *What you have described is similar in many respects to the analytical review carried out by the auditors. We do much more than merely check the bookkeeping entries and the paperwork. We are looking at whether the balance sheet makes sense and whether any items have changed without sufficient explanation.*

LO4 10.6 Measurement and recording

Liabilities are measured at the amount originally received from the lender of finance or supplier of goods and services, plus any additional charges incurred such as rolled-up interest added to a loan. This is generally agreed to be a useful measure of the obligation to transfer economic benefits from the company.

From the accounting equation it may be seen that an increase in a liability must be related either to an increase in an asset or a decrease in the ownership interest. Usually any related decrease in the ownership interest will be reported in the balance sheet as an expense.

The most significant current liabilities for most companies are bank borrowing and trade creditors. Both of these are essential sources of finance for small companies and are an important aspect, if not essential, for larger companies.

L04

Activity 10.3

Write down the documentation you would expect to see as evidence of the money amount of the following liabilities:

● *bank overdraft;*
● *amount owing to a trade supplier.*

Now read the next sections and find whether your answer matches the information in the text.

10.6.1 Bank overdraft finance

Banks provide short-term finance to companies in the form of an overdraft on a current account. The advantage of an overdraft is its flexibility. When the cash needs of the company increase with seasonal factors, the company can continue to write cheques and watch the overdraft increase. When the goods and services are sold and cash begins to flow in, the company should be able to watch the overdraft decrease again. The most obvious example of a business which operates in this pattern is farming. The farmer uses the overdraft to finance the acquisition of seed for arable farming, or feed through the winter for stock farming and to cover the period when the crops or animals are growing and maturing. The overdraft is reduced when the crops or the animals are sold.

The main disadvantage of an overdraft is that it is repayable on demand. The farmer whose crop fails because of bad weather knows the problem of being unable to repay the overdraft. Having overdraft financing increases the worries of those who manage the company. The other disadvantage is that the interest payable on overdrafts is variable. When interest rates increase, the cost of the overdraft increases. Furthermore, for small companies there are often complaints that the rate of interest charged is high compared with that available to larger companies. The banks answer that the rates charged reflect relative risk and it is their experience that small companies are more risky.

10.6.2 Trade creditors

It is a strong feature of many industries that one enterprise is willing to supply goods to another in advance of being paid. Most suppliers will state terms of payment (e.g. the invoice must be paid within 30 days) and some will offer a discount for prompt payment. In the United Kingdom it has not been traditional to charge interest on overdue accounts but this practice is growing as companies realise there is a high cost to themselves of not collecting cash from their customers.

Trade creditors rarely have any security for payment of the amount due to them, so that if a customer fails to pay they must wait in the queue with other suppliers and hope for a share of some distribution. They are described as *unsecured creditors*. Some suppliers will include in the contract a condition that the goods remain the property of the supplier should the customer fail to pay. This is called *retention of title* and will be noted in the balance sheet of a company which has bought goods on these terms. Retention of title may offer some protection to the unpaid supplier but requires very prompt action to recover identifiable goods in the event of difficulty.

Some suppliers send goods to a customer on a *sale-or-return* basis. If there are no conditions to prevent return then the goods will not appear as stock in the balance sheet of the customer and there will be no indication of a liability. This practice is particularly common in the motor industry where manufacturers send cars to showrooms for sale or return within a specified period of time. Omitting the stock and the related potential liability is referred to as *off-balance sheet finance*, a topic explored further in Chapter 15.

Suppliers send *invoices* to the customer showing the amount due for payment. These invoices are used in the customer's accounts department as the source of information for liabilities. At the end of the month the suppliers send *statements* as a reminder of unpaid invoices. Statements are useful as additional evidence of liabilities to suppliers.

Measurement of trade creditors is relatively straightforward because the company will know how much it owes to short-term creditors. If it forgets the creditors, they will soon issue a reminder.

Recording requires some care because omission of any credit transaction will mean there is an understatement of a liability. In particular, the company has to take some care at the end of the year over what are called *cut-off procedures*. Take the example of raw materials provided by a supplier. The goods arrive at the company's store by delivery van but the invoice for their payment arrives a few days later by mail. The accounts department uses the supplier's invoice as the document which initiates the *recording* of the asset of stock and the liability to the supplier. In contrast, the event which *creates* the liability is the acceptance of the goods. (It is difficult for the accounts department to use the delivery note as a record of the liability because it shows the quantities but not the price of the goods delivered.) So, at the end of the accounting year the accounts department has to compare the most recent delivery notes signed by the storekeeper with the most recent invoices received from the supplier. If goods have been received by the company, the balance sheet must include the asset of stock and the related liability. Using a similar line of reasoning, if a supplier has sent an invoice ahead of delivery of the goods, it should not be recorded as a liability because there is no related asset.

The recording of purchases of goods for resale is shown in Chapter 6. In the illustration of the process for recording the transactions of M. Carter there is a purchase of goods from the supplier, R. Busby, on credit terms. Payment is made later in the month. The purchase of the goods creates the asset of stock and the liability to the supplier. Payment to the supplier reduces the asset of cash and eliminates the liability to the supplier.

L05 10.7 Accruals and the matching concept

At the balance sheet date there will be obligations of the company to pay for goods or services which are not contained in the accounting records because no document has been received from the supplier of the goods or services. It is essential that all obligations are included at the balance sheet date because these obligations fall under the definition of liabilities even although the demand for payment has not been received. The process of including in the balance sheet all obligations at the end of the period is called the *accrual of liabilities* and is said to reflect the *accruals concept* (*see* Chapter 4).

The argument contained in the previous paragraph is based on the definition of a liability, but some people prefer to arrive at the same conclusion using a different argument. They say that all expenses of the accounting period must be matched against the revenue earned in the period. If a benefit has been consumed, the effect must be recorded whether or not documentation has been received. This argument is referred to as the *matching concept*.

In the *Statement of Principles*, the ASB explains that matching has two forms: time matching and revenue/expenditure matching. Time matching involves recognising an expense or loss over the period of time in which it occurs. Revenue/expenditure matching involves recognising an expense in the profit and loss account to match the revenue to which it relates.[4] Matching is not the main driver of the *Statement of Principles* because it could be used to delay recognition of expenses with the risk that hoped-for benefits never actually happen.[5]

The accruals concept and the matching concept are, for most practical purposes, different ways of arriving at the same conclusion. (There are exceptions but these are well beyond the scope of a first-level text.) A definition which expresses both ideas is as follows:

Definition The *accruals* (or *matching*) *concept* states that all income and charges relating to the financial year to which the accounts relate shall be taken into account, without regard to the date of receipt and payment.[6]

10.7.1 The distinction between the expense of the period and the cash paid

A company starts business on 1 January Year 1. It has a financial year-end of 31 December Year 1. During Year 1 it receives four accounts for electricity, all of which are paid ten days after receiving them. The dates of receiving and paying the accounts are as follows:

Date invoice received	Amount of invoice £	Date paid
31 Mar. Year 1	350	10 Apr. Year 1
30 June Year 1	180	10 July Year 1
30 Sept. Year 1	280	10 Oct. Year 1
31 Dec. Year 1	340	10 Jan. Year 2
	1,150	

The company has used electricity for the entire year and therefore should match against revenue the full cost of £1,150. Only three invoices have been paid during the year, the final invoice not being paid until the start of Year 2. That is important for cash flow but is not relevant for the measurement of profit. The transactions during the year would be recorded as shown in Exhibit 10.1. The arrival of the electricity invoice causes a record to be made of the increase in the liability and the increase in the expense (decreasing the ownership interest). The payment of the amount due requires a separate record to be made of the decrease in the liability and the decrease in the asset of cash.

Exhibit 10.1

Spreadsheet analysis of transactions relating to the expense of electricity consumed, Year 1

Date	Transactions with electricity company	Asset	Liability	Ownership interest:profit of the period
		Cash	Electricity company	Electricity expense
Year 1		£	£	£
Mar. 31	Invoice received £350		350	(350)
Apr. 10	Pay electricity company £350	(350)	(350)	
June 30	Invoice received £180		180	(180)
July 10	Pay electricity company £180	(180)	(180)	
Sept. 30	Invoice received £280		280	(280)
Oct. 10	Pay electricity company £280	(280)	(280)	
Dec. 31	Invoice received £340		340	(340)
	Totals	(810)	340	(1,150)

The payment made to the electricity company in January Year 2 is not recorded in Exhibit 10.1 because it is not a transaction of Year 1. It will appear in a spreadsheet for January Year 2. The totals at the foot of the spreadsheet show that the transactions of Year 1 have caused the cash of the company to decrease by £810. There remains a liability of £340 to the electricity company at the end of Year 1. The profit and loss account for the year will show an expense of £1,150. The spreadsheet satisfies the accounting equation because there is a decrease in an asset, amounting to £810, and an increase in a liability amounting to £340. These together equal the decrease of £1,150 in the ownership interest:

Asset ↓	–	**Liability** ↑	=	**Ownership interest** ↓
– £810		+ £340		– £1,150

That one needs a little careful thought because several things are happening at once. You might prefer to think about it one stage at a time. You know from earlier examples in Chapters 2, 5 and 6 that a decrease in an asset causes a decrease in the ownership interest. You also know that an increase in a liability causes a decrease in the ownership interest. Put them together and they are both working in the same direction to decrease the ownership interest.

10.7.2 Accrual where no invoice has been received

Now consider what might happen if the final electricity invoice for the year has not been received on 31 December Year 1. If no invoice has been received then there will be no entry in the accounting records. That, however, would fail to acknowledge that the electricity has been consumed and the company knows there is an obligation to pay for that electricity. In terms of the matching concept, only nine months' invoices are available to match against revenue when there has been 12 months' usage. The answer is that the company must make an *estimate* of the *accrual* of the liability for electricity consumed. Estimates will seldom give the true answer but they can be made reasonably close if some care is taken. If the company keeps a note of electricity meter readings and knows the unit charge, it can calculate what the account would have been.

The entries in the spreadsheet at the end of the month are shown in Exhibit 10.2. They will be the same numerically as those in the final line of Exhibit 10.1 but the item shown at 31 December will be described as an accrual.

Exhibit 10.2
Spreadsheet entry for accrual at the end of the month

Date	Transactions with electricity company	Asset	Liability	Ownership interest:profit of the period
		Cash	Electricity company	Electricity expense
Year 1		£	£	£
Dec. 31	Accrual for three months		340	(340)

10.7.3 The nature of estimates in accounting

Making an accrual for a known obligation, where no invoice has been received, requires estimates. In the example given here it was a relatively straightforward matter to take a meter reading and calculate the expected liability. There will be other examples where the existence and amount of an expense are both known with reasonable certainty. There will be some cases where the amount has to be estimated and the estimate is later found to be incorrect. That is a normal feature of accounting, although not all users of financial statements realise there is an element of uncertainty about the information provided. If a liability is unintentionally understated at the end of a period, the profit will be overstated. In the next accounting period, when the full obligation becomes known, the expense incurred will be higher than was anticipated and the profit of that period will be lower than it should ideally be. If the error in the estimate is found to be such that it would change the views of the main users of financial statements, a *prior year adjustment* may be made by recalculating the profits of previous years and reporting the effect, but that is a relatively rare occurrence.

L05 **Activity 10.4**

Write down five types of transaction where you might expect to see an accrual of expense at the year-end. Against each transaction type write down the method you would use to estimate the amount of the accrued expense.

L06 # 10.8 Liabilities for taxation

In the balance sheet of a company there are two main categories of liability related directly to the company. The first is the *corporation tax* payable, based on the taxable profits of the period, the second is *deferred taxation*. Each of these will be discussed here. You will also see in the current liabilities section of a balance sheet the words 'other tax and social security payable'. This refers to the amounts deducted from employees' salaries and wages by the company on behalf of the Inland Revenue and paid over at regular intervals. In respect of such amounts the company is acting as a tax collecting agent of the Inland Revenue.

10.8.1 Corporation tax

Companies pay corporation tax based on the taxable profit of the accounting period (usually one year). The taxable profit is calculated according to the rules of tax law. That in itself is a subject for an entire textbook but one basic principle is that the taxable profit is based on profit calculated according to commercially accepted accounting practices. So, apart from some specific points of difference, the accounting profit is usually quite close to the taxable profit. Assume that the corporation tax rate is 30 per cent of the taxable profit. (The tax rate each year is set by the Chancellor of the Exchequer.) Analysts will evaluate the tax charge in the profit and loss account as a percentage of taxable profit and start to ask questions when the answer is very different from 30 per cent. The explanation could be that there are profits earned abroad where the tax rate is different, but it could also be that there has been some use of provisions or adjustments for accounting purposes which are not allowed for tax purposes. That will lead to more probing by the analysts to establish whether they share the doubts of the tax authorities.

Large companies must pay corporation tax by four quarterly instalments. A company with a year-end of 31 December Year 1 will pay on 14 July Year 1, 14 October Year 1, 14 January Year 2 and 14 April Year 2. The amount of tax due is estimated by making a forecast of the profit for the year. As the year progresses the forecast is revised and the tax calculation is also revised. This means that at the end of the accounting year there is a liability for half that year's tax bill. A 'large' company is any company that pays corporation tax at the full rate. Small companies, which have a special, lower, rate of corporation tax, pay their tax bill nine months after the end of the accounting period. The precise limits for defining 'large' and 'small' companies change with tax legislation each year. (You will be given the necessary information in any exercise that you are asked to attempt.) Suppose the taxable profit is £10m and the tax payable at 30 per cent is £3m. During the year £1.5m is paid in total on the first two instalment dates. At the balance sheet date there will remain a liability of £1.5m to be paid in total on the final two instalment dates.

	Assets	–	Liabilities	=	Ownership interest
During year	↓ £1.5m Cash				↓ £1.5m (Tax expense)
At end of year			↑ £1.5m Tax liability		↓ £1.5m (Tax expense)

10.8.2 Deferred taxation liability

It was explained earlier in this section that the taxable profit is based on the accounting profit unless there are taxation rules which indicate otherwise. There are taxation rules which allow companies to defer the payment of some taxation on the full accounting profit. (*Deferring* means paying much later than the normal period of nine months.) The deferral period might be for a few months or it might be for a few years. The obligation to pay tax eventually cannot be escaped but the liability becomes long term. This is reflected, in terms of the accounting equation, by reporting the decrease in ownership claim in the profit and loss account but showing the deferred liability as a separate item under *liabilities due after one year*.

10.9 Summary

Now score your view of your confidence in achieving the learning outcomes of the chapter.

1 = Very confident about knowledge, application, problem solving and evaluation.

2 = Confident about knowledge and application, less sure about problem solving and evaluation.

3 = Need to read again to be more certain of basic knowledge and application.

LO1 You have learned the definition of a liability and the features that distinguish liabilities due within one year.

1 ☐ 2 ☐ 3 ☐

LO2 You can now explain the conditions for recognition of liabilities, and particularly the risks of failing to recognise a liability that ought to be reported in the balance sheet.

1 ☐ 2 ☐ 3 ☐

LO3 You have learned to explain, using the example of Safe and Sure, how the information on liabilities presented in a company's balance sheet and notes meets the needs of users.

1 ☐ 2 ☐ 3 ☐

LO4 You are now able to explain the features of current liabilities and the approach to measurement and recording of these.

1 ☐ 2 ☐ 3 ☐

LO5 You are able to explain the terms 'accruals' and 'matching concept' and you have learned how to apply these ideas to recording the expenses of the period in an accounting equation spreadsheet.

1 ☐ 2 ☐ 3 ☐

LO6 You are now able to explain how liabilities for taxation arise in companies.

1 ☐ 2 ☐ 3 ☐

LO7 If you wish to learn how to prepare the ledger accounts to record accruals, you should now turn to the Supplement.

1 ☐ 2 ☐ 3 ☐

If your scores are all 1 or 2, try the questions in the series A, B and C. This will give you feedback on your assessment of how well you have achieved the learning outcomes. Read again any sections of the chapter where you find your knowledge and understanding are less comprehensive than you first estimated.

   If your scores include some at 3, try the series A questions to find where the problems lie. Read the relevant sections again, work through any illustrative examples and case studies, then try the questions in the series B. Once you feel confident at that level of knowledge and application, move on to try some or all of the series C questions.

International perspective

Accruals accounting is widely used. The attitude to prudence, verging on strong conservatism, may affect the recognition of liabilities and the balance between recognition as a liability and disclosure as a contingent liability.

Test your understanding

Skills outcomes
S01 Application of technical skills   S02 Problem solving and evaluation skills   S03 Communication skills

L01, S01   **A10.1** What is the definition of a liability?

L01, S01   **A10.2** What is the distinction between a long-term liability and a current liability?

L02, S01   **A10.3** What is the effect of understatement of liabilities?

L02, S01   **A10.4** What is a contingent liability?

L03, S01   **A10.5** What information do users of financial statements need to have concerning current liabilities of a company?

L04, S01   **A10.6** How are the current liabilities for (a) bank overdraft and (b) trade creditors measured?

L05, S01   **A10.7** What is meant by an accrual? How is it recorded?

L05, S01   **A10.8** Explain what is meant by the matching concept.

L04, S01   **A10.9** On reviewing the financial statements, the company accountant discovers that a supplier's invoice for an amount of £10,000 has been omitted from the accounting records. The goods to which the invoice relates are held in the warehouse and are included in stock. What will be the effect on the profit and loss account and the balance sheet when this error is rectified?

L04, S01   **A10.10** On reviewing the financial statements, the company accountant discovers that a payment of £21,000 made to a supplier has been omitted from the cash book and other internal accounting records. What will be the effect on the profit and loss account and the balance sheet when this omission is rectified?

L05, S01   **A10.11** On reviewing the financial statements, the company accountant discovers that an invoice for the rent of £4,000 owed to its landlord has been recorded incorrectly as rent receivable of £4,000 in the company's accounting records. What will be the effect on the profit and loss account and the balance sheet when this error is rectified?

Application

L05, S01   **B10.1** White Ltd commenced trading on 1 July Year 3 and draws up its accounts for the year ended 30 June Year 4. During its first year of trading the company pays total telephone expenses of £3,500. The three-month bill paid in May Year 4 includes calls of £800 for the quarter up to 30 April Year 4 and advance rental of £660 to 31 July Year 4. The bill received in August Year 4 includes calls of £900 for the quarter up to 31 July Year 4 and advance rental of £660 to 31 October Year 4.

Required

Show calculations of the telephone expense to be recorded in the profit and loss account of White Ltd for its first year of trading.

L05, S01 B10.2 Plastics Ltd pays rent for a warehouse used for storage. The quarterly charge for security guard services is £800. The security firm sends an invoice on 31 March, 30 June, 30 September and 31 December. Plastics Ltd always pays the rent five days after the invoice is received. The security services have been used for some years. Plastics Ltd has an accounting year-end of 31 December.

Required

Prepare a spreadsheet to show how the transactions of one year in respect of security services are recorded.

L06, S01 B10.3 The accountant of Brown Ltd has calculated that the company should report in its profit and loss account a tax charge of £8,000 based on the taxable profit of the period. Of this amount, £6,000 will be payable nine months after the accounting year-end but £2,000 may be deferred for payment in a period estimated at between three and five years after the accounting year-end. Using the accounting equation explain how this information will be reported in the financial statements of Brown Ltd.

Problem solving and evaluation

L05, S02 C10.1 The following file of papers was found in a cupboard of the general office of Green Ltd at the end of the accounting year. Explain how each would be treated in the financial statements and state the total amount to be reported as an accrued liability on the balance sheet date. The year-end is 31 December Year 1.

Item	Description	Amount £
1	Invoice dated 23 December for goods received 21 December.	260
2	Invoice dated 23 December for goods to be delivered on 3 January Year 2.	310
3	Foreman's note of electricity consumption for month of December – no invoice yet received from electricity supply company.	100
4	Letter from employee claiming overtime payment for work on 1 December and note from personnel office denying entitlement to payment.	58
5	Telephone bill dated 26 December showing calls for October to December.	290
6	Telephone bill dated 26 December showing rent due in advance for period January to March Year 2.	90
7	Note of payment due to cleaners for final week of December (to be paid on 3 January under usual pattern of payment one week in arrears).	48
8	Invoice from supplier for promotional calendars received 1 December (only one-third have yet been sent to customers).	300
9	Letter dated 21 December Year 1 to customer promising a cheque to reimburse damage caused by faulty product – cheque to be sent on 4 January Year 2.	280
10	Letter dated 23 December promising donation to local charity – amount not yet paid.	60

Activities for study groups

Turn to the annual report of a listed company which you have used for activities in previous chapters. Find every item of information about current liabilities. (Start with the financial statements and notes but look also at the operating and financial review, chief executive's review and other non-regulated information about the company.)

Divide into two groups. One group should take on the role of the purchasing director and one should take on the role of a company which has been asked to supply goods or services to this company on credit terms.

- *Supplier group:* What questions would you ask to supplement what you have learned from the annual report?
- *Purchasing director:* What questions would you ask about the supplier? What might you learn about the supplier from the annual report of the supplier's company?

Notes and references

1 ASB (1999) *Statement of Principles for Financial Reporting*, ch. 4, 'The elements of financial statements', para. 4.23.
2 ASB (1998) FRS 12, *Provisions, Contingent Liabilities and Contingent Assets*, Accounting Standards Board, para. 2.
3 *Ibid.*, para. 91.
4 ASB (1999) *Statement of Principles for Financial Reporting*, ch. 5, para. 5.28.
5 *Ibid.*, para. 5.29.
6 ASB (2000) FRS 18, *Accounting Policies*, App. II, para. 3(d).

Bookkeeping entries for accruals

In the main part of the chapter the accruals for electricity were analysed. Now consider the debit and credit recording. The following transactions are to be recorded.

A company starts business on 1 January Year 1. It has a financial year-end of 31 December Year 1. During Year 1 it receives three accounts for electricity, all of which are paid ten days after receiving them. The dates of receiving and paying the accounts are as follows:

Amount of invoice £	Date invoice received	Date paid
350	31 Mar. Year 1	10 Apr. Year 1
180	30 June Year 1	10 July Year 1
280	30 Sept. Year 1	10 Oct. Year 1

At 31 December the final invoice for the year has not arrived because of delays in the mail but the amount due for payment is estimated at £340.

L07 **Activity 10.5**

Before you read further, attempt to write down the debit and credit entries for: each of the three invoices received; the payments of those three invoices; and the estimated amount due for payment at the end of the year. You may find help in looking back to Exhibits 10.1 and 10.2.

Exhibit 10.3
Analysis of debit and credit aspect of each transaction and event

Date	Transaction	Debit	Credit
Year 1			
Mar. 31	Receive invoice for electricity £350	Expense (electricity)	Liability to supplier
Apr. 10	Pay supplier £350	Liability to supplier	Cash
June 30	Receive invoice for electricity £180	Expense (electricity)	Liability to supplier
July 10	Pay supplier £180	Liability to supplier	Cash
Sept. 30	Receive invoice for electricity £280	Expense (electricity)	Liability to supplier
Oct. 10	Pay supplier £280	Liability to supplier	Cash
Dec. 31	Estimate amount owing to supplier £340	Expense (electricity)	Accruals

Exhibit 10.3 sets out the debit and credit aspect of each transaction and event. The amount of the liability to the supplier cannot be recorded until the invoice is received. The credit entry for the estimate of the amount owing to the supplier is therefore shown in a separate account called *accruals* which will be the basis for the amount shown in the balance sheet under that heading.

The ledger accounts required here are:

L1 Expense (electricity)
L2 Liability to supplier
L3 Accrual

Also required to complete the double entry, but not shown here as a ledger account, are:

L4 Cash
L5 Profit and loss account

L1 Expense (Electricity)

Date	Particulars	Page	Debit	Credit	Balance
Year 1			£	£	£
Mar. 31	Invoice from supplier	L2	350		350
June 30	Invoice from supplier	L2	180		530
Sept. 30	Invoice from supplier	L2	280		810
Dec. 31	Estimated accrual	L3	340		1,150
Dec. 31	Transfer to profit and loss account	L5		(1,150)	nil

LEONA: *The electricity account for the year shows a full 12 months' expense which is transferred to the profit and loss account at the end of the year.*

L2 Liability to supplier

Date	Particulars	Page	Debit	Credit	Balance
Year 1			£	£	£
Mar. 31	Invoice for electricity expense	L1		350	(350)
Apr. 10	Cash paid	L4	350		nil
June 30	Invoice for electricity expense	L1		180	(180)
July 10	Cash paid	L4	180		nil
Sept. 30	Invoice for electricity expense	L1		280	(280)
Oct. 10	Cash paid	L4	280		nil

LEONA: *The supplier's account is showing a nil liability because all invoices received have been paid. We know there is another invoice on the way but the bookkeeping system is quite strict about only making entries in the ledger when the documentary evidence is obtained. The document in this case is the supplier's invoice. Until it arrives the liability has to be recognised as an accrual rather than in the supplier's account.*

L3 Accruals

Date	Particulars	Page	Debit	Credit	Balance
Year 1			£	£	£
Dec. 31	Estimate of electricity expense	L1	340	(340)	

LEONA: *The balance sheet will record a nil liability to the supplier but will show an accrual of £340 for electricity. When the supplier's invoice arrives in January of Year 2, the debit and credit entries will be:*

Date	Transaction	Debit	Credit
Year 2			
Jan. 4	Receive invoice for electricity £340	Accrual	Liability to supplier

In this way the liability remaining from Year 1 is recorded without affecting the expense account for Year 2. The credit balance on the accrual account at the end of Year 1 is eliminated by being matched against the debit entry at the start of Year 2.

L07, S01 Test your understanding

S10.1 Prepare bookkeeping records for the information in question **B10.1**.

S10.2 Prepare bookkeeping records for the information in question **B10.2**.

S10.3 Prepare bookkeeping records for the information in question **B10.3**.

S10.4 Prepare bookkeeping records for the information in question **C10.1**.

Chapter 11

Provisions and long-term liabilities

Contents

After studying this chapter you should be able to:

LO1 Define a long-term liability.

LO2 Explain the needs of users for information about long-term liabilities.

LO3 Explain the different types of long-term loan finance which may be found in the balance sheets of major companies.

LO4 Understand the purpose of provisions and explain how provisions are reported in financial statements.

LO5 Understand the nature of deferred income and explain how it is reported in financial statements.

LO6 Know the main types of loan finance and capital instruments used by companies and understand the principles of reporting information in the financial statements.

Additionally, for those who choose to study the Supplement to this chapter:

LO7 Prepare the ledger accounts to record provisions and deferred income.

LO1   # 11.1 Introduction

Chapter 10 has provided basic information on the definition and recognition of liabilities and has expanded in more detail in the case of current liabilities including accruals. In Chapter 10 there is a list of the headings for the liabilities section of the balance sheet formats. These are:

E   Creditors: amounts falling due within one year.
H   Creditors: amounts falling due after more than one year.
I   Provisions for liabilities and charges.
J   Accruals and deferred income.

In this chapter we deal with sections H and I of the formats and also explain the treatment of deferred income which appears in section J. For each of these sections we follow the pattern established in earlier chapters by asking:

- What are the rules for defining and recognising these items?
- What are the information needs of users in respect of the particular items?
- What information is currently provided by companies to meet these needs?
- Does the information show the desirable qualitative characteristics of financial statements?
- What are the rules for measuring, and processes for recording, these items?

This chapter looks first at provisions, then turns to long-term liabilities and finally covers deferred income. General principles of definition and recognition of liabilities are dealt with in Chapter 10 and you should ensure you have read and understood that chapter before embarking on this one. For convenience the definitions are repeated here.

Definitions

Liabilities are defined as the obligations of an entity to transfer economic benefits as a result of past transactions or events.[1]

Long-term liabilities are those liabilities expected to extend beyond one year from the balance sheet date.

L02

11.2 Users' needs for information

There are two aspects of information needed in relation to liabilities. The first relates to the amount owed (sometimes called the *principal sum* or the *capital amount*) and the second relates to the cost of servicing the loan (usually the payment of *interest*).

Owners of a company need to know how much the company owes to other parties because the owners are at the end of the queue when it comes to sharing out the assets of the company if it closes down. Lenders to the company want to know how many other lenders will have a claim on assets if the company closes down and how much the total claim of lenders will be. They may want to take a *secured loan*, where the agreement with the company specifies particular assets which may be sold by the lender if the company defaults on payment.

Cash flow is important to a range of users. Interest payments are an expense to be reported in the profit and loss account, but paying interest is a drain on cash as well as affecting the ownership interest by a reduction in profit. Owners of the company want to know if there will be sufficient cash left to allow them a dividend (or drawings for partnerships and sole traders) after interest has been paid. Lenders want to be reassured that the company is generating sufficient cash flow and profit to cover the interest charges.

Both owners and lenders want to see the impact of borrowing on future cash flows. They need to know the scheduled dates of repayments of loans (sometimes referred to as the *maturity profile of debt*), the currency in which the loan must be repaid and the structure of interest rates (e.g. whether the loan period is starting with low rates of interest which are then stepped up in future years).

Finally, owners and lenders are interested in the *gearing* of the company. This means the ratio of loan capital to ownership interest in the balance sheet or the ratio of interest payments to net profit in the profit and loss account. Chapter 13 will provide more detail on the calculation and interpretation of gearing.

L02 | **Activity 11.1**

Imagine you are a shareholder in a company which is financed partly by long-term loans. Write down the information needed by users in the order of importance to you as a shareholder and explain your answer.

L03   11.3 Information provided in the financial statements

The balance sheet of Safe and Sure plc, set out in Chapter 7, contains the following information in relation to long-term liabilities:

		Notes	Year 7 £	Year 6 £
Liabilities due	Creditors	9	(2.7)	(2.6)
after one year	Bank and other borrowings	10	(0.2)	(0.6)
	Provisions for liabilities and charges	11	(20.2)	(22.2)

Notes to the balance sheet explain more about the balance sheet items. Note 9 gives some indication of the type of creditors due after more than one year.

Note 9		Year 7 £m	Year 6 £m
Creditors due	Deferred consideration on acquisition	0.6	–
after more than	Other creditors	2.1	2.6
one year		2.7	2.6

Note 10 distinguishes secured and unsecured loans among the borrowings due after one year and also gives a schedule of repayment over the immediate and medium-term or longer-term future. For this company, bank borrowings all mature within five years. Note 10 also confirms that commercial rates of interest are payable.

Note 10		Year 7 £m	Year 6 £m
Bank and other	Secured loans	–	0.3
borrowings due	Unsecured loans	0.2	0.3
after more than		0.2	0.6
one year			
	Loans are repayable by instalments:		
	Between one and two years	0.1	0.2
	Between two and five years	0.1	0.4
		0.2	0.6

Interest on long-term loans, which are denominated in a number of currencies, is payable at normal commercial rates appropriate to the country in which the borrowing is made. The last repayment falls due in Year 11.

Note 11 gives information on provisions for liabilities which will occur at a future date, as a result of past events or of definite plans made.

Note 11		Year 7 £m	Year 6 £m
Provisions	*Provisions for treating contaminated site:*		
	At 1 January	14.2	14.5
	Utilised in the year	(2.2)	(0.3)
	At 31 December	12.0	14.2
	Provisions for restructuring costs:		
	At 1 January	4.2	–
	Created in year	1.0	4.3
	Utilised in year	(1.0)	(0.1)
	At 31 December	4.2	4.2
	Provision for deferred tax:		
	At 1 January	3.8	2.7
	Transfer to profit and loss account	0.5	1.2
	Other movements	(0.3)	(0.1)
	At 31 December	4.0	3.8
	Total provision	20.2	22.2

Finally, note 33 sets out contingent liabilities. (Contingent liabilities are defined and explained in Chapter 10.) Two contingent items have the amount quantified. The impact of litigation (legal action) is not quantified. The company may think that to do so would be seen as an admission of legal liability.

Note 33	
Contingent liabilities	The company has guaranteed bank and other borrowings of subsidiaries amounting to £3.0m (Year 6: £15.2m). The group has commitments, amounting to approximately £41.9m (Year 6: £28.5m), under forward exchange contracts entered into in the ordinary course of business.
	Certain subsidiaries have given warranties for service work. These are explained in the statement on accounting policies.
	There are contingent liabilities in respect of litigation. None of the actions is expected to give rise to any material loss.

The accounting policy statement contains three items relevant to liabilities:

Accounting policies

Deferred tax

Provision for deferred tax receivable and payable is made at rates currently expected when income, expenditure or depreciation fall into different periods for accounting and for taxation purposes, to the extent that it is probable that a benefit or charge will crystallise.

Warranties

Some service work is carried out under warranty. The cost of claims under warranty is charged against the profit and loss account of the year in which the claims are settled.

Deferred consideration

For acquisitions involving deferred consideration, estimated deferred payments are accrued in the balance sheet. Interest due to vendors on deferred payments is charged to the profit and loss account as it accrues.

Because the level of borrowing is low in this company, and therefore would not create any concern for investors or new lenders, the finance director has very little to say about it in his report. To some extent the chairman takes the initiative earlier in the annual report:

Finance

Once again, during Year 7 we had a strong operating cash flow, amounting to £196.7m (up from £163.5m in Year 6). This funded expenditure of £24.6m on acquisition of other companies and businesses (after allowing for £3.1m received from a disposal of a company) and the group still ended the year with an increase in its cash balances.

David Wilson has already commented in Chapters 4 and 7 on some aspects of the liabilities in the financial statements of Safe and Sure plc. Here he is explaining to Leona, in the coffee bar at the health club, his views on liabilities in particular.

DAVID: *Where do I start in explaining how I look at liabilities? Well, I always read the accounting policy notes before I look at any financial statements. This company provides three accounting policy notes relating to matters of liabilities. The policy on warranties is interesting because it confirms that the company does not record any expected liability on warranties. The first time I saw this in the annual report I was quite concerned about lack of prudence, but on my first visit to the company I was shown the warranty settlement file. There are very few claims under warranty because the company has lots of procedures which have to be followed by employees who carry out service work. Warranty claims are relatively unusual and unpredictable for this company so there is no previous pattern to justify setting up a liability in the form of a provision for future claims.*

The deferred consideration arises because this company has acquired another business and wants to look into all aspects of the newly acquired investment before making full payment.

Deferred tax provisions are common to many companies. They are an attempt to line up the accounting profit with the tax charge based on taxable profits, which are usually different. I don't understand the technical details but my test of importance is to look at the amount charged to the profit and loss account for the year. It is less than 1 per cent of the profit after tax, so I shan't be giving it much attention on this occasion.

Provisions for restructuring are my real headache. These are a measure of the costs expected when the company plans a restructuring such as changing the management structure with redefinition of the role of some employees and redundancy for others. It sounds reasonable to give warning of what all this will cost but apparently it has been linked to some creative accounting in the profit and loss account. Whatever the cause was, I know the ASB has recently produced a new standard which tightens up on this kind of provision. Have you read it?

LEONA: *Yes. On the one hand, you would like to know that a company is prudent in reporting in the profit and loss account now the likely losses which will arise in future years because of a decision to reorganise. On the other hand, you would not like to think that a company has loaded the profit and loss account with lots of bad news this year so that it can make next year look much better when the results are published. The ASB's standard is targeting those companies which are being excessively prudent. I could explain more but not at this time on a Friday night. What do you see in the balance sheet and the other information provided by the company?*

DAVID: *After reading and thinking about the items in the accounting policy notes I look to the breakdown between current liabilities and longer-term liabilities. I also look to the amount of long-term finance compared with the amount of the shareholders' funds. The borrowings in this company are relatively low in relation to shareholders' funds, so there is not a high financial risk, but I still want to look for unexplained changes since the previous year. Again, there is nothing which springs to the eye.*

The contingent liability note is usually quite interesting. One of my senior colleagues says that you should start at the end of the annual report and read it backwards. Then you find the best parts first. The contingent liability note is always near the end. I would be asking lots of questions about the forward exchange contracts, if I had not already asked the financial controller. He confirmed in more detail what the finance director says rather briefly. The forward exchange contracts are used as part of prudent financial management to put a limit on any potential loss through adverse currency movements on transactions in different countries.

LEONA: *Much of what you say is reflected in what auditors carry out by way of analytical review. What we don't provide is a view to the future. What are your thoughts there?*

DAVID: *This is a cash-rich company and it has very little in the way of complicated financial structures. For a major company that is probably unusual, but it means I can concentrate on the operating aspects of the business and on whether it will continue to generate cash. It uses cash generated to buy other businesses and expand further, but I wonder what will happen when the scope for that expansion ceases. It is unlikely to be a problem in the near future because the company has a foothold in expanding markets in Asia. When that scope for expansion comes to an end the company may have to start borrowing to finance expansion rather than relying on internal cash flows.*

L04 | 11.4 Provisions for liabilities and charges

Making a provision for a liability or a charge is an accounting process similar to that of making accrual for a known obligation.

Definition | A *provision* is defined as a liability of uncertain timing or amount.[2]

The distinguishing feature of a provision often lies in the larger element of uncertainty which surrounds a provision. Such a provision will appear in the liabilities section of a balance sheet. (This textbook has already considered in Chapter 8 the provision for depreciation and in Chapter 9 the provision for doubtful debts. These are examples of what is regarded as an adjustment to the reported value of an asset, rather than an adjustment for significant uncertainty. They are therefore reported as adjustments to the asset and do not appear in the liabilities section.) Examples of provisions which may be found in the liabilities sections of published accounts are for the following:

- losses on contracts
- obsolescence of stock
- costs related to closure of a division of the company
- costs of decommissioning an oil rig
- cost of landscaping a site at the end of the period of use
- warranties given for repair of goods.

Recording a provision is relatively straightforward. The ownership interest is reduced by an expense in the profit and loss account and a liability is created under the name of the provision:

Assets – **Liabilities** ↑	equals	**Ownership interest ↓ (expense)**

When the provision is no longer required it is released to the profit and loss account as an item of revenue which increases the ownership interest and the liability is reduced:

Assets – **Liabilities** ↓	equals	**Ownership interest** ↑

The provision may also be released to the profit and loss account so as to match an expense which was anticipated when the provision was made. The effect on the accounting equation is an increase in the ownership interest – the same effect as results from regarding the release of the provision as an item of revenue.

Example

During the year ending 31 December Year 5, a company's sales of manufactured goods amounted to £1m. All goods carry a manufacturer's warranty to rectify any faults arising during the first 12 months of ownership. At the start of the year, based on previous experience, a provision of 2.5 per cent of sales was made (estimating the sales to be £1m). During Year 5 repairs under warranty cost £14,000. There could be further repair costs incurred in Year 6 in respect of those items sold part-way through Year 5 whose warranty extends into Year 6.

Using the accounting equation, the effect of these events and transactions may be analysed. When the provision is established there is an increase in a liability and an expense to be charged to the profit and loss account:

Assets   –   **Liabilities** $\uparrow$ =   **Ownership interest** $\downarrow$ **(expense)**

$$\boxed{+£25,000} \qquad\qquad\qquad \boxed{-£25,000}$$

As the repairs under warranty are carried out, they cause a decrease in the asset of cash and a decrease in the provision. They do not directly affect the profit and loss account expense:

Asets $\downarrow$ –   **Liabilities** $\downarrow$ =   Ownership interest

$$\boxed{-£14,000} \qquad\qquad \boxed{-£14,000}$$

The overall effect is that the profit and loss account will report an expense of £25,000 but the provision will only be used to the extent of £14,000, leaving £11,000 available to cover any further repairs in respect of Year 5 sales. The repairs, when paid for, decrease the asset of cash but are not seen as decreasing the ownership interest. They are seen as meeting a liability to the customer (rather like making a payment to meet a liability to a supplier). The creation of the provision establishes the full amount of the liability and the decrease in the ownership interest which is to be reported in the profit and loss account.

The spreadsheet for analysis is contained in Exhibit 11.1.

Exhibit 11.1
Spreadsheet for analysis of provision for warranty repairs

Date	Transaction or event	Asset	Liability	Ownership interest
		Cash	Provision	Profit and loss account
Year 5		£	£	£
Jan. 1	Provision for repairs		25,000	(25,000)
Jan.–Dec.	Repairs under warranty	(14,000)	(14,000)	
	Totals	(14,000)	11,000	(25,000)

L04

Activity 11.2

Test your understanding of the previous section by analysing the following information and entering it in a spreadsheet to show analysis of the impact of the information on the accounting equation:

Jan. 1 Year 1   Make a provision for repairs, £50,000.
During Year 1   Spend £30,000 against the provision and carry the rest forward.
Jan. 1 Year 2   Make a further provision for repairs, £10,000.
During Year 2   Spend £25,000 against the provision and carry the rest forward.
Jan. 1 Year 3   Reduce the remaining provision to £3,000.

L05

11.5 Deferred income

For companies located in areas of the country where there are particular problems of unemployment or a need to encourage redevelopment of the location, the government may award grants as a contribution to the operating costs of the company or to the cost of buying new fixed assets.

Consider the award of a government grant to a company, intended to help with the cost of training employees over the next three years. The asset of cash increases, but there is no corresponding effect on any other asset or liability. Consequently, the ownership interest is increased. The obvious label for this increase is *revenue*. However, the benefit of the grant will extend over three years and it would therefore seem appropriate to spread the revenue over three years to match the cost it is subsidising. The accounting device for producing this effect is to say that the cash received as an asset creates a liability called *deferred income*. This does not meet the definition of a liability stated at the start of this chapter because the practice of deferring income is dictated by the importance of *matching revenues and costs* in the profit and loss account. It is one of the cases where established custom and practice continues because it has been found to be useful although it does not fit neatly into the conceptual framework definitions.

Example

A company receives a grant of £30,000 towards the cost of employee retraining. The retraining programme will last for three years and the costs will be spread evenly over the three years.

The profit and loss account will show revenue of £10,000 in each year. At the outset the deferred income will be recorded in the balance sheet as £30,000. By the end of Year 1 the deferred income will be reduced to £20,000. At the end of Year 2 the deferred income will be reduced to £10,000. At the end of Year 3 the deferred income is reduced to nil. The accounting records are shown in Exhibit 11.2.

Exhibit 11.2
Recording deferred income and transfer to revenue

Date	Transaction or event	Asset	Liability	Ownership interest
		Cash	Deferred income	Revenue
Year 1		£	£	£
Jan. 1	Receiving the grant	30,000	30,000	
Dec. 31	Transfer to profit and loss account of first year's revenue		(10,000)	10,000
Year 2				
Dec. 31	Transfer to profit and loss account of second year's revenue		(10,000)	10,000
Year 3				
Dec. 31	Transfer to profit and loss account of third year's revenue		(10,000)	10,000

Where grants are received towards the acquisition of fixed assets there is a similar approach of spreading the grant over the period during which the company will benefit from use of the asset. Some companies show the revenue as a separate item in the profit and loss account while others deduct it from the depreciation charge. This is a matter of presentation which makes no difference to the overall profit. The balance sheet treatment is more controversial. Some companies report separately the net book value of the asset and the deferred income. Others deduct the deferred income from the net book value of the asset. This does not affect the ownership interest but shows a lower amount in the fixed assets section of the balance sheet. In consequence, the user who calculates profit as a percentage of fixed assets or a percentage of total assets will obtain a higher answer where a company shows the lower amount for net assets. Most companies report the asset and deferred income separately, but some argue for the *net approach* which sets one against the other. (There is a view that they may not be complying with the Companies Act 1985 and so relatively few UK companies take the net approach.) The choice will be set out in the notes on accounting policies. This is a useful illustration of the importance of reading the note on accounting policies.

L05 Activity 11.3

Consider a grant received as a contribution to staff retraining costs over the next three years. Write down three arguments in favour of reporting the entire grant in the profit and loss account in the year it is received and write down three arguments in favour of spreading the grant across the period of retraining. Which set of arguments do you find more persuasive?

L06 | 11.6 Long-term liabilities

The balance sheet requires a separate heading for all liabilities payable after one year. Users of financial statements need information about when the liabilities will be due for repayment (the *maturity* pattern). The Companies Act requires financial statements to show separately:

- Liabilities falling due within five years of the balance sheet date.
- Liabilities falling due beyond five years from the balance sheet date.

Users also need to know about the nature of the liability and any risks attaching to expected outflows of economic benefit from the liability. The risks lie in: the interest payable on the loan; the currency of the loan; and the eventual amount to be repaid to the lender. Interest payable may be at a fixed rate of interest or a variable rate of interest. The currency of borrowing is important when foreign exchange rates alter. Repayment amounts may equal the amount borrowed initially, in some cases. In other cases there may be a *premium* (an extra amount) payable in addition to the sum borrowed. There are some very complex accounting aspects to reporting long-term liabilities, the technical aspects of which are well beyond the capacity of a first-level text, but they are all directed towards ensuring that liabilities are recorded in full and the matching concept is observed in relation to interest charges.[3]

Users want to know about the risks of sacrificing particular assets if the loan is not repaid on the due date. A claim to a particular asset may be made by a creditor who has a loan *secured* on a particular asset or group of assets.

11.6.1 Recording and measurement

This section concentrates on the terminology of long-term liabilities and the general issues of recording and measurement that they raise. The basic feature of long-term loan finance is that it is provided by a lender who expects payment of interest at an agreed rate at agreed points in time and repayment of the loan on an agreed date or dates.

The names given to loan capital vary depending on the type of lender, the possibility that the loan will be bought and sold like ordinary shares, the currency in which the loan has been provided and the legal form of the documents creating the loan. Some of the names you will see are: loan stock, debentures, bonds, commercial paper, loan notes and bank facility.

- *Loan stock.* The word *stock* is used in more than one context in accounting, which is potentially confusing. In Chapter 9 you saw the word used to describe goods held by a company for use or sale to customers. In the phrase *loan stock* it is used to describe an investment held by a lender. In the United States the problem is avoided by having different words. The goods held for use or sale are called *inventory* and the loan stock is called a *bond*. If a company shows loan stock in its balance sheet this usually indicates that the stock is available for purchase and sale, in a manner similar to the purchase and sale of shares in a company.

- *Debenture.* The legal meaning of the term *debenture* is *a written acknowledgement of a debt*. This means there will be a contract, in writing, between the company and the lender. The contract is called the debenture deed and is held by a *trustee* who is required to look after the needs of the lenders. If the company does not pay interest, or repay capital, on the due date, the trustee must take action to recover what is owed to the lenders. Debentures may be secured or unsecured, depending on what is stated in the debenture deed.
- *Bond.* The term *bond* has been in common use in the United States for some time as a name for loan capital. It is now found increasingly frequently in the balance sheets of UK companies, particularly when they are raising finance in the international capital markets where the US terminology is more familiar.
- *Commercial paper, loan notes* and *bank facility.* These are all names of short- to medium-term financing provided by banks or similar organisations. The interest payable is usually variable and the loans are unsecured.

This is only a sample of the main variations of names given to loan finance. It is not exhaustive because the name does not matter greatly for the purposes of accounting records and interpretation. The essential information needed for the users of accounting information is the answer to five questions:

1 How much was borrowed (the *capital* sum)?
2 How much has to be repaid (the capital sum plus any additional interest charge)?
3 When is repayment required?
4 What are the interest payments required?
5 Has the lender sought any security for repayment of the interest and the capital sum?

The Companies Act meets this need by requiring disclosure of:

- The total amount in respect of which any security has been given, and an indication of the nature of the security.
- The interest payable and terms of repayment for each category of loan.

11.6.2 Secured and unsecured loans

- *Unsecured loan.* An unsecured loan is one where the lender has no first claim on any particular assets of the company and, in the event of default, must wait for payment alongside all the other unsecured creditors. If there is no wording to indicate that the loan is secured, then the reader of financial statements must assume it is unsecured.
- *Secured loan.* Where any loan is described as *secured*, it means that the lender has first claim to named assets of the company. Where a debenture is secured, and the company defaults on payment, the trustee for the debenture will take possession of the asset and use it to make the necessary repayment. Having this claim on an asset is given the legal term of a *charge on the asset*. Some loans are secured by a *floating charge*, so called because it floats over all the assets of the company and only settles to earth when the default occurs. (The term *crystallisation* is often used in practice, using the simile of crystals clinging to the

sides and base of a glass dish as they fall out of a solution.) At that moment the trustee for the debenture holders may take possession of any assets which will be sufficient to meet the amount due. A floating charge is a flexible form of security which allows the company to buy and sell fixed assets in the normal course of business without the permission of the lender but provides security to the lender if needed.

In the event of the company not being able to pay all the amounts it owes, secured lenders come before unsecured lenders in the queue for repayment.

L06

Activity 11.4

A financial weekly magazine contains the following sentence:

'Textiles plc has this week issued a 5.75 per cent loan 2011 at nominal value, secured by a floating charge.'

Explain each part of the sentence.

11.6.3 Loan having a range of repayment dates

When a loan is made to a business, conditions will be negotiated regarding the amount and date of repayment. Some banks are willing to offer a range of repayment dates, say any time between 10 and 15 years hence, with the company being allowed to choose when it will repay. If the company needs the money and the interest rate is favourable, the company will borrow for the longest period allowed under the contract. If the company finds it no longer needs the money, or else the interest rate is burdensome, the company will repay at the earliest possible opportunity. For balance sheet purposes the preparer of accounts has to decide which date to use as a basis for classification.

The general principle is that if there is an obligation to transfer economic benefits, there will be a liability in the balance sheet. Where there is a range of possible dates for repayment, the maturity date will be taken as the earliest date on which the lender can require repayment.[4]

11.6.4 Change in the nature of finance source

Some types of finance provided to a business may be arranged so as to allow a change in the nature of the source during the period of financing. As an example, consider the case of convertible loans.

A convertible loan is a source of finance which starts its life as a loan but, at some point in the future, may be converted to ordinary shares in the company (for example the lender is promised 5 shares per £100 of loan capital). At the date of conversion, the lender becomes a shareholder. This kind of financial arrangement is attractive to those providing finance because it provides the reassurance of loan finance and a payment of interest in the early years of a new development, with the option of switching to shares if the project is successful. If the project is not successful and the share price does not perform as expected, then the lender will not convert and will look for repayment of the loan on the due date. For the company there are some tax advantages of issuing loan finance. Also, the rate of interest required by investors in a convertible loan is usually lower than that required for a straight (non-convertible) loan because investors see potential additional rewards in the convertible loan.

While a convertible loan remains unconverted it is reported as a loan. Companies are not allowed to say 'We are almost certain there will be a conversion' and report the convertible loan as share finance from the outset. However, there is an awareness that the eventual conversion will dilute the existing shareholders' claim on future profits and so the company will report the earnings per share before and after taking into account the effect of this dilution. Consequently, you will see 'fully diluted earnings per share' at the foot of the profit and loss account.

11.6.5 Interest payable on the loan

Companies and their banks may negotiate a variety of patterns for interest payment on loans. The pattern of interest payment might be based on a low percentage charge in earlier years and a higher percentage charge in later years, because the company expects that profits will be low initially but will rise later to cover the higher interest payments. For many years the profit and loss account would have reported the interest charge based on the amount paid in each year, but in 1994 the ASB stated its preference for reporting the interest charge as it would be if a compound interest rate were applied over the life of the loan.

The reasoning behind the ASB's approach is that, for purposes of reporting profit, the flexibility of negotiation of interest payment patterns makes comparability difficult to achieve. The banks will, however, ensure that they receive the overall compound interest they require and this gives a commercially relevant basis for comparability in the matching of interest charges against the profits of the period.

The general principle is that the amount shown as the expense of interest payable in the profit and loss account should be based on the compound rate of interest applying over the entire period of the loan.[5]

This will not always be the same as the amount of interest paid in cash during the period. The spreading of interest charges over the period of the loan is an application of the accruals or matching concept. As an example, consider stepped bonds and deep discount bonds.

Stepped bonds

A *stepped bond* is a form of lending where the interest rate increases over the period of the loan. Take as an example a loan of £5m which carries a rate of interest of 8 per cent per annum for the first three years, 10 per cent per annum for the next three years and 13 per cent per annum for the final four years. The cash payment for interest starts at £400,000 and by the tenth year has risen to £650,000. The overall payments may be shown to be equivalent to a compound rate of 10.06 per cent per annum. Exhibit 11.3 shows that the profit and loss account charge of £503,000 would start higher than the cash amount, £400,000. By the final year the profit and loss account charge of £517,000 would be lower than the cash amount,

£650,000. The pattern followed on each line of Exhibit 11.3 is to start with the amount owing, add interest at 10.06 per cent and deduct the amount of the cash payment, leaving the amount owing at the end of the period which becomes the amount owing at the start of the next period. By the end of the ten years the amount owing is exactly £5,000,000, the amount required by the lender.

Exhibit 11.3

Calculation of profit and loss account charge for interest based on compound interest calculation

Year	Loan at start	Profit and loss account charge	Cash payment record	
		Interest at 10.06%	Cash paid	Loan at end
	(a)	(b)	(c)	(a) + (b) − (c)
	£000s	£000s	£000s	£000s
1	5,000	503	400	5,103
2	5,103	513	400	5,216
3	5,216	525	400	5,341
4	5,341	537	500	5,378
5	5,378	541	500	5,419
6	5,419	545	500	5,464
7	5,464	550	650	5,364
8	5,364	540	650	5,254
9	5,254	529	650	5,133
10	5,133	517	650	5,000
Total		5,300	5,300	

It may be seen from Exhibit 11.3 that the profit and loss account charge has a smoother pattern than that of the cash payments. Over the life of the loan the total profit and loss account charge must equal the total of the cash payments. The accounting processes for recording these amounts are too complex for a first-level textbook. The important point to note is that all companies are required to use this approach in calculating the interest charge for the profit and loss account. The cash flow implications of interest payments may be quite different and it will be necessary to look to the cash flow statement for evidence of the cash flow effect.

Deep discount bonds

A *deep discount bond* is issued at a price lower than (*at a discount to*) its repayment amount. The interest rate paid during the life of the loan may be very low (a *low coupon bond*) or there may be no interest paid at all during the period of the loan (a *zero coupon bond*). As an example, consider a zero coupon bond issued at £28m with a redemption value of £41m in four years' time. The cash payments of interest are zero but the profit and loss account would show an annual charge of 10 per cent per annum (starting at £2.8m in Year 1 and rising to £3.73m by Year 4). If there were no pattern of annual interest the entire discount of £13m would be shown as an expense of Year 4, distorting the underlying pattern of trading profit. Exhibit 11.4 shows the pattern of interest charges for the profit and loss account.

Exhibit 11.4

Schedule of interest charges for zero coupon bond

Year	Loan at start £m	Interest £m	Loan at end £m
1	28.00	2.80	30.80
2	30.80	3.08	33.88
3	33.88	3.39	37.27
4	37.27	3.73	41.00
Total		13.00	

In the balance sheet the amount recorded for the liability will start at £28m and rise to £41m as shown in the final column of Exhibit 11.4, so that the liability at the end represents the total amount due.

LO6 | **Activity 11.5**

A three-year loan of £100,000 will be repaid at the end of three years as £133,100. No interest is payable during the three-year period. The interest included in the loan repayment arrangement is equivalent to a compound annual charge of 10 per cent per annum. Explain how this transaction would appear in the profit and loss account and balance sheet over the three-year period.

11.6.6 Complex capital instruments

It is impossible to read the balance sheet of most major listed companies without realising rapidly that there is a bewildering array of capital instruments being used to raise money for business. The reasons are complex but lie in the need to provide conditions which are attractive to both borrower and lender when they may be based in different countries and may have different perspectives on interest rates and currency exchange rates. This section explains the term 'interest rate swaps', which are increasingly used by companies, and takes an illustration from a major company to indicate the variety of capital instruments (sources of finance) in use. Detailed descriptions and discussion are beyond the scope of this text but would be found in a finance manual.

Interest rate swaps

Suppose there are two companies, A and B. Both have identical amounts of loan finance. Company A is paying fixed rates of interest, but would prefer to be paying variable rates, while Company B is paying variable rates of interest, but would prefer to be paying fixed rates. The reasons could be related to patterns of cash flow from trading, cash flow from investments or beliefs about future directions of interest rates. Whatever the reason, it would seem quite acceptable for them to swap (exchange) so that A pays the variable interest on behalf of B and B pays the fixed interest on behalf of A. This type of arrangement has to be explained carefully because neither company can escape from the legal obligation on the loans taken out initially. The explanation will usually be found in a note to the accounts which gives information on the legal obligation and on the actual impact on the profit and loss account of implementing the swap.

Capital instruments of a listed company

The following illustration is based upon the balance sheet of a major UK listed company:

Note on borrowings:	Year 2 £m	Year 1 £m
Unsecured borrowings:		
10^{1}/$_{2}$% euro-sterling bonds Year 17	100.0	100.0
Loan stocks		
13.625% Year 16	25.0	25.0
5.675% − 9.3% Year 3/Year 10	5.9	6.1
Zero coupon bonds Year 3	96.6	87.2
Variable rate multi-option bank facility	15.8	155.2
Bank loans, overdrafts, commercial paper, short- and medium-term notes	257.0	244.8

. . . the nominal value of the zero coupon bonds is £100m and the effective annual rate of interest is 10.85% . . .

Comment. The euro-sterling bonds and the loan stocks are reported at the amount due for repayment at the end of the loan period. The euro-sterling bonds are loans raised in the eurobond market, repayable in sterling. Those loans which have fixed rates of interest are indicated in the table by a fixed percentage rate. Zero coupon means a zero percentage rate of annual interest payable. That does not mean the company escapes interest payment altogether. The liability on the zero coupon bonds increases by 10.85 per cent each year as indicated in the extract note at the foot of the table. It is presumably due for repayment part-way through Year 3 since the liability shown at the end of Year 2 is quite close to the £100m amount due (called the *nominal value* in the note). The remaining loans are variable rate and so the annual interest charge depends on current rates of interest. Professional investors might want to know more about the nature of the bank facility and also the breakdown of the various components of the figure £257m.

11.7 Summary

Now score your view of your confidence in achieving the learning outcomes of the chapter.

1 = Very confident about knowledge, application, problem solving and evaluation.

2 = Confident about knowledge and application, less sure about problem solving and evaluation.

3 = Need to read again to be more certain of basic knowledge and application.

		1	2	3
LO1	You are now able to define a long-term liability.	☐	☐	☐
LO2	You can explain the needs of users for information about long-term liabilities.	☐	☐	☐
LO3	You are able to explain the types of long-term loan finance most frequently found in the balance sheets of major companies.	☐	☐	☐
LO4	You now understand the purpose of provisions and can explain how provisions are reported in financial statements.	☐	☐	☐
LO5	You now understand the nature of deferred income and can explain how it is reported in financial statements.	☐	☐	☐
LO6	You now know the main types of loan finance and capital instruments used by companies and you understand the principles of reporting information in the financial statements.	☐	☐	☐
LO7	Those who wish to be able to prepare the ledger accounts to record provisions and deferred income should now turn to the Supplement.	☐	☐	☐

If your scores are all 1 or 2, try the questions in the series A, B and C. This will give you feedback on your assessment of how well you have achieved the learning outcomes. Read again any sections of the chapter where you find your knowledge and understanding are less comprehensive than you first estimated.

If your scores include some at 3, try the series A questions to find where the problems lie. Read the relevant sections again, work through any illustrative examples and case studies, then try the questions in the series B. Once you feel confident at that level of knowledge and application, move on to try some or all of the series C questions.

International perspective

Of the topics covered in this chapter, provisions give the greatest scope for international variation in accounting treatment. In countries where the accounting system and the tax system are linked, there may be specific rules about the level and nature of provisions allowed. In countries that have a strong culture of conservatism (strong prudence) the provisions may be used to understate profit. The problem with such an approach is that the unnecessary provision may then be released in a year when profits would otherwise be lower. This has the effect of 'smoothing' out the peaks and troughs of profit. The UK standard setting body believes that provisions should only be used under tightly regulated conditions. This approach also applies in the USA.

Test your understanding

L04, S01   **A11.1** Explain why a provision may be required.

L04, S01   **A11.2** Give three examples of situations which may lead to provisions.

L05, S01   **A11.3** Explain how deferred income is recorded.

L05, S01   **A11.4** Is it justifiable to report deferred income under the category of liability?

L06, S01   **A11.5** Explain what is meant by each of the following terms:

(a) loan stock;
(b) debenture;
(c) bond;
(d) maturity date; and
(e) convertible loan stock.

L05, S01   **A11.6** On reviewing the financial statements, the company accountant discovers that a grant of £60,000 towards expenditure of the current year plus two further years has been reported entirely as revenue of the period. What will be the effect on the profit and loss account and the balance sheet when this error is rectified?

L04, S01   **A11.7** On reviewing the financial statements, the company accountant discovers that there has been no provision made for urgent repairs to external doors and window frames, already identified as being of high priority on grounds of health and safety. The amount of £50,000 should be provided. What will be the effect on the profit and loss account and the balance sheet when this error is rectified?

Application

L04, S01   **B11.1** The Washing Machine Repair Company gives a warranty of no-cost rectification of unsatisfactory repairs. It has turnover from repair contracts recorded as:

Year	Amount of turnover
	£
1	80,000
2	90,000

Based on previous experience the manager makes a provision of 10 per cent of turnover each year for warranty costs. In respect of the work done during years 1 and 2, repairs under warranty are carried out as follows:

Date of repair work	Amount in respect of Year 1 turnover	Amount in respect of Year 2 turnover	Total
	£	£	£
1	4,500		4,500
2	3,200	4,800	8,000
3		5,000	5,000

Required
(a) Show how this information would be recorded in the financial statements of the Washing Machine Repair Company.
(b) Explain how the financial statements would appear if the company made no provision for warranty costs but charged them to profit and loss account when incurred.

LO5, S01 **B11.2** General Engineering Ltd receives a government grant for £60,000 towards employee training costs to be incurred evenly over the next three years. Explain how this transaction will be reported in the financial statements.

Problem solving and evaluation

LO4, S02 **C11.1** Explain why each of the following is recognised as a provision in the balance sheet of a telecommunications company:

(a) On 15 December Year 2, the Group announced a major redundancy programme. Provision has been made at 31 December Year 2 for the associated costs. The provision is expected to be utilised within 12 months.
(b) Because of the redundancy programme, some properties have become vacant. Provision has been made for lease payments that cannot be avoided where sub-letting is not possible. The provision will be utilised within 15 months.
(c) There is a legal claim against a subsidiary in respect of alleged breach of contract. Provision has been made for this claim. It is expected that the provision will be utilised within 12 months.

LO4, S02 **C11.2** (Refer also to Chapter 10, section 10.3.2, on Contingent liabilities.)
Explain why each of the following is reported as a contingent liability but not recognised as a provision in the balance sheet.

(a) Some leasehold properties which the group no longer requires have been sub-let to third parties. If the third parties default, the group remains responsible for future rent payments. The maximum liability is £200,000.
(b) Group companies are defendants in the United States in a number of product liability cases related to tobacco products. In a number of these cases, the amounts of compensatory and punitive damages sought are significant.
(c) The Department of Trade and Industry has appointed Inspectors to investigate the company's flotation 10 years ago. The directors have been advised that it is possible that circumstances surrounding the flotation may give rise to claims against the company. At this stage it is not possible to quantify either the probability of success of such claims or of the amounts involved.

Activities for study groups

Turn to the annual report of a listed company which you have used for activities in previous chapters. Find every item of information about liabilities. (Start with the financial statements and notes but look also at the operating and financial review, chief executive's review and other non-regulated information about the company.)

As a group, imagine you are the team of fund managers in a fund management company. You are holding a briefing meeting at which each person explains to the others some feature of the companies in which your fund invests. Today's subject is liabilities. Each person should make a short presentation to the rest of the team covering:

(a) The nature and significance of liabilities in the company.
(b) The effect on profit of a 10 per cent error in estimation of any one of the major categories of liability.
(c) The company's comments, if any, on its future obligations.
(d) The risks which might attach to the liabilities of the company.
(e) The liquidity of the company.
(f) The trends in liabilities since last year (or over five years if a comparative table is provided).
(g) The ratio of current assets to current liabilities.

Notes and references

1 ASB (1999) *Statement of Principles for Financial Reporting*, ch. 4, 'The elements of financial statements', para. 4.23.
2 ASB (1998) Financial Reporting Standard (FRS 12), *Provisions, Contingent Liabilities and Contingent Assets*, Accounting Standards Board.
3 ASB (1993) Financial Reporting Standard (FRS 4), *Capital Instruments*, Accounting Standards Board.
4 *Ibid.*, para. 34.
5 *Ibid.*, para. 28.

Bookkeeping entries for provisions and deferred income

Provisions

In the main text of this chapter there is an example based on the recording of provision for repairs under warranty. The analysis of the transactions and events is set out in Exhibit 11.1. The ledger account will appear as follows:

L3 Provision for warranty repairs

Date	Particulars	Page	Debit	Credit	Balance
Year 5			£	£	£
Jan. 1	Provision in respect of Year 5	L2		25,000	(25,000)
Jan.–Dec.	Repairs carried out	L1	14,000		(11,000)

LEONA: *At the start of the year (or possibly in practice at the end of each month) the provision is recorded by debiting the profit and loss account (L2) and crediting the provision. When the repairs are carried out there is a credit entry in the cash account (L1) and a debit entry in the provision account. Nothing is recorded as a profit and loss account expense at that time. The overall effect is that the profit and loss account carries an expense of £25,000 and the provision account shows a potential liability of £11,000 to cover any further repairs arising from work done during Year 5 (since some of the goods sold will remain under warranty into Year 6).*

Deferred income

In the main text of this chapter there is an example based on the recording of deferred income arising under a grant. The analysis of the transactions and events is set out in Exhibit 11.2. The ledger account will appear as follows:

L3 Deferred income (balance sheet)

Date	Particulars	Page	Debit	Credit	Balance
Year 1			£	£	£
Jan. 1	Grant received	L1		30,000	(30,000)
Dec. 31	Transfer to profit and loss account	L2	10,000		(20,000)
Year 2					
Dec. 31	Transfer to profit and loss account	L2	10,000		(10,000)
Year 3					
Dec. 31	Transfer to profit and loss account	L2	10,000		nil

LEONA: *The deferred income account is reported as a liability in the balance sheet. It is established by a credit entry matched by a debit in the cash account (L1). Each year there is a transfer of one-third to the profit and loss account (L2) so that the revenue is spread evenly over the period.*

L07, S01 Test your understanding

S11.1 Prepare bookkeeping records for the information in question **B11.1**.

S11.2 Prepare bookkeeping records for the information in question **B11.2**.

Chapter 12

Ownership interest

After reading this chapter you should be able to:

LO1 Define ownership interest.

LO2 Explain and demonstrate how the ownership interest is presented in company accounts.

LO3 Understand the nature and purpose of the statement of total recognised gains and losses and the reconciliation of movements in shareholders' funds.

LO4 Explain the needs of users for information about the ownership interest in a company.

LO5 Read and interpret the information reported by companies in their annual reports, in respect of the ownership interest.

LO6 Explain the accounting treatment of dividends.

LO7 Understand the methods by which a company's shares may be issued when the company has a Stock Exchange listing.

LO8 Show that you understand the impact of transactions and events on ownership interest in company accounts.

Additionally, for those who choose to study the Supplement:

LO9 Record end-of-period adjustments as debit and credit adjustments to a trial balance taken from the ledger accounts and produce figures for financial statements.

12.1 Introduction

The final element of the accounting equation has been reached. It was explained in Chapter 2 that the ownership interest is the residual amount found by deducting all liabilities of the entity from all of the entity's assets:

Assets minus **Liabilities**	equals	**Ownership interest**

The terminology was also explained in Chapter 2. The words *equity* and *net assets* both appear in the press and in commentaries in connection with the ownership interest. *Equity* is a word used to describe the ownership interest in the assets of the business after all liabilities are deducted. This is also referred to as the *net assets*, calculated as the assets minus the liabilities.

The structure which has been adopted for Chapters 8 to 12 is based on a series of questions:

- What are the rules for defining and recognising these items?
- What are the information needs of users in respect of the particular items?
- What information is currently provided by companies to meet these needs?
- Does the information show the desirable qualitative characteristics of financial statements?
- What are the rules for measuring, and processes for recording, these items?

These questions will be addressed in turn.

L01 | 12.2 Definition and recognition

The definition of *ownership interest* was presented in Chapter 2 as: *'the residual amount found by deducting all of the entity's liabilities from all of the entity's assets'*.

Because the ownership interest is the residual item of the equation, it can only increase or decrease if something happens to an asset or to a liability. Recognition conditions are applied to assets and liabilities but there cannot be any additional recognition criteria applied to the ownership interest.

Events which change assets or liabilities include:

- Making a profit (or loss) through the operations of the business – earning revenue and incurring expenses.
- A contribution of cash by incoming shareholders purchasing new shares.
- Holding an asset which increases or decreases in value.
- Holding a liability which increases or decreases in value.

Each one of these events is important to the users of the financial statements and affects the claims of owners on the assets of the business. Since owners are the user group most interested in the ownership interest, this chapter will focus primarily on the information which is helpful to them. Reporting a profit or a loss has been dealt with in some length in previous chapters. In this chapter we concentrate on the issue of new shares and on the events which cause increases or decreases in assets and liabilities which are *not* reported in the profit and loss account.

L02 | 12.3 Presentation of ownership interest

Chapters 7 to 11 have concentrated primarily on the limited liability company. For any limited liability company the *profit and loss account* is the primary financial statement which reports the revenues and expenses of the business that arise through operations.

The change in value of an asset or liability while it is *held* by the company gives more cause for debate. If the asset has increased in value while still being held by the company, then there may be an increase in the valuation for financial reporting purposes. That is not a *realised* gain and so cannot be reported in the profit and loss account. There is another primary financial statement, the *statement of total recognised gains and losses*, which companies must use to report unrealised gains.

Example of an unrealised gain

A business buys a building at a cost of £10m. One year later similar buildings are selling for £13m. The business does not intend to sell but would like to report the potential increase in the market value of the asset. Because there is no sale, the £3m estimate of the increase in value is *unrealised*. It may not be reported in the profit and loss account but may be reported in the statement of total recognised gains and losses.

The presentation of the ownership interest is therefore a potentially complex affair, using more than one financial statement. There is information about the current position of the ownership interest contained in the *balance sheet* and the related *notes to the accounts*. There is information about changes in the ownership interest in the *profit and loss account* and the *statement of total recognised gains and losses*. The approach taken in this chapter is first of all to 'walk through' the early years of operating a limited liability company and the various types of ownership interest which arise.

12.3.1 Issue of shares at the date of incorporation

When the company first comes into existence it issues *shares* to the owners, who become *shareholders*. The date on which the company comes into existence is called the *date of incorporation*.

Each share has a *named value* which is called its *nominal value*. Sometimes it is referred to as the *par value*. This amount is written on the *share certificate* which is the document given to each owner as evidence of being a shareholder. Exhibit 12.1 shows the share certificate issued by a company which confirms that J. A. Smith is the owner of 100,000 ordinary shares of 25p nominal value each. This means that J. A. Smith has paid £25,000 to the company and that is the limit of this person's liability if the company fails.

Exhibit 12.1
Share certificate issued by a company

Certificate number 24516

Public Company plc

SHARE CERTIFICATE

This is to certify that

J. A. Smith

is the registered owner of 100,000 ordinary shares of 25 pence each.
Given under Seal of the Company the 15th day of August 20XX

Signed *P McDowall*
Company Secretary

J Jones
W Brown
Directors

All share certificates are recorded in the share register by the company secretary. The share certificate is a piece of paper which may be sold by the existing owner to another person who wishes to become a shareholder. The person who wishes to become a shareholder is often referred to as a *prospective investor*. That is not a legal term but is a useful way of indicating a person who has an interest in finding out more about the company, without having the legal rights of ownership. When the new owner has acquired the shares, the term 'investor' may continue to be used as a description which emphasises that this person now has a financial interest in knowing that the company is performing well.

The issue of 100,000 shares at a price of 25 pence each will collect £25,000 cash for the company. The effect on the accounting equation is that the *asset of cash increases* by £25,000 and the *ownership interest is increased* by £25,000.

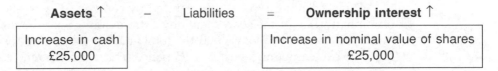

Assets ↑	–	Liabilities	=	**Ownership interest** ↑
Increase in cash £25,000				Increase in nominal value of shares £25,000

For a company, the ownership interest created by the issue of new shares at their nominal value is recorded as *share capital*.

L01

Activity 12.1

Look at the financial pages of a newspaper. Find the daily list of share prices. What information does the newspaper provide about shares in each company? Which of these items of information would you expect to find in the annual report of the company? Give reasons for your answer.

12.3.2 Buying and selling shares

The company itself has no concern about the purchase and sale of shares from one owner to another, other than having to record the new owner's name in the share register. The purchase and sale may take place by private arrangement or may take place in an established *stock market* (also called a *stock exchange*) if the company is a public limited company. If the shares are traded in an established stock market they are called *listed* shares because the daily prices are listed on screens for buyers and sellers to see. If there is high demand for the shares, their price will rise. If there is little demand, the price will fall. The market price on any day will depend on investors' expectations about the future of the company. Those expectations will be influenced by announcements from the company, including financial information but also covering a much wider range of company news. The expectations may also be influenced by information about the industry in which the company operates. One of the main purposes of a well-regulated stock exchange is to ensure that all investors have access to the same information at the same time so that no one has an advantage.

12.3.3 Issue of further shares after incorporation

As time goes by, the company may wish to raise new finance and to issue new shares. This could be intended to buy new fixed assets, or even to provide cash so that the company may purchase the shares of another company and create a larger group.

Although the nominal value remains the same, the market value may be quite different. Suppose a company has shares of nominal value 25 pence but finds that its shares are selling in the market at 80 pence each. If the company issues 200,000 new shares it will collect £160,000 in cash. That is the important piece of information for the company because it can use the cash to buy new assets and expand the activities of the business. The *asset of cash has increased* by £160,000 and the *ownership interest has increased* by £160,000.

The accounting records are required by company law to show separately the nominal value of the shares and any extra amount over the nominal value. The nominal value is 25 pence and the total amount collected per share is 80 pence. So the extra amount collected is 55 pence. This extra amount is called a *premium* (the word means 'something extra'). So the £160,000 increase in the ownership interest is recorded as two separate items, namely the *nominal value* of £50,000 and the *share premium* of £110,000.

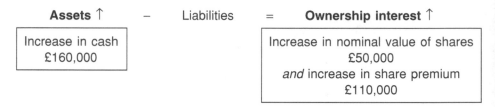

12.3.4 Revaluation of fixed assets

Suppose a company buys a hotel costing £560,000. The hotel is run successfully for a period of three years and at the end of that period a professional valuer confirms that the hotel, if sold, would probably result in sale proceeds of £620,000 because of the change in property values and the reputation which the hotel has established. The directors of the company may wish to tell shareholders about this increased market value of the company's fixed asset.

There are two ways of informing shareholders in the financial statements. One is to continue to record the balance sheet value at £560,000 (the historical cost) but to include a note to the balance sheet explaining that the market value has been confirmed as £620,000 by an expert. That information would allow the investor to think, 'That makes me feel better off by £60,000'.

This feeling of investor happiness is surrounded by a note of caution, because the gain in value is not *realised*. The asset has not in fact been sold in the market. It only needs a rumour of pollution on the local beach to depress the market value of all the hotels in the town. Some companies feel that this note of caution is conveyed by providing the information on the increase in value in the notes to the accounts rather than the balance sheet itself.

Other companies take a bolder view and decide that, in the interests of providing information which is relevant to the needs of users, the company should apply the accounting equation on behalf of the readers of the financial statement. These companies then have a problem of deciding on the name to be given to describe this £60,000 increase in the ownership interest. It cannot be called revenue and included in the profit and loss account because it has not been realised by the operations of the business. It represents a new ownership interest as a newly identified 'reserve' of wealth. The wealth lies in the asset, but the interest in that wealth is a claim which belongs to the owners. The increased wealth is caused by revaluation of the asset, and so the name chosen for this claim is *revaluation reserve*. In terms of the accounting equation there is an *increase in the value of an asset* and an *increase in the ownership interest*.

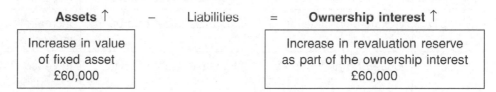

Assets ↑	−	Liabilities	=	**Ownership interest** ↑
Increase in value of fixed asset £60,000				Increase in revaluation reserve as part of the ownership interest £60,000

Example

A company, Office Owner Ltd, is formed on 1 January Year 1 by the issue of 4m ordinary shares of 25 pence nominal value each. The cash raised from the issue is used on 2 January to buy an office block which is rented to a customer for an annual rent of £50,000. The tenant carries all costs of repairs. The company's administration costs for the year are £10,000. At the end of the year the office block is valued by an expert at £1,015,000. On the last day of the year the company issues a further 2m ordinary shares at a price of 40 pence each, to raise cash in Year 2 for expansion plans.

L02 | **Activity 12.2**

For the analysis of each transaction you should look back to the previous sections where each type of transaction is dealt with in detail. Write down the effect of each transaction on the accounting equation. Check your answer against Exhibit 12.2. When you are satisfied that you understand Exhibit 12.2 look to Exhibit 12.3 where you will find the amounts entered in the spreadsheet.

Exhibit 12.2

Office Owner Ltd – analysis of transactions for Year 1

Date	Transaction or event	Effect on assets	Effect on ownership interest
Year 1			
Jan. 1	Issue of shares at nominal value	Increase asset of cash	Increase share capital at nominal value
Jan. 2	Purchase of office block	Increase asset of property	Decrease asset of cash
Jan.–Dec.	Rent received	Increase asset of cash	Revenue of the period
Jan.–Dec.	Administration costs	Decrease asset of cash	Expense of the period
Dec. 31	Revaluation of asset	Increase asset of property	Increase ownership interest by revaluation
Dec. 31	Issue of further shares	Increase asset of cash	Increase share capital at nominal value and increase share premium

Entering the amounts in the spreadsheet of Exhibit 12.3 shows, in the final line, that the accounting equation is satisfied and allows a balance sheet to be prepared as in Exhibit 12.4.

Exhibit 12.3

Office Owner Ltd – spreadsheet of transactions for Year 1

Date	Transaction or event	Cash	Office block	Share capital	Share premium	Profit and loss account	Revaluation reserve
Year 1		£000s	£000s	£000s	£000s	£000s	£000s
Jan. 1	Issue of shares	1,000		1,000			
Jan. 2	Purchase of office block	(1,000)	1,000				
Jan.–Dec.	Rent received	50				50	
Jan.–Dec.	Administration costs	(10)				(10)	
Dec. 31	Revaluation of asset		15				15
Dec. 31	Issue of further shares	800		500	300		
		840	1,015	1,500	300	40	15

└── 1,855 ──┘ └──────── 1,855 ────────┘

Exhibit 12.4
Office Owner Ltd – balance sheet at end of Year 1

Office Owner Ltd Balance sheet at end of Year 1	
	£000s
Fixed asset: Office block (at valuation)	1,015
Current asset: Cash	840
Net assets	1,855
Share capital	1,500
Share premium	300
Revaluation reserve	15
Profit and loss account	40
	1,855

L02 **Activity 12.3**

Suppose you note that a company has revalued its land and buildings as reported in the balance sheet. What evidence would you expect to see as justification for the amount of the revaluation? What questions might you ask about the basis of revaluation?

12.3.5 Changes in exchange rates of foreign currency

All information in the financial statements of a UK company is shown in £ sterling. Where exchange rates alter, a company may lose or gain purely because of the exchange rate movement. That loss or gain must be reported.

The accounting process is called *translation*. Translation from one currency to another is particularly important when the financial statements of companies in a group are added together and so must all be restated in a common currency. The word 'translation' is used because the process is comparable to translating words from one language to another.

There are different methods of reporting depending on the type of transaction or event. Two different stories are considered here. The first is the purchase of an asset located in a foreign country. The second is the purchase, by a group of companies, of the share capital of a company in a foreign country.

Purchase of an asset

Take first of all the example of a UK company which buys a factory in Sweden. The factory is priced at Kr10,000,000. At the date of purchase of the factory the exchange rate is Kr10 = £0.70. The UK company has agreed to pay for the factory on the day of the transfer of legal title.

For accounting purposes the cost of the factory is recorded at the amount paid at the date of purchase. This is calculated as:

$$\frac{0.70}{10} \times Kr10,000,000 = £700,000$$

The effect of the transaction on the balance sheet of the UK company is:

Assets ↑↓   –   Liabilities   =   Ownership interest

Increase in asset of factory £700,000   Decrease in asset of cash £700,000

That is the end of the story so far as the UK company is concerned. The exchange rate between the krona and the £ may fluctuate, and this may affect the company's view of the price for which the factory might eventually be sold, but that information will not appear in the financial statements of the UK company until such time as the factory is sold.

Purchase of shares in another company

Suppose now that a UK group of companies has decided to purchase the entire share capital of a Swedish company whose only asset is the same factory. The purchase price is Kr10,000,000. The Swedish company distributes its entire profit as dividend each year so that the only item remaining in its balance sheet is the factory at a cost of Kr10,000,000. (This is a very simplistic example but is sufficient to illustrate the exchange rate problem.)

At the date of purchase of the investment, the factory will be recorded in the group balance sheet at £700,000.

Assets ↑↓   –   Liabilities   =   Ownership interest

Increase in sterling equivalent of group's asset of factory £700,000   Decrease in group's asset of cash £700,000

One year later the exchange rate has altered to Kr10 = £0.68. The factory is the only asset of the subsidiary. In the Swedish accounts it remains at Kr10,000,000 but, translated into £ sterling, this now represents only £680,000:

$$\frac{0.68}{10} \times Kr10,000,000 = £680,000$$

This represents a potential loss of £20,000 on the translated value of the asset at the start of the year. The loss is unrealised but as a matter of prudence the fall in the translated asset value should be reported. However, there have been strong feelings expressed by companies over many years that the unrealised loss should not affect the reported profit of the period. Consequently the relevant accounting standard[1] allows the effect on the ownership interest to be shown in reserves.

Assets ↓	–	Liabilities	=	Ownership interest ↓
Reduction in sterling equivalent of assets of subsidiary £20,000				Decrease in reserves £20,000

The reporting of the reduction in the asset value as a decrease in reserves is controversial because less attention is sometimes paid to reserves than is paid to the profit and loss account. This means that the impact on the ownership interest may pass unnoticed.

This practice of translation is required by the accounting standard on the subject. In group accounting there is considerable complexity to the technical aspects of which exchange rate effects must pass through the profit and loss account and which may pass through the reserves. The important message for the reader of the annual reports is to be alert to the possibility of exchange rate effects on the ownership interest being reported in reserves.

L03   12.4 Additional primary financial statements

In Chapter 7 it was noted that the ASB's *Statement of Principles* names four primary financial statements:

- the balance sheet;
- the profit and loss account;
- the cash flow statement; and
- the statement of total recognised gains and losses.

The first three were dealt with in that chapter. The statement of total recognised gains and losses is now explained.

12.4.1 Statement of total recognised gains and losses

The *statement of total recognised gains and losses* (STRGL) was introduced by the Accounting Standards Board[2] as a result of well-publicised company failures where it was apparent that important information about changes in the ownership interest had not been understood fully by the users of the financial statements. In particular, losses caused by exchange rate fluctuations had been reported in the notes on reserves, apparently without the expert observers pointing to the fact that these losses cancelled out the profits gained from operating activities.

As well as exchange rate gains and losses, the STRGL will report unrealised gains and losses arising on revaluation of fixed assets of a period. Its purpose is to show the extent to which shareholders' funds have increased or decreased from all the various gains and losses recognised in the period. (There is an example later in the chapter, taken from the annual report of Safe and Sure plc.)

Definition
> The *statement of total recognised gains and losses* shows the extent to which share-holders' funds have increased or decreased from all the various gains and losses recognised in the period.

12.4.2 Reconciliation of movements in shareholders' funds

In addition to the statement of total recognised gains and losses the Accounting Standards Board also requires a *reconciliation of movements in shareholders' funds.* It may also be presented as a primary financial statement,[3] so that it has comparable prominence with other important information, or may be presented as a note to the financial statements. Most companies appear to be giving this reconciliation the prominence of a primary financial statement. (An example from the annual report of Safe and Sure plc appears later in the chapter.)

Definition
> The *reconciliation of movements in shareholders' funds* is a statement which presents all items causing a change in shareholders' funds during a period of time.

L04 ## 12.5 Users' needs for information

The owners of a company, and potential investors in a company, are primarily interested in whether the business will make them better off or worse off. They also want to be reassured that the business has taken care of the resources entrusted to it (carrying out the function of *stewardship*). The first source of an increase in the ownership interest is the *profit* generated by the company. Professional investors will use the phrase *quality of earnings* to refer to the different components of profit. They tend to regard profits generated by the main operating activity as being of higher quality than windfall gains such as profits on the sale of fixed assets which are not a regular feature of the company's activity.

Owners of a company expect to receive a reward for ownership. One form of reward is to watch the business grow and to know that in the future a sale of shares will give them a satisfactory gain over the period of ownership. That requires a long-term horizon. Some investors prefer to see the reward more frequently in the form of a dividend. They want to know that the ownership interest is adequate to support the dividend and yet leave sufficient assets in the business to generate further profits and dividends.

Creditors of a company know that they rank ahead of the shareholders in the event of the company being wound up, but they want to know that the company is generating sufficient wealth for the owners to provide a cushion against any adverse events. Therefore creditors will also be concerned with the ownership interest and how it is being maintained or is growing.

Employees, suppliers and customers similarly look for reassurance as to the strength of the business to continue into the future. The ownership interest is a convenient focus which summarises the overall impact of the state of assets and liabilities, although what employees are really interested in is the preservation of the earnings capacity of the business.

L05   12.6 Information provided in the financial statements

In Chapter 7 the balance sheet of Safe and Sure plc was presented. The final section of that balance sheet presented information on the capital and reserves representing the claim of the shareholders on the assets.

		Notes	Year 7 £m	Year 6 £m
Capital and reserves	Called-up share capital	12	19.6	19.5
	Share premium account	13	8.5	5.5
	Revaluation reserve	14	4.6	4.6
	Other reserves	15	9.1	7.2
	Profit and loss account	16	393.0	309.2
	Shareholders' funds		434.8	346.0

In the discussion contained in Chapter 7 it was emphasised that the most important feature of this information is that, in total, it represents the shareholders' legal claim. There is nothing to see, touch, count or hold. If the company were to cease trading at the balance sheet date, sell all its assets for the balance sheet amount and pay off all liabilities, the shareholders would be left with £434.8m to take away. The shareholders have the *residual claim*, which means that if the assets were to be sold for more than the balance sheet amount, the shareholders would share the windfall gain. If the assets were sold for less than the balance sheet amount, the shareholders would share the loss.

The total ownership interest is a claim which is described by this company as *shareholders' funds*. It is equal to the *net assets* of the company. The total claim is subdivided so as to explain how the various parts of the claim have arisen. This section now considers each part of the claim in turn.

12.6.1 Share capital

The information shown by the company at note 12 is as follows:

Note 12		Year 7 £m	Year 6 £m
Share capital	Ordinary shares of 2 pence each		
	Authorised: 1,050,000,000 shares		
	(Year 6: 1,000,000,000)	21.0	20.0
	Issued and fully paid: 978,147,487 shares	19.6	19.5

Certain senior executives hold options to subscribe for shares in the company at prices ranging from 33.40p to 244.33p under schemes approved by shareholders at various dates. Options on 3,479,507 shares were exercised during Year 7 and 66,970 options lapsed. The number of shares subject to options, the years in which they were purchased and the years in which they will expire are:

Purchase	Expiry	Numbers
All	Year 8	13,750
purchased	Year 9	110,000
10 years	Year 10	542,500
before	Year 11	1,429,000
expiry	Year 12	2,826,600
	Year 13/14	3,539,942
	Year 15	3,690,950
	Year 16	2,279,270
	Year 17	3,279,363
		17,711,375

Called-up means that the company has called upon the shareholders who first bought the shares to make payment in full. When a new company is brought to the stock market for the first time, investors may be invited to buy the shares by paying an instalment now and the rest later. That was quite common in the 1980s when former nationalised industries, such as electricity and water companies, were being sold to the private sector. The *prospectus,* which is issued to invite the purchase of shares, specifies the dates on which the company would make a call for the rest of the share price due. After all the cash has been received by the company, the shares are described as *fully paid.*

Ordinary shareholders are entitled to vote at meetings, usually in proportion to the number of shares held. That means that the power of the individual shareholder depends on the number of shares held. For most large companies there are relatively small numbers of shareholders who control relatively large proportions of the share capital. A company which is part of a larger group of companies is required to report in the notes to the accounts the name and country of the ultimate parent company. Companies which are listed on the Stock Exchange are required to disclose in the directors' report the name of any shareholder interested in 3 per cent or more of the company's issued share capital.

Before the directors of a company may issue new shares, they must be *authorised* to do so by the existing shareholders. The existing shareholders need to be aware that their claim will be diluted by the incoming shareholders. (If there are 50 shares owned equally by two persons, each controls 50 per cent of the company. If 25 new shares are issued to a third person, then all three have 33.3 per cent each, which *dilutes* the voting power of the first two persons.)

One of the controversial aspects of share capital in recent years has been the privilege of share options taken by directors and other employees (usually senior employees of the business but sometimes spreading to the wider employee range). A share option allows the person holding the option to buy shares in the company, at any future date up to a specified limit in time, at an agreed fixed price. The argument in favour of such an arrangement is that it gives senior management an incentive to make the company prosperous because they want the share price to increase above the price they have agreed to pay. The argument against it is that they have no very strong incentive because the worst that can happen to directors and other employees is that they decide not to take up the option when the share price has not performed well. Until 1995 there were also some personal tax advantages in taking options rather than a normal portion of salary, but since then, the tax rules have limited such benefits.

Major companies now disclose, in the directors' report, the options held by each of the directors. (Chapter 15 explains the influence of the Greenbury Committee on the reporting of directors' remuneration.)

The analyst's view

David and Leona are on the plane flying from London to Aberdeen for a week's holiday in the Cairngorms. David has brought the annual report of Safe and Sure plc as a precaution against inclement weather disturbing their plans for outdoor activities. While they wait for lunch to be served, David turns to the annual report and finds it is quite helpful to have Leona alongside him.

DAVID: *At the present time nothing seems to excite more comment from the financial journalists than the salaries paid to the directors and the options they hold. I have to confess that it's something I look for in the annual report. Maybe I'm looking for my future earning potential! One of my more cynical colleagues says that directors can't lose on options. If the share price rises they make money, which we don't mind because our investment is rising in value. What happens if the share price falls? The directors take new options at the lower price and then wait for the market to rise again so that they make a profit! We can't do that for our investment.*

I always look at the note on share capital to see whether new shares have been issued during the year. It reminds me to find out the reason. In this case the increase is £0.1m and the reason is explained in the accounts as being due entirely to the issue of options.

12.6.2 Share premium

It was explained earlier in this chapter that when shares are issued by a company it may well be that the market price of the shares is greater than the nominal value. What really matters to the company is the amount of cash contributed by the new shareholders but company law insists that the claim of these new shareholders is split into *nominal amount* and *share premium* (the amount received in excess of the nominal amount).

Note 13		Year 7	Year 6
		£m	£m
Share premium	At 1 January	5.5	3.6
account	Premium on shares issued during the		
	year under the share option schemes	3.0	1.9
	At 31 December	8.5	5.5

DAVID: *I look at the share premium account only as a check on the amount of cash raised by issuing shares during the year. If I add the £3.0m shown in this note to the £0.1m shown as an increase in nominal value, then I know that £3.1m was raised in total by the issue of shares. I can check that in the* cash flow statement *and in the* reconciliation of movements in shareholders' funds (*a statement which follows close to the profit and loss account*).

12.6.3 Revaluation reserve

Earlier in the chapter the effect of revaluing assets was explained in terms of the accounting equation. It was also explained that the effects of foreign currency exchange rates may appear in reserves. The note to the accounts of Safe and Sure plc appears as follows:

Note 14		Year 7	Year 6
		£m	£m
Revaluation	At 1 January	4.6	4.7
reserve	Exchange adjustments	0.1	(0.1)
	Transfer to profit and loss account	(0.1)	—
	At 31 December	4.6	4.6

DAVID: *I always look at the reserves note to see what is happening to the overall shareholders' claim. In this case there are no significant changes but it is interesting to note that this year the ownership interest has benefited by £0.1m from exchange rate adjustments whereas last year it lost £0.1m for the same reason.*

The transfer to profit and loss account is quite interesting. It would appear that an extra amount of £0.1m in profit has been added to this year's profit and loss account by an accounting entry. I hadn't noticed that until now but I will put it on my list of questions to the company next year.

LEONA: *You needn't be in suspense – I can enlighten you. When a fixed asset is revalued the gain is regarded as unrealised because the asset has not been sold. However, the asset will gradually grow older and will move closer to being sold. When it is sold the unrealised gain will become realised. Some people believe that this move towards realisation should be dealt with by transferring a portion of the unrealised gain to realised gains over the life of the asset.*

In fact, that extra amount of £0.1m is not *in this year's profit and loss account. That would be frowned upon by any reputable auditor. The transfer is to the accumulated profit of past years. Take a look at Note 16 and you'll see it there. Now you see that it can be quite useful to have the auditor's expertise on hand.*

Note 16		Year 7	Year 6
		£m	£m
Profit and loss	At 1 January	309.2	249.5
account	Exchange adjustments	4.1	(5.6)
	Profit for the year retained	81.1	66.8
	Transfer to other reserves	(1.5)	(1.5)
	Transfer from revaluation reserves	0.1	
	At 31 December	393.0	309.2

DAVID: *Well I recognise the retained profit for the year £81.1m as agreeing with the profit and loss account. (See* Chapter 7.) *And I can see some more exchange adjustments. But now you're losing me even more. The transfer from the revaluation reserve is now clear to me but there is a new transfer of £1.5m from here to something called 'other reserves'. What is that all about?*

LEONA: *The balance sheet reference for 'other reserves' is to Note 15. Let's see what it says.*

Note 15		Year 7	Year 6
		£m	£m
Other	At 1 January	7.2	6.0
reserves	Exchange adjustments	0.4	(0.3)
	Transfer from profit and loss account	1.5	1.5
	At 31 December	9.1	7.2

DAVID: *Now I can see the transfer of £1.5m to this reserve. But why is the transfer made? What is the purpose of 'other reserves'? And look, there is another exchange adjustment. Why have all these different reserves?*

LEONA: *Even I have to admit that I have no answer to this one. If I were the auditor, I would know. As an outside reader I can see nothing more than you can. There is no explanation of what 'other reserves' means. That is something you would have to clear up by phoning the group's financial controller.*

DAVID: *Aha! I've won! I knew that there were limits on auditors. Now you are telling me that there are secrets which the company and the auditor know but they don't tell the reader.*

LEONA: *There is the important word 'materiality'. Do you, as an investor, care very much about £9.1m compared with wealth of £393m accumulated through the profit and loss account reserves? You have to be careful not to become too tied up with detail. It can make a person slightly boring. In any event, the Accounting Standards Board has tried to help busy readers like you by creating a new primary financial statement called the statement of total recognised gains and losses. It ignores all the transfers into and out of reserves but highlights the items which cause an overall decrease or increase in the ownership interest. Turn back to the page immediately following the profit and loss account. You'll see that all the exchange rate adjustments are brought together in one amount and the transfers into and out of reserves are ignored.*

12.6.4 Statement of total recognised gains and losses

Safe and Sure plc Statement of total recognised gains and losses		
	Year 7 £m	Year 6 £m
Profit attributable to shareholders	114.8	94.6
Exchange rate adjustments	4.6	(6.0)
Total recognised gains for the year	119.4	88.6

In case you need even more help, the Accounting Standards Board also requires a reconciliation of movements in shareholders' funds. That is usually on the same page as, or very close to, the statement of total recognised gains and losses.

12.6.5 Reconciliation of movements in shareholders' funds

Safe and Sure plc Reconciliation of movements in shareholders' funds		
	Year 7 £m	Year 6 £m
Profit attributable to shareholders	114.8	94.6
Dividends	(33.7)	(27.8)
New share capital issued	3.1	2.0
Exchange rate adjustments	4.6	(6.0)
Net change in shareholders' funds	88.8	62.8
Opening shareholders' funds	346.0	283.2
Closing shareholders' funds	434.6	346.0

Now you really can start to tie things together. Look at the balance sheet. (See Chapter 7.) The final line there shows the closing shareholders' funds which appear as the final line in this reconciliation. The profit and the dividends you can see in the profit and loss account. (See Chapter 7.) The new share capital issued is £3.1m which is a combination of the increase of £3.0m in share premium (Note 13) and the increase of £0.1m in nominal share capital (Note 12). That is really tricky to sort out from the Notes – it's very helpful to have the reconciliation give the information in one place. The exchange adjustments have been brought together already in the statement of total recognised gains and losses.

DAVID: *You have given me plenty to think about. I can see the drinks trolley on its way – what would you like?*

L06 12.7 Dividends

Shareholders who invest in a company do so because they want the value of their shares to increase over time and return greater wealth when eventually sold. In the meantime the shareholders look for an income to spend each year. That comes to some of them by means of dividends.

Companies are not obliged to pay dividends and may decide not to do so if there is a shortage of cash or it is needed for other purposes. The directors make a recommendation to the shareholders in the annual general meeting. The shareholders may vote against taking the dividend but that happens only very rarely. Final dividend payments usually take place soon after the annual general meeting. Some companies also pay an interim dividend during the accounting year. Major UK companies have in past years ensured that a dividend was paid every year, however small, because it allowed the shares to be regarded as sufficiently 'safe' for investors such as trustees of charitable institutions.

When a company decides it wants to pay a dividend, there are two essential tests. The first is, 'Does the company have the cash resources to pay a dividend?' The second is, 'Has the company made sufficient profits, adding this year to previous years, to justify the dividend as being paid out of wealth created by the business?'

Even where the company has cash in the bank from which to pay the dividend, it must look forward and ensure that there are no other commitments in the near future which will also need cash. The company may decide to borrow short term to finance the dividend. In such a situation the company has to weigh the interest cost of borrowing against the risk of its shares being undervalued because of lack of interest from shareholders. These are all problems of cash management (more often called 'treasury management').

Company law imposes a different viewpoint. It takes the view that a company should not return to shareholders, during the life of the company, a part of the capital contributed by the shareholder body. Accordingly there is a requirement that dividends must be covered by accumulated reserves of past profit in excess of accumulated reserves of past losses. It is not required that the dividend is covered by the profit of the year. A company might choose to smooth things over by maintaining the dividend reasonably constant even where profits are fluctuating.

The dividend declared by the company is usually expressed in pence per share. Shareholders receive dividend calculated by multiplying the dividend in pence per share by the number of shares held. For the company there is a reduction in the asset of cash and a reduction in the ownership claim. The management of the company may regard the dividend as an expense of the business but it is more properly regarded as a reduction in the claim which the owners have on the net assets as a whole.

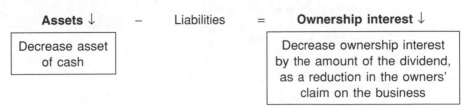

343

At the end of the accounting period the company will calculate profit and then declare a recommended dividend. The dividend is recommended by the directors to the shareholders. The shareholders may accept or decline but are not allowed to increase the amount. This recommended dividend is an obligation of the company, shown with creditors due for payment within 12 months of the balance sheet date. In the financial statements at the end of the year there will be an accrued liability for the dividend payable.

Assets	–	Liabilities ↑	=	Ownership interest ↓
		Increase current liability of dividend payable		Decrease ownership interest by the amount of the dividend, as a reduction of the owners' claim on the business

L07

12.8 Issue of further shares on the Stock Exchange

Once a company has a listing on the Stock Exchange it may decide to issue further shares. There are different methods by which this may be done, depending on the company's motive for the action. This section describes: an offer for sale, a capitalisation issue and a rights issue.

12.8.1 Offer for sale

When a company seeks a listing of its shares for the first time, it must offer those shares to the public (using the services of a member firm of the Stock Exchange as a sponsor) and issue a prospectus setting out information about itself. Some of the information to be included in the prospectus is required by the Companies Act but this is expanded upon by the *Listing Rules*. The prospectus is a highly informative document, revealing far more about a company than would be found in the annual report. There is a requirement for an accountant's report which includes a three-year history of the financial statements. In particular, there must be a specific statement confirming the adequacy of working capital.

There may also be a forecast of the expected profits for the next accounting period. The reporting accountants will be asked to give an opinion on the forecast. Particularly interesting are the assumptions on which the forecast is based. The reporting accountants will confirm that the amounts in the forecast are consistent with the assumptions but the reader will have to decide how appropriate the assumptions themselves are.

Exhibit 12.5 contains an example of a statement of assumptions taken from a company prospectus.

Exhibit 12.5

Assumptions on which profit forecast is based

> The forecasts have been prepared on a basis consistent with the accounting policies normally accepted by the Group and on the following principal assumptions:
>
> (i) there will be no changes in taxation or other legislation or government regulations or policies which will have a significant effect on the Group; and
> (ii) the operations of the Group and its suppliers will not be significantly affected by weather conditions, industrial action or civil disturbances.

You may be surprised to learn that the wording in Exhibit 12.5 is extracted from the prospectus of a company retailing high quality chocolates. You may be further surprised to learn that very similar wording appeared in the prospectus of a company offering dry cleaning services. There is no regulation which says that the statement of assumptions has to be helpful to the user of the annual report.

12.8.2 Capitalisation issue

After the shares have been listed for some time, the market value may have grown to the point where the shares are less marketable because the price of each is too large for convenient trading in small lots. The company may decide to increase the number of shares held by shareholders without making any change to the assets or liabilities of the company. One way of achieving this is to convert reserves into share capital. Take the simplified balance sheet in Exhibit 12.6. The company decides to convert £1m of reserves into share capital. It writes to each shareholder saying 'You will receive one new share for each share already held'. The balance sheet now becomes as shown in Exhibit 12.7.

Exhibit 12.6

Balance sheet of company prior to capitalisation

	£m
Assets	7
Liabilities	(4)
	3
Share capital, in shares of 25 pence each	1
Reserves	2
	3

Exhibit 12.7

Balance sheet of company after capitalisation

	£m
Assets	7
Liabilities	(4)
	3
Share capital, in shares of 25 pence each	2
Reserves	1
	3

The shareholder now holds twice as many shares by number but is no better or worse off financially because the total value of the company has not changed. The shares will each be worth one-half of the market price of an old share at the moment of issue. This process is sometimes referred to as a *bonus issue* because the shareholders receive new share certificates, but in reality there is no bonus because no new wealth is created.

In terms of the accounting equation the effect on the balance sheet is:

$$\text{Assets} \quad - \quad \text{Liabilities} \quad = \quad \textbf{Ownership interest} \uparrow\downarrow$$

> Increase in share capital £1m
> Decrease in reserves £1m

12.8.3 Rights issue

Once a company has a market listing it may decide that it needs to raise further finance on the stock market. The first people it would ask are the existing shareholders, who have already shown their commitment to the company by owning shares in it. Furthermore, it is desirable to offer them first chance because if strangers buy the shares the interests of the existing shareholders may be diluted. Suppose the company in Exhibit 12.6 wishes to raise £3m new finance. It will offer existing shareholders the right to pay for, say, 2m new shares at 150 pence each. There are already 4m shares of 25p nominal value in issue, so the letter to the shareholders will say: 'The company is offering you the right to buy 1 new share at a price of 150p for every 2 existing shares you hold.' Existing shareholders will be attracted by this offer provided the market price stays above 150 pence for existing shares. They may take up the rights themselves or sell the right to someone else. In either event, the company will receive £3m cash, the company will issue 2m new shares at 150 pence each and the balance sheet will appear as in Exhibit 12.8.

Exhibit 12.8
Balance sheet after rights issue

	£m
Assets	7.0
New cash	3.0
	10.0
Liabilities	(4.0)
	6.0
Share capital, in shares of 25 pence each	1.5
Share premium	2.5
Reserves	2.0
	6.0

The issue price of 150 pence is split for accounting purposes into the nominal value of 25 pence and the premium of 125 pence. In terms of the accounting equation the effect of the rights issue on the balance sheet is:

Assets ↑	−	Liabilities	=	Ownership interest ↑
Increase in cash £3m				Increase in share capital £0.5m Increase in share premium £2.5m

L07 **Activity 12.4**

Look in the financial section of a newspaper for the list of recent issues of new shares. Obtain the address of one company from a trade directory and write politely to ask for a copy of the prospectus. If you are sufficiently fortunate to obtain a copy of a prospectus, look at the accounting information and compare it with the amount and type of information published in the annual report. Why are they not the same?

12.9 Summary

Now score your view of your confidence in achieving the learning outcomes of the chapter.

1 = Very confident about knowledge, application, problem solving and evaluation.

2 = Confident about knowledge and application, less sure about problem solving and evaluation.

3 = Need to read again to be more certain of basic knowledge and application.

L01 You can now define ownership interest as the residual item in the accounting equation, representing the ownership claim on assets after all liabilities to third parties have been met.

1 2 3
☐ ☐ ☐

LO2 You can explain and demonstrate how the ownership interest is presented in company accounts, as share capital and reserves of all types. You can give this explanation for an initial issue of shares, a subsequent issue of shares, a revaluation and the effect of changing exchange rates using the accounting equation.

1 2 3
☐ ☐ ☐

LO3 You now understand the nature and purpose of the statement of total recognised gains and losses and the reconciliation of movements in shareholders' funds.

1 2 3
☐ ☐ ☐

LO4 You can explain the needs of users for information about the ownership interest in a company.

1 2 3
☐ ☐ ☐

LO5 You can read and interpret the information reported by companies in their annual reports, in respect of the ownership interest, using an example such as Safe and Sure to illustrate your explanation.

1 2 3
☐ ☐ ☐

LO6 You can explain the accounting treatment of dividends, both interim and final.

1 2 3
☐ ☐ ☐

LO7 You now understand, and can explain by simple calculation, the methods by which a company's shares may be issued when the company has a Stock Exchange listing.

1 2 3
☐ ☐ ☐

LO8 The knowledge you have gained in Chapters 8 to 12 allows you to use a spreadsheet of the type illustrated in Chapters 5 and 6 to show that you understand the impact of transactions and events on ownership interest in company accounts. Examples for you to try are provided in the Lecturer's Guide that accompanies this textbook.

1 2 3
☐ ☐ ☐

LO9 You should now turn to the Supplement if you wish to learn how to record end-of-period adjustments as debit and credit adjustments to a trial balance taken from the ledger accounts and produce figures for financial statements.

1 2 3
☐ ☐ ☐

If your scores are all 1 or 2, try the questions in the series A, B and C. This will give you feedback on your assessment of how well you have achieved the learning outcomes. Read again any sections of the chapter where you find your knowledge and understanding are less comprehensive than you first estimated.

If your scores include some at 3, try the series A questions to find where the problems lie. Read the relevant sections again, work through any illustrative examples and case studies, then try the questions in the series B. Once you feel confident at that level of knowledge and application, move on to try some or all of the series C questions.

International perspective

It has been explained in this chapter that the proposed dividend should be reported as a current liability at the end of the year. If you look at the balance sheet of a US company you will not find this liability recorded. US companies take the view that the liability does not exist until the dividend is agreed by shareholders in the Annual General Meeting, which takes place after the year-end. There is an International Accounting Standard which makes no mention of the dividend liability. It is likely that UK practice will change to reflect international practice.

The chapter has also explained the accounting processes for revaluing fixed assets. Such revaluation is not allowed in the USA or Germany. In other countries, such as France, it is allowed but rarely used. Revaluation is permitted by the IASB but is not a requirement.

The ownership interest consists of share capital plus all reserves. The reserves are given different names in different countries. In some there is a legally defined reserve with a tax-deductible transfer to the reserve from the profit and loss account. It requires careful reading of the ownership interest section of the balance sheet.

Test your understanding

Skills outcomes
SO1 Application of technical skills   **SO2** Problem solving and evaluation skills   **SO3** Communication skills

L01, SO1   **A12.1** What is the definition of ownership interest?

L01, SO1   **A12.2** Why may it be said that the ownership interest is the residual item in the accounting equation?

L02, SO1   **A12.3** What is the effect on the accounting equation where new shares are issued for cash?

L02, SO1   **A12.4** Why does the company not record the buying and selling of shares in its balance sheet?

L02, SO1   **A12.5** What is a share premium? How is it recorded?

L02, SO1   **A12.6** How is the revaluation of a fixed asset reported?

L03, SO1   **A12.7** Why may the revaluation of a fixed asset not be reported in the profit and loss account?

L03, SO1   **A12.8** Where may the reader of the annual report find out about the effect of movements in foreign exchange rates?

L03, SO1   **A12.9** What is the purpose of the statement of total recognised gains and losses?

L03, SO1   **A12.10** What is the purpose of the reconciliation of movements in shareholders' funds?

L06, SO1   **A12.11** How is a proposed dividend recorded in the financial statements of a company?

L07, SO1   **A12.12** What is meant by:

(a) offer for sale;
(b) capitalisation issue; and
(c) rights issue?

Explain the effect of each of the above on the balance sheet of a company.

Application

L02, S01 **B12.1** Explain the effect on the accounting equation of each of the following transactions:

(a) At the start of Year 1, Bright Ltd issues 200,000 shares at nominal value 25 pence per share, receiving £50,000 in cash.

(b) At the end of Year 2, Bright Ltd issues a further 100,000 shares to an investor at an agreed price of 75 pence per share, receiving £75,000 in cash.

(c) At the end of Year 3 the directors of Bright Ltd obtain a market value of £90,000 for a company property which originally cost £70,000. They wish to record this in the balance sheet.

L06, S01 **B12.2** Explain the effect on the accounting equation of the following transactions and decisions regarding dividends:

(a) The company pays a dividend of £20,000 during the accounting period.

(b) The directors recommend a dividend of £30,000 at the end of the accounting year. It will be paid following shareholder approval at the Annual General Meeting, held two months after the accounting year-end.

L07, S01 **B12.3** The following is a summarised balance sheet of Nithsdale Ltd.

	£000s
Cash	20
Other assets less liabilities	320
	340
Ordinary shares (400,000 of 25 pence each)	100
Share premium	40
Reserves of retained profit	200
	340

The company is considering three possible changes to its capital structure:

(a) issue for cash 50,000 additional ordinary shares at £1 per share, fully paid; or

(b) make a 1 for 4 capitalisation issue of ordinary shares; or

(c) make a 1 for 5 rights issue at £3 per share.

Show separately the impact of each change on the balance sheet of the company.

L02, S01 **B12.4** Fragrance plc has owned a factory building for many years. The building is recorded in the balance sheet at £250,000, being historical cost of £300,000 less accumulated depreciation of £50,000. The recent report of a professional valuer indicated that the property is valued at £380,000 on an open market basis for its existing use. Explain the effect this information will have on the reported financial statements.

L02, L03, S01 **B12.5** Suppose the factory building in question **B12.4** was valued by the professional expert at £240,000. What effect would this information have on the reported financial statements?

Problem solving and evaluation

This question reviews your understanding of Chapters 8–12 and the effect of transactions on ownership interest.

L08, S02 **C12.1** Set out below is a summary of the accounting records of Titan Ltd at 31 December Year 1:

	£000s	£000s
Assets		
Land and buildings	200	
Plant and machinery	550	
Investment in shares	150	
Stock	250	
Trade debtors	180	
Cash	150	
Liabilities		
Trade creditors		365
Debenture loan 10% nominal rate of interest		250
Ownership interest		
Share capital		600
Profit and loss account reserve at 1 Jan. Year 1		125
Revenue		
Sales		1,815
Cost of goods sold	1,505	
Expenses		
Overhead expenses	145	
Debenture interest paid	25	
Totals	3,155	3,155

The summary of the accounting records includes all transactions which have been entered in the ledger accounts up to 31 December, but investigation reveals further adjustments which relate to the accounting period up to, and including, that date.

The adjustments required relate to the following matters:

(i) No depreciation has been charged for the year in respect of buildings, plant and machinery. The depreciation of the building has been calculated as £2,000 per annum and the depreciation of plant and machinery for the year has been calculated as £55,000 for the year.

(ii) The company is aware that electricity consumption during the months of November and December, Year 1, amounted to around £5,000 in total, but no electricity bill has yet been received.

(iii) Overhead expenses include insurance premiums of £36,000 which were paid at the start of December, Year 1, in respect of the 12-month period ahead.

(iv) The stock amount is as shown in the accounting records of items moving into and out of stock during the year. On 31 December a check of the physical stock was made. It was discovered that raw materials recorded as having a value of £3,000 were, in fact, unusable. It was also found that an employee had misappropriated stock worth £5,000.

(v) The company proposes to pay a dividend of £30,000.

(vi) The corporation tax payable in respect of the profits of the year is estimated at £45,000, due for payment on 30 September, Year 2.

Required

(a) Explain how each of the items (i) to (vi) will affect the ownership interest.

(b) Calculate the amount of the ownership interest after taking into account items (i) to (vi). (*Hint: First calculate the profit of the year.*)

Activities for study groups

Turn to the annual report of a listed company which you have used for activities in earlier chapters. Find every item which relates to the ownership interest (including any discussion in the non-regulated part of the annual report).

As a group, imagine you are shareholders in this company. You are holding a meeting of the shareholders' action group calling for clarity of information about your total interest in the business. Make lists of the good points and weak points in the quality of information available to you and then arrange the weak points in descending order of importance. Then draft an action plan for improved communication with shareholders which you would propose sending to the company.

Notes and references

1 ASC (1983) Statement of Standard Accounting Practice (SSAP 20), *Foreign Currency Translation*, Accounting Standards Committee.

2 ASB (1992) Financial Reporting Standard (FRS 3), *Reporting Financial Performance*, Accounting Standards Board; and ASB (1999) *Statement of Principles for Financial Reporting*, ch. 7.

3 ASB (1992) FRS 3, para. 59.

A spreadsheet for adjustment to a trial balance at the end of the accounting period

End-of-period adjustments and the ownership interest

If you look back to Chapter 6 you will see that it finished with a trial balance and a promise that the trial balance would be used later as the starting point for preparation of financial statements. The moment has now arrived where the trial balance is used as a starting point for making end-of-period adjustments to show the change in the ownership interest during the period.

The accruals concept (or the parallel argument of matching in the profit and loss account) requires all items relevant to the period to be included in the financial statements of the period. Most items will be included because they will have been recorded in the ledger and hence in the financial statements. However, there will be some items of information, emerging from enquiry at the end of the period, which have not yet resulted in a transaction but which are undoubtedly based on events relevant to the period.

The enquiry will take a routine form of:

- estimating the depreciation of fixed assets where this has not already been recorded;
- examining fixed assets for signs of obsolescence beyond the amount allowed for in the depreciation charge;
- counting the stock of raw materials, work-in-progress and finished goods, for comparison with the accounting record;
- evaluating the doubtful debtors;
- checking files for any purchase invoices received but not yet recorded;
- checking files for any sales invoices for goods sent out but not yet recorded;
- considering whether any resource has been consumed, or service received, for which a supplier has not yet sent an invoice.

Returning to the trial balance contained in Exhibit 6.15 of Chapter 6, it may be noted that the depreciation for the month has been charged, there are no debtors and therefore no concerns about doubtful debts, and it would appear from the list of transactions for the month that all sales and purchases have been recorded carefully. Suppose, however, that when M. Carter checks the stock of goods at the end of the month it is found that the roof has been leaking and rainwater has damaged goods worth £500. Furthermore, the business uses gas to heat a water boiler and it is estimated that consumption for the month amounts to £80.

These items of information are called *end-of-period adjustments*. Both events could, and would, be recorded in the ledger accounts by the business. If you were presented with this information as a class exercise, or you were the auditor taking the trial balance and adjusting it for this further information, you would use a spreadsheet which set out the trial balance and then provided further columns for the end-of-period adjustments. The spreadsheet for this example is set out in Exhibit 12.9 but before looking at that you should read through the next section which explains the recording of end-of-period adjustments. In this case a one-month period is covered and so the adjustments are referred to as *month-end adjustments*.

Analysis of the month-end adjustments

Before any entries may be made in the adjustments columns of the spreadsheet, the effect of each adjustment on the accounting equation must be considered so that the debit and credit entries may be identified.

(a) At the end of the month it is found that the roof has been leaking and rainwater has damaged goods worth £500

The loss of stock causes the ownership interest to decrease and is recorded as a debit entry in the expense of cost of goods sold. The decrease in the stock is recorded as a credit entry in the ledger account.

Dr	Cost of goods sold	£500	
Cr	Stock of goods		£500

(b) The business uses gas to heat a water boiler and it is estimated that consumption for the month amounts to £80

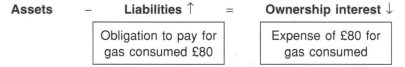

The event of consuming the gas causes the ownership interest to decrease and is recorded as a debit entry in an expense account for gas consumed. The obligation to pay for the gas at a future time is recorded as a credit entry in the ledger account for accruals.

Dr	Expense of gas	£80	
Cr	Accruals		£80

The spreadsheet

Exhibit 12.9 contains, in the left-hand pair of debit and credit columns, the trial balance of Exhibit 6.15 from Chapter 6. The next pair of columns contains the debit and credit entries necessary for the end-of-period adjustments. The third pair of columns shows the resulting amounts on each line of profit and loss account items. The final pair of columns shows the resulting amounts on each line of balance sheet items. The entire spreadsheet could be thought of as a series of ledger accounts stretched across the page, with one line for each ledger account.

Exhibit 12.9

Trial balance of M. Carter at the end of May, before month-end adjustments

Ledger account title	Trial balance		Adjustments		Profit and loss account		Balance sheet	
	Dr	Cr	Dr	Cr	Expense	Revenue	A	L + C
	£	£	£	£	£	£	£	£
L3 Buildings	30,000						30,000	
L4 Equipment	5,750						5,750	
L5 Stock of goods	8,000			500 (a)			7,500	
L11 R. Welsby	nil							
L1 Cash	6,400						6,400	
Accruals				80 (b)				80
L6 R. Busby		nil						
L2 Ownership interest		49,000						49,000
Subtotal	50,150	49,000					49,650	49,080
Difference: profit of the month								570
L10 Sales		7,000				7,000		
L9 Cost of goods sold	3,500		500 (a)		4,000			
L7 Electricity	100				100			
Gas			80 (b)		80			
L8 Wages	2,000				2,000			
L12 Depreciation	250				250			
Subtotal	5,850	7,000			6,430	7,000		
Difference: profit of the month					570			
Total of each column	56,000	56,000	580	580	7,000	7,000	49,650	49,650

The debit and credit entries identified by the foregoing analysis are shown in the adjustments columns of the spreadsheet with identifying letters in brackets alongside. Where no suitably named line exists, a new line may be inserted. The use of a new line is shown here for accruals and the expense of gas. If the exercise is being carried out using a computer spreadsheet package, the insertion of an extra line is not a problem. For a handwritten exercise it may be necessary to leave spaces at possible insertion points.

Once all adjustments have been entered, each of the adjusted amounts can be carried across to one of the final four columns, depending on whether the item belongs to the profit and loss account or the balance sheet. Each pair of columns is added and the difference between the totals in the profit and loss account columns should equal the difference between the totals in the balance sheet columns. If that is not the case, it means that an error has taken place at some point in the spreadsheet and must be found.

Revised statement of profit

The statement of profit before adjustments is shown in section 6.6.2 of Chapter 6 and the balance sheet is in section 6.6.3. From the final four columns of the spreadsheet in Exhibit 12.9, these could now be restated as follows:

M Carter, Wholesaler		
Profit and loss account (adjusted) for the month of May Year XX		
	£	£
Sales		7,000
Cost of goods sold		4,000
Gross profit		3,000
Other expenses		
Wages	2,000	
Electricity	100	
Gas	80	
Depreciation	250	
		2,430
Net profit		570

Statement of financial position: the balance sheet

Accounting equation	M Carter, Wholesaler Balance sheet (adjusted) at 31 May Year XX	£
	Fixed assets	
	Buildings	30,000
	Equipment	6,000
		36,000
	Depreciation	(250)
FA	Depreciated cost of fixed assets	35,750
	Current assets	
	Stocks	7,500
	Cash at bank	6,400
CA		13,900
CL	Accruals	(80)
	Net current assets	13,820
A – L	Net assets	49,570
	Ownership interest	
	Capital at start	50,000
	Add profit	570
	Less drawings	(1,000)
OI	**Total ownership interest**	49,570

This completes the study of double entry bookkeeping in this book. You are now in a position to be able to carry out the following tasks in relation to the business of a sole trader:

- Record transactions in ledger accounts.
- Prepare a trial balance.
- Make end-of-period adjustments to the trial balance.
- Prepare a profit and loss account and balance sheet.

L09, S01 Test your understanding

S12.1

(a) Using the information provided in question **C12.1**, prepare a spreadsheet containing a trial balance, adjustment and resulting figures for profit and loss account and balance sheet items. (Exhibit 12.9 provides a pattern to follow.)

(b) Present the profit and loss account for the year and the balance sheet at the end of the year in an informative and useful manner.

Part 4

Performance analysis

Chapter 13

Ratio analysis

After reading this chapter you should be able to:

LO1 Define, calculate and interpret ratios that help analyse and understand (a) performance for investors, (b) management performance, (c) liquidity and working capital, and (d) gearing.

LO2 Explain investors' views of the balance of risk and return, and the risks of investing in a geared company when profits are fluctuating.

LO3 Explain how the pyramid of ratios helps integrate interpretation.

LO4 Describe the uses and limitations of ratio analysis.

LO5 Carry out a practical exercise of calculating and interpreting ratios.

13.1 Introduction

Ratios are widely used as a tool in the interpretation of financial statements. The ratios selected and the use of the resulting information depend on the needs of the person using the information. What investors really want to do is choose the best moment to sell shares when the share price is at its highest. To choose that best moment, the investors will monitor the company's performance. Bankers lending to the company will also monitor performance, and look for indicators of solvency and ability to repay interest and capital.

Many users will rely on others to monitor ratios on their behalf. Employees will look to their advisers, perhaps union officials, to monitor performance. Small private investors with limited resources will rely heavily on articles in the financial sections of newspapers. Professional fund managers will look to their own research resources and may also make use of the analysts' reports prepared by the brokers who act for the fund managers in buying and selling shares. Each broker's analyst seeks as much information as possible about a company so that he or she can sell information which is of better quality than that of any other broker's analyst. There is fierce competition to be a highly rated analyst because that brings business to the broking firm and high rewards for the analyst.

In monitoring performance the expert analysts and fund managers will use ratios rather than absolute amounts. A figure of £100m for sales means nothing in isolation. The reader who knows that last year's sales were £90m sees immediately an increase of 11.1 per cent. The reader who knows that fixed assets remained constant at £75m knows that the fixed assets this year have earned their value in sales 1.33 times ($100/75 = 1.33$) whereas last year they earned their value in sales 1.2 times ($90/75 = 1.2$). Ratios show changes in relationships of figures which start to create a story and start to generate questions. They do not provide answers.

The fund managers and analysts all have their own systems for calculating ratios and some keep these a carefully guarded secret so that each may hopefully see an important clue before the next person does so. That means there is no standard system of ratio analysis. There are, however, several which are used frequently. A selection of these will be used here as a basic framework for analysis. As you start to read more about company accounts you will find other ratios used but you should discover that those are largely refinements of the structure presented here.

L01 ## 13.2 Systematic approach to ratio analysis

A systematic approach to ratio analysis seeks to establish a broad picture first of all, and then break that broad picture down until there are thumbnail sketches of interesting areas. Four key headings commonly encountered in ratio analysis are:

Investor ratios. Ratios in this category provide some measure of how the price of a share in the stock market compares to key indicators of the performance of the company.

Analysis of management performance. Ratios in this category indicate how well the company is being run in terms of using assets to generate sales and how effective it is in controlling costs and producing profit based on goods and services sold.

Liquidity and current assets. The management of cash and current assets and the preservation of an adequate, but not excessive, level of liquidity is an essential feature of business survival especially in difficult economic circumstances.

Gearing (referred to in American texts as 'leverage'). Gearing is a measure of the extent to which there is financial risk indicated in the balance sheet and in the profit and loss account (*see* later section on risk and return). Financial risk means the risk associated with having to pay interest and having an obligation to repay a loan.

In the following sections key ratios for each of these aspects of a systematic analysis are specified by the name of the ratio and the definition in words. Below each definition there is a brief discussion of the meaning and interpretation of the ratio.

13.2.1 Investor ratios

Investors who buy shares in a company want to be able to compare the benefit from the investment with the amount they have paid, or intend to pay, for their shares. There are two measures of benefit to the investors. One is the profit of the period (usually give the name 'earnings' when referring to the profit available for ordinary shareholders). The other is the dividend which is an amount actually paid to the shareholders. Profit indicates wealth created by the business. That wealth may be accumulated in the business or else paid out in the form of dividend. Four ratios are presented with a comment on each.

Earnings per share	$\dfrac{\text{Profit after tax for ordinary shareholders}}{\text{Number of ordinary shares}}$

Comment. This is the most frequently quoted measure of company performance and progress. The percentage change from year to year should be monitored for the trend. Criticisms are that this strong focus on annual earnings may cause 'short-termism' among investors and among company managers. The ASB has tried, in the accounting standard FRS 3 *Reporting Financial Performance*, to turn companies and users of accounts away from reliance on earnings per share as a single performance measure, but the earnings per share remains a strong feature of comments on company results.

Price–earnings ratio	$\dfrac{\text{Share price}}{\text{Earnings per share}}$

Comment. The price–earnings ratio (often abbreviated to *p/e ratio*) compares the amount invested in one share with the earnings per share. It may be interpreted as the number of years for which the currently reported profit is represented by the current share price. The p/e ratio reflects the market's confidence in future prospects of the company. The higher the ratio, the longer is the period for which the market believes the current level of earnings may be sustained.

In order to gain some feeling for the relative magnitude of the p/e ratio of any individual company, it should be compared with the average p/e ratio for the industry, given daily in the *Financial Times*. The p/e ratio is quite commonly used as a key item of input information in investment decisions or recommendations.

Dividend cover (payout ratio)	$\dfrac{\text{Profit after tax for ordinary shareholders}}{\text{Ordinary dividend of the period}}$

Comment. Companies need cash to enable them to pay dividends. For most companies the profits of the business must generate that cash. So the dividend decision could be regarded as a two-stage question. The first part is, 'Have we made sufficient profits?' and the second stage is, 'Has that profit generated cash which is not needed for reinvestment in fixed or current assets?' The dividend cover helps in answering the first of these questions. It shows the number of times the dividend has been covered by the profits of this year. It could be said that the higher the dividend cover, the 'safer' is the dividend. On the other hand, it could be argued that a high dividend cover means that the company is keeping new wealth to itself, perhaps to be used in buying new assets, rather than dividing it among the shareholders.

Dividend per share	$\dfrac{\text{Dividend payable to ordinary shareholders}}{\text{Number of issued shares}}$

Comment. The dividend per share is one of the key measures announced by the company at the end of the financial year (and sometimes as an interim dividend during the year as well). Shareholders immediately know how much to expect in total dividend, depending on the number of shares held. The figure of dividend per share is the cash amount paid by the company. It may or may not be subject to tax in the hands of the recipient, depending on whether or not the recipient is a taxpayer.

The dividend policy of the company is a major decision for the board of directors. Many companies like to keep to a 'target' dividend cover with only minor fluctuations from one year to the next. The evidence from finance research is that company managers have two targets, one being the stability of the dividend cover but the other being a desire to see the dividend per share increase, or at least remain stationary, rather than decrease. Dividends are thought to carry a signal to the market of the strength and stability of the company.

Dividend yield	$\dfrac{\text{Dividend per share}}{\text{Share price}} \times 100\%$

Comment. The dividend yield is a very simple ratio comparing dividend per share with the current market price of a share. It indicates the relationship between what the investor can expect to receive from the shares and the amount which is invested in the shares. Many investors need income from investments and the dividend yield is an important factor in their decision to invest in, or remain in, a company. It has to be noted that dividends are not the only benefit from share ownership. Section 14.5 on risk and return presents a formula for return (yield) which takes into account the growth in share price as well as the dividend paid. Investors buy shares in expectation of an increase in the share price. The directors of many companies would take the view that the dividend yield should be adequate to provide an investment income, but it is the wealth arising from retained profits that is used for investment in new assets which in turn generate growth in future profits.

13.2.2 Analysis of management performance

Management of a business is primarily a function requiring stewardship, meaning careful use of resources for the benefit of the owners. There are two central questions to test this use of resources: How well did the management make use of the investment in assets to create revenue, and how carefully did the management control costs so as to maximise the profit derived from that revenue?

Return on shareholders' equity	$\dfrac{\text{Profit after tax}}{\text{Share capital + Reserves}} \times 100\%$

Comment. A key measure of success, from the viewpoint of shareholders, is the success of the company in using the funds provided by shareholders to generate profit. That profit will provide new wealth to cover their dividend and to finance future expansion of the business. The return on shareholders' equity is therefore a measure of company performance from the shareholders' perspective. It is essential in this calculation to use the profit for ordinary shareholders, which is the profit after tax and after interest charges.

Return on capital employed	$\dfrac{\text{Profit before interest and tax}}{\text{Total assets} - \text{Current liabilities}} \times 100\%$

Comment. A broader measure than return on shareholders' equity is the ratio which measures the performance of a company as a whole in using all sources of long-term finance. Profit before interest and tax is used in the numerator as a measure of operating results. It is sometime called 'earnings before interest and tax' and is abbreviated to EBIT. Return on capital employed is often seen as a measure of management efficiency. The denominator could equally well be written 'Ordinary share capital plus reserves plus long-term loans'. The ratio is a measure of how well the long-term finance is being used to generate operating profits.

Return on total assets	$\dfrac{\text{Profit before interest and tax}}{\text{Total assets}} \times 100\%$

Comment. Calculating the return on total assets is another variation on measuring how well the assets of the business are used to generate operating profit before deducting interest and tax.

Net profit on sales	$\dfrac{\text{Net profit (before interest and tax)}}{\text{Sales (turnover)}} \times 100\%$

Comment. The ratio of net profit as a percentage of sales is also referred to as the *net profit margin*. The aim of many a successful business manager is to make the margin as high as possible. The margin reflects the degree of competitiveness in the market, the economic situation, the ability to differentiate products and the ability to control expenses. At the end of this section it is shown that companies are not obliged to seek high profit margins. Some cannot, because of strong competitive factors. Yet they still make a satisfactory return on capital employed by making efficient use of the capital equipment.

Gross profit percentage	$\dfrac{\text{Gross profit}}{\text{Sales (turnover)}} \times 100\%$

Comment. The gross profit as a percentage of sales is also referred to as the *gross margin*. It has been seen in earlier chapters that the gross profit is equal to sales minus all cost of sales. That gross profit may be compared with sales as shown above. The gross profit percentage concentrates on costs of making goods and services ready for sale. Small changes in this ratio can be highly significant. There tends to be a view that there is a 'normal' value for the industry or for the product that may be used as a benchmark against which to measure a company's performance.

Because it is such a sensitive measure, many companies try to keep secret from their competitors and customers the detailed breakdown of gross profit for each product line or area of activity. Companies do not want to give competitors any clues on how much to undercut prices and do not want to give customers a chance to complain about excessive profits.

Total assets usage	$\dfrac{\text{Turnover}}{\text{Total assets}}$

Comment. Total assets usage indicates how well a company has used its fixed and current assets to generate sales. Such a ratio is probably most useful as an indication of trends over a period of years. There is no particular value which is too high or too low but a sudden change would prompt the observer to ask questions.

Fixed assets usage	$\dfrac{\text{Turnover}}{\text{Fixed assets}}$

Comment. A similar measure of usage, but one which concentrates on the productive capacity as measured by fixed assets, indicates how successful the company is in generating sales (turnover) from fixed assets. The fixed asset usage ratio may be interpreted as showing how many £s of sales have been generated by each £ of fixed assets.

13.2.3 Liquidity and working capital

Liquidity is a word which refers to the availability of cash in the near future after taking account of immediate financial commitments. Cash in the near future will be available from bank deposits, cash released by sale of stocks and cash collected from customers. Immediate financial commitments are shown in current liabilities. The first ratio of liquidity is therefore a simple comparison of current assets with current liabilities.

Current ratio	Current assets : Current liabilities

Comment. If the current assets amount to £20m and the current liabilities amount to £10m the company is said, in words, to have 'a current ratio of 2 to 1'. Some commentators abbreviate this by saying 'the current ratio is 2'. Mathematically that is incorrect wording but the listener is expected to know that the words 'to 1' have been omitted from the end of the sentence.

The current ratio indicates the extent to which short-term assets are available to meet short-term liabilities. A current ratio of 2 : 1 is regarded, broadly speaking, as being a reasonable order of magnitude. As with other ratios, there is no 'best' answer for any particular company and it is the trend in this ratio which is more important. If the ratio is worsening over time, and especially if it falls to less than 1 : 1, the observer would look closely at the cash flow. A company can survive provided it can meet its obligations *as they fall due*. Some companies therefore operate on a very tight current ratio because they are able to plan the timing of inflows and outflows of cash quite precisely.

Companies which generate cash on a daily basis, such as retail stores, can therefore operate on a lower current ratio. Manufacturing businesses which have to hold substantial stocks would operate on a higher current ratio.

Acid test	(Current assets minus stock) : Current liabilities

Comment. In a crisis, where short-term creditors are demanding payment, the possibility of selling stocks to raise cash may be unrealistic. The acid test takes a closer look at the liquid assets of the current ratio, omitting the stocks. For many companies this ratio is less than 1 : 1 because it is unlikely that all creditors will require payment at the same time. As with the current ratio, an understanding of the acid test has to be supported by an understanding of the pattern of cash flows. Analysts in particular will often ask companies about the peak borrowing requirements of the year and the timing of that peak in relation to cash inflows.

Stock holding period	$\dfrac{\text{Average stock held}}{\text{Cost of sales}} \times 365$

Comment. The stock holding period measures the average period during which stocks of goods are held before being sold or used in the operations of the business. It is usually expressed in days, which is why the figure of 365 appears in the formula. If months are preferred, then the figure 12 should be substituted for the figure 365. One point of view is that the shorter the period, the better. Another point of view is that too short a period may create a greater risk of finding that the business is short of a stock item.

In calculating the stock holding period it is preferable to use the average of the stock held at the start of the year and the stock held at the end of the year. Some analysts use only the year-end figure if the start-of-year figure is not available. Whatever variation is used, it is important to be consistent from one time period to the next.

Debtors collection period	$\dfrac{\text{Trade debtors}}{\text{Credit sales}} \times 365$

Comment. The debtors collection period measures the average period of credit allowed to credit customers. An increase in this measure would indicate that a company is building up cash flow problems, although an attempt to decrease the period of credit allowed might deter customers and cause them to seek a competitor who gives a longer period of credit. It is important to be aware of the normal credit period for the industry. Some companies offer discount for prompt payment. Any offer of discount should weigh the cost of the discount against the benefit of earlier receipt of cash from customers.

Creditors payment period	$\dfrac{\text{Trade creditors}}{\text{Credit purchases}} \times 365$

Comment. The creditors payment period measures the average period of credit taken from suppliers of goods and services. An increase in this measure could indicate that the supplier has allowed a longer period to pay. It could also indicate that the company is taking longer to pay, perhaps because of cash flow problems. If payment is delayed then the company may lose discounts available for prompt payments. A reputation for being a slow payer could make it more difficult to obtain supplies in future. Some large companies have gained a reputation for delaying payment to smaller suppliers. Company law now requires company directors to make a statement of policy in relation to creditor payment.

Companies do not usually report purchases directly, so the figure must be calculated as follows:

Purchases = Cost of goods sold + closing stock − opening stock

Working capital cycle	Stock holding period + Debtors collection period − Creditors payment period

Comment. You saw in Chapter 9 the working capital cycle whereby stocks are purchased on credit, then sold to customers who eventually pay cash. The cash is used to pay suppliers and the cycle starts again. We can now put some timings into the diagram. The working capital represents the long-term finance needed to cover current assets that are not matched by current liabilities. The longer the total of the stock holding period and debtors collection period, compared to the creditors payment period, the greater the need for working capital to be financed long term.

13.2.4 Gearing

The term *gearing* is used to describe the mix of loan finance and equity finance in a company. It is more properly called *financial gearing* and in American texts is called *leverage*. There are two main approaches to measuring gearing. The first looks at the balance sheet and the second looks at the profit and loss account.

Debt/equity ratio	$\dfrac{\text{Long-term loans}}{\text{Ordinary share capital} + \text{Reserves}} \times 100\%$

Comment. From the balance sheet perspective the gearing measure considers the relative proportions of long-term loans and equity in the long-term financing of the business. The precise meaning of 'long-term loans' will vary from one company to the next. It is intended to cover the loans taken out with the aim of making them a permanent part of the company's financing policy. As they come due for repayment, they are replaced by further long-term finance. The starting point is the section 'creditors due for payment after more than one year'. However the accounting rules require separate reporting of loans due for repayment within one year. It is necessary to look in the 'current liabilities' for bank loans that are becoming due for repayment. In some companies the bank overdraft is a semi-permanent feature and so is included in this ratio calculation.

Different industries have different average levels, depending on the types of assets held and the stability or otherwise of the stream of profits. A low gearing percentage indicates a low exposure to financial risk because it means that there will be little difficulty in paying loan interest and repaying the loans as they fall due. A high gearing percentage indicates a high exposure to financial risk because it means that there are interest charges to be met and a requirement to repay the loans on the due date.

Interest cover	$\dfrac{\text{Profit before interest and tax}}{\text{Interest}}$

Comment. The importance of being able to meet interest payments on borrowed funds is emphasised by measuring gearing in terms of the profit and loss account. If the profit generated before interest and tax is sufficient to give high cover for the interest charges, then it is unlikely that the company is overcommitting itself in its borrowing. If the interest cover is falling or is low, then there may be increasing cause for concern.

L01

L02

13.3 Investors' views on risk and return

Uncertainty about the future means that all investments contain an element of risk. For investors who are averse to risk, there is a fear of income falling below an acceptable level and a fear of losing the capital invested in the company. Given a choice between two investments offering the same expected return, risk-averse investors will choose the least risky investment.

13.3.1 Return

The word *return* has many meanings but for an investor the basic question is 'What have I gained from owning these shares?' One simple formula which answers that question is:

$$\frac{(Market\ price\ of\ share\ today - Price\ paid\ for\ share) + Dividends\ received}{Price\ paid\ for\ share} \times 100\%$$

Investors in a company which is in a low-risk industry may be willing to accept a low rate of return. Investors in a company which is in a high-risk industry will be seeking a higher rate of return to compensate for the additional risk they take.

Research has shown that share prices react very rapidly to any item of information which is sufficiently important to affect investors' decisions. This phenomenon is sometimes referred to as the *efficient markets hypothesis*, which is a statement that share prices react immediately to make allowance for each new item of information made available. The annual results of a listed company are announced through the Stock Exchange by means of a document called a *preliminary announcement*, issued approximately two months after the accounting year-end. The annual report then goes to the printers and is distributed to shareholders about three months after the related year-end.

When investors evaluate share price by calculating return, they take the most up-to-date price available.

13.3.2 Risk

There are two main types of risk: operating risk and financial risk. *Operating risk* exists where there are factors which could cause sales to fluctuate or cause costs to increase. Companies are particularly vulnerable to operating risk when they have a relatively high level of fixed operating costs. These fixed costs are incurred independently of the level of activity. If sales fall, or the direct costs of sales increase, the fixed costs become a greater burden on profit. *Financial risk* exists where the company has loan finance, especially long-term loan finance where the company cannot relinquish its commitment. Loan finance carries an obligation to pay interest charges and these create a problem similar to the fixed costs problem. If the sales are strong and the direct costs of sales are well under control, then interest charges will not be a problem. If sales fall, or the direct costs of sales rise, then a company may find that it does not have the cash resources to meet the interest payments as they fall due. Repaying the loan could become an even greater worry.

Both operating risk and financial risk are important to the company's shareholders because they have the residual claim on assets after all liabilities are met. If the company's assets are growing then these risks will not pose a problem but if the business becomes slack then the combination of high fixed operating costs and high interest charges could be disastrous. As a rule of thumb, investors look for low financial risk in companies which have high operating risk and, conversely, will tolerate a higher level of financial risk where there is relatively low operating risk.

The terms *operating gearing* and *financial gearing* are frequently used to describe the extent of operating risk and financial risk. (Financial gearing has been explained in the previous section.) In terms of the profit and loss account they are defined as follows:

Operating gearing	$\dfrac{\text{Profit before fixed operating costs}}{\text{Fixed operating costs}}$

Financial gearing	$\dfrac{\text{Profit before interest charges}}{\text{Interest charges}}$

In analysis of published accounting information, it is not possible to estimate the operating gearing because detailed information on fixed costs is not provided. Thus the term *gearing* is applied only in measuring financial gearing. Despite the lack of published information, professional investors will be aware of the importance of operating gearing and will try to understand as much as possible about the cost structure of the company and of the industry. The next section illustrates the benefits to shareholders of having gearing present when operating profits are rising and the risks when operating profits are falling.

13.3.3 Impact of gearing when profits are fluctuating

In a situation of fluctuating profits the presence of a fixed charge, such as an interest payment, will cause the profit for ordinary shareholders to fluctuate by a greater percentage. Exhibit 13.1 illustrates this fluctuation. Company X has no gearing but company Y has loan finance in its capital structure.

The conclusion to be drawn from Exhibit 13.2 (a) and (b) is that a 20 per cent increase or decrease in operating profit causes a corresponding 20 per cent increase or decrease in profit for ordinary shareholders in the ungeared company but a 40 per cent increase or decrease in profit for ordinary shareholders in the geared company. It would appear preferable to be a shareholder in a geared company when profits are rising but to be a shareholder in an ungeared company when profits are falling.

Exhibit 13.1

Data to illustrate the effect of gearing on profits for ordinary shareholders

	X plc £m	*Y plc* £m
Summary balance sheet		
Total assets minus current liabilities	1,000	1,000
Ordinary shares (£1 nominal value per share)	1,000	500
Loan stock (10% per annum)	–	500
	1,000	1,000
Expected level of profit		
Operating profit	100	100
Interest	–	50
Net profit for ordinary shareholders (A)	100	50

Exhibit 13.2

Fluctuations in profit

(a) Effect of 20% decrease in operating profit		
Operating profit	80	80
Interest		50
Net profit for ordinary shareholders (B)	80	30
Percentage decrease of (B) on (A)	20%	40%
(b) Effect of 20% increase in operating profit		
Operating profit	120	120
Interest	–	50
Net profit for ordinary shareholders (C)	120	70
Percentage increase of (C) on (A)	20%	40%

L03   13.4 Pyramid of ratios

The various ratios which contribute to the analysis of management performance may be thought of as forming a pyramid, as in Exhibit 13.3.

The apex is the return on capital employed (measuring capital employed here as total assets). As the pyramid spreads out there are more detailed explanations of how the pyramid is built up. Net profit as a percentage of total assets has two components. One is the net profit as a percentage of sales and the other is sales as a multiple of total assets. Multiply these two together and you return to the net profit as a percentage of total assets. This relationship indicates that there could be two quite different types of business, both of which may be highly successful. One business trades on low margins, charging prices which look highly competitive, and succeeds by having a high level of sales so that the assets are

Exhibit 13.3

Pyramid of ratios for analysis of management performance

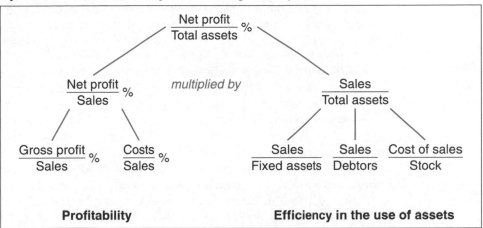

being used very effectively. The other business trades on high margins and makes sales less frequently. You could contrast the discount furniture store on the outskirts of town, where the car park is always full and the prices are unbeatable, with the old-world charm of the retail furnisher in the town centre whose prices look high but which attracts customers preferring extra service and attention. Both businesses are able to earn sufficient return on total assets to satisfy the owners.

The pyramid then spreads out into two areas: profitability and efficiency in the use of assets. The relationships here are additive – each component explains a little of the profitability of sales or the efficiency in the use of assets. The pyramid is a useful tool of detective work to trace the cause of a change in return on capital employed.

L04 13.5 Use and limitations of ratio analysis

The important feature of ratios is that they indicate trends and deviations from expected patterns. Ratios taken in isolation for a single company or a single period of time are of limited usefulness. The first requirement is to find a benchmark against which to compare ratios calculated for one period only.

13.5.1 Evaluating ratios by comparison

The comparison could be made with any or all of the following:

- the company's prior expectations of the outcome
- external observers' prior expectations of the outcome
- ratios based on previous years' figures for this company
- ratios calculated from this year's figures for other companies
- ratios calculated from previous years' figures for other companies
- industry averages published by commercial organisations.

The company's prior expectations are set out in a budget which is usually kept confidential. It is therefore unlikely that the user of the financial statements will have access to such a high-quality source of comparison. External observers may also have prior expectations. Professional analysts make forecasts of profits to help them or their clients in making investment decisions. The forecasts may be sent to clients of professional advisers, by way of investment advice bulletins. There are directories which publish such forecasts.

In the absence of information based on expectations, the user of the annual report may have to rely on the past as a possible predictor of the future, or on comparisons with other companies and industry norms. Professional investment advisers will collect data from annual reports and calculate ratios in their preferred manner. Advisory services will process the information and sell the results in the form of directories, on-line search facilities or CD-ROM with regular updates. One of the most widely used sources of ratio analysis of company accounts is Datastream, available in many colleges and universities but also used commercially. Organisations such as Reuters publish regular analyses of company information. Newspapers and weekly journals such as the *Financial Times* and the *Investors Chronicle* are yet another source of information which will include ratios.

It could be argued that companies should themselves publish the norms against which their own particular results may be compared, but most would claim that their business is unique and no comparisons would be entirely valid.

13.5.2 Limitations

No two companies are exactly alike in the nature of their operations. Comparisons must make allowances for differences in the types of business or the relative weighting of different types of business. Many companies operate in more than one industry so that comparison with industry norms has to be treated with care.

Accounting numbers are used in ratio analysis and it has been a theme of the preceding chapters that accounting numbers may be affected by different accounting policies. The most common causes of variation due to accounting policy differences lie in depreciation and stock valuation, both of which are highly subjective.

Ratios are primarily a starting point from which to identify further questions to ask about the present position and future directions of the operations and the financing of a company. They do not provide answers in themselves.

L05   13.6 Worked example of ratio analysis

In the following worked example, information is provided about a company buying and selling television and video equipment. Data are given for the current year in the first pair of columns and there are comparative figures for the previous year in the second pair of columns. Ratios are calculated for the two years as an indication of trends. Tentative comments are provided as to the possible interpretation of the resulting figures.

13.6.1 Financial statements to be analysed

Peter (Television) plc

Profit and loss account
for the year ended 31 December Year 2

	Year 2		Year 1	
	£m	£m	£m	£m
Turnover		720		600
Cost of sales		432		348
Gross profit		288		252
Distribution costs	72		54	
Administrative expenses	66		60	
		138		114
Operating profit		150		138
Interest payable		45		45
Profit before taxation		105		93
Taxation		42		37
Profit after taxation		63		56
Dividends (proposed)		30		25
Retained profit		33		31

Balance sheet as at 31 December Year 2

	£m	£m	£m	£m
Fixed assets:				
Land and buildings		600		615
Plant and equipment		555		503
		1,155		1,118
Current assets:				
Stock	115		82	
Trade debtors	89		61	
Prepayments	10		9	
Bank	6		46	
	220		198	
Current liabilities				
Trade creditors	45		30	
Taxation	21		19	
Proposed dividend	30		25	
Accruals	29		25	
	125		99	
Net current assets		95		99
		1,250		1,217
12% debentures		375		375
		875		842
Ordinary shares of £1 each		500		500
Retained profits		375		342
		875		842

13.6.2 Share price information

When investors evaluate share price, they take the most up-to-date price available. However, for the exercise of comparing financial ratios it is useful to take the share prices immediately after the preliminary announcement at the end of February or beginning of March, when the accounting information has not become too much out of date.

Market price at 1 March Year 2	202 pence
Market price at 1 March Year 3	277 pence

13.6.3 Presenting the ratio calculations

Because there are so many variations on the methods of calculating ratios in accounting, it is extremely important to practise a useful and informative layout. That must include, at a minimum:

- the name of each ratio
- the formula in words
- the workings to show how the formula has been applied
- the value of the ratio
- a narrative comment.

Exhibits 13.4 to 13.7 present this information in a set of ratio calculations for Peter (Television) plc, each exhibit covering one of the main headings explained earlier. The calculations are given first for the more recent year, Year 2, followed by the comparative figures for Year 1. A commentary is provided for each exhibit.

L05 | **Activity 13.2**

Use the ratios explained in this chapter to carry out a full analysis of the Year 2 column of the accounts of Peter (Television) plc. Prepare your analysis before you read Exhibits 13.4 to 13.7. When you have finished, compare your analysis with the ratios calculated. Where your answers differ, be sure that you understand whether it is due to an arithmetic error or a more fundamental point. Keep a note of your score of the number of items calculated correctly.

Then go back to Year 1 and repeat the exercise. Hopefully your score of correct items will have increased.

Exhibit 13.4
Investor ratios

Ratio	Definition in words	Year 2		Year 1	
		Workings	Result	Workings	Result
Earnings per share	$\dfrac{\text{Profit after tax for ordinary shareholder}}{\text{Number of ordinary shares}}$	$\dfrac{63}{500}$	12.6 pence	$\dfrac{56}{500}$	11.2 pence
Price earnings ratio	$\dfrac{\text{Share price}}{\text{Earnings per share}}$	$\dfrac{277}{12.6}$	22	$\dfrac{202}{11.2}$	18
Dividend cover (payout ratio)	$\dfrac{\text{Profit after tax for ordinary shareholder}}{\text{Ordinary dividends}}$	$\dfrac{63}{30}$	2.1 times	$\dfrac{56}{25}$	2.24 times
Dividend per share	$\dfrac{\text{Dividend payable to ordinary shareholders}}{\text{Number of issued shares}}$	$\dfrac{30}{100}$	6.0 pence	$\dfrac{25}{500}$	5.0 pence
Dividend yield	$\dfrac{\text{Dividend per share}}{\text{Share price}} \times 100$	$\dfrac{6.0}{277} \times 100\%$	2.17%	$\dfrac{5.0}{202} \times 100\%$	2.48%

Comment. Earnings per share increased over the period, indicating an improved profit performance for shareholders. The price–earnings ratio rose, indicating greater confidence in the stock market about the sustainability of this new level of profit. The dividend cover has fallen marginally, but is still more than twice covered. This marginal decrease in dividend cover is caused by increasing the dividend per share from 5 pence to 6 pence. The dividend yield has fallen, despite the increased dividend per share, because the market price has risen. The fall in yield may not be significant if it reflects a general trend in the market where, possibly, all shares have risen in price over the year. To say anything more about these ratios requires comparative figures for the industry and for the market as a whole. Both types of data would be found in the *Financial Times*.

Exhibit 13.5
Analysis of management performance

Ratio	Definition in words	Year 2		Year 1	
		Workings	Result	Workings	Result
Return on shareholders' equity	$\dfrac{\text{Profit after tax}}{\text{Share capital} + \text{Reserves}} \times 100\%$	$\dfrac{63}{875} \times 100\%$	7.2%	$\dfrac{56}{842} \times 100\%$	6.65%
Return on capital employed	$\dfrac{\text{Profit before interest and tax}}{\text{Total assets} - \text{Current liabilities}} \times 100\%$	$\dfrac{150}{1{,}250} \times 100\%$	12.0%	$\dfrac{138}{1{,}217} \times 100\%$	11.4%
Net profit on sales	$\dfrac{\text{Profit before interest and tax}}{\text{Sales (turnover)}} \times 100\%$	$\dfrac{150}{720} \times 100\%$	20.8%	$\dfrac{138}{600} \times 100\%$	23%
Gross profit percentage	$\dfrac{\text{Gross profit}}{\text{Sales (turnover)}} \times 100\%$	$\dfrac{288}{720} \times 100\%$	40%	$\dfrac{252}{600} \times 100\%$	42%
Total assets usage	$\dfrac{\text{Turnover}}{\text{Total assets}}$	$\dfrac{720}{(1{,}155 + 220)}$	0.52 times	$\dfrac{600}{(1{,}118 + 198)}$	0.46 times
Fixed assets usage	$\dfrac{\text{Turnover}}{\text{Fixed assets}}$	$\dfrac{720}{1{,}155}$	0.62 times	$\dfrac{600}{1{,}118}$	0.54 times

Comment. The return on shareholders' equity and the return on capital employed both show an improvement on the previous year. This is due to an improvement in the use of assets (total assets and fixed assets) which more than offsets a fall in the net profit as a percentage of sales. The gross profit percentage fell by a similar amount, which suggests that the price charged for goods and services is not keeping pace with increases in costs. The company should look carefully at either increasing prices or attempting to control costs of goods sold more effectively.

Exhibit 13.6

Liquidity and working capital

Ratio	Definition in words	Year 2			Year 1		
		Workings	Result		Workings	Result	
Current ratio	Current assets : Current liabilities	220 : 125	1.76 : 1		198 : 99	2.0 : 1	
Acid test	(Current assets − Stock) : Current liabilities	(220 − 115) : 125	0.84 : 1		(198 − 82) : 99	1.17 : 1	
Stock holding period (closing stock only available)	$\dfrac{\text{Average stock held}}{\text{Cost of sales}} \times 365$	$\dfrac{(115 + 82)/2}{432}$	83.2 days		$\dfrac{(*82 + 82)/2}{348}$	86 days	
Debtors collection period	$\dfrac{\text{Trade debtors}}{\text{Credit sales}} \times 365$	$\dfrac{89}{720} \times 365$	45.1 days		$\dfrac{61}{600} \times 365$	37.1 days	
Creditors payment period	$\dfrac{\text{Trade creditors}}{\text{Credit purchases}} \times 365$	$\dfrac{45}{432 + 115 - 82} \times 365$	35.3 days		$\dfrac{61}{348 + 82 - *82} \times 365$	31.5 days	

Note: *Assuming the opening stock is the same as the closing stock.

Comment. The liquidity has fallen over the period, as indicated by both the current ratio and the acid test. The ratios may still be within acceptable ranges (although this needs to be confirmed by comparison with industry norms). One cause appears to be in lengthening the period of credit taken by customers and this should be investigated as a matter of urgency. There is a marginal decrease in the stock holding period but it remains relatively long, compared to the creditors payment period.

Exhibit 13.7
Gearing (leverage)

Ratio	Definition in words	Year 2		Year 1	
		Workings	Result	Workings	Result
Debt/equity ratio	$\dfrac{\text{Debt} + \text{Preference share capital}}{\text{Ordinary share capital} + \text{Reserves}} \times 100\%$	$\dfrac{375}{875} \times 100\%$	42.9%	$\dfrac{375}{842} \times 100\%$	44.5%
Interest cover	$\dfrac{\text{Profit before interest and tax}}{\text{Interest}}$	$\dfrac{150}{45}$	3.33 times	$\dfrac{138}{45}$	3.07 times

Comment. Gearing in the balance sheet has remained almost constant and the interest cover has increased marginally. The relative stability of the position indicates that there is probably no cause for concern but the ratios should be compared with those for similar companies in the industry.

13.7 Summary

It is essential to treat ratio analysis with great caution and to understand the basis of calculation and the nature of the data used. For that reason the illustrations have been set out in detail using a layout that allows you to demonstrate your knowledge of the formula, your ability to collect data for calculation, and the result of that calculation which can then be interpreted. In this chapter all the information has been made available to you as and when you required it. In Chapter 14 we move on to consider published financial statements where more exploration may be required to find the most useful information.

Now score your view of your confidence in achieving the learning outcomes of the chapter.

1 = Very confident about knowledge, application, problem solving and evaluation.

2 = Confident about knowledge and application, less sure about problem solving and evaluation.

3 = Need to read again to be more certain of basic knowledge and application.

L01 You are now able to define, calculate and interpret ratios that help analyse and understand (a) performance for investors, (b) management performance, (c) liquidity and working capital and (d) gearing.

1 2 3
☐ ☐ ☐

L02 You can explain investors' views of the balance of risk and return, and the risks of investing in a geared company when profits are fluctuating.

1 2 3
☐ ☐ ☐

L03 You can describe the uses and limitations of ratio analysis.

1 2 3
☐ ☐ ☐

L04 You are able to carry out a practical exercise of calculating and interpreting ratios, using simple balance sheets and profit and loss accounts.

1 2 3
☐ ☐ ☐

If your scores are all 1 or 2, try the questions in the series A, B and C. This will give you feedback on your assessment of how well you have achieved the learning outcomes. Read again any sections of the chapter where you find your knowledge and understanding are less comprehensive than you first estimated.

If your scores include some at 3, try the series A questions to find where the problems lie. Read the relevant sections again, work through any illustrative examples and case studies, then try the questions in the series B. Once you feel confident at that level of knowledge and application, move on to try some or all of the series C questions.

The general principles explained in this chapter can be applied to the annual report of any profit-seeking business. The precise formulae may require adaptation to suit particular national characteristics. However international comparison requires great caution. Accounting policies and practices are not yet harmonised entirely. If the underlying data are not comparable then neither are the ratios. The key is to ask first, 'What value do we expect for this ratio?' Then calculate the ratio and seek an interpretation of the similarity or difference.

Test your understanding

> **Skills outcomes**
> SO1 Application of technical skills   SO2 Problem solving and evaluation skills   SO3 Communication skills

L01, S01   **A13.1** Which ratios provide information on performance for investors?

L01, S01   **A13.2** Which ratios provide information on management performance?

L01, S01   **A13.3** Which ratios provide information on liquidity and working capital?

L01, S01   **A13.4** Which ratios provide information on gearing?

L02, S01   **A13.5** What is the view of investors on risk and return?

L02, S01   **A13.6** Why is financial gearing important to a company which has fluctuating profits?

L03, S01   **A13.7** Explain the use of the pyramid of ratios in analysis of performance.

L04, S01   **A13.8** What are the limitations of ratio analysis?

Application

L05, S01   **B13.1** The following financial statements relate to Hope plc:

Profit and loss account for the year ended 30 June Year 4

	£000s	£000s
Turnover		6,200
Cost of sales		2,750
Gross profit		3,450
Administration and selling expenses	2,026	
Debenture interest	252	2,278
Profit before taxation		1,172
Taxation		480
Profits after taxation		692
Dividends paid and proposed		330
Retained profit		362

Balance sheet as at 30 June Year 4

	£000s	£000s	£000s
Fixed assets (net of depreciation)			1,750
Current assets:			
Stocks and work-in-progress	620		
Trade debtors	1,540		
Cash	200	2,360	
less: Creditors due within one year:			
Trade creditors	300		
Other creditors and accruals	940		
Proposed dividend	90	1,330	
Net current assets			1,030
Total assets *less* current liabilities			2,780
Creditors due after one year			
18% debentures			1,400
Total net assets			1,380
Share capital and reserves			
Issued share capital:			
900,000 ordinary shares of 50p nominal value			450
Profit and loss account			930
			1,380

Required

(a) Calculate ratios which measure:
    (i) liquidity and the use of working capital;
    (ii) management performance; and
    (iii) gearing.
(b) Explain how each ratio would help in understanding the financial position and results of the company.
(c) The market price is currently 1,100 pence per share. Calculate ratios which are useful to investors.

L05, S01 **B13.2** The following financial statements relate to Charity plc:

Profit and loss account for year ended 30 September Year 4

	£000s	£000s
Turnover		2,480
Cost of sales		1,100
Gross profit		1,380
Administration and selling expenses	634	
Debenture interest	75	709
Profit before taxation		671
Taxation		154
Profits after taxation		517
Dividends paid and proposed		155
Retained profit		362

Balance sheet as at 30 September Year 4

	£000s	£000s	£000s
Fixed assets (net of depreciation)			785
Current assets:			
Stocks and work-in-progress	341		
Trade debtors	801		
Cash	110	1,252	
less: Creditors due within one year:			
Trade creditors	90		
Other creditors and accruals	654		
Proposed dividend	33	777	
Net current assets			475
Total assets *less* current liabilities			1,260
Creditors due after one year			
17% debentures			440
Total net assets			820
Share capital and reserves			
Issued share capital			
(1,360,000 ordinary shares of 25p nominal value)			340
Profit and loss account			480
			820

Required

(a) Calculate ratios which measure:
  (i) liquidity and the use of working capital;
  (ii) management performance; and
  (iii) gearing.
(b) Explain how each ratio would help in understanding the financial position and results of the company.
(c) The market price of one share is 800 pence. Calculate ratios which will be of interest to investors.

Chapter 14

Analysis of corporate performance

After reading this chapter you should be able to:

LO1 Explain the importance of the operating and financial review as a component of the annual report of a company.

LO2 Describe and explain other useful information in the annual report that is relevant to analysis of corporate performance.

LO3 Relate the interpretation of ratios to the information in a cash flow statement.

LO4 Explain how segmental information is useful to the analysis of corporate performance.

14.1 Introduction

You have learned from Chapter 13 the basic techniques of ratio analysis that may help you to interpret the performance of a company relative to other companies or other periods of time. It might be helpful to users of annual reports if companies themselves would carry out some analysis and interpretation of this type. There was a time when it was felt that the role of the company stops at the presentation of the financial statements. Today, however, there is an expectation that companies will recognise the need to give more information to users, such as an objective discussion to be included in the annual report, plus highlights statements and trends of data. The cash flow statement, illustrated in Chapters 5 and 6 and discussed briefly in Chapter 7, is a useful source of information that complements the understanding of ratios. Group accounts, also outlined in Chapter 7, are quite complex and so analysts like to receive segmental information that breaks the total information into key areas of activity of the business.

LO1 # 14.2 Operating and Financial Review

The operating and financial review (OFR) has been a feature of the annual reports of many listed companies since 1993.[1] It has some similarities to the management discussion and analysis (MD&A) produced for many years by larger companies in the United States, but with the important difference that the OFR is voluntary. The ASB hopes that giving companies wide discretion will encourage the development of best practice in reporting rather than a slavish adherence to rules which may result in a lacklustre document.

There is guidance as to the key features of the OFR. In particular the company should provide the reader with a strong sense of the 'top-down' structure of the business. The reader of the annual report should readily gain an overview of the business within the first minutes of reading. Many companies achieve this 'top-down' message by presenting a 'highlights' statement and then using graphics or summary tables at the start of each subsequent section to draw attention to the key financial figures.

The discussion should be objective, balancing good and bad news. It should analyse and explain the main features and should give the reader a sense of the dynamics of the operating activities and the financial position. The dynamics of the operations relate to the principal risks and uncertainties of the main lines of business. The dynamics of the financial position encompass the sources of liquidity and their application, including the implications of the financing requirements arising from the capital expenditure plans of the business.

A forward-looking aspect is particularly important. There are some trends and factors underlying the business that have affected the results but are not expected to continue in the future. There are other known events, trends and uncertainties that are expected to have an impact on the business in the future. The management is encouraged to identify those factors expected to have an impact on the future. A forecast is not required.

14.2.1 Structure of the OFR

There is no prescribed format for the OFR. The ASB sets out principles but urges companies to use their judgement as to the most suitable method of presentation. To gain a full sense of the intended content of the OFR it is essential to read the full Statement issued by the ASB.

The following lists are indicative of the types of information to be found in operating review and financial review sections of the OFR:

Operating review

There should be a discussion of the main factors and influences that may have a major effect on future results, such as:

- scarcity of raw materials
- skill shortages
- patents, licences or franchises
- dependence on major suppliers or customers
- product liability
- health and safety
- environmental protection costs and potential environmental liabilities
- self-insurance
- exchange rate fluctuations
- rates of inflation as these affect costs and revenues in different countries or markets.

There should also be an indication of expenditure which creates an investment for the future. This may include capital expenditure to acquire new fixed assets, but could also include expenses reported in the profit and loss account which generate benefits for the future. Examples would be research expenditure, marketing, major repairs and staff development programmes. The existence of a future benefit implies that there is a possibility of meeting the definition of an asset, but the uncertainties are such that the item is recognised in the profit and loss account rather than the balance sheet. Drawing attention to such items in the OFR is a compromise in not reporting an asset but giving a strong indication of the potential benefit.

Financial review

In addition to highlighting issues from the current year that are relevant to future prospects the financial review section of the OFR might be expected to report:

- interest cover and gearing
- treasury policy
- capital structure and maturity profile of borrowing
- major financing transactions
- interest costs and rate charges
- tax charges
- cash flows
- liquidity at the end of the period and peak level of borrowing
- capital expenditure commitments.

14.2.2 Presentation of the OFR

Companies have evolved different forms of presentation. Some report the OFR as a single document. Others prefer to separate the operating review and the financial review because different directors are responsible for the different activities contributing to each. In some annual reports the OFR effectively begins with the chairman's statement and the chief executive's statement. They present the key messages and give the forward-looking aspects. The finance director follows with the particular aspects of the financial review, and then the directors of each business area give their reports on the activities of the business.

The number of pages in the OFR varies from 2 to over 20, depending on the nature of the business, but many have settled down to between 4 and 6 pages. Many companies use graphics in the margin or within the text as an aid to understanding.

A growing development is to split the annual report so that the statutory financial statements and notes are in a second part while the aspects of wider interest, including the OFR, are contained in the first part together with summary financial statements. Shareholders in such companies are offered the first part of the report as a routine mailing and are invited to request the statutory information in the second part, should that be of interest to them. The OFR is thus becoming a leading source of information for those who lack the time or expertise to delve into the statutory information. It also provides a base for more searching questions from those who have explored the numbers in detail.

14.2.3 Company Law Review

Chapter 7, section 7.9.2, has explained some aspects of the Company Law Review reported in June 2001. One recommendation of the Review is that the Operating and Financial Review should become a mandatory statement in the annual report of all public companies and most of the large private companies. The law will list some items that must always be disclosed and some others that should be disclosed if they are material. This is an example of the legislators observing the voluntary development of good practice and then deciding to make it compulsory for all. We do not yet know how or when the legislation will be introduced, but it seems likely that eventually the OFR will pass into statute law. One criticism of the present form of OFR is that it is not covered by the audit process, beyond a general overview for consistency with the financial statements. The Company Law Review proposes that the law should require the auditors to review the OFR. They would not give a direct opinion on the content of the OFR but would review the process by which it is prepared.

L01   **Activity 14.1**

> *Read through the section on the OFR again. How much of the information suggested for the OFR is extracted directly from the financial statements? How much of the information suggested for the OFR provides additional understanding which is not available from the financial statements?*

L02 ## 14.3 Other guidance in analysis

In Chapter 7, Figure 7.1, there is a list of 'accompanying information' that may be found in the annual report. The first item listed there is the Operating and Financial Review, explained in section 14.2. The second item is the Chairman's statement, which usually appears at the start of the annual report, as a short narrative lasting no more than a page and often preceded by a 'Highlights' statement of key financial measures. The Chairman sets out key features as an introduction to the detail that follows in later pages. The third item listed there is the Directors' report, which is usually found part-way through the annual report. Its contents are required partly by the Companies Act, partly by the UK Listing Agreement and partly by the Code of Corporate Governance. The fourth item is the historical summaries that allow trends to be seen over several years, with some companies giving five-year trends and others giving ten-year trends. The final item is 'non-accounting and non-financial information'. This covers the rest of the annual report and often provides the most interesting aspects for the reader who wants to understand the company in its entirety.

In this section we will consider the highlights statement and the trend analysis.

14.3.1 Highlights statement

Safe and Sure plc presents Highlights of Year 7 as follows:

		Year 7 £m	Increase %	Year 6 £m
Turnover	United Kingdom	323.4	31.1	*246.7*
	Europe	164.3	7.0	*153.5*
	North America	124.5	36.7	*91.1*
	Asia Pacific and Africa	122.4	12.3	*109.0*
	Total turnover	734.6	22.4	*600.3*

		Year 7 £m	Increase %	Year 6 £m
Profit	United Kingdom	76.9	28.8	59.7
	Europe	45.3	12.4	40.3
	North America	17.0	22.3	13.9
	Asia Pacific and Africa	35.5	17.9	30.1
	Net interest income	2.3		3.0
	Profit before tax	177.0	20.4	147.0
Earnings	Earnings per share	11.74p	20.9	9.71p
Dividends	Dividends per share	3.45p	21.1	2.85p

The Highlights statement shows what the company regards as important information for investors as the primary users of the annual report. Turnover is a measure of the size of operations, with growth of turnover being an indicator of expansion. Profit is the reward for shareholders, with growth again being an important indicator. Segment figures are provided for both turnover and profit. This company has a target profit growth of 20 per cent per annum and so is emphasising that it has more than met the target. Earnings per share and dividend per share are the key indicators from which investors can calculate yields based on the current market price. There is no regulation of highlights statements and so other companies may give different information. Together with the Chairman's statement, the Highlights present the key messages of the annual report.

14.3.2 Historical summaries and trend analysis

Listed companies usually provide a historical summary of the financial statements of previous years. The historical summary for Safe and Sure may be found in Appendix I. The analyst may use this table to establish trends of:

- year-on-year growth of turnover and operating profit
- growth rates adjusted for annual inflation
- key ratios.

The company does not usually carry out the ratio analysis; this is left to the analysts to calculate and interpret. On relatively rare occasions the company will provide ratios but it is not always clear which formula has been used.

14.3.3 Finance director's review

There are relatively few references to ratios in the annual reports of companies. Some finance directors claim that interpretation of ratios is a very complex matter. They say that if they provide ratio calculations in the annual report, then they will have to provide detailed explanation, which will make the report too lengthy. So in general they leave the ratios for others to calculate and interpret. Sometimes they will comment on a ratio where they know the expert users will ask questions.

In the operating and financial review of Safe and Sure plc the finance director states:

The pleasing return on our tangible net assets (45.3 per cent per annum before tax on average net assets) reflects the high value of the intangible assets of the Safe and Sure brand and of businesses built up over the years. Such value is not reported in the balance sheet.

Is it possible to check on the finance director's calculation? He has used pre-tax profit which is £177m and the average of the tangible net assets. The respective figures for Year 7 and Year 6 are £434.8m and £346.0m. The average net assets figure is therefore £390.4m. The calculation of the ratio is:

$$\frac{177}{390.4} \times 100\% = 45.3\%$$

which confirms the figure given by the finance director. (It should be noted that confirming ratios reported in annual reports is not always so straightforward, although it ought to be.) We need other evidence before we can agree that 45.3 per cent is a 'pleasing' return.

In the next section, David aims to explain his approach to using ratios to pinpoint target areas for probing by way of questions to the company, while Leona explains how ratios are useful to the auditor.

14.3.4 The analyst and the auditor

DAVID: *We subscribe to the major on-line database sources of information about companies, so I don't very often sit down to calculate ratios. I'm more interested in the interpretation. There are a few key ratios that I look at for major clues as to strange goings-on and then I scan a more detailed ratio report for unusual changes. We can program in an instruction to set a warning flag against any ratio which has altered by more than a specified range since the previous figures, or over a given period of time.*

What do I look to first? Gross margins on turnover and net margins on turnover, with as much segmental detail as I can find. Segmental information is an area where often we do have to carry out our own analysis using our skills, experience and specialist sources of information. Not many databases break down the company's results by segment. Then I'll check the tax charge as a percentage of the taxable profit. It should be around 30 per cent if the company's accounts have been accepted for tax purposes, but if there are items which the tax authorities don't allow, then the percentage will be different. I'm always interested in what appears in the profit and loss account but is not accepted by the tax rules. Depreciation is a notoriously variable figure and is difficult to spot because the accounting rules say that a change in depreciation rate or useful asset life is not a change in policy. Companies have to draw attention to a change in policy and explain the impact. Depreciation escapes that rule. So I calculate the depreciation charge as a percentage of total asset value. If that percentage changes then I start asking questions.

Common-size statements are very useful. That means turning all items in the financial statements to percentages with the total assets represented by 100 per cent in the balance sheet and the turnover represented by 100 per cent in the profit and loss account. It is also useful to have percentage changes from one year to the next. That is all relatively easy when you are using spreadsheets.

Over a period of time I monitor the variability of a ratio for a particular company. I calculate this as:

$$\frac{\text{Maximum value} - \text{Minimum value}}{\text{Mean value of ratio}}$$

Again I am looking for unusual movements outside an expected range.

LEONA: *The auditors don't rely on anyone else's calculations. We carry out our own ratio analysis as part of our analytical review. For commercial, manufacturing and service companies we monitor a standard list of ratios which is:*

- *acid test ratio*
- *current ratio*
- *debtor days*
- *rate of stock movement*
- *gearing*
- *interest cover*
- *return on capital employed*
- *return on total assets*
- *gross profit margin.*

We are looking at these with a focus on the particular concerns of the auditor. Possible liquidity crises or working capital shortages could raise a question as to whether the company is a going concern. Debtor days ratios are a clue to whether the doubtful debt provision is adequate. Rate of stock movement may indicate a need for provision for slow-moving stock. Gearing and interest cover are further indicators of financial stability or otherwise in relation to the going concern issue. Return on capital employed and on total assets may show inefficient use of assets and perhaps point to assets which have no future benefit. Gross margins may cause us to ask questions about incorrect records of sales or stocks if the margins are different from the norms.

For listed companies we also look at the dividend cover and the Altman Z-score. The Z-score is a model developed for use in predicting insolvency. You need to read a finance textbook to get the details, but basically it is a combined score based on a list of key variables all pointing to potential insolvency problems. We have to be able to say that the business is a going concern, so that kind of information is important to us.

DAVID: *That's OK for the current year. What about trends?*

LEONA: *Yes, trends are an important part of our review. We try to use a predictive approach and estimate the current year's figure from the previous data rather than merely compare this year with last. Taking a predictive approach encourages us to challenge fluctuations and to seek persuasive explanations. We use all the familiar forms of trend analysis – graphical representation, moving averages and simple regression analysis.*

DAVID: *How much reliance do you place on these analytical procedures?*

LEONA: *It can range from conclusive reliance to no reliance at all. It depends very much on the nature of the assertions being tested, the plausibility and predictability of the relationships involved, and the extent to which data is available and reliable.*

DAVID: *Maybe I have underestimated auditors in the past. None of the activities you describe is really apparent from the audit report. Perhaps y ou undersell your work.*

LEONA: *I probably have to admit that our work stops when we have gained sufficient assurance to write the audit report. We don't give information to the reader – that is not the function of the audit.*

DAVID: *You and I need to spend more time together on this question of analysis in depth. Analysts with insight command top ratings and that's what I'm looking for. And I think the benefit would not all be one-way – I can help you with broader awareness of the strategies used by management in giving the markets the messages they want to convey.*

LEONA: *Sounds fine to me.*

L03 14.4 Linking ratios to the cash flow statement

In Chapter 7 the cash flow statement of a company was illustrated and discussed. Any ratio analysis which seeks to interpret liquidity, management performance or financial structure should be related to the information provided by the cash flow statement. Ratios give a measure of position at a particular point in time while the cash flow statement gives some understanding of the movements in cash and cash-related items.

The operating cash flow will be explained by a note showing the movements in working capital and these may usefully be linked to changes in the rate of movement of stock or the period of credit allowed to customers and taken from suppliers. The ratio will give the change in terms of number of days, while the cash flow statement will indicate the overall impact on liquid resources.

If the efficiency in the use of fixed assets appears to have fallen, it may be that new assets were acquired during the year which, at the balance sheet date, were not fully effective in generating sales. That acquisition will appear in the cash flow statement. If the gearing has changed, the impact on cash flow will be revealed in the cash flow statement.

L03 Activity 14.2

Read again the sections of Chapters 3, 4 and 7 on cash flow statements. What is the purpose of the cash flow statement? What are the main headings? Which ratios may be used in conjunction with the cash flow statement to help understand the financial position of the company?

14.4.1 Explanation of a cash flow statement

The cash flow statement in Exhibit 14.1 is calculated from the balance sheets and profit and loss account of Peter (Television) plc in Chapter 13, section 13.6. It is presented using headings similar to those of Safe and Sure in Chapter 7. The headings are taken from the UK accounting standard FRS 1. In Chapters 3, 5 and 6 you saw simple cash flow statements prepared using the information entered in the cash column of a spreadsheet. Those were examples of what is called the *direct* method of preparing a cash flow statement because the figures came directly from the cash column of the transaction spreadsheet. The cash flow statement in Exhibit 14.1 is said to be prepared using the *indirect* method because it takes an indirect route of starting with an accruals-based profit figure and then making adjustments to arrive at the cash figure. Consider each line in turn.

Exhibit 14.1
Cash flow statement

Peter (Television) plc
Cash flow statement
for the year ended 31 December Year 2

Note: Assume depreciation charge for year is £50m.
   No fixed assets were sold

[The words and figures printed in italics are not normally shown in published cash flow statements – they are to help you with interpretation]

	£m	£m
Operating profit		150
Add back items not involving a flow of cash:		
Depreciation		50
		200
Increase in stocks *(115 – 82)*	33	
Increase in debtors *(89 – 61)*	28	
Increase in prepayments *(10 – 9)*	1	
Reduction in cash due to increases in current assets	62	
Increase in trade creditors	(15)	
Increase in accruals	(4)	
Increase in cash due to increases in liabilities	(19)	
Reduction in cash due to working capital changes		(43)
Net cash inflow from operating activities		157
Returns on investment and servicing of finance		(45)
		112
Taxation *(42 + 19 – 21)*		(40)
		72
Capital expenditure *1,155 – 1,118 + 50*		(87)
		(15)
Equity dividends paid *(previous year's liability)*		(25)
		(40)
Financing *(share or loan issue)*		nil
Decrease in cash		(40)

Check in balance sheet Decrease in bank (46 – 6) = 40

One purpose of the cash flow statement is to answer the question, 'Why do we have a cash problem despite making an operating profit?' We saw in Exhibit 3.7 of Chapter 3 that profit and cash flow can be different because the cash generated in making a profit is spent in various ways. The cash flow statement emphasises ways in which cash has come into, or moved out of, the company. So we start with operating profit of £150m.

Depreciation is an expense in the profit and loss account which represents cost being shared across accounting periods. There is no cash flow and so there should be no deduction for this item. To correct the position, depreciation of £50m is 'added back' to the accounting profit. Next we consider how changes in working capital have affected cash flow.

Looking first at current assets, we find that the stock has increased from £82m to £115m. Allowing stock to increase reduced the cash available for other purposes. Debtors have increased from £61 to £89. This means the cash is flowing less fast and so cash is reducing. Prepayments have increased from £9m to £10m. This is also using up cash. In total the increases in current assets have used up £62m of the cash generated in making profit.

Looking next at current liabilities, we see that trade creditors have increased from £30m to £45m. If creditors are increasing, it means they are not being paid. This helps cash flow by not spending it. Accruals have increased by £4m, again helping cash flow by not making a payment. It is not a good idea to help cash flow indefinitely by not paying creditors, but where stocks and debtors are expanding to use up cash flow, it is helpful if current liabilities are expanding in a similar way to hold back cash flow.

The taxation payment involves more calculation. Cash has been required to meet the liability of £19m remaining in the Year 1 balance sheet, and also to pay half of the tax expense of Year 2, which is £21m. The calculation is: tax expense of the year, minus liability at the end of the year, plus liability at the start of the year.

Capital expenditure is calculated by comparing the book values at the beginning and end of the year and adjusting for changes during the year. We are told there were no sales of fixed assets so any increase must represent an addition. The balance started at £1,118m, fell by £50m for depreciation, increased by the unknown figure for additions, and finished at £1,155m. The missing figure is calculated as £87m.

The dividend paid was the current liability at the end of Year 1. We know there was no interim dividend because the dividend charged in the Year 2 profit and loss account is the same as the liability at the end of Year 2.

There were no financing changes in either share capital or long-term loans and so the final line of the cash flow statement is nil.

Finally the right-hand column is added and produces a figure of £40m which is then checked against the balance sheet figures. This shows that cash has fallen from £46m to £6m and so the calculation is confirmed as being correct.

14.4.2 Analyst's commentary

Here is the comment made by one analyst in a briefing note to clients.

Despite making an operating profit of £150,000, the cash balances of the company have decreased by £40,000 during the year.

The cash generated by operating profit is calculated by adding back depreciation of £50,000 because this is an accounting expense which does not involve an outflow of cash. The resulting cash flow of £200,000 was eroded by allowing current assets to increase by more than the increase in current liabilities. This suggests that we should ask questions about the rate of usage of stock and the period of credit allowed to debtors. Our analysis [Chapter 13, section 13.6] shows that the stock holding period reduced marginally from 86 to 83 days, which is not unexpected in the industry. The period of credit taken from suppliers increased by 4 days but the debtors collection period increased by 18 days. Our attention should focus on the control of debtors to look for any weaknesses of credit control and a potential risk of bad debts.

After paying interest charges and taxation the company was still in cash surplus at £72,000 but swung into cash deficit through capital expenditure of £87,000. Taking in the dividend payment of £25,000 the positive cash flow of £72,000 changed to a negative cash flow of £40,000.

We take the view that in the short run it is reasonable to run down cash balances in this way. The company probably had excessive liquidity at the end of Year 1. However if there is to be a further major investment in fixed assets we would want to see long-term finance being raised, either through a share issue or through a new long-term loan.

14.4.3 EBITDA

EBITDA stands for Earnings before interest, taxation, depreciation and amortisation. It is increasingly used by analysts as a measure of cash flow because it removes the non-cash expenses of depreciation and amortisation from profit. Instead of a price–earnings multiple based on earnings per share, the analyst will relate share price to EBITDA. The reason appears to be a desire to get away from the subjectivity of accruals-based profit and closer to cash flow as something objectively measured.

L04   14.5 Segmental information

In Chapter 7, sections 7.7 and 7.8, you have read about the group structure used by many companies, and you have seen the method of construction of consolidated financial statements. Safe and Sure presents consolidated financial statements, which are discussed in section 7.4. The process of consolidation of financial information in group accounts is intended to be an improvement on sending the parent company shareholders a bundle of the separate financial statements of each member of the group. It lets them see, in one set of financial statements, the full picture of the group. On the negative side, the process of aggregation causes a loss of information about the various different activities of the group. In order to balance the benefits of aggregation with the need for detail, accounting provides additional information about the various segments of the group on a year-by-year basis.

14.5.1 Users' needs for information

Consolidated financial statements are a very convenient means of bringing together a large volume of data, but they suffer a major defect in losing much of the rich detail available from seeing each constituent company separately. It is particularly important for users of financial statements to know how the results of various activities compare, where the group of companies is involved in more than one product line and more than one type of market.

Segmental reporting has developed as a means of supplementing the consolidated financial statements by providing more insight into the activities of the group. The purpose of segmental reporting is viewed as providing information to assist the users of financial statements

(a) to appreciate more thoroughly the results and financial position of the entity by permitting a better understanding of the entity's past performance and thus a better assessment of its future prospects; and

(b) to be aware of the impact that changes in significant components of a business may have on the business as a whole.[2]

The accounting standard which deals with segmental reporting requires the group to define in its financial statements each reported class of business and geographical segment. Turnover should be disclosed by location of operations (i.e. indicating the geographical source of products or services) as well as by the geographical destination of the output. The profit before taxation should also be disclosed for each segment, analysed by source. The net assets of each segment should be reported. These items of information, taken together, allow comparison of turnover to net assets, profit to net assets and profit to turnover. They also assist those who believe that the past provides a clue to making predictions about the company for the future.

The standard allows companies considerable freedom to define segments as they see fit and to vary the definitions from one year to the next. It also allows the discretion of non-disclosure to directors where, in their opinion, the disclosure of segmental information would be seriously prejudicial to the reporting entity. The extent to which application of the segmental reporting standard leaves matters in the hands of the directors means that segmental information may have to be treated with caution on some occasions. However, if a company were found to be consistently misleading the market, the share price might eventually suffer.

14.5.2 Information provided in the financial statements

The group balance sheet and profit and loss account of Safe and Sure plc are presented in full in Chapter 7 and have been explored in more detail in subsequent chapters. Consequently you are already familiar with much of the information about the assets and liabilities of the group.

Parent company

In the published annual report of Safe and Sure plc there are further columns for the parent company balance sheet which have not been set out in the illustrations for this textbook in order to avoid giving too much information at one time. The parent company balance sheet confirms that the parent is primarily a holding company whose main asset is the investment in its subsidiaries. It owns some of the group's land and buildings and a small portion of the vehicle fleet. Its current assets consist mainly of amounts owed by subsidiaries and dividends due from subsidiaries. Its current liabilities consist mainly of amounts owed to subsidiaries and dividends payable to its own shareholders. The parent company has some long-term liabilities for money borrowed to purchase subsidiaries. Most of the cash used for purchase of new subsidiaries is provided by the new wealth generated by the group as a whole.

Group

Information about the Safe and Sure group is very much more interesting than information about the parent company alone. That is why the preceding chapters have used the group information about Safe and Sure to explain the treatment of assets, liabilities and ownership interest. There are a few particular items of interest in respect of acquisitions of new subsidiaries and the use of the goodwill reserve. There is also some interesting information about the various segments of the business which contribute to the overall picture. This section summarises those particular features of the annual report.

David and Leona have returned from their holiday and are again working on Leona's flat. In the middle of a less than successful attempt to fit a carpet, David pauses for coffee and explains how he looked at the segmental information presented by the company.

14.5.3 Segmental information in Safe and Sure

As an illustration of the type of segmental information available, the note to the profit and loss account of Safe and Sure plc is set out in Note 17 to the financial statements.

Note 17: Segmental analysis

	Turnover		Profit		Net assets	
	Year 7 £m	Year 6 £m	Year 7 £m	Year 6 £m	Year 7 £m	Year 6 £m
Geographical analysis						
United Kingdom	323.4	246.7	76.9	59.7	30.9	48.2
Continental Europe	164.3	153.5	45.3	40.3	43.7	19.4
North America	124.5	91.1	17.0	13.9	2.5	(3.3)
Asia Pacific and Africa	122.4	109.0	35.5	30.1	31.5	29.5
	734.6	600.3	174.7	144.0	108.6	93.8
Interest receivable (net)			2.3	3.0		
Net cash					67.0	15.6
Total	734.6	600.3	177.0	147.0	175.6	109.4

	Disposal and recycling		Security and cleaning		Total	
	Year 7 £m	Year 6 £m	Year 7 £m	Year 6 £m	Year 7 £m	Year 6 £m
Business sector analysis						
Turnover						
United Kingdom	186.2	150.8	137.2	95.9	323.4	246.7
Continental Europe	161.2	150.0	3.1	3.5	164.3	153.5
North America	65.3	61.1	59.2	30.0	124.5	91.1
Asia Pacific and Africa	116.2	104.1	6.2	4.9	122.4	109.0
Turnover by service	528.9	466.0	205.7	134.3	734.6	600.3
Operating profit by service	156.1	129.6	18.6	14.4	174.7	144.0
Net operating assets by service	98.9	72.8	9.7	21.0	108.6	93.8

The above analysis of turnover is based on the country in which the order is received. It would not be materially different if based on the country in which the customer is located.

Disposal and recycling includes all aspects of collection and safe disposal of industrial and commercial waste products.

Security and cleaning is undertaken by renewable annual contract, predominantly for hospitals, other healthcare premises and local government organisations.

The information contained in Note 17 relates to a service business, so it might be expected that the net assets would be relatively low compared to the turnover and operating profit. Professional analysts would be particularly interested in the relationships and trends underlying these figures.

DAVID: *The first thing I did here was to feed all these tables of segmental information into our spreadsheet package. I asked for two printouts initially. The first calculated the turnover as a multiple of net assets, the operating profit as a multiple of net assets and the profit as a percentage of turnover. That is shown in Exhibit 14.2. The second printout converted the business sector analysis to percentage increases and decreases on the previous year, as shown in Exhibit 14.3.*

Exhibit 14.2
Turnover and operating profit, each as a multiple of net assets

	Turnover as a multiple of net assets		Profit as a multiple of net assets		Profit as a % of turnover	
	Year 7	Year 6	Year 7	Year 6	Year 7 %	Year 6 %
Geographical analysis						
United Kingdom	10.5	*5.1*	2.5	*1.2*	23.8	*24.2*
Continental Europe	3.8	*7.9*	1.0	*2.1*	27.6	*26.3*
North America	49.8	*n/a*	6.8	*n/a*	13.7	*15.3*
Asia Pacific and Africa	3.9	*3.7*	1.1	*1.0*	29.0	*27.6*
	6.8	*6.4*	1.6	*1.5*	23.8	*24.0*

Exhibit 14.3
Percentage changes on previous year

	Disposal and recycling Year 7 % on Year 6	Security and cleaning Year 7 % on Year 6	Total Year 7 % on Year 6
Business sector analysis			
Turnover			
United Kingdom	23.5	43.0	31.1
Continental Europe	7.5	(11.4)	7.0
North America	6.9	97.3	36.7
Asia Pacific and Africa	11.6	26.5	12.3
Turnover by service	13.5	53.2	22.4
Operating profit by service	20.4	29.2	21.3
Net operating assets by service	35.9	(53.8)	15.8

Then I turned to the front of the annual report. The importance of segmental information becomes apparent as soon as you start to read the chairman's statement and it continues through the business reviews, presented on a segmental basis with some helpful illustrations to reinforce the message. The chief executive's review continues the segmental theme strongly and gives further information to augment the basic tables which I have already analysed. That attention to detail in their reports is a reflection of the thorough questioning which these people receive from the fund managers and analysts who follow the company closely. I know one analyst who would put Sherlock Holmes in the shade. She collects the accounts of each individual UK company in the group, and as many overseas subsidiary companies as she can get hold of. She puts them all together like a jigsaw and then starts to ask intensive questions based on what she has and what she can deduce about the missing pieces. Seasoned finance directors wilt visibly under her interrogation!

LEONA: *Segmental reporting is an area where the auditor sometimes has to give way to the directors because of the discretion allowed by the accounting standard. The directors are expected to review annually their definitions of segments and may redefine these when appropriate. The auditors may find it difficult to argue on the question of what is 'appropriate' but they can make sure that the effect of the change is fully disclosed. Some companies operating in global markets do genuinely have problems. How do you define a geographical segment for an airline company? Is it based on the country in which the passenger starts the journey? Is it based on the country in which the booking office is located? Is it based on the country in which the passenger finishes the journey?*

I know of a couple of companies which assert that they have only one business operation but then give analytical information on sub-units. They avoid describing these sub-units as segments and therefore do not have to apply the disclosure rules for segments.

Segmental reporting is an area where you and your analyst friends probably put more pressures on the companies than we can as auditors. That's a good example of market forces at work, but it does assume that the information you prise out of the company is made available more widely. Companies make use of the operating and financial review to answer the questions which they know the investors ask on a regular basis.

14.6 Summary

Now score your view of your confidence in achieving the learning outcomes of the chapter.

1 = Very confident about knowledge, application, problem solving and evaluation.

2 = Confident about knowledge and application, less sure about problem solving and evaluation.

3 = Need to read again to be more certain of basic knowledge and application.

L01 You are now able to explain the importance of the operating and financial review as a component of the annual report of a company. You also understand that the flexibility of presentation allowed by the ASB's guidance can mean that the reader must be equally flexible in locating the relevant information. You are also aware that the Company Law Review has recommended a compulsory OFR for large unlisted companies in addition to listed companies.

1	2	3
☐	☐	☐

LO2 You can describe and explain the 'accompanying information' in the annual report that is relevant to analysis of corporate performance. Features of particular interest are the highlights statement and the historical trend information.

1	2	3
☐	☐	☐

LO3 You can now relate the interpretation of ratios to the information presented in a cash flow statement and prepare a report suitable for non-specialists.

1	2	3
☐	☐	☐

LO4 You can explain how segmental information is useful to the analysis of corporate performance.

1	2	3
☐	☐	☐

If your scores are all 1 or 2, try the questions in the series A, B and C. This will give you feedback on your assessment of how well you have achieved the learning outcomes. Read again any sections of the chapter where you find your knowledge and understanding are less comprehensive than you first estimated.

If your scores include some at 3, try the series A questions to find where the problems lie. Read the relevant sections again, work through any illustrative examples and case studies, then try the questions in the series B. Once you feel confident at that level of knowledge and application, move on to try some or all of the series C questions.

International perspective

The use of regulated narrative reporting is found in other countries. In the USA there is a requirement for a Management Discussion and Analysis in the annual report submitted to the Securities and Exchange Commission by a listed company. In some continental European countries there is a requirement for a Management Report. Narrative reports are usually a mixture of regulated content and voluntary disclosures chosen by the company to present its chosen image. The cash flow statement used internationally has a three-component presentation (operating, investment and financing cash flows). Segmental reporting which meets the international accounting standard must disclose external revenue by business segment; revenue from transactions with other segments; segment results, assets, liabilities and acquisition of fixed assets each analysed by business segment, location of assets and location of customers. That list leads to several combinations of matrix presentation.

Test your understanding

Skills outcomes
SO1 Application of technical skills   SO2 Problem solving and evaluation skills   SO3 Communication skills

L01, S01   **A14.1** What is the purpose of the Operating and Financial Review?

L01, S01   **A14.2** Why is there no prescribed format for the OFR?

LO1, SO1 **A14.3** What are the main items that may be found in the Operating Review?

LO1, SO1 **A14.4** What are the main items that may be found in the Financial Review?

LO1, SO1 **A14.5** Why might companies be reluctant to disclose forward-looking information in the Financial Review?

LO1, SO1 **A14.6** What has the Company Law Review proposed for the OFR?

LO2, SO1 **A14.7** What is the purpose of a Highlights statement?

LO2, SO1 **A14.8** How does a five-year summary of historical results help investors?

LO3, SO1 **A14.9** How does an increase in stock affect cash flow?

LO3, SO1 **A14.10** How does an increase in trade debtors affect cash flow?

LO3, SO1 **A14.11** How does an increase in trade creditors affect cash flow?

LO3, SO1 **A14.12** What is meant by EBITDA?

LO4, SO1 **A14.13** How does segmental information help the users of financial statements?

LO4, SO1 **A14.14** Which items are reported on a segmental basis?

Application

LO3, SO1 **B14.1** D Ltd has an operating profit of £12m, which includes a depreciation charge of £1m. During the year the trading stock has increased by £4m, trade debtors have increased by £3m and trade creditors have increased by £5m. Prepare a statement of cash flow from operations.

LO3, SO1 **B14.2** E Ltd has an operating profit of £16m, which includes a depreciation charge of £2m. During the year the trading stock has increased by £1m, trade debtors have decreased by £3m and trade debtors have decreased by £2m. Prepare a statement of cash flow from operations.

Problem solving and evaluation

The following questions link Chapter 13 and Chapter 14.

LO5 of Ch. 13, LO1–4 of Ch. 14, SO2, SO3 **C14.1** Carry out a ratio analysis of Safe and Sure plc, using the financial statements set out in Appendix I (at the end of this book) and applying the method of analysis set out in Chapter 13, section 13.6. Making a comparison of Year 7 with Year 6, write a short commentary on each ratio separately and then summarise the overall themes emerging from the ratios. Assume a share price of 260 pence is applicable at 31 December Year 7 and a share price of 210 pence is applicable at 31 December Year 6.

LO5 of Ch. 13, LO2 of Ch. 14, SO2, SO3 **C14.2** Carry out a trend analysis on Safe and Sure plc, using the historical summary set out in Appendix I (at the end of the book). Write a short report on the key features emerging from the trends.

Activities for study groups

Activities 14.1

Turn to the annual report of a listed company which you have used for activities through-out the previous chapters. Split the group to take two different roles: one half of the group should take the role of the finance director and the other half should take the role of the broker's analyst writing a report on the company.

Look through the annual report for any ratio calculations performed by the company and check these from the data in the financial statements, so far as you are able. Prepare your own calculations of ratios for analysis of all aspects of performance. Find the current share price from a current newspaper.

Once the data preparation is complete, the finance director sub-group should prepare a short report to a meeting with the analysts. The analysts should then respond with questions arising from the ratio analysis. The finance directors should seek to present answers to the questions using the annual report. Finally make a joint report to the class on problems encountered in calculating and interpreting financial ratios.

Activity 14.2

Turn to the annual report of a listed company which you have used for activities in previous chapters. Is this a group? How do you know? Where is the list of subsidiary companies?

If you do not have a group report, obtain another annual report which is for a group of companies (nearly all large listed companies operate in group form). As a group, imagine that you are a team of analysts seeking to break down the component segments of the group for analytical purposes. How much information can you find about the segments? What are the problems of defining segments in this group? If you can obtain the annual report for the previous year, compare the definitions of segments. Are they consistent from one year to the next?

Based on your analysis, prepare a short talk to the class on the subject: 'The usefulness of segmental information in the analysis of group performance'.

Notes and references

1   ASB (1993) Statement, *Operating and Financial Review*, Accounting Standards Board.
2   ASC (1990) Statement of Standard Accounting Practice (SSAP 25), *Segmental Reporting*, Accounting Standards Committee.

Part 5

Current developments

Chapter 15

Developing issues in financial reporting

Learning outcomes

After studying this chapter you should be able to:

LO1   Explain the processes of international harmonisation and convergence with international standards.

LO2   Explain the difficulty of defining what is meant by the phrase 'a true and fair view'.

LO3   Identify and explain some of the issues that are currently of interest in the standard-setting process, namely:
(a) measurement of value;
(b) off-balance-sheet finance;
(c) related parties.

LO4   Explain how accounting practice is constantly evolving new types of, and approaches to, disclosure, in:
(a) social and environmental disclosures;
(b) the reporting cycle;
(c) summary financial statements.

LO5   Understand some of the current developments in influencing and enforcing the regulatory process, particularly:
(a) corporate governance;
(b) the Financial Reporting Review Panel.

LO6   Question the validity of the stakeholder perspective of accounting standard setting.

15.1 Introduction

Accounting is a subject which develops faster than most textbooks can be written. The basic core of knowledge which endures from one year to the next is contained in these chapters but that basic core is constantly modified as new events give rise to new opportunities. Above all, there are strong forces towards international harmonisation of accounting practice for companies listed on stock exchanges around the world. The word currently favoured is 'convergence' of accounting standards. The chapter begins by explaining why there is a need for harmonisation and discussing the barriers that may limit harmonisation.

The never-ending process of change has been summarised neatly by those who argue that the true and fair view required of financial statements is dynamic in nature. The words stay the same but they are applied in a context of changing social and economic values.

Because of the unstoppable rate of change, the standard-setting bodies must be constantly reviewing existing practice and developing new work. Examples of issues currently under the microscope of standard setting are: the measurement of value, off-balance sheet assets and liabilities, and related parties.

Demand for disclosure is also relentless in wanting greater variety. Environmental reporting is an example of an area where external pressure groups have worked to extract from companies information which they would not, in some cases, have given willingly. The users of information about a company need information earlier and more frequently than they can obtain it by waiting for the annual report to be published. Preliminary announcements are made in order to give the first news about results. Interim reports give information on a half-yearly or quarterly basis. Summary financial statements are an attempt to bring down to a manageable volume the complexities of the requirements of law.

Accounting information is produced within a strongly regulated setting and at present that regulation seems set to increase rather than diminish. The responsibilities of directors regarding corporate governance are widely debated. The Financial Reporting Review Panel attempts to hold the line of good reporting in compliance with the law and accounting standards.

Finally, it should be noted that this entire book on financial accounting has been built on a model of user needs which itself is the basis of the *Statement of Principles*. That meets general acceptance in the accounting profession from those who set accounting standards, but you need to be aware that further study of the academic literature will encourage you to question the *user needs* model.

All the issues outlined in this introduction are now discussed as illustrations of the constantly changing nature of accounting. The list is by no means exhaustive, but hopefully it will encourage those who intend to study further by showing that there is greater depth to the subject. Hopefully it will also encourage others, who do not intend to study further in a formal manner, to maintain a current awareness by regular reading of the financial press with particular attention to accounting issues.

The structure of the chapter is set out below:

Structure of
Chapter 15

International harmonisation and convergence

Dynamic nature of the true and fair view

Some current issues addressed by the ASB
Measurement of value
Assets which are not recognised – off-balance-sheet finance
Related parties

Changes in type and manner of disclosure
Social and environmental disclosures
Preliminary announcements and interim results
Summary financial statements

Enforcing and influencing the regulatory process
Corporate governance
Financial Reporting Review Panel

Users' needs
How valid is the stakeholder model?

L01

15.2 International harmonisation and convergence

Accounting practice has evolved in different ways in different countries around the world. This might not be a problem if all countries kept their borders tightly closed and there were no international trade, but that economic situation vanished long ago. Unfortunately, the accounting differences did not vanish, because accounting serves a variety of complex purposes which have only been hinted at in earlier chapters of this text. The *Statement of Principles*, which has guided the structure of this text, views users of financial statements as a list of individuals or organisations. That is what the economists would call a *microeconomic* approach to analysis. In any country these individuals and organisations operate in different ways with different balances of power and influence. The economic systems of countries therefore may be very different. This is what the economists would call a *macroeconomic* approach to analysis.

15.2.1 Causes of accounting differences

In some countries the finance needed by business is provided mainly by banks, whereas in others there is a substantial amount of equity financing where a wide spread of shareholders support business needs for finance. Banks tend to seek accounting information about the security of their investment and the capacity to pay interest, while equity investors want information about growth of the investment and the capacity to pay dividends. In some countries the tax system dictates the way in which accounts are prepared, while in other countries the tax rules are separate from the accounting rules. Tax systems have complex rules which govern the revenue to be taxed and expenditure allowed. Companies use the accounts to make the best of the tax rules and do not disclose information which could be adverse to the tax position. Some countries have a cultural background in which secrecy is seen as a virtue, while other countries operate a spirit of openness in disclosure because the people of those countries believe in openness. Some countries operate under governments which regulate strongly from the centre, while the governments of other countries set the framework through legislation but then encourage self-regulating bodies to work out the details.

The previous paragraph contains only four separate points of differences between countries. Each point made offers two contrasting characteristics. There are 16 different ways of combining these characteristics. It does not take a great deal of imagination to see that extending the list of differences and adding some variation within each type of difference would soon create sufficient combinations to explain why accounting practices have developed in different ways. The differences exist, and the task on an international scale is to reduce the different accounting practices so that international business uses one accounting language. This process of moving closer is called *harmonisation*.

15.2.2 Convergence with international standards

Much of what you have learned about the accounting equation and its application to financial statements would be recognised by accounting practitioners around the world. Where this text has focused on financial reporting in annual reports, it has taken a UK perspective. Safe and Sure, for example, is typical of the financial statements of UK listed companies. The regulatory processes described in Chapters 4 and 7 are primarily those of the UK, although there is sufficient detail to give you some understanding of the influence of the European Union.

By the year 2005 it is expected that listed companies in all EU Member States will apply the accounting standards set by the International Accounting Standards Board (IASB Standards). This target has been set by the European Commission, which is putting in place the legislative procedures to achieve the target.

The IASB Standards were called International Accounting Standards (IAS) until 2000; from that date they are called International Financial Reporting Standards (IFRS).

What differences will we see in UK companies as 2005 approaches?

Many of the IASB Standards are similar to the existing UK accounting standards. The trend towards convergence has taken place over several years and the UK's ASB has been a leading participant in the process of developing IASB Standards. Where possible in recent years, the ASB standards have moved closer to IASB Standards. Fixed assets, current assets, liabilities and ownership interest are accounted for in similar ways under both sets of standards. The ASB's Statement of Principles was drafted with the benefit of already having the IASB's Conceptual Framework as a guide. So, while the technical references will change by 2005, the essence of the approach will change relatively little at the level we are studying in introductory accounting.

The European Commission continues to act as gatekeeper for regulation of listed companies in Member States. It will scrutinise and approve all IASB Standards for use by European companies. Section 7.2.3 explains how it will be helped in this by a technical advisory committee whose participants are drawn from experts across the Member States.

European companies will continue to use the reporting formats described in Chapter 7. One area where the International Standards are ahead of the EU regulation is that of segmental reporting. We may in future see more detailed segmental reporting in many European companies' annual reports.

15.2.3 Reporting international differences

Until convergence is complete, some regulatory authorities will continue to require a formal statement explaining ('reconciling') accounting differences. In particular, the regulations of the US stock markets (imposed by the Securities and Exchange Commission, SEC) provide a useful opportunity for users of financial statements to observe the extent to which different accounting rules give a different picture of the same economic circumstances. Foreign companies which seek a listing for their shares on a US stock exchange are required to report to the SEC on what is called 'Form 20F'. This is a lengthy document but includes a statement showing the profit which would be reported under US rules and the profit which would be reported under the rules of the company's home country. There are between 40 and 50 UK companies in any one year reporting on Form 20F. Because of the different accounting rules they generally report a lower profit in the United States (although that cannot be taken as a definite rule because individual circumstances are quite important).

There was considerable surprise when the first German company to obtain a listing showed in its report on Form 20F that a reported profit under German accounting rules turned into a reported loss under US rules. It had been generally thought that German accounting is more conservative than other accounting systems, but this case showed that the conservatism manifests itself in smoothing out good and bad times through provisions, not all of which were permissible under US rules.

In recent years there has been an increase in foreign registrants taking a US listing. (You can find an up-to-date list on the website of the New York Stock Exchange, www.nyse.com.)

The remaining sections of this chapter explain issues that are continuing to develop in the UK and are also relevant in an international context. They will all attract continuing attention in future from national and international regulators.

L01 **Activity 15.1**

Choose any two countries which you know something about (you don't need to know anything about their accounting practices). Write down a list of all the factors which make one country different from the other. Then go back through the list and put a cross against any factor which might cause the accounting practices of those two countries to be different. To what extent have you identified matters of law, the economy, culture of the country, culture of individuals, and religious beliefs? Research has shown that all these factors have an influence on accounting practices.

L02 15.3 Dynamic nature of the true and fair view

The Companies Act 1985 requires that financial statements of companies should show *a true and fair view*. The Act provides no definition of the meaning of 'a true and fair view'. Consequently from time to time those who set accounting standards have sought the opinion of expert legal advisers. The lawyers have put forward the view that the requirement for a true and fair view is a dynamic concept which changes its nature as the general values of society change. Although the words stay the same, the meaning of the words changes because the opinions of society in general change.

15.3.1 What do the lawyers say?

What does that mean in practice? The lawyers have provided an example.[1] The Bill of Rights 1688 prohibited 'cruel and unusual punishments'. The dictionary definition of 'cruel' has changed little since that time but a judge today would characterise as 'cruel' some punishments which a judge of 1688 would not have regarded as cruel. The meaning of the word remains the same but the facts to which it is applied have changed. Based on reasoning of that type, the lawyers have argued that the words 'true and fair' may carry the same dictionary meaning from one time to another but the accounting principles and practice contributing to a true and fair view will change as circumstances change.

One very important issue is the question of whether society, and the public interest, would expect the application of *accounting standards* to be necessary as evidence of intent to apply a true and fair view. Legal advice provided to the ASB analysed the role of an accounting standard:

> What is the purpose of an accounting standard? The initial purpose is to identify proper accounting practice for the benefit of preparers and auditors of accounts. However, because accounts commonly comply with accounting standards, the effect of the issue of standards has also been to create a common understanding between users and preparers of accounts as to how particular items should be treated in accounts and accordingly an expectation that, save where good reason exists, accounts will comply with applicable accounting standards.[2]

Accounting standards have, over a period of years, become regarded as an authoritative source of accounting practice. The legal opinion given to the ASB is that accounting standards provide very strong evidence of the proper practice which should be adopted. The 'true and fair view' is seen as a dynamic concept:

> Thus what is required to show a true and fair view is subject to continuous rebirth and in determining whether the true and fair requirement is satisfied the Court will not in my view seek to find synonyms for the words 'true and fair' but will seek to apply the concepts which those words imply.[3]

15.3.2 Who is responsible for the true and fair view?

Under company law, it is the directors who are responsible for ensuring that the accounts are prepared in such a way as to show a true and fair view. The auditors state whether, in their opinion, the accounts show a true and fair view. If you turn back to Chapter 4 you will see an example of the statement of directors' responsibilities which now appears in many company reports and also a copy of the auditors' report. Both contain the phrase 'a true and fair view' and emphasise the different types of responsibility held by directors and auditors.

15.3.3 How specific is the 'true and fair' concept?

You should have gained an understanding, from various chapters of this book, that there is more than one accounting treatment for many transactions and events. It is a great puzzle to many people that companies could produce different accounting statements for one particular period of time, each of which would show a true and fair view. The answer lies in one very small word. The requirement of law is for 'a true and fair view' but not for 'the true and fair view'. Thus the directors do not have to find 'the very best true and fair view', which may surprise some users of financial statements. It also becomes very difficult for auditors to enter into dispute with directors where there are two acceptable alternatives, either of which could result in a true and fair view. To be successful in contradicting the directors, the auditors need to show that a particular practice does *not* show a true and fair view. If they can successfully argue that opinion then the company has the choice of revising the proposed treatment or facing a *qualified* audit opinion. Here is an example of a qualified audit opinion where the auditor and directors were in disagreement:

> **Qualified audit opinion**
> We found that the company has made no provision for doubtful debts, despite circumstances which indicate that such a provision is necessary.
>   In our opinion the accounts do not give a true and fair view . . .

It is therefore essential, in reading the annual report, to read the auditors' report at an early stage in order to be aware of any problems with the financial statements. It is also essential to realise that the meaning of 'true and fair' is highly subjective and changes over a period of time.

15.3.4 International perspective

The phrase 'true and fair' was taken into European Directives when the UK joined as a Member State but it has never found an exact equivalent in the underlying meaning. For example the French wording 'image fidèle' is closer to 'a faithful picture'. The US wording is 'faithful representation'. The UK position is that it may be necessary for individual companies to take action which contravenes legal rules, in the interest of presenting 'a true and fair view'. The international position is generally that the law prevails and any questions about fair presentation should be analysed within the legal framework.

L02 | **Activity 15.2**

> Looking back through Chapters 8 to 12, identify matters of accounting practice where more than one accounting policy is permitted. If you were an auditor, how would you decide whether one or other of the permitted choices gave a true and fair view?

L03a | # 15.4 Measurement of value

Throughout the majority of this financial accounting text the value of assets and liabilities has been measured at historical cost. That means the price paid, or the liability agreed, when the transaction was first undertaken. In times when prices are changing, that information about the cost at the date of the transaction will become less *relevant* to the needs of users (although it may be seen as a *reliable* measure).

15.4.1 Stages of recognition and measurement

At the moment when the transaction takes place, the historical cost is also the current value, where current value is regarded as the value of the item at the accounting date. In the *Statement of Principles* this is identified as the point of *initial recognition*. If an asset or a liability is involved, then there will be various points at which it may be appropriate to remeasure the amount at which the asset or liability is recorded. This is referred to as *subsequent remeasurement*. Finally there may come a point at which the asset or liability should be removed from the financial statements. This is referred to as *derecognition*.[4]

The conditions to be applied in deciding on initial recognition have been explained in Chapter 2. Derecognition reverses the conditions so that an asset or a liability should cease to be recognised if there is no longer sufficient evidence that the entity has access to future economic benefits or an obligation to transfer economic benefits.[5]

15.4.2 Limitations of historical cost accounting

Throughout this text you have studied historical cost accounting where the acquisition of assets is recorded at the amount paid at the time of acquisition. The academic literature is bursting at the seams with criticisms of historical cost accounting, but the practice has proved hard to change. There were brief practical attempts in the United Kingdom to apply a different approach for a period from the mid-1970s to the mid-1980s but the rate of inflation then became less of a problem and interest waned.

Critics of historical cost accounting have said that in the balance sheet there is the addition of items bought at different times and with £s of different purchasing power. That is not a satisfactory procedure. In the profit and loss account the costs are matched against revenue without regard for the fact that goods were bought and expenses paid for at an earlier point in time. Sales are therefore matched against outdated costs. The tax system takes the accounting profit as its starting point and therefore the tax payable is dictated by outdated accounting figures.

Supporters of historical cost accounting point to its reliability and objectivity because the monetary amount of the transaction is known. Verifiability is straightforward because documentation exists. The preference for historical cost values remains strong; if companies do decide to revalue fixed assets then the ASB requires them to keep the current values up to date in each year's balance sheet.[6]

15.4.3 Subsequent remeasurement

Subsequent remeasurement poses more problems and is one of the more controversial aspects of the *Statement of Principles*. It is suggested that there should be a change in the amount at which an asset or liability is recorded if there is sufficient evidence that: (a) the amount has changed and (b) the new amount can be measured with sufficient reliability.[7] In times of inflation (when prices generally are increasing), the idea of remeasurement becomes particularly important. Even when inflation is not a major problem, there may be one particular asset whose value increases through scarcity of supply or decreases through lack of demand.

That leads into an extremely controversial question: 'How do you measure value?' Chapter 6 of the *Statement of Principles* outlines some approaches to value.

15.4.4 Entry price and exit price

Taking fixed assets and stocks as the main examples to begin with, it could be said that there are two different categories of measures of value. There is a price which the organisation will have to pay to acquire the asset and there is a price at which the organisation will be able to sell the asset to someone else. If you have ever tried buying and selling second-hand goods you will know that the buying price and the selling price are often quite different. The student who tries to sell an outdated personal computer through an advertisement on the college noticeboard knows that any enquirer will try to push the price downwards. The student attempting to enquire about a similar item of equipment knows that the seller will try to keep the price high. Somehow the price for which you are able to sell your second-hand possessions invariably appears to be lower than the price someone else is asking for their unwanted belongings.

The price paid by a business to acquire an asset is called in accounting the *entry price* and the price at which the business would be able to sell the asset is called the *exit price*. Academic authors will argue long and hard on both sides of the case and if you pursue the study of accounting further you will meet that academic debate. In the real world a decision has to be made. In the United Kingdom, that decision was made by the standard-setting body at the beginning of the 1980s, when SSAP 16 required companies to use the entry price approach and to measure the value of fixed assets and stocks at the *cost of replacement* at the balance sheet date.[8] That approach was used to provide additional information in annual reports of the United Kingdom for the first half of the 1980s, but gradually the enthusiasm of companies waned and by the late 1980s they had reverted to their traditional practice of using primarily historical cost for most aspects of measurement.

15.4.5 Current practice

Despite the general adherence to historical cost, some exceptions have persisted. Companies which own land and buildings may choose to revalue them periodically using the open market value of the land and buildings in their existing form of use. Some businesses holding investments in shares may choose to value these at the market price rather than the historical cost. Thus many companies say in their accounting policy notes: 'These accounts have been prepared on a modified historical cost basis.'

Prior to the issue of FRS 15, *Measurement of Tangible Fixed Assets*, there was no accounting standard dealing with how and when to revalue fixed assets; companies were at liberty to revalue as and when they chose. The desire to show good news rather than bad news may have encouraged company directors to revalue where there had been an increase in value but to wait for the upturn where temporary decreases occurred. Users of financial statements may often not have known what policy the company had applied in deciding which assets to revalue, or in deciding the timing of revaluation.

FRS 15 has imposed greater consistency and clarity of disclosure where fixed assets are revalued (*see* Chapter 8).

15.4.6 Moving forward: the ASB's ideas

Chapter 6 of the *Statement of Principles* is the first stage in moving away from the limitations of historical cost accounting. In a current value system, changes in value are recorded as they occur. This idea, if accepted, puts quite a large hole in the concept of *realisation*, which is at the heart of traditional accounting practice. It has been the practice to record changes in ownership interest only when the change in an asset or liability is realised, in the form either of cash or of other assets the ultimate realisation of which can be assessed with reasonable certainty.[9] That practice finds support in the Companies Act 1985 which states that the profit and loss account may report only those profits which are realised.

However, the Accounting Standards Board has created a statement of total recognised gains and losses in which a company may report changes in assets and liabilities which are not realised (*see* Chapter 12). There is therefore a place in which to report changes in current value, but the question of how to measure value is still unanswered.

The argument favoured by the ASB, as indicated in the *Statement of Principles*, is the one which leads to a measurement system based on *value to the business*. Those who support this idea start by asking: What is the worst that can happen to a person, or business, which owns a fixed asset or item of trading stock? The answer is that they may be *deprived* of the item, perhaps by theft, fire, obsolescence or similar cause. The next question is: What would the owners need in order to be returned to the position they enjoyed previously? The answer, in most cases, is that they need to be provided with the cost of replacement of a similar item so that they may continue with the activity of the business. In a few rare cases, where the owners may have decided to sell rather than continue using the asset, the selling price is the measure of deprival.

From this analysis it is argued that the *value to the business* of a fixed asset or an item of stock is usually the *replacement cost* at the accounting date. The replacement cost is that of a similar item in a similar state. Such a replacement cost might be found in a catalogue of prices of used equipment or it could be estimated by starting with the cost of a new item and applying an appropriate proportion of depreciation.

15.4.7 Making the idea work

The ASB cannot afford to experience a repetition of the situation of the 1980s when companies decided to cease applying current cost accounting as required by SSAP 16. Consequently, it is exploring the acceptability of a gradual move away from historical cost to current values, looking first for those assets where revaluation will cause least argument. These could be:

- properties (i.e. land and buildings but excluding fixed assets, such as factories or plant, which are specific to the business)
- investments which have a Stock Exchange listing
- stocks of commodities where a market of sufficient depth exists.[10]

The common features of these items are that the Companies Act already requires supplementary information on current values (in the directors' report or in the notes to the accounts) and also that there is trading on a ready market.

It is not possible at this time to predict exactly how or when UK companies might report current values of fixed assets, but it is clear that there is a determination to persuade both preparers and users of financial statements that it is not in their interests to remain so closely blinkered by historical cost.

15.4.8 International perspective

There is some way to go in gaining international agreement about the use of valuations beyond historical cost. The Fourth Directive permits Member States to include a revaluation clause in national legislation. Germany chose not to do this and so German companies must adhere to historical cost accounting. The IASB Standard permits revaluation but does not require it. In some countries, such as France, revaluation is permitted but rarely used by companies. The IASB has developed new standards requiring the use of 'fair value' in particular cases; the European Union published a new Directive in 2001 allowing fair value to be used in Member States. There is a tendency internationally to see 'fair value' in exit price terms as being linked to the market value of the asset; there is a UK view that arguments based on 'value to the business' or 'deprival value' would support an entry price value. The debate continues.

LO3a

Activity 15.3

Look at the items you possess. These might include a house or a flat or a car but equally well they could be a bicycle and some modest items of furniture. Whatever their nature, write down on a piece of paper a figure in £s which answers the question: What is the value of these possessions? Now think about how you arrived at that figure. Did you use the original cost because that was the amount you paid to acquire them? Did you use replacement cost because that is the amount you would have to pay to replace them? Did you use selling price because that is the amount you could collect in cash for conversion to other uses? Did you have some other method? What was the reason for the method you chose? Would you obtain the same answer using all the methods listed for this activity? Which answer is the most relevant for your information needs? Which is the most reliable? Is there any conflict here between relevance and reliability? Would other students answer these questions as you have done?

LO3b

15.5 Off-balance-sheet finance

One major problem for UK accounting emerged in the 1980s in a period of business expansion. To finance expansion, companies were borrowing and therefore increasing their gearing ratios. Some companies looked for ways of avoiding disclosing in the balance sheet the full extent of the commitment on borrowed funds. Omitting the item from the balance sheet could not remove the commercial obligation but it could reduce the questions arising from those who would read the financial statements.

The accounting question is: How do you remove, or fail to include, a liability so that no one will notice? The answer, as with all accounting questions, starts in the accounting equation. To keep the equation in balance, any removal of a liability must be matched by removal of an asset of equal amount.

Many ingenious schemes emerged, but one of the least complex is the sale and leaseback of land and buildings.

15.5.1 Sale and leaseback of property

Consider the following scenario. A company has the following balance sheet:

	£m
Land and buildings	20
Other assets, *less* current liabilities	15
	35
Less long-term loan	(20)
Net assets	15
Share capital	15

The company sells the land and buildings for £20m and repays the loan. The balance sheet now appears to contain no gearing:

	£m
Other assets, *less* current liabilities	15
Share capital	15

However, enquiry behind the scenes reveals a complex arrangement. The land and buildings were sold to a consortium of finance companies, but on the same day a lease was signed that allowed the company to continue occupying the property at a rental payment which would vary according to current rates of interest and would be calculated as a percentage of the £20m cash received. In five years' time the company would have the option to repurchase the land and buildings at £20m and the consortium of finance companies would have the option to force the company to repurchase at £20m. These options would mean that if the price rose over the next five years the company would wish to buy at £20m. If the price fell over the next five years the consortium would insist on repurchase.

Now ask yourself, where do the benefits and risks of this contract lie? The benefits of a rise in value and the risks of a decrease in value remain with the company, as they would if the company had remained the owner. The company will pay a rental which looks very much like an interest payment on a loan of £20m. If the company fails to meet its obligations, then the consortium will claim the asset. The commercial effect of this transaction is that of a loan based on the security of the asset of land and buildings.

15.5.2 Action to improve practice

After some years of consultation and discussion with interested parties, the Accounting Standards Board has decided that such transactions do not change the commercial substance of the transaction and it is the commercial substance which matters. So a transaction of this type would now have to be reported on the balance sheet[11] in the form of an asset and matching liability.

The story remains of interest to those using financial statements because it indicates the problem of a situation where the *reader* never knows what is not being reported. The pressure for bringing transactions on to the balance sheet came from some auditors who saw what was happening but had no standard to call upon. The story also illustrates the problem of determining what presents a true and fair view where there is no backing from an accounting standard. The auditors were unable to argue against the directors of companies in the absence of a standard to back up the argument.

15.5.3 International perspective

The problems associated with off-balance-sheet finance received high public profile at the end of 2001, running into 2002, with the failure of a large US company called Enron. Because of the size of the company and the political impact of its failure, hearings were called by the US Congress at which witnesses gave evidence on accounting practices, among other matters. One of the accounting issues discussed was the question of 'off-balance-sheet finance'. The Chief Accountant of the Securities and Exchange Commission described to the House of Representatives how money could be borrowed at advantageous rates of interest using a 'special purpose entity' which was not consolidated with the rest of the group accounts. Provided the assets of the special purpose entity retained sufficient value, the lender would be content with the arrangement. If the assets fell in value then the lender would look to the parent company for reimbursement. Shareholders in the parent would be unaware of the extent of such borrowing until the lenders demanded repayment. At the time of the failure of Enron the US standard-setting body (the Financial Accounting Standards Board) was still in the process of providing guidance on consolidation of such special purpose entities. The International Accounting Standards Board had no standard that directly addressed such entities.

LO3b   **Activity 15.4**

> *Off-balance-sheet finance is one example of information which would never come to the attention of the users of financial statements but for the concern of some auditors. Make a list of other types of information which may be evident to the auditors but which are unlikely to be conveyed to the readers. Consider this list in the light of the requirement that financial statements must show a true and fair view. To what extent is the reader of financial statements reliant on the directors and the auditors?*

LO3c   # 15.6 Related parties

One of the areas in which readers of financial statements have lacked information is that of the relationships between the company and other persons or organisations which may influence the performance and position of the company. These relationships are not necessarily against the company's interests but they may be undesirable. Whatever the good and bad points, the user of the financial statements should be aware of related parties so that a judgement may be formed.

15.6.1 Nature of related parties

Related parties come in several forms. They include:

- the parent company, any subsidiary and any fellow subsidiary undertakings
- directors of the company
- associates and joint venture companies
- pension funds established on behalf of the company's employees.

Other forms of relationship may also be presumed to be related parties, such as:

- key management personnel
- shareholders controlling more than 20 per cent of the voting rights
- one entity being managed by another entity under a management contract
- close family of directors and key personnel
- partnerships, companies or trusts in which a related party has a controlling interest.

15.6.2 Problems of related parties

What undesirable activities might related parties pursue? Some of the worst examples only come out into the open after disaster has struck and investigators are sent to find the cause. Such investigations are carried out by accountants and lawyers appointed as inspectors by the Department of Trade and Industry. The inspectors write lengthy reports, usually referred to as *DTI Reports.* These make fascinating reading on the shortcomings of persons involved in failed companies. Some of the activities uncovered which have involved related parties are as follows:

1 The director of a company took investment certificates belonging to the employees' pension fund and used these certificates as security for borrowing more money to prop up his ailing company. The banks that lent the money were not aware that the certificates belonged to the pension funds because they were bearer bonds, which are regarded as being the property of the person who carries them ('bears them') at any time. It was clearly undesirable that the director of the company also had access to the investment certificates of the pension fund.

2 A person was a director of company X and a major shareholder in company Y. The goods produced by Y were of adequate quality but priced more highly than those of competitors. The person concerned used his position as director of company X to authorise purchase of goods from company Y, rather than seek the most competitive price in the market.

3 The figure of trade debtors for company Z included a loan to a customer which proved, on investigation, to be a business owned by the husband of the sales director.

The first two cases are clearly undesirable situations because there is loss to one or more parties. The third case may be a perfectly sound transaction but the facts should be known so that users of the financial statements may form a judgement.

15.6.3 Auditing and accounting actions

This problem of the existence of related parties and the potential for transactions which are not at arm's length is not a new one. It is, however, another example of information which is only discovered by the auditor. If there is no accounting standard the auditor cannot insist on disclosure. In 1995, therefore, the ASB introduced a new Financial Reporting Standard, FRS 8, *Related Party Disclosures.* At the same time the Auditing Practice Board issued a Statement of Auditing Standards, SAS 460, *Related Parties.*

The FRS requires companies to disclose:

- names of some related parties and their relationships
- descriptions of the transactions and amounts involved
- amounts due at the balance sheet date.

The SAS requires auditors to plan the audit work with the objective of obtaining sufficient audit evidence regarding the adequacy of disclosure of related party transactions and control of the entity in the financial statements.

Will FRS 8 prevent the determined fraudster from removing the assets of a company? It is probably unrealistic to suggest that any regulatory process will deter those who are determined to disobey it. It is, however, hoped that the uncertainty will be removed in cases where unnecessary suspicion may previously have been created by secrecy. It is also thought that the existence of the standard will create a new atmosphere of open disclosure regarding the stewardship of the company.

15.6.4 International perspective

The definition of 'related party' is dependent to some extent on the business culture and structure of companies in any particular country. Concepts of family loyalties, extended families and interrelated business may all make particular types of relationship significant in various countries. The IASB has a standard dealing with related parties but it is generally not as rigorous as the UK standard in its disclosure requirements. However in one respect the IASB is more demanding because it expects companies to disclose the pricing policy of related party transactions. The US enquiry into Enron, mentioned in section 15.5.3, may well lead to stronger international rules on declaring related party interests.

LO3c

> ## Activity 15.5
>
> *In FRS 8 the ASB defines close family as 'those family members, or members of the same household, who may be expected to influence, or be influenced by, that person (an identified related party) in their dealings with the reporting entity'. Consider the practical problems facing directors and auditors in reporting transactions with such persons where these persons deny that they exercise influence on a person who has already been identified as a related party. How would you feel if your transactions with a company were reported in the financial statements because you are living in the same household as a senior manager of a company? Are the information needs of shareholders in a company more important than the sensitivities of any individual person affected by an accounting rule?*

LO4a

15.7 Social and environmental disclosures

Companies disclose in their annual reports more information than is represented only in financial statements. Depending on social attitudes or pressures, companies may voluntarily disclose additional information intended to confirm the company's sense of social responsibility. In some instances, the provisions of law eventually catch up with the values of society and disclosures become mandatory.

Investors are increasingly asking questions about the corporate social responsibility of the companies in which they invest. Many investors want to be reassured that the businesses in which they have a stake adopt ethical business practices towards employees, the community and the environment. You will see increasing numbers of what are described as 'ethical investment funds' which make careful enquiry before buying shares. Some ethical investors feel that they are best placed to influence a company if they become shareholders; others feel that they should not become shareholders until the company has a sound policy.

15.7.1 Types of disclosure

Examples of social disclosure on mandatory topics would be: information about pensions for employees, employees' share option schemes, policy regarding employment of disabled persons, donations to charity and consultation with employees. Social disclosure on a voluntary basis would cover: information about employee matters, health and safety, community work, energy and the environment.

In terms of relative volume, the amount of information disclosed about employee-related matters exceeds other types of social and environmental disclosures, but the area where there is the fastest growth in interest is that of environmental issues. Many leading companies now have an 'environment' section in the annual report and some go even further in producing a separate environmental report. Research shows a growth in reporting such work over a period of some years.[12]

Below are extracts from the 'environment' section of the report of the directors of Safe and Sure plc, the company used for illustration throughout this text.

Safe and Sure is committed to the provision of services and products which improve the quality of life, both for our customers and the community, using working practices designed to protect the environment.

Heightened awareness of environmental issues and increased legislation provide a focal point for developing greener techniques and solutions to problems, both in our more traditional businesses and also in offering opportunities to develop new businesses.

Antibacterial deep cleaning of premises, in particular high-risk areas such as washrooms, drains and food production and preparation areas, has been developed to meet increased legislation and concern as to health and food safety.

It is the responsibility of the company and all its employees to ensure that all services and products are procured, produced, packaged and delivered, and waste materials ultimately disposed of, in ways which are appropriate from an environmental viewpoint. It is the responsibility of our employees to carry out their work in a manner that will not cause damage to the environment.

15.7.2 Need for measurement

Social and environmental disclosures in annual reports have so far centred on narrative description in the directors' report or in the non-statutory part of the document. There is little evidence of impact on the accounting numbers but that may be the next step. Environmental obligations create liabilities. An oil rig in the North Sea will eventually have to be removed. The liability may be regarded as existing now because the event creating the obligation was the original act of positioning the rig in the oil field. But what will eventual removal cost? Will the rig be dismantled to a few hundred feet below the surface, out of the way of fishing nets? Will it be dismantled down to the sea bed with the debris left behind? Will the rig be towed away for dismantling elsewhere? Until these questions can be answered, the liability cannot be measured as a money amount and therefore cannot be recognised in the balance sheet. Most oil companies make a provision each year towards the ultimate cost of removal of the rig and they accumulate the provision in the balance sheet. They do not, in general, report the full liability at the outset.

15.7.3 Company Law Review

The Company Law Review report of 2001 proposed that the new form of Operating and Financial Review should include a section dealing with the company's policies and performance on environmental, community, social, ethical and reputational issues including compliance with relevant laws and regulations. This could include any social or community programmes; policies for the business on environmental and ethical issues and their impact for the business; policies on international trade and human rights issues; and any political and charitable contributions. This looks to be quite a formidable list but there is a clause 'required to the extent that it is material' so it remains to be seen how the materiality condition is applied if and when these proposals become legislation.

15.7.4 International perspective: the Kyoto Protocol

International agreements on supporting sustainable development have consequences for accounting. One example is seen in the Kyoto Protocol, an agreement resulting from a conference held in Kyoto, Japan in 1997. It set out measures for dealing with problems of climate change by reducing greenhouse gas emissions. Some countries were more reluctant than others to sign the agreement; by 2001 there were 178 in agreement, although the US government was still not committed. The agreement requires action to be taken to reduce carbon-based emissions (particularly carbon dioxide) over a defined time-scale. This in turn creates new assets and liabilities for individual companies. The liabilities are easier to see: companies which do not reduce emissions will face penalties. However there will also be opportunities to take actions that prevent emissions and extract value from the new carbon market. If these actions meet the definition and recognition criteria, they will be regarded as assets. One interesting feature of the Kyoto agreement is that companies will be given 'allowances to emit'. The allowance, in the form of a licence, will be capable of being transferred from one company to another. The entity that buys a licence to emit will acquire an asset.

There is no international accounting standard dealing directly with accounting for the environment and sustainable development but there are interested groups working on the accounting issues in various countries.

LO4a

Write down the accounting equation: Assets minus Liabilities equals Ownership interest. Suppose you are the accountant for an oil company and you have been asked to record the full liability for dismantling an oil rig in 20 years' time. How would you make the accounting equation balance?

LO4b

15.8 The reporting cycle

The annual report is a regulated base of information on which a reporting cycle is built. The cycle begins when the company makes its first announcement of the results of the financial year. This announcement is made in a manner dictated by Stock Exchange rules and is called a 'preliminary announcement' because it is a preliminary to the issue of the full annual report. It is also called a 'press release' because it forms the basis of the information which first appears in the financial press.

The cycle continues with reports being issued in the period between annual reports. These are called 'interim reports'. The London Stock Exchange requires half-yearly reports. The regulators of the US stock exchanges require quarterly reports. All UK listed companies provide half-yearly reports and some voluntarily provide quarterly reports.

Company law does not prescribe the content of the preliminary announcement or the interim report. The Company Law Review report of 2001 (*see* section 7.9.2) recommended that regulation of the preliminary announcement was best carried out by the market regulator rather than by parliamentary legislation. The report did suggest that company law should require that the preliminary announcement be published on the company's website, with electronic notification to shareholders.

The guidance to listed companies, formerly provided by the Stock Exchange but transferred to the Financial Services Authority in 2000, leaves scope for flexibility in disclosure and measurement. That has caused the Accounting Standards Board to write non-mandatory guidance on good practice. This section explains some features of the ASB guidance on preliminary announcements and interim reports.

15.8.1 Preliminary announcements

The preliminary announcement is the first external communication of the financial performance and position of a company in relation to the financial year most recently completed. The institutional shareholders and their advisers will form expectations about the position and performance in advance of the announcement. They look carefully at the preliminary announcement in comparison with their expectations.

There is no obligation on companies to send these preliminary announcements to shareholders so that in practice only the institutional shareholders and their advisers see them. The ASB suggests that it would be fairer if all shareholders were entitled to request a copy of the announcement. Companies are also encouraged to use ways of publicising the preliminary announcements which will make them more readily available to the private investor.

Reliability is a key requirement of the preliminary announcement. The Stock Exchange requires the company's auditors to agree to the release of the preliminary announcement. There is an expectation that the information in the preliminary announcement will be consistent with the annual report when it eventually appears.

The rules of the Financial Services Authority and the Stock Exchange do not regulate the content of the preliminary announcement other than the requirement for profit and loss information and any significant information necessary for the purpose of assessing the results being announced. In practice many of these announcements include more information than the profit and loss account. The ASB recommends a narrative commentary, a summarised profit and loss account, a summarised balance sheet and a summarised cash flow statement. Increasingly it is found that companies are using the text of the Operating and Financial Review as the basis for the narrative comment in the preliminary announcement.

In general the ASB wishes to improve the timeliness, quality, relevance and consistency of preliminary announcements within the constraints of reliability. It could be that in the longer term the preliminary announcement would increasingly take over the role of the annual report. The delay in publishing the annual report is related to the need to publish a paper-based document. The Company Law Review report recommends that electronic means of communication could speed up the process considerably.

15.8.2 Interim reports

For some time listed companies have been required to report their profit figures on a half-yearly basis between one annual report and the next. The Committee on the Financial Aspects of Corporate Governance (the 'Cadbury Committee' – *see* section 15.10) recommended in 1992 that the ASB should work with the Stock Exchange to clarify the accounting principles to be used in the preparation of interim reports. It also proposed that a balance sheet should accompany the profit and loss account.

One interesting accounting question is how to measure the results of half a year. One view is that the results of half a year should represent the actual events of that half-year. This is called the 'discrete' method. A different view is that the result for six months should represent half of the results of the full year. This is called the 'integral' method. Why does this make a difference? Imagine a company which manufactures and sells fireworks. The costs will fall evenly through the year but most of the sales will arise in the months leading to 5 November. Using the discrete method, the first six months of the calendar year will show low profits or perhaps losses. The second six months will show relatively high profits. Using the integral method each half-year will show the same profit at 50 per cent of the total figure of the year.

The ASB recommends that the discrete method should be used as far as possible. Some expense items, such as taxation, may have to be spread evenly over the year.

In matters of disclosure the ASB recommends that the interim report should include a management commentary, although less detailed than the operating and financial review. A summarised balance sheet and a summarised cash flow statement are also recommended.

15.8.3 International perspective

The ASB's recommendations are similar to the International Accounting Standard, IAS 34, *Interim Reporting*, providing some evidence of a willingness to harmonise practice where this is acceptable to the national standard setter.

LO4b **Activity 15.7**

Obtain the interim report and the annual report of a major listed company. Compare the interim report with the annual report. What are the information items in the interim report? How do they compare with the full year in the annual report? What statements of accounting policy are made in the interim report?

LO4c ## 15.9 Summary financial statements

In 1989, the Companies Act was amended to allow listed companies to send a summary financial statement to shareholders who do not wish to receive the full accounts. The legislation prescribes a minimum list of disclosures, covering the basic elements of the directors' report, the profit and loss account and the balance sheet. The notes to the profit and loss account and the balance sheet do not appear in the summary financial statement.

It is a requirement that there must be an explanation in the summary financial statement which reminds readers that it is only a summary and that they are entitled to request the full version. There must also be a warning that the summary does not contain sufficient information to allow for a full understanding of the results and state of affairs of the company or group concerned. The auditors must report on whether, in their opinion, the summary is consistent with the full accounts and complies with the legal requirements.

The reason for introducing the summary financial statement in 1989 was related to the privatisation of several large companies which had been in public ownership (such as gas, electricity and telephone companies). There had been widespread interest in buying shares and consequently the share registers held an unusually large number of names. It is an expensive business to print and distribute a full version of the annual report and so the summary financial statement was devised as a means of cost saving.

Summary financial statements do not necessarily make financial statements more readable for the user. There have been restrictions on the form of wording which may be used for items in the financial statements (because of the requirement for 'consistency'). Thus the description 'simplified' may be more appropriately rewritten as 'shortened'.

The benefits of summary financial statements are therefore a cost saving for the company and, possibly, a more readable summary for the shareholder. The limitations lie in the absence of the explanatory notes. The overall picture conveyed to the reader may be too simplistic and may give the impression that financial statements may be analysed in a few simple ratios such as gearing or earnings per share.

In practice, relatively few companies appear to have taken the simplified annual report approach, but increasingly they are providing a 'split' annual report. There is no regulation of the precise contents except that the part which contains a summary of the financial statements must contain a reference to the full document. A pattern is appearing where the second part of the annual report contains the regulated information of directors' report and statutory accounts while the first part contains the chairman's statement, the chief executive's report, the operating and financial report and summary financial statements.

The Company Law Review report (*see* section 7.9.2) tested opinions on various alternatives to the summary financial statements and finally concluded that the arrangements in place should continue. Abolition was not favoured, but legal regulation was also rejected. The report recommended the facility for summary financial statements should extend to all companies, whether public or private. The summary statement should include a summary OFR and the guidance on the form and content should be given by the ASB. The Financial Reporting Review Panel should have the power to consider the summary statement as well as the annual report.

LO4c | **Activity 15.8**

Suppose you are a company shareholder and you receive a letter asking whether you would prefer to receive the summary financial statement but not receive the full annual report. What would be your reply? What are your reasons for this reply?

LO5a | ## 15.10 Corporate governance

The term *corporate governance* is used to describe the way in which companies are directed and controlled. In Chapter 1 the idea of stewards and their agents was put forward briefly as a model of the relationship between shareholders and the directors of a company. It could be argued that these two groups could be left together to work out their fate, but a series of well-publicised corporate failures and financial scandals of the 1980s raised concern that such a system does not always work and the public interest may suffer as a result.

There has therefore been considerable interest in intervening to improve the quality of corporate governance. The issue has been high on the agenda in several of the English-speaking countries and the ideas have strong international interest although perhaps translated into different words and phrases. In the United Kingdom, the government has taken some action through legislation but has largely followed the traditional route of encouraging the self-regulatory approach. One of the most important aspects of this self-regulatory approach was the 1992 report of what is usually referred to as the Cadbury Committee.[13]

The Cadbury Committee was set up by the Financial Reporting Council, the London Stock Exchange and the accountancy profession. It was asked to report on a range of issues concerned with the way directors run their companies and auditors monitor those companies, considering also the links between directors, auditors and shareholders. The recommendations of the Cadbury Committee were wide-ranging but included proposed improvements in financial reporting such as:

- more detail in the interim reports
- clearer information about directors' remuneration
- effective use of the operating and financial review
- the effectiveness of the internal control procedures used by the business
- reassurance that the business is a going concern
- a statement of the responsibilities of directors.

Although the report was issued in 1992 it took some time for further working parties to agree on the manner of reporting on internal controls and the going concern confirmation. By the end of 1995 these were in place and 1996 saw the start of a review of the first three years of implementing the Cadbury Report.

The review was chaired by Sir Ronald Hampel, so that the report which eventually appeared in 1998 was called 'The Hampel Report'.[14] It took as its starting point the view that good corporate governance was not merely a matter of complying with a number of hard and fast rules. There was seen to be a need for broad principles. It was important to take account of the diversity of circumstances and experience among companies, and within the same company over time. On this basis Hampel suggested that the true safeguard for good corporate governance lay in the application of informed and independent judgement by experienced and qualified individuals – executive and non-executive directors, shareholders and auditors.

Relatively little was said about financial reporting, beyond the assertion that the board of directors should present a balanced and understandable assessment of the company's position and prospects (Hampel Report, Principle DI).

Following the Hampel Report, the Stock Exchange issued a Combined Code (1998) for listed companies containing recommendations on directors; directors' remuneration; relations with shareholders; and accountability and audit. The accountability section emphasised the responsibilities of directors in respect of financial reporting. They should present a balanced and understandable assessment of the company's position and prospects. In particular they should explain their responsibilities and they should also report that the business is a going concern.

15.10.1 Directors' remuneration

If one item of accounting information eclipsed all others during the mid-1990s it must have been directors' remuneration. The prime item of interest for any financial journalist was the salary of the highest paid director and the amount that person was gaining through share option schemes. These schemes allow directors to obtain each year the option to buy shares at an agreed price. If the share price rises subsequently the directors exercise the option, buy the share at the agreed price and may sell immediately at a profit. This scheme is not applied only to directors. Some companies offer such options to some or all of their employees by way of encouraging loyalty to the company and supplementing cash salaries.

In response to well-publicised concerns about the need to disclose and control the level of directors' remuneration, a study group chaired by Sir Richard Greenbury (1995) produced a code of best practice on disclosure and remuneration policy.[15] In particular there should be a remuneration committee of non-executive directors which should make a report to shareholders each year. That report should include full details of all elements in the remuneration package of each individual director, by name.

15.10.2 Company Law Review

Matters of corporate governance featured strongly in the Company Law Review report (*see also* section 7.9.2). An accounting proposal was that a new form of operating and financial review would include a section on corporate governance covering corporate governance values and structures. This would describe the group's systems and structures for controlling and focusing the powers of management and securing an effective working relationship between members, directors and senior management. This type of information is already provided voluntarily in the corporate governance statements of larger listed companies but the Company Law Review proposals would apply to all companies, public and private.

L05a   **Activity 15.9**

> *Obtain the annual report of a listed company. Turn to the report on corporate governance. What does the company say about corporate governance? What do the auditors say about the report on corporate governance? What is disclosed about the remuneration committee? What information is given elsewhere in the annual report, relating to directors' remuneration?*

L05b   ## 15.11 Financial Reporting Review Panel

The role of the Financial Reporting Review Panel (FRRP) as a mechanism for enforcing accounting standards is outlined in Chapter 4. It is useful to look at the record of the FRRP's work as an indication of where the problems have arisen. Sources of information are qualified audit reports or disclosed non-compliance with accounting standards, as well as complaints from individuals or corporate bodies and press comment.

Information on activity of the FRRP (from the annual reports of the Financial Reporting Council)			
	Year to:		
	December 2001	*December 1997*	*December 1996*
Accounts of companies drawn to the attention of the Panel	53	24	49
Cases considered:			
Brought forward from previous period	9	13	15
New cases in current period	53	24	49
	62	37	64
Not pursued beyond initial examination	24	11	24
Action concluded*	27	21	27
Still under consideration at end of period	11	5	13
	62	37	64
*Public statements issued regarding these cases	7	5	8

15.11.1 Press notices

When the FRRP has taken action on a complaint it may decide to issue a Press Notice. (These can be downloaded from the website www.frrp.org.uk.) Seven press notices were issued in 2001 relating to companies. The accounting matters covered: treatment of goodwill (press notice 64), revenue recognition, development expenditure, pension costs, debtors, financial instruments and earnings per share (press notice 65), treatment of volume-related rebates (press notice 67), cost of acquisition of a subsidiary (press notice 68), presentation of the profit and loss account (press notice 69) and tangible fixed assets (press notices 70 and 71). In all cases the press notice names the company and outlines the accounting issue together with the remedy required.

The FRRP has received criticism from some quarters on the relatively few cases that receive publicity in this way. In contrast it has also been criticised for issuing press notices about relatively trivial matters. To respond on the latter concern, the Panel developed in 2001 an 'Improvement Letter' procedure in which the Panel chairman writes to the company pointing out the matter for concern. The letter explains that on this occasion the Panel will be satisfied if the matter is dealt with by correction of comparative figures in the next annual report, and no publicity will be given to the case. This allows the press notices to focus on more significant issues where the true and fair view is called into question.

Press notices are also used for generic issues (where several complaints of a similar kind are received). Press notice 66 dealt with a new standard on financial instruments where it appeared that some companies were not applying the term 'financial instrument' correctly. In the generic cases the companies are not named.

15.11.2 Effectiveness of the process

The FRRP operates on a reactive basis. It responds to complaints and enquiries rather than initiating enquiries (a proactive approach). It reported in 2001 on an enquiry into its own processes. There appeared to be no enthusiasm for following the example of the Securities and Exchange Commission in the USA where the staff are actively involved in setting up proactive investigations. This response may reflect the reality of the more limited resources available to the FRRP; it is likely that there will continue to be suggestions that the FRRP should be at least partly proactive in its work. As part of its self-investigation the FRRP commissioned a study of a sample of annual reports to look for issues that ought to have come to its attention. The study found no evidence that significant concerns were escaping investigation but it did find evidence of non-compliance that had not been reported.

The chairman suggested, in the 2001 report, that the FRRP should not be judged merely by the bare statistics. It should be judged on whether it is effective in reinforcing the commitment to good financial reporting of those involved in preparing financial statements.

15.11.3 Company Law Review

The Company Law Review report (2001) concluded that the most effective way to maintain the proposed new regime would be to build on the strengths of the Financial Reporting Council, the Accounting Standards Board and the Financial Reporting Review Panel. The FRRP's remit might be widened to include non-financial responsibilities in respect of the new OFR.

15.11.4 International perspective

The move towards convergence of accounting standards has also encouraged consideration of enforcement mechanisms. Discussions in the European context point to the FRRP as a possible model that others might adopt to enforce and monitor compliance with the international accounting standards. A committee considering reform in the German legal system has pointed to the FRRP as an example that might be followed.

L05b | **Activity 15.10**

Consider whether you feel greater or lesser reassurance when you know that a regulatory mechanism such as the FRRP exists but you also know that its powers of asking for action by the courts of law have not been exercised. Does this lead you to conclude that the FRRP has done a good job if the power of the law is not needed? Does it lead you to believe that the FRRP has exercised discretion in compromise rather than face a confrontation? What further evidence would you require to form a firm opinion in one direction or the other?

L06 ## 15.12 How valid is the stakeholder model?

In this textbook we take as our starting point the ASB's *Statement of Principles*, and we constantly return to that *Statement* for explanation or discussion of the accounting practices explained in various chapters. The *Statement of Principles* is, in its turn, built on a model which sees the objective of accounting as serving the needs of a wide range of users. Those users are sometimes referred to as *stakeholders* and the *Statement of Principles* is regarded as an example of a *stakeholder model* of the process of regulating accounting.

There are, however, those who would argue that the stakeholder model is the wrong place to start and therefore the significant problems of accounting will not be solved using a statement of principles of this type. At the basic level of understanding existing accounting practice, which is the limit of this textbook, the validity of one model versus another may not be a critical issue, but you should be aware that there are views that more complex accounting problems may not be solved using a stakeholder approach (although the ASB might not subscribe to such views).

Those who argue against the 'user needs' approach suggest that accounting regulation is a much more complex process of social interaction. Standard setters producing accounting rules in a self-regulatory environment need to be sure of a consensus of opinion supporting the proposed rules. They will therefore seek out a range of opinions and will undoubtedly be subjected to lobbying (letters of comment and personal contact) by persons or organisations seeking to put forward a particular viewpoint. Indeed, part of the UK standard-setting process involves issuing an exposure draft for comment before a financial reporting standard is issued, although there is no way of knowing what lobbying occurs behind the scenes.

The process of standard setting may therefore be regarded as one of negotiating and balancing various interests. There has been research after the event, both in the United Kingdom and in other countries, which has shown that the standard-setting bodies were influenced by one or more powerful forces. One particularly clear example may be seen in the development of an accounting standard to tighten up practices in reporting expenditure on research and development.[16] There is a significant amount of academic literature on factors influencing the process of setting accounting standards.

Those who have identified these 'political' pressures would suggest that the accounting standard-setting process should openly admit that there are influential factors such as: the relative balance of power among those who prepare and those who use accounting information; relative dependency of some on others; the balance of individual liberty against collective need; and the ideology observed in particular systems of social relations. (Ideology means that a group in society may hold strong beliefs which make it genuinely unable to appreciate different positions taken by others.)

Thus claims that the standard-setting process is neutral in its impact on the economy or on society may be unrealistic. This textbook does not seek to impose any particular view on its readers. It has used the *Statement of Principles* as a consistent basis for explaining current practice, but it leaves to the reader the task of taking forward the knowledge of external financial reporting and the understanding of what influences the future development of external financial reporting.

15.13 Summary

The issues selected for discussion in this final chapter are all matters on which there is no firm conclusion and on which there will be further developments over a period of years. They pursue a consistent theme of the dynamic nature of accounting practice, with a background of changing economic conditions and changing social values. From this point a study of accounting may, for some, take a route towards establishing a technical expertise in increasingly complex matters. For others it may take a route towards academic literature which variously draws on the theory of economics, finance, and social and political order to understand, explain and predict the development of the subject and the behaviour of those who practise the subject. For yet another group the further study of accounting may be in the nature of maintaining general awareness. Whichever group you find yourself in, you have gained a thorough basic knowledge and should feel confident in reading and understanding the financial statements of companies. From here, a constantly questioning approach and a reluctance to accept without fully understanding will be an invaluable way to take forward this basic knowledge.

Now score your view of your confidence in achieving the learning outcomes of the chapter.

1 = Very confident about knowledge, application, problem solving and evaluation.

2 = Confident about knowledge and application, less sure about problem solving and evaluation.

3 = Need to read again to be more certain of basic knowledge and application.

L01 Explain the processes of international harmonisation and convergence with international standards.

1 ☐ 2 ☐ 3 ☐

L02 Explain the difficulty of defining what is meant by the phrase 'a true and fair view'.

1 ☐ 2 ☐ 3 ☐

L03 Identify and explain some of the issues that are currently of interest in the standard-setting process, namely:

(a) measurement of value;
(b) off-balance-sheet finance;
(c) related parties.

1 ☐ 2 ☐ 3 ☐

L04 Explain how accounting practice is constantly evolving new types of, and approaches to, disclosure, in:

(a) social and environmental disclosures;
(b) the reporting cycle;
(c) summary financial statements.

1 ☐ 2 ☐ 3 ☐

LO5 Understand some of the current developments in influencing and enforcing the regulatory process, particularly:

(a) corporate governance;
(b) the Financial Reporting Review Panel.

1	2	3
☐	☐	☐

LO6 Question the validity of the stakeholder perspective of accounting standard setting.

1	2	3
☐	☐	☐

If your scores are all 1 or 2, try the questions in the series A, B and C. This will give you feedback on your assessment of how well you have achieved the learning outcomes. Read again any sections of the chapter where you find your knowledge and understanding are less comprehensive than you first estimated.

If your scores include some at 3, try the series A questions to find where the problems lie. Read the relevant sections again, work through any illustrative examples and case studies, then try the questions in the series B. Once you feel confident at that level of knowledge and application, move on to try some or all of the series C questions.

Further reading

Cairns, D. and Nobes, C. (2000) *The convergence handbook. A comparison between International Accounting Standards and UK financial reporting requirements.* The Institute of Chartered Accountants in England and Wales.

Davies, M., Paterson, R. and Wilson, A. (2001) *UK and International GAAP: Generally Accepted Accounting Practice in the United Kingdom and under the International Accounting Standards,* 7th edn, Butterworths Tolley.

Gadd, F. K. and Lowen, J. (2001) 'Accounting for Kyoto', *Accountancy*, September, p. 105.

Gray, R., Bebbington, J. and Walters, D. (1993) *Accounting for the Environment*, Paul Chapman Publishing.

Gray, R. and others (1998) *Valuation of Assets and Liabilities: Environmental Law and the Impact of the Environmental Agenda on Business*, The Institute of Chartered Accountants of Scotland.

Parker, R. H. and Nobes, C. W. (1994) *An International View of True and Fair Accounting*, Routledge.

Testimony Concerning Recent Events Relating to Enron Corporation, by Robert K. Herdman, Chief Accountant, US Securities and Exchange Commission, before the Subcommittee on Capital Markets, Insurance and Government Sponsored Enterprises and the Subcommittee on Oversight and Investigation, Committee on Financial Services, US House of Representatives.
www.sec.gov/news/testimony/121201tsrkh.htm

Useful websites

www.iasb.org.uk

www.ifad.net (contains GAAP 2001, a comparison of international accounting standards with national accounting practice).

Test your understanding

> **Skills outcomes**
> **SO1** Application of technical skills   **SO2** Problem solving and evaluation skills   **SO3** Communication skills

L01, S01 **A15.1** Explain the problems of harmonising accounting practice internationally.

L02, S01 **A15.2** Why has it been found impossible to write a definitive guide on the meaning of 'a true and fair view'?

L03a, S01 **A15.3** What are the limitations of historical cost accounting?

L03a, S01 **A15.4** Why is it desirable to remeasure assets and liabilities subsequent to acquisition?

L03a, S01 **A15.5** Explain what is meant by *entry price* and *exit price*.

L03b, S01 **A15.6** Why is off-balance-sheet finance a problem in accounting?

L03c, S01 **A15.7** Why is it important to report information about related party transactions?

L04a, S01 **A15.8** What are the problems of reporting matters of social and environmental concern in the annual report of a company?

L04b, S01 **A15.9** What is the role of the preliminary announcement and the interim report?

L04c, S01 **A15.10** What are the benefits and limitations of summary financial statements?

L05a, S01 **A15.11** What is meant by *corporate governance*?

L05a, S01 **A15.12** How does financial reporting help to improve corporate governance?

L05b, S01 **A15.13** What is the role of the Financial Reporting Review Panel?

L06, S01 **A15.14** Should accounting standards focus primarily on the needs of users?

Activity for study groups

Divide the group into sections to take on four different roles: a private shareholder in a company; a financial journalist; a finance director of a company; and a broker's analyst providing an advisory service to clients.

In each section develop your opinion on the subject: *Taking the user needs perspective will solve all the problems of accounting.*

Arrange a meeting to present all four opinions and then discuss the extent to which the Accounting Standards Board will be able to obtain the co-operation of all parties in solving accounting problems.

Notes and references

1 Hoffman, L. and Arden, M. H. (1983) 'Legal opinion on "true and fair"', *Accountancy*, November, pp. 154–6.
2 ASB (1993) *Foreword to Accounting Standards*, appendix, 'Accounting Standards Board: the true and fair requirement', para. 4. Opinion prepared by Mary Arden, barrister of Erskine Chambers, Lincoln's Inn, London.

3 *Ibid.*, para. 14.
4 ASB (1999) *Statement of Principles for Financial Reporting*, ch. 5, 'Recognition in financial statements', paras 5.22–5.25.
5 *Ibid.*, para. 5.23.
6 ASB (1999) Financial Reporting Standard (FRS 15), *Measurement of Tangible Fixed Assets*, Accounting Standards Board, paras 43–52.
7 *Ibid.*, para. 6.19.
8 ASC (1980) Statement of Standard Accounting Practice (SSAP 16), *Current Cost Accounting*, Accounting Standards Committee (issued March 1980 and withdrawn July 1988).
9 ASB (2000) Financial Reporting Standard (FRS 18), *Accounting Policies*, para. 28, Accounting Standards Board.
10 ASB (1993) *The Role of Valuation in Financial Reporting*, discussion paper, Accounting Standards Board.
11 ASB (1994) Financial Reporting Standard (FRS 5), *Reporting the Substance of Transactions*, Accounting Standards Board.
12 Gray, R., Kouhy, R. and Lavers, S. (1995) 'Corporate social and environmental reporting', *Accounting, Auditing and Accountability Journal*, **8** (2), pp. 44–77.
13 The Committee on the Financial Aspects of Corporate Governance (1992) *The Financial Aspects of Corporate Governance* (The Cadbury Report), December. The Committee chairman was Sir Adrian Cadbury.
14 *The Committee on Corporate Governance Final Report* (1998), Gee Publishing Ltd. (The Committee chairman was Sir Ronnie Hampel.)
15 *Report of a Study Group on Directors' Remuneration* (1995) (The Greenbury Report), Gee Publishing Ltd.
16 Hope, T. and Gray, R. (1982) 'Power and policy making: the development of an R&D standard', *Journal of Business Finance and Accounting*, **9** (4), pp. 531–58.

Glossary of financial accounting terms

The definition of one term may require the use of another term which is defined elsewhere in the glossary. Italics are used to indicate that such a definition is available.

accountancy firm A business partnership (or possibly a limited company) in which the partners are qualified accountants. The firm undertakes work for clients in respect of audit, accounts preparation, tax and similar activities.

accountancy profession The collective body of persons qualified in accounting, and working in accounting-related areas. Usually they are members of a professional body, membership of which is attained by passing examinations.

accounting policies Accounting methods which have been judged by business enterprises to be most appropriate to their circumstances and adopted by them for the purpose of preparing their financial statements.

accounting standards Definitive statements of best practice issued by a body having suitable authority.

Accounting Standards Board The authority in the United Kingdom which issues definitive statements of best accounting practice.

accruals concept The accruals (or matching) concept states that revenues and expenses are recognised as they are earned or incurred and not as money is received or paid.

acquisition An acquisition takes place where one company acquires control of another, usually through purchase of shares.

agency A relationship between a principal and an agent. In the case of a limited liability company, the shareholder is the principal and the director is the agent.

agency theory A theoretical model, developed by academics, to explain how the relationship between a principal and an agent may have economic consequences.

amortisation Process similar to *depreciation*, usually applied to intangible fixed assets.

annual report A document produced each year by limited liability companies containing the acccounting information required by law. Larger companies also provide information and pictures of the activities of the company.

articles of association Document setting out the relative rights of shareholders in a limited liability company.

articulation The term 'articulation' is used to refer to the impact of transactions on the balance sheet and profit and loss account through application of the accounting equation.

assets Rights or other access to future economic benefits controlled by an entity as a result of past transactions or events.

associated company One company exercises significant influence over another, falling short of complete control.

audit An audit is the independent examination of, and expression of opinion on, financial statements of an entity.

audit manager An employee of an accountancy firm, usually holding an accountancy qualification, given a significant level of responsibility in carrying out an audit assignment and responsible to the partner in charge of the audit.

balance sheet A statement of the financial position of an entity showing assets, liabilities and ownership claim.

bond The name sometimes given to loan finance (more commonly in the United States).

broker (stockbroker) Member of a stock exchange who arranges purchase and sale of shares and may also provide an information service giving buy/sell/hold recommendations.

broker's report Bulletin written by a stockbroking firm for circulation to its clients, providing analysis and guidance on companies as potential investments.

business cycle Period (usually twelve months) during which the peaks and troughs of activity of a business form a pattern which is repeated on a regular basis.

business entity A business which exists independently of its owners.

capital Amount of finance provided to enable a business to acquire assets and sustain its operations.

cash flow projections Statements of cash expected to flow into the business and cash expected to flow out over a particular period.

chairman The person who chairs the meetings of the board of *directors* of a company (preferably not the chief executive).

chief executive The *director* in charge of the day-to-day running of a company.

close season Period during which those who are 'insiders' to a listed company should not buy or sell shares.

Companies Act The Companies Act 1985 as modified by the Companies Act 1989. Legislation to control the activities of limited liability companies.

conceptual framework A statement of principles providing generally accepted guidance for the development of new reporting practices and for challenging and evaluating the existing practices.

consolidation Consolidation is a process that aggregates the total assets, liabilities and results of the parent and its subsidiaries (the group) so that the consolidated financial statements present financial information about the group as a single reporting entity.

corporate governance The system by which companies are directed and controlled. Boards of directors are responsible for the governance of their companies.

corporate recovery department Part of an accountancy firm which specialises in assisting companies to recover from financial problems.

current asset An asset that is expected to be converted into cash within the trading cycle.

cut-off procedures Procedures applied to the accounting records at the end of an accounting period to ensure that all transactions for the period are recorded and any transactions not relevant to the period are excluded.

debenture A written acknowledgement of a debt – a name used for loan financing taken up by a company.

default Failure to meet obligations as they fall due for payment.

deferred asset An asset whose benefit is delayed beyond the period expected for a current asset, but which does not meet the definition of a fixed asset.

depreciation The measure of the cost or revalued amount of economic benefits of the tangible fixed asset that have been consumed during the period. Consumption includes the wearing out, using up or other reduction in the useful life of a tangible fixed asset, whether arising from use, effluxion of time or obsolescence through either changes in technology or demand for the goods and services produced by the asset.

Directive A document issued by the European Union requiring all Member States to adapt their national law to be consistent with the Directive.

director(s) Person(s) appointed by shareholders of a limited liability company to manage the affairs of the company.

disclosed An item which is reported in the notes to the accounts is said to be disclosed but not *recognised*.

dividend Amount paid to a shareholder, usually in the form of cash, as a reward for investment in the company. The amount of dividend paid is proportionate to the number of shares held.

earnings for ordinary shareholders Profit after deducting interest charges and taxation and after deducting preference dividends (but before deducting extraordinary items).

earnings per share *Earnings for ordinary shareholders* divided by the number of shares which have been issued by the company.

entity Something that exists independently, such as a business which exists independently of the owner.

equities analyst A person who investigates and writes reports on ordinary share investments in companies (usually for the benefit of investors in shares).

equity shares Shares in a company which participate in sharing dividends and in sharing any surplus on winding up, after all liabilities have been met.

eurobond market A market in which bonds are issued in the capital market of one country to a non-resident borrower from another country.

expense An expense is caused by a transaction or event arising during the ordinary activities of the business which causes a decrease in the ownership interest.

external reporting Reporting financial information to those users with a valid claim to receive it, but who are not allowed access to the day-to-day records of the business.

external users (of financial statements) Users of financial statements who have a valid interest but are not permitted access to the day-to-day records of the company.

fair value The amount at which an asset or liability could be exchanged in an arm's-length transaction between a willing buyer and a willing seller.

financial accounting A term usually applied to *external reporting* by a business where that reporting is presented in financial terms.

financial adaptability The ability of the company to respond to unexpected needs or opportunities.

financial information Information which may be reported in money terms.

Financial Reporting Standard Title of an accounting standard issued by the UK *Accounting Standards Board* as a definitive statement of best practice (issued from 1990 onwards – predecessor documents are Statements of Standard Accounting Practice, many of which remain valid).

financial risk Exists where a company has loan finance, especially *long-term loan finance* where the company cannot relinquish its commitment. The risk relates to being unable to meet payments of interest or repayment of capital as they fall due.

financial statements Documents containing accounting information which is expected to have a useful purpose.

financial viability The ability to survive on an ongoing basis.

fixed asset An asset that is held by an enterprise for use in the production or supply of goods or services, for rental to others, or for administrative purposes on a continuing basis in the reporting entity's activities.

fixed capital Finance provided to support the acquisition of *fixed assets*.

fixed cost One which is not affected by changes in the level of output over a defined period of time.

floating charge Security taken by lender which floats over all the assets and crystallises over particular assets if the security is required.

format A list of items which may appear in a *financial statement*, setting out the order in which they are to appear.

forward exchange contract An agreement to buy foreign currency at a fixed future date and at an agreed price.

fund manager A person who manages a collection (portfolio) of investments, usually for an insurance company, a pension fund business or a professional fund management business which invests money on behalf of clients.

gearing (financial) The ratio of debt capital to ownership claim.

general purpose financial statements Documents containing accounting information which would be expected to be of interest to a wide range of user groups. For a limited liability company there would be: a balance sheet, a profit and loss account, a statement of recognised gains and losses and a cash flow statement.

going concern basis The assumption that the business will continue operating into the foreseeable future.

goodwill Goodwill on acquisition is the difference between the price paid for an investment in a *subsidiary* and the *fair value* of the net assets acquired.

gross Before making deductions.

gross margin Sales minus cost of sales before deducting administration and selling expenses (another name for *gross profit*). Usually applied when discussing a particular line of activity.

gross profit Sales minus cost of sales before deducting administration and selling expenses (see also *gross margin*).

Inland Revenue The UK government's tax-gathering organisation.

insider information Information gained by someone inside, or close to, a listed company which could confer a financial advantage if used to buy or sell shares. It is illegal for a person who is in possession of inside information to buy or sell shares on the basis of that information.

institutional investor An organisation whose business includes regular investment in shares of companies, examples being an insurance company, a pension fund, a charity, an investment trust, a unit trust, a merchant bank.

interest (on loans) The percentage return on *capital* required by the lender (usually expressed as a percentage per annum).

internal reporting Reporting financial information to those users inside a business, at various levels of management, at a level of detail appropriate to the recipient.

investors Persons or organisations which have provided money to a business in exchange for a share of ownership.

joint and several liability (in a partnership) The partnership liabilities are shared jointly but each person is responsible for the whole of the debts of the partnership in the event that any other partner is unable to contribute.

liabilities Obligations of an entity to transfer economic benefits as a result of past transactions or events.

limited liability A phrase used to indicate that those having liability in respect of some amount due may be able to invoke some agreed limit on that liability.

limited liability company Company where the liability of the owners is limited to the amount of *capital* they have agreed to contribute.

liquidity The extent to which a business has access to cash or items which can readily be exchanged for cash.

listed company A company whose shares are listed by the Stock Exchange as being available for buying and selling under the rules and safeguards of the Exchange.

listing requirements Rules imposed by the Stock Exchange on companies whose shares are listed for buying and selling.

loan covenants Agreement made by the company with a lender of *long-term finance*, protecting the loan by imposing conditions on the company, usually to restrict further borrowing.

loan creditors Persons who have lent money to a business.

long-term finance Money lent to a business for a fixed period, giving that business a commitment to pay interest for the period specified and to repay the loan at the end of the period.

management Collective term for those persons responsible for the day-to-day running of a business.

management accounting Reporting accounting information within a business, for *management* use only.

market value (of a share) The price for which a share could be transferred between a willing buyer and a willing seller.

matching concept The matching (or accruals) concept states that revenues and expenses are recognised as they are earned or incurred and not as money is received or paid. Expenses are matched against revenues in the period they are incurred.

maturity profile of debt The timing of loan repayments by a company in the future.

memorandum (for a company) Document setting out main objects of the company and its powers to act.

merger Two organisations agree to work together in a situation where neither can be regarded as having acquired the other.

minority interest The *ownership interest* in a company held by persons other than the *parent company* and its *subsidiary* undertakings.

net After making deductions.

net assets *Assets* minus *liabilities* (equals *ownership interest*).

net realisable value The proceeds of selling an item, less the costs of selling.

nominal value (of a share) The amount stated on the face of a share certificate as the named value of the share when issued.

operating and financial review Section of the annual report of many companies which explains the main features of the financial statements.

operating risk Exists where there are factors which would cause profits to fluctuate through changes in operating conditions.

ordinary shares Shares in a company which entitle the holder to a share of the dividend declared and a share in net assets on closing down the business.

ownership interest The residual amount found by deducting all of the entity's liabilities from all of the entity's assets.

parent company Company which controls one or more subsidiaries in a group.

partnership Two or more persons in business together with the aim of making a profit.

partnership deed A document setting out the agreement of the partners on how the partnership is to be conducted (including the arrangements for sharing profits and losses).

partnership law Legislation which governs the conduct of a partnership and which should be used where no partnership deed has been written.

portfolio (of investment) A collection of investments.

portfolio of shares A collection of shares held by an investor.

preference shares Shares in a company which give the holder a preference (although not an automatic right) to receive a dividend before any ordinary share dividend is declared.

preliminary announcement The first announcement by a listed company of its profit for the most recent accounting period. Precedes the publication of the full annual report. The announcement is made to the entire stock market so that all investors receive information at the same time.

premium An amount paid in addition, or extra.

price-sensitive information Information which, if known to the market, would affect the price of a share.

primary financial statements The balance sheet, profit and loss account, statement of total recognised gains and losses and cash flow statement.

principal (sum) The agreed amount of a loan, on which interest will be charged during the period of the loan.

private limited company (Ltd) A company which has *limited liability* but is not permitted to offer its shares to the public.

public limited company (plc) A company which has *limited liability* and offers its shares to the public.

qualified audit opinion An audit opinion to the effect that: the accounts do *not* show a true and fair view; or the accounts show a true and fair view *except for* particular matters.

realised profit A profit arising from revenue which has been earned by the entity and for which there is a reasonable prospect of cash being collected in the near future.

recognised An item is recognised when it is included by means of words and amount within the main financial statements of an entity.

Registrar of Companies An official authorised by the government to maintain a record of all annual reports and other documents issued by a company.

reserves The claim which owners have on the *assets* of a company because the company has created new wealth for them over the period since it began.

return (in relation to investment) The reward earned for investing money in a business. Return may appear in the form of regular cash payments (dividends) to the investor, or in a growth in the value of the amount invested.

revaluation reserve The claim which owners have on the *assets* of the business because the market value of an asset is greater than its historical cost.

revenue Revenue is created by a transaction or event arising during the ordinary activities of the business which causes an increase in the ownership interest.

risk (in relation to investment) Factors that may cause the profit or cash flows of the business to fluctuate.

secured loan Loan where the lender has taken a special claim on particular assets or revenues of the company.

share capital Name given to the total amount of cash which the shareholders have contributed to the company.

share premium The claim which owners have on the assets of a company because shares have been purchased from the company at a price greater than the *nominal value*.

shareholders Owners of a *limited liability company*.

shareholders' funds Name given to total of *share capital* and *reserves* in a company balance sheet.

shares The amount of share capital held by any shareholder is measured in terms of a number of shares in the total capital of the company.

short-term finance Money lent to a business for a short period of time, usually repayable on demand and also repayable at the choice of the business if surplus to requirements.

sole trader An individual owning and operating a business alone.

specific purpose financial statements Documents containing accounting information which is prepared for a particular purpose and is not normally available to a wider audience.

stakeholders A general term devised to indicate all those who might have a legitimate interest in receiving financial information about a business because they have a 'stake' in it.

Statement of Principles A document issued by the *Accounting Standards Board* in the United Kingdom setting out key principles to be applied in the process of setting accounting standards.

stewardship Taking care of resources owned by another person and using those resources to the benefit of that person.

stock exchange An organisation which has the authority to set rules for persons buying and selling shares. The term 'stock' is used loosely with a meaning similar to that of 'shares'.

subsidiary company Company in a group which is controlled by another (the parent company). (*See* Chapter 7 for full definition.) Sometimes called *subsidiary undertaking*.

tangible fixed assets A *fixed asset* which has a physical existence.

trade creditors Persons who supply goods or services to a business in the normal course of trade and allow a period of credit before payment must be made.

turnover The sales of a business or other form of revenue from operations of the business.

unsecured creditors Those who have no claim against particular assets when a company is wound up, but must take their turn for any share of what remains.

unsecured loan Loan in respect of which the lender has taken no special claim against any assets.

variance The difference between a planned, budgeted or standard cost and the actual cost incurred. An *adverse variance* arises when the actual cost is greater than the standard cost. A *favourable variance* arises when the actual cost is less than the standard cost.

working capital Finance provided to support the short-term assets of the business (stocks and debtors) to the extent that these are not financed by short-term creditors. It is calculated as current assets minus current liabilities.

Appendix I

Information extracted from annual report of Safe and Sure plc, used throughout Financial Accounting

Safe and Sure plc
Consolidated balance sheet at 31 December

		Notes	Year 7 £m	Year 6 £m
Fixed assets	Intangible assets	1	260.3	237.6
	Tangible assets	2	137.5	121.9
	Investments	3	2.8	2.0
			400.6	361.5
Current assets	Stocks	4	26.6	24.3
	Debtors	5	146.9	134.7
	Short-term deposits and cash		107.3	90.5
			280.8	249.5
Current liabilities due within one year	Creditors	6	(189.3)	(170.2)
	Bank and other borrowings	7	(40.1)	(74.3)
			(229.4)	(244.5)
	Net current assets		51.4	5.0
Deferred assets	Taxation recoverable	8	5.9	4.9
	Total assets *less* current liabilities		457.9	371.4
Liabilities due after one year	Creditors	9	(2.7)	(2.6)
	Bank and other borrowings	10	(0.2)	(0.6)
	Provisions for liabilities and charges	11	(20.2)	(22.2)
	Net assets		434.8	346.0
Capital and reserves	Called-up share capital	12	19.6	19.5
	Share premium account	13	8.5	5.5
	Revaluation reserve	14	4.6	4.6
	Other reserves	15	9.1	7.2
	Profit and loss account	16	393.0	309.2
	Shareholders' funds		434.8	346.0

Safe and Sure plc
Consolidated profit and loss account for the years ended 31 December

	Notes	Year 7 £m	Year 6 £m
Turnover			
Continuing operations		701.1	589.3
Acquisitions		13.5	
		714.6	
Discontinued operations		20.0	11.0
Turnover	17	734.6	600.3
Cost of sales	18	(531.5)	(427.3)
Gross profit		203.1	173.0
Distribution expenses		(2.2)	(2.5)
Administrative expenses	19	(26.2)	(26.5)
Operating profit			
Continuing operations		192.5	154.0
Acquisitions		2.7	
		195.2	
Discontinued operations		(20.5)	(10.0)
Profit on ordinary activities before interest		174.7	144.0
Interest receivable (net)	20	2.3	3.0
Profit on ordinary activities before tax	21	177.0	147.0
Tax on profit on ordinary activities	22	(62.2)	(52.4)
Profit attributable to ordinary shareholders		114.8	94.6
Dividends		(33.7)	(27.8)
Retained profit for the year		81.1	66.8
Earnings per share	23	11.74	9.71

Safe and Sure plc
Statement of total recognised gains and losses

	Year 7 £m	Year 6 £m
Profit attributable to shareholders	114.8	94.6
Exchange rate adjustments	4.6	(6.0)
Total recognised gains for the year	119.4	88.6

Safe and Sure plc
Reconciliation of movements in shareholders' funds

	Year 7 £m	Year 6 £m
Profit attributable to shareholders	114.8	94.6
Dividends	(33.7)	(27.8)
New share capital issued	3.1	2.0
Exchange adjustments	4.6	(6.0)
Net change in shareholders' funds	88.8	62.8
Opening shareholders' funds	346.0	283.2
Closing shareholders' funds	434.8	346.0

Safe and Sure plc
Consolidated cash flow statement for the years ended 31 December

		Notes	Year 7 £m	Year 6 £m
Operating activities	Net cash flow from operating activities	24	196.7	163.5
Returns on investments and servicing of finance	Interest received		5.0	5.9
	Interest paid		(3.1)	(2.4)
	Net cash inflow from returns on investments and servicing of finance		1.9	3.5
Taxation	UK corporation tax paid		(20.1)	(18.3)
	Overseas tax paid		(30.5)	(26.5)
	Total tax paid		(50.6)	(44.8)
Capital expenditure and financial investments	Purchase of tangible fixed assets		(60.0)	(47.5)
	Sale of tangible fixed assets		12.0	10.1
	Net capital expenditure		(48.0)	(37.4)
Acquisitions and disposals	Purchase of companies and businesses	25	(27.7)	(90.1)
	Sale of a company		3.1	–
	Net payment for acquisitions		(24.6)	(90.1)
Equity dividends paid	Dividends paid to shareholders		(29.5)	(24.4)
Management of liquid resources	Net movement of short-term deposits		(30.7)	36.3
	Net loan movement (excluding overdraft)	26	16.2	(24.0)
	Net cash movement on liquid resources		(14.5)	12.3
Financing activities	Issue of ordinary share capital	27	3.1	2.0
Cash movement	Increase/decrease in cash and deposits repayable on demand, net of bank overdrafts	28	34.5	(15.4)

Accounting policies (extracts)

Intangible fixed assets

Purchased goodwill is calculated as the difference between the fair value of the consideration paid for an acquired entity and the aggregate of the fair values of that entity's identifiable assets and liabilities. The useful economic life of purchased goodwill is considered to be significantly in excess of 20 years and accordingly an impairment review has been undertaken at the balance sheet date.

Freehold and leasehold property

Freehold and leasehold land and buildings are stated either at cost or at their revalued amounts less depreciation. Full revaluations are made at five-year intervals with interim valuations in the intervening years, the most recent being in Year 0.

Provision for depreciation of freehold land and buildings is made at the annual rate of 1 per cent of cost or the revalued amounts. Leasehold land and buildings are amortised in equal annual instalments over the periods of the leases subject to a minimum annual provision of 1 per cent of cost or the revalued amounts. When properties are sold the difference between sales proceeds and net book value is dealt with in the profit and loss account.

Other tangible fixed assets

Other tangible fixed assets are stated at cost less depreciation. Provision for depreciation is made mainly in equal annual instalments over the estimated useful lives of the assets as follows:

4 to 5 years   vehicles
5 to 10 years   plant, machinery and equipment

Stocks and work-in-progress

Stocks and work-in-progress are stated at the lower of cost and net realisable value, using the first-in-first-out principle. Cost includes all direct expenditure and related overheads incurred to the date of the balance sheet.

Deferred tax

The provision for deferred tax recognises a future liability arising from past transactions and events. Tax legislation allows the company to defer settlement of the liability for several years.

Warranties

Some service work is carried out under warranty. The cost of claims under warranty is charged against the profit and loss account of the year in which the claims are settled.

Deferred consideration

For acquisitions involving deferred consideration, estimated deferred payments are accrued in the balance sheet. Interest due to vendors on deferred payments is charged to the profit and loss account as it accrues.

Notes to accounts

Note 1 Intangible fixed assets

	Year 7 £m	Year 6 £m
Goodwill at 1 January	237.6	139.1
Additions in year	24.3	98.5
Reductions in year	(1.6)	–
Goodwill at 31 December	260.3	237.6

The reduction of £1.6m results from the annual impairment review.

Note 2 Tangible fixed assets

	Land and buildings £m	Plant and equipment £m	Vehicles £m	Total £m
Cost or valuation				
At 1 January Year 7	28.3	96.4	104.8	229.5
Additions at cost	3.9	18.5	37.8	60.2
On acquisitions	0.3	1.0	0.7	2.0
Disposals	(0.6)	(3.1)	(24.7)	(28.4)
At 31 December Year 7	31.9	112.8	118.6	263.3
Aggregate depreciation				
At 1 January Year 7	2.2	58.8	46.6	107.6
Depreciation for the year	0.5	13.5	19.2	33.2
On acquisitions	0.1	0.7	0.6	1.4
Disposals	(0.2)	(2.8)	(13.4)	(16.4)
At 31 December Year 7	2.6	70.2	53.0	125.8
Net book value at 31 December Year 7	29.3	42.6	65.6	137.5
Net book value at 31 December Year 6	26.1	37.6	58.2	121.9

Analysis of land and buildings at cost or valuation

	Year 7 £m	Year 6 £m
At cost	10.4	7.1
At valuation	21.5	21.2
	31.9	28.3

The majority of the group's freehold and long-term leasehold properties were revalued during Year 5 by independent valuers. Valuations were made on the basis of the market value for existing use. The book values of the properties were adjusted to the revaluations and the resultant net surplus was credited to the revaluation reserve.

Analysis of net book value of land and buildings

	Year 7 £m	Year 6 £m
Freehold	24.5	21.0
Leasehold:		
Over 50 years unexpired	2.1	2.4
Under 50 years unexpired	2.7	2.7
	29.3	26.1

If the revalued assets were stated on the historical cost basis the amounts would be:

	Year 7 £m	Year 6 £m
Land and buildings at cost	15.7	14.5
Aggregate depreciation	(2.2)	(1.9)
	13.5	12.6

Note 3

Relates to investments in subsidiary companies and is not reproduced here.

Note 4 Stocks

	Year 7 £m	Year 6 £m
Raw materials	6.2	5.4
Work-in-progress	1.9	1.0
Finished products	18.5	17.9
	26.6	24.3

Note 5 Debtors

	Year 7 £m	Year 6 £m
Trade debtors	128.1	117.0
Other debtors	10.9	9.8
Prepayments and accrued income	7.9	7.9
	146.9	134.7

Note 6 Creditors due within one year

	Year 7 £m	Year 6 £m
Deferred consideration on acquisition	1.1	4.3
Trade creditors	23.6	20.4
Dividends payable	23.8	19.6
Corporation tax	31.5	26.5
Other tax and social security payable	24.5	21.2
Other creditors	30.7	23.8
Accruals and deferred income	54.1	54.4
	189.3	170.2

Note 7 Bank and other borrowings due within one year

	Year 7 £m	Year 6 £m
Bank loans and overdrafts due within one year or on demand:		
Secured	0.4	0.4
Unsecured	39.7	73.9
	40.1	74.3

Interest on bank loans and overdrafts, and on other loans due within one year, which are denominated in a number of currencies, is payable at normal commercial rates appropriate to the country where the borrowing is made. Bank loans amounting to £0.4m (Year 6: £0.4m) are secured on certain assets of the group.

Note 8

Explains the nature of taxation recoverable and is not reproduced here.

Note 9 Creditors due after more than one year

	Year 7 £m	Year 6 £m
Deferred consideration on acquisition	0.6	–
Other creditors	2.1	2.6
	2.7	2.6

Note 10 Bank and other borrowings due after more than one year

	Year 7 £m	Year 6 £m
Secured loans	–	0.3
Unsecured loans	0.2	0.3
	0.2	0.6
Loans are repayable by instalments:		
Between one and two years	0.1	0.2
Between two and five years	0.1	0.4
	0.2	0.6

Interest on long-term loans, which are denominated in a number of currencies, is payable at normal commercial rates appropriate to the country in which the borrowing is made. The last repayment falls due in Year 11.

Note 11 Provisions

	Year 7 £m	Year 6 £m
Provisions for treating contaminated site:		
At 1 January	14.2	14.5
Utilised in the year	(2.2)	(0.3)
At 31 December	12.0	14.2
Provisions for restructuring costs:		
At 1 January	4.2	–
Created in year	1.0	4.3
Utilised in year	(1.0)	(0.1)
At 31 December	4.2	4.2
Provision for deferred tax:		
At 1 January	3.8	2.7
Transfer to profit and loss account	0.5	1.2
Other movements	(0.3)	(0.1)
At 31 December	4.0	3.8
Total provision	20.2	22.2

Note 12 Share capital

	Year 7 £m	Year 6 £m
Ordinary shares of 2 pence each		
Authorised: 1,050,000,000 shares		
(Year 6: 1,000,000,000)	21.0	20.0
Issued and fully paid: 978,147,487 shares	19.6	19.5

Certain senior executives hold options to subscribe for shares in the company at prices ranging from 33.40p to 244.33p under schemes approved by shareholders at various dates. Options on 3,479,507 shares were exercised during Year 7 and 66,970 options lapsed. The number of shares subject to options, the years in which they were purchased and the years in which they will expire are:

Purchase	Expiry	Numbers
	Year 8	13,750
All	Year 9	110,000
purchased	Year 10	542,500
10 years	Year 11	1,429,000
before	Year 12	2,826,600
expiry	Year 13/14	3,539,942
	Year 15	3,690,950
	Year 16	2,279,270
	Year 17	3,279,363
		17,711,375

Note 13 Share premium account

	Year 7 £m	Year 6 £m
At 1 January	5.5	3.6
Premium on shares issued during the year under the share option schemes	3.0	1.9
At 31 December	8.5	5.5

Note 14 Revaluation reserve

	Year 7 £m	Year 6 £m
At 1 January	4.6	4.7
Exchange adjustments	0.1	(0.1)
Transfer to profit and loss account	(0.1)	—
At 31 December	4.6	4.6

Note 15 Other reserves

	Year 7 £m	Year 6 £m
At 1 January	7.2	6.0
Exchange adjustments	0.4	(0.3)
Transfer from profit and loss account	1.5	1.5
At 31 December	9.1	7.2

Note 16 Profit and loss account

	Year 7 £m	Year 6 £m
At 1 January	309.2	249.5
Exchange adjustments	4.1	(5.6)
Profit for the year retained	81.1	66.8
Transfer to other reserves	(1.5)	(1.5)
Transfer from revaluation reserves	0.1	—
At 31 December	393.0	309.2

Note 17 Segmental analysis

	Turnover Year 7 £m	Turnover Year 6 £m	Profit Year 7 £m	Profit Year 6 £m	Net assets Year 7 £m	Net assets Year 6 £m
Geographical analysis						
United Kingdom	323.4	246.7	76.9	59.7	30.9	48.2
Continental Europe	164.3	153.5	45.3	40.3	43.7	19.4
North America	124.5	91.1	17.0	13.9	2.5	(3.3)
Asia Pacific & Africa	122.4	109.0	35.5	30.1	31.5	29.5
	734.6	600.3	174.7	144.0	108.6	93.8
Interest receivable (net)			2.3	3.0		
Net cash					67.0	15.6
Total	734.6	600.3	177.0	147.0	175.6	109.4

	Disposal and recycling		Security and cleaning		Total	
	Year 7	Year 6	Year 7	Year 6	Year 7	Year 6
	£m	£m	£m	£m	£m	£m
Business sector analysis						
Turnover:						
United Kingdom	186.2	150.8	137.2	95.9	323.4	246.7
Continental Europe	161.2	150.0	3.1	3.5	164.3	153.5
North America	65.3	61.1	59.2	30.0	124.5	91.1
Asia Pacific & Africa	116.2	104.1	6.2	4.9	122.4	109.0
Turnover by service	528.9	466.0	205.7	134.3	734.6	600.3
Operating profit by service	156.1	129.6	18.6	14.4	174.7	144.0
Net operating assets by service	98.9	72.8	9.7	21.0	108.6	93.8

The above analysis of turnover is based on the country in which the order is received. It would not be materially different if based on the country in which the customer is located.

Disposal and recycling includes all aspects of collection and safe disposal of industrial and commercial waste products.

Security and cleaning is undertaken by renewable annual contract, predominantly for hospitals, other healthcare premises and local government organisations.

Notes 18–23

Contain supporting details for the profit and loss account and are not reproduced here.

Note 24 Cash flow from operating activities

Reconciliation of operating profit to net cash flow from operating activities

	Year 7	Year 6
	£m	£m
Operating profit	174.7	144.0
Depreciation charge	33.2	30.1
Increase in stocks*	(1.9)	(1.1)
Increase in debtors*	(7.4)	(5.3)
Decrease in creditors*	(0.4)	(3.6)
Net cash inflow from continuing activities	198.2	164.1
Cash outflow in respect of discontinued item	(1.5)	(0.6)
Net cash inflow from operating activities	196.7	163.5

*Note: It is not possible to reconcile these figures with the balance sheet information because of the effect of acquisitions during the year.

Note 25 Information on acquisitions (extract)

	£m
Net assets of subsidiaries acquired, as shown in their balance sheets	4.1
Adjustments made by directors of Safe and Sure plc	(3.4)
Fair value of net assets acquired (a)	0.7
Cash paid for subsidiaries (b)	25.0
Goodwill (b − a)	24.3

Notes 26–28

Contain supporting detail for the cash flow statement and are not reproduced here.

Note 29 Cash flow and net liquid funds

Reconciliation of cash flow for the year to the balance sheet items

	Year 7 £m	Year 6 £m
Balance sheet items		
Short-term deposits and cash	107.3	90.5
Short-term borrowings	(40.1)	(74.3)
Long-term borrowings	(0.2)	(0.6)
Net liquid funds	67.0	15.6
Cash flow per cash flow statement	34.5	
Exchange adjustments	2.4	
Increase in other liquid resources	14.5	
	51.4	
Add net liquid funds at start of period	15.6	
Net liquid funds at end of period	67.0	

Notes 30–32

Contain various other items of information required by company law and are not reproduced here.

Note 33 Contingent liabilities

The company has guaranteed bank and other borrowings of subsidiaries amounting to £3.0m (Year 6: £15.2m). The group has commitments, amounting to approximately £41.9m (Year 6: £28.5m), under forward exchange contracts entered into in the ordinary course of business.

Certain subsidiaries have given warranties for service work. These are explained in the statement on accounting policies. There are contingent liabilities in respect of litigation. None of the actions is expected to give rise to any material loss.

Note 34

Contains commitments for capital expenditure and is not reproduced here.

Five-year summary

	Year 3	Year 4	Year 5	Year 6	Year 7
	£m	£m	£m	£m	£m
Group turnover	309.1	389.0	474.1	600.3	734.6
Group profit before tax	74.4	90.4	114.5	147.0	177.0
Tax	(27.2)	(33.9)	(44.3)	(52.4)	(62.2)
Group profit after tax	47.2	56.5	70.2	94.6	114.8
Dividends	(12.7)	(16.4)	(22.4)	(27.8)	(33.7)
Retained profit in the group	34.5	40.1	47.8	66.8	81.1
Earnings per share	4.88p	6.23p	8.02p	9.71p	11.74p
Dividends per share	1.32p	1.69p	2.31p	2.85p	3.45p
	£m	£m	£m	£m	£m
Share capital	19.4	19.4	19.4	19.5	19.6
Reserves	160.8	195.3	265.4	326.5	415.2
Capital employed	180.2	214.7	284.8	346.0	434.8

Operating and Financial Review (extract)

CHIEF EXECUTIVE'S REVIEW OF OPERATIONS
Group results

Group turnover in Year 7 increased by 22.4 per cent to £734.6m, while profits before tax increased by 20.4 per cent to £177.0m. Earnings per share increased by 20.9 per cent to 11.74 pence. These results show the benefits of our geographic diversification across the major economies of the world. We have achieved excellent growth in the UK, together with continued good growth in North America. Growth in Europe continued to be constrained by depressed economies, while excellent results in Australia were held back by disappointing growth in South East Asia. Segmental results are set out in detail in Note 17 to the financial statements.

Turnover in Disposal and Recycling improved turnover by 13.4 per cent and profits improved by 20.4 per cent. Turnover in Security and Cleaning improved by 53.2 per cent and profits improved by 29.2 per cent.

Organisation

We continue to be organised into four geographic regions, each headed by a regional managing director. Group services are provided for finance, legal, research and development, corporate affairs, business development and management development.

Strategy

Our ultimate objective is to achieve for our shareholders a high rate of growth in earnings and dividends per share each year. Our strategies are to provide customers with the highest standards of service and to maintain quality of service as we enter new fields. We also operate a prudent financial policy of managing our businesses to generate a strong operating cash flow.

Disposal and recycling

Disposal and recycling includes all aspects of collection and safe disposal of industrial and commercial waste products. During Year 7 all our operational landfill sites gained certification to the international environment management standard. Organic waste deposited in landfill sites degrades naturally and gives off a gas rich in methane which has to be controlled for environmental reasons. However, landfill sites can also be a cheap, clean and highly efficient source of renewable energy. Through strategic long-term contracts we are generating 64MW of electricity each year from landfill waste to energy schemes. New waste transfer and recycling centres in Germany and France were added to the Group's network during Year 7.

Security and cleaning

Security and cleaning is undertaken by renewable annual contract, predominantly for hospitals, other healthcare premises and local government organisations. During Year 7 we acquired a security company in the UK and some smaller operations in Switzerland and Spain. Improved margins in contract cleaning reflected continued demands for improved hygiene standards and our introduction of new techniques to meet this need.

FINANCE DIRECTOR'S REVIEW

Profits

Operating profits rose to £174.7m in Year 7, up from £144.0m in Year 6. Interest income fell £0.7m to £2.3m in Year 7, as a result of the cash spent on acquisitions towards the end of Year 6. At constant average Year 6 exchange rates, the Year 7 profit before tax would have been £0.6m higher at £177.6m, an increase of 20.8 per cent over the reported Year 6 figures.

Cash flow

The Group's businesses are structured to utilise as little fixed and working capital as is consistent with the profit and earnings growth objective in order to produce a high cash flow. Working capital was held to an increase in Year 7 of £9.7m (Year 6: £10.0m).

A net cash flow of £196.7m was generated from operating activities. That was boosted by other amounts of cash from interest received. After paying interest and tax, the Group had £148.0m remaining. Fixed assets required £48.0m (after allowing for the proceeds of selling some of our vehicle fleet in the routine replacement programme. That left £100m from which £24.6m was required to pay for acquisitions. The remaining £75.4m covered dividends of £29.5m leaving £45.9m. We raised £3.1m in ordinary share capital to give a net inflow of liquid funds in the year of £49.0m. Out of that amount, short-term deposits have increased by £14.5m, leaving an increase in cash of £34.5m.

Foreign currency

The year-end net cash is stated after deducting £35.2m of foreign currency bank borrowings incurred to fund overseas acquisitions. The main borrowings were £26.8m in US dollars and £8.4m in yen (to fund our Japanese associate investment). The borrowings are mainly from banks on a short-term basis with a maturity of up to one year. We have fixed the interest rate on $20m of the US dollar loans through to November Year 8 at an overall cost of 4.5 per cent.

All material foreign currency transactions are matched back into the currency of the Group company undertaking the transaction. It is not the Group's current practice to hedge the translation of overseas profits or assets back into sterling, although overseas acquisitions may be financed by foreign currency borrowings.

Capital expenditure

The major items of capital expenditure are vehicles, equipment used on customers' premises and office equipment, particularly computers. Disposals during the year were mainly of vehicles being replaced on a rolling programme.

Taxation

The overall Group taxation charge comprises tax at 30 per cent on UK profits and an average rate of 38 per cent on overseas profits, reflecting the underlying rates in the various countries in which the Group operates.

Prospects

Once again, in Year 7 Safe and Sure met its declared objective of increasing its pre-tax profits and earnings per share by at least 20 per cent per annum. The board expects a return to much better growth in Europe and a substantially improved performance in the USA to underpin good Group growth for the year.

Appendix II

Solutions to numerical and technical questions in Financial Accounting

Note that solutions are provided only for numerical and technical material since other matters are covered either in the book or in the further reading indicated.

Chapters 1 and 15 have no solutions given in this Appendix because there are no numerical questions.

Chapter 2

Application

B2.1 Classify each of the items in the following list as: asset; liability; neither an asset nor a liability:

Cash at bank	Asset
Loan from the bank	Liability
Letter from the bank promising an overdraft facility at any time in the next three months	Neither
Trade debtor (a customer who has promised to pay later)	Asset
Trade debtor (a customer who has promised to pay later but has apparently disappeared without leaving a forwarding address)	Neither
Supplier of goods who has not yet received payment from the business	Liability
Stock of finished goods (fashion clothing stored ahead of the spring sales)	Asset
Stock of finished goods (fashion clothing left over after the spring sales)	Neither, unless value remains
Investment in shares of another company where the share price is rising	Asset
Investment in shares of another company where the share price is falling	Asset while there is still some benefit expected
Lender of 5-year loan to the business	Liability
Customer to whom the business has offered a 12-month warranty to repair goods free of charge	Liability
A motor vehicle owned by the business	Asset
A motor vehicle rented by the business for one year	Neither
An office building owned by the business	Asset
An office building rented by the business on a 99-year lease, with 60 years' lease period remaining	Asset, but may not be shown

B2.2 Yes to all, except the rented building where risks and benefits are mainly for the owners, not the users.

B2.3

A letter from the owner of the business, addressed to the bank manager, promising to guarantee the bank overdraft of the business.	Transaction is between owner and bank, not with business.
A list of the customers of the business.	Has benefit for the future but no event, also not measurable with reliability.
An order received from a customer.	Future benefit expected but insufficient evidence that it will be obtained.
The benefit of employing a development engineer with a high level of 'know-how' specifically relevant to the business.	Future benefit exists but not measurable with sufficient reliability.
Money spent on an advertising campaign to boost sales.	Future benefit exists but not measurable with sufficient reliability.
Structural repairs to a building.	Repairs put right the problems of the past – do not create future benefits.

Chapter 3

Application

B3.1

Sunshine Wholesale Traders
Balance sheet at 30 June Year 2

	£	£
Fixed assets		
Fleet of delivery vehicles		35,880
Furniture and fittings		18,800
Total fixed assets		54,680
Current assets		
Debtors	34,000	
Bank deposit	19,000	
Total current assets	53,000	
Current liabilities		
Trade creditors	8,300	
Current assets less current liabilities		44,700
Net assets		99,380
Ownership interest at the start of the year		56,000
Profit of the year		43,380
Ownership interest at end of year		99,380

Note that ownership interest at the start of the year is entered as the missing item.

Sunshine Wholesale Traders
Profit and loss account for the year ended 30 June Year 2

	£	£
Revenues		
Sales		294,500
Expenses		
Cost of goods sold		188,520
Gross profit		105,980
Wages and salaries	46,000	
Transport costs	14,200	
Administration costs	1,300	
Depreciation	1,100	
Total expenses		62,600
Net profit of the year		43,380

B3.2

Balance sheet at . . .

	£	£
Fixed assets		
Land and buildings		95,000
Vehicles		8,000
Total fixed assets		103,000
Current assets		
Stock of goods for resale	35,000	
Cash at bank	9,000	
Total current assets	44,000	
Liabilities due within one year		
Trade creditors	43,000	
Wages due	2,000	
	45,000	
Current liabilities less current assets		(1,000)
		102,000
Liabilities due after one year		(20,000)
		82,000
Ownership interest		82,000

(a) Decrease liability to employees £2,000, decrease asset of cash £2,000.
(b) Decrease ownership interest by £8,750, decrease asset of stock by £8,750.
(c) Increase asset of stock £5,000, increase liability of trade creditors £5,000.

Test your understanding

S3.1
(a) Debit liability to employees £2,000, credit asset of cash £2,000.
(b) Debit asset of stock £5,000, credit liability of trade creditors £5,000.
(c) Debit ownership interest £8,750, credit asset of stock £8,750.

Chapter 4

Application

B4.1 This requires a narrative answer based on section 4.5.2.

Additionally, students may wish to refer to documents produced by the Accounting Standards Board, which may be found in any text containing the accounting standards. The particular documents are the *Statement of Aims* and the *Foreword to Accounting Standards*.

The *Statement of Aims* states that accounting standards will be issued or amended in response to evolving business practices, new economic developments and deficiencies being identified in current practice. The *Foreword to Accounting Standards* states that accounting standards are authoritative statements of how particular types of transactions and other events should be reflected in financial statements and accordingly compliance with accounting standards will normally be necessary for financial statements to show a true and fair view.

B4.2 This requires a narrative answer based on section 4.3. The more difficult aspect of this question is explaining how each convention affects current accounting practice. One example of each would be:

- *Going concern*: In historical cost accounting the fixed assets of an enterprise are recorded in the balance sheet at the historical cost, after deducting depreciation, rather than at estimated selling price, because the enterprise is a going concern and it is expected that the fixed assets will be held for long-term use.
- *Accruals*: The expense of electricity consumed during a period includes all units of electricity used, irrespective of whether an invoice has been paid.
- *Consistency*: It would be inconsistent, in a balance sheet, to measure trading stock at selling price at one point of time and at cost at another point of time.
- *Prudence*: It is prudent to measure stock of goods at cost, rather than at selling price, because to value at selling price would anticipate a sale which may not take place.

B4.3 This is an essay which shows the student's understanding of the issues in the chapter and the ability to think about them in the context of a variety of users' needs. It requires the student to link the information in Chapter 4 with the ideas set out in Chapter 1, section 1.5.

Chapter 5

Test your understanding

A5.1

Transaction	Asset	Liability	Ownership interest
(a) Owner puts cash into the business	Increase^		Increase
(b) Buy a vehicle for cash	Increase and decrease^		
(c) Receive a bill for electricity consumed		Increase	Decrease*
(d) Purchase stationery for office use, paying cash	Increase and decrease^		
(e) Pay the electricity bill in cash	Decrease^	Decrease	
(f) Pay rental for a computer, used for customer records	Decrease^		Decrease*
(g) Buy spare parts for cash, to use in repairs	Increase and decrease^		
(h) Buy spare parts on credit terms	Increase	Increase	
(i) Pay garage service bills for van, using cash	Decrease^		Decrease*
(j) Fill van with petrol, using credit account at local garage, to be paid at the start of next month		Increase	Decrease*
(k) Carry out repairs for cash	Increase^		Increase*
(l) Carry out repairs on credit terms	Increase		Increase*
(m) Pay wages to an employee	Decrease^		Decrease*
(n) Owner takes cash for personal use	Decrease^		Decrease

A5.2 Symbol * shows items which will have an effect on a profit and loss account.

A5.3 Symbol ^ shows items which will have an effect on a cash flow statement.

A5.4 All items other than those asterisked will have a direct effect on a balance sheet. The asterisked items will collectively change the accumulated profit which will increase the ownership interest reported in the balance sheet.

A5.5 Transactions analysed to show the two aspects of the transaction:

	£		
Apr. 1	60,000	Increase asset of cash	Increase ownership interest
Apr. 1	800	Decrease asset of cash	Decrease ownership interest (expense)
Apr. 2	35,000	Increase asset of equipment	Decrease asset of cash
Apr. 3	5,000	Increase asset of supplies	Increase liability to trade creditor
Apr. 4	1,200	Increase asset of cash	Increase ownership interest (revenue)
Apr. 15	700	Decrease asset of cash	Decrease ownership interest (expense)
Apr. 20	500	Decrease asset of cash	Decrease ownership interest (voluntary)

	£		
Apr. 21	2,400	Increase asset of cash	Increase ownership interest (revenue)
Apr. 29	700	Decrease asset of cash	Decrease ownership interest (expense)
Apr. 29	1,900	Increase asset of debtor	Increase ownership interest (revenue)
Apr. 30	80	Decrease asset of cash	Decrease ownership interest (expense)
Apr. 30	*1,500	Decrease asset of supplies	Decrease ownership interest (expense)

*Stock acquired £5,000, less amount remaining £3,500 = £1,500 asset used in period.

Application

B5.1

		Cash and bank	Other assets	Liabilities	Capital contributed or withdrawn	Revenue	Expenses
		£	£	£	£	£	£
April 1	Jane Gate commenced her dental practice on April 1 by depositing £60,000 in a business bank account.	60,000			60,000		
April 1	Rent for a surgery was paid, £800, for the month of April.	(800)					800
April 2	Dental equipment was purchased for £35,000, paying in cash.	(35,000)	35,000				
April 3	Dental supplies were purchased for £5,000, taking 30 days' credit from a supplier.		5,000	5,000			
April 4	Fees of £1,200 were collected in cash from patients and paid into the bank account.	1,200				1,200	
April 15	Dental assistant was paid wages for two weeks, £700	(700)					700
April 20	Jane Gate withdrew £500 cash for personal use.	(500)			(500)		
April 21	Fees of £2,400 were collected in cash from patients and paid into the bank.	2,400				2,400	
April 29	Dental assistant was paid wages for two weeks, £700.	(700)					700
April 29	Invoices were sent to patients who are allowed 20 days' credit, for work done during April amounting to £1,900.		1,900			1,900	
April 30	Telephone bill for April was paid, £80.	(80)					80
April 30	Dental supplies unused were counted and found to be worth £3,500, measured at cost price (i.e. stock decreased by £1,500).		(1,500)				1,500
	Totals	25,820	40,400	5,000	59,500	5,500	3,780

AII.8

Accounting equation:

Cash	plus	other assets	less	liabilities		
25,820	+	40,400	−	5,000	=	61,220

Capital contributed or withdrawn	plus	revenue	less	expenses		
59,500	+	5,500	−	3,780	=	61,220

B5.2

Dental Practice of Jane Gate
Cash flow statement for the month of April Year XX

	£
Operating activities	
Inflow from fees	3,600
Outflow: rent paid	(800)
wages	(1,400)
telephone	(80)
Net inflow from operations	1,320
Investing activities	
Payment for equipment	(35,000)
Net outflow for investing activities	(35,000)
Financing activities	
Capital contributed by owner	60,000
Capital withdrawn as drawings	(500)
Net inflow from financing activities	59,500
Increase in cash at bank over period	25,820

Dental Practice of Jane Gate
Profit and loss account for the month of April Year XX

	£	£
Fees charged		5,500
Dental supplies used	1,500	
Wages	1,400	
Rent	800	
Telephone	80	
		3,780
Profit		1,720

Dental Practice of Jane Gate
Balance sheet at 30 April Year XX

	£
Fixed assets	
Dental equipment at cost	35,000
Current assets	
Dental supplies	3,500
Debtors	1,900
Cash at bank	25,820
	31,220
Current liabilities	
Trade creditors	(5,000)
Current assets less current liabilities	26,220
Net assets	61,220
Capital at start	60,000
Add profit	1,720
Less drawings	(500)
Total ownership interest	61,220

Chapter 6

Test your understanding

A6.1

(a) Profit is only reported when there is a sale. The number of items sold is 60. Each one gives a profit of £5 so the total profit is £300.

(b) When the 200 items are purchased there is an increase of £4,000 in the asset of stock of spare parts and a decrease of £4,000 in the asset of cash. When the 60 items are sold for £1,500 there is an increase in the asset of cash and an increase in the ownership interest reported as revenue. The 60 items cost £1,200 to purchase and so at the date of sale there is a reduction in the asset of stock amounting to £1,200 and a decrease in the ownership interest due to the expense of cost of goods sold £1,200.

A6.2

(a) Transactions summarised by spreadsheet

	Cash	Stock	Revenue	Expense
	£	£	£	£
Purchase 200 items @ £20 each	(4,000)	4,000		
Sell 60 items @ £25	1,500		1,500	
Cost of goods sold 60 @ £20		(1,200)		1,200
Totals	(2,500)	2,800	1,500	1,200

(b) Stock increases by £2,800 while cash decreases by £2,500, overall increase in assets amounting to £300. Ownership interest increases by £300 when expenses of £1,200 are set against revenue of £1,500.

A6.3

(a) Calculation of profit on sale:

	£
Sale of 50 trays for £8 each	400
Cost of 50 trays at £5.50 each	275
Profit on sale	125

(b) Analysis of transactions using the accounting equation

	£		
June 1	300	Increase asset of stock of raw materials.	Decrease asset of cash.
June 3	210	Decrease asset of stock of raw materials.	Increase asset of work-in-progress.
June 5	175	Decrease asset of cash.	Increase asset of work-in-progress.
June 6	385	Increase asset of finished goods.	Decrease asset of work-in-progress.
June 11	275	Decrease ownership interest: expense of cost of goods sold.	Decrease asset of finished goods.
June 14	400	Increase asset of cash.	Increase ownership interest: revenue.

A6.4

Date	Amount		
	£		
Apr. 1	60,000	Increase asset of cash.	Increase ownership interest.
Apr. 2	20,000	Increase asset of buildings.	Decrease asset of cash.
Apr. 4	12,000	Increase asset of equipment.	Decrease asset of cash.
Apr. 6	8,500	Increase asset of stock.	Decrease asset of cash.
Apr. 7	7,000	Increase asset of stock.	Increase liability to supplier.
Apr. 11	7,000	Decrease liability to supplier.	Decrease asset of cash.
Apr. 14	400	Decrease ownership claim (expense).	Decrease asset of cash.
Apr. 17	5,500	Decrease ownership claim (expense).	Decrease asset of stock.
Apr. 17	6,000	Increase asset of cash.	Increase ownership claim (revenue).
Apr. 17	4,200	Increase asset of debtor.	Increase ownership claim (revenue).
Apr. 24	4,200	Increase asset of cash.	Decrease asset of debtor.
Apr. 28	2,700	Decrease ownership claim (voluntary withdrawal).	Decrease asset of cash.
Apr. 30	2,800	Decrease ownership claim (expense).	Decrease asset of cash.
Apr. 30	550	Decrease ownership claim (expense of depreciation).	Decrease asset of equipment.

Application

B6.1 (a)

		Cash at bank	Fixed assets and debtors	Stock of goods	Trade creditor	Capital contributed or withdrawn	Revenue	Expenses
		£	£		£	£	£	£
Apr. 1	The owner pays cash into a bank account for the business.	60,000				60,000		
Apr. 2	The business acquires buildings for cash.	(20,000)	20,000					
Apr. 4	The business acquires equipment for cash.	(12,000)	12,000					
Apr. 6	The business purchases a stock of goods for cash.	(8,500)		8,500				
Apr. 7	The business purchases a stock of goods on credit from R. Green and receives an invoice.			7,000	7,000			
Apr. 11	The business pays R. Green in cash for the goods it acquired on credit.	(7,000)			(7,000)			
Apr. 14	The business pays a gas bill in cash.	(400)						400
Apr. 17	Some of the goods purchased for resale (items costing £5,500) are removed from the store because sales have been agreed with customers for this date.			(5,500)				5,500
Apr. 17	The business sells goods for cash.	6,000					6,000	
Apr. 17	The business sells goods on credit to P. Weatherall and sends an invoice.		4,200				4,200	
Apr. 24	P. Weatherall pays in cash for the goods obtained on credit.	4,200	(4,200)					
Apr. 28	The owner draws cash from the business for personal use.	(2,700)				(2,700)		
Apr. 30	The business pays wages to employees, in cash.	(2,800)						2,800
Apr. 30	The business discovers that its equipment has fallen in value over the month.		(550)					550
	Totals	16,800	31,450	10,000	nil	57,300	10,200	9,250

(b)
Accounting equation:

Assets	–	Liabilities	=	Ownership interest
16,800 + 31,450 + 10,000		nil	=	57,300 + 10,200 – 9,250
58,250				58,250

B6.2

Peter Gold, furniture supplier
Cash flow statement for the month of April Year XX

	£
Operating activities	
Cash from customers	10,200
Outflow: payment for goods	(8,500)
payment to supplier (R. Green)	(7,000)
wages	(2,800)
gas	(400)
Net outflow from operations	(8,500)
Investing activities	
Payment for buildings	(20,000)
Payment for equipment	(12,000)
Net outflow for investing activities	(32,000)
Financing activities	
Capital contributed by owner	60,000
Capital withdrawn as drawings	(2,700)
Net inflow from financing activities	57,300
Increase in cash at bank over period	16,800

Peter Gold, furniture supplier
Profit and loss account for the month of April Year XX

	£	£
Sales		10,200
Cost of goods sold		5,500
Gross profit		4,700
Other expenses		
Wages	2,800	
Gas	400	
Depreciation	550	
		3,750
Net profit		950

Peter Gold, furniture supplier
Balance sheet at 30 April Year XX

	£
Fixed assets	
Buildings	20,000
Equipment	12,000
	32,000
Depreciation	(550)
Depreciated cost of fixed assets	31,450
Current assets	
Stocks	10,000
Cash at bank	16,800
	26,800
Net assets	58,250
Capital at start	60,000
Add profit	950
Less drawings	(2,700)
Total ownership interest	58,250

Chapter 7

Application

The questions at the end of Chapter 7 provide opportunities for writing about accounting informa-tion. The Accounting Standards Board has a practice of writing an 'Explanation' section to each of its Financial Reporting Standards (FRSs). So, for Question B7.2 you could look at the Explanation section of FRS 3, while for Question B7.3 you could look at the Explanation section of FRS 1.

To write a short essay for Question B7.1 or Question B7.3 the first two chapters of the *Statement of Principles* would be very helpful.

Problem solving and evaluation

Question C7.1 requires you to show that you have thought about all the material in the first seven chapters of the book. A reader of your essay might expect to find some or all of the fol-lowing questions addressed:

(a) This is a listed company and so shares are bought and sold through the stock market. Does your answer show that you have thought about this active market process?
(b) In giving advice on principles have you made use of the *Statement of Principles*, especially Chapters 1 and 2?
(c) Have you given examples of the kind of information which would be relevant to the *Statement of Principles*? Furthermore, have you carried out some research on company annual reports so that you can provide first-hand examples or illustrations?

Chapter 8

Application

B8.1

(a) The amount of £8,000 has been reported as an asset. Since this is a repair it must be removed from the assets. Removing an asset causes a decrease in the ownership interest through an additional expense of £8,000 in the profit and loss account.

Problem solving and evaluation

C8.1 The Biscuit Manufacturing Company

(a) Depreciation calculated on a straight-line basis: $\dfrac{22,000 - 2,000}{4} = £5,000$ per annum

		Assets			Ownership interest	
	Transaction or event	Machine at cost	Accumulated depreciation of van	Cash	Capital contributed or withdrawn	Profit = Revenue minus expenses
Year 1		£	£	£	£	£
1 Jan.	Owner contributes cash			22,000	22,000	
1 Jan.	Purchase biscuit machine	22,000		(22,000)		
All year	Collected cash from customers			40,000		40,000
All year	Paid for wages, other costs			(17,000)		(17,000)
31 Dec.	Calculate annual depreciation		(5,000)			(5,000)
	Totals	22,000	(5,000)	23,000	22,000	18,000

		Assets			Ownership interest		
	Transaction or event	Machine at cost	Accumulated depreciation of machine	Cash	Ownership interest at start of year	Capital contributed or withdrawn	Profit = Revenue minus expenses
Year 2		£	£	£	£	£	£
1 Jan.	Amounts brought forward at start of year	22,000	(5,000)	23,000	40,000		
All year	Collected cash from customers			40,000			40,000
All year	Paid for wages, fuel, etc.			(17,000)			(17,000)
31 Dec.	Calculate annual depreciation		(5,000)				(5,000)
	Totals	22,000	(10,000)	46,000	40,000		18,000

		Assets			Ownership interest		
	Transaction or event	Machine at cost	Accumulated depreciation of machine	Cash	Ownership interest at start of year	Capital contributed or withdrawn	Profit = Revenue minus expenses
Year 3		£	£	£	£	£	£
1 Jan.	Amounts brought forward at start of year	22,000	(10,000)	46,000	58,000		
All year	Collected cash from customers			40,000			40,000
All year	Paid for wages, fuel, etc.			(17,000)			(17,000)
31 Dec.	Calculate annual depreciation		(5,000)				(5,000)
	Totals	22,000	(15,000)	69,000	58,000		18,000

	Transaction or event	Assets			Ownership interest		
		Machine at cost	Accumulated depreciation of machine	Cash	Ownership interest at start of year	Capital contributed or withdrawn	Profit = Revenue minus expenses
Year 4		£	£	£	£	£	£
1 Jan.	Amounts brought forward at start of year	22,000	(15,000)	69,000	76,000		
All year	Collected cash from customers			40,000			40,000
All year	Paid for wages, fuel, etc.			(17,000)			(17,000)
31 Dec.	Calculate annual depreciation		(5,000)				(5,000)
	Totals	22,000	(20,000)	92,000	76,000		18,000

(b)

Biscuit Manufacturing Company
Balance sheet at 31 December Year 3

	£
Fixed assets	
Machine at cost	22,000
Accumulated depreciation	(15,000)
Net book value	7,000
Current assets	
Cash	69,000
Total assets	76,000
Ownership interest	
Ownership interest at the start of the year	58,000
Profit of the year	18,000
	76,000

Biscuit Manufacturing Company
Profit and loss account
for the year ended 31 December Year 3

	£	£
Revenue		
Sale of biscuits		40,000
Expenses		
Wages, ingredients and running costs	(17,000)	
Depreciation	(5,000)	
		(22,000)
Net profit		18,000

AII.18

C8.2 (a)

	Transaction or event	Assets			Ownership interest		
		Machine at cost	Accumulated depreciation of machine	Cash	Ownership interest at start of year	Capital contributed or withdrawn	Profit = Revenue minus expenses
Year 4		£	£	£	£	£	£
1 Jan.	Amounts brought forward at start of year	22,000	(15,000)	69,000	76,000		
All year	Collected cash from customers			40,000			40,000
All year	Paid for wages, fuel, etc.			(17,000)			(17,000)
31 Dec.	Calculate annual depreciation		(5,000)				(5,000)
31 Dec.	Machine disposal	(22,000)	20,000	3,000			1,000
	Totals	nil	nil	95,000	76,000		19,000

Note that at the end of Year 4 the net book value is £2,000 (cost £22,000 less accumulated depreciation £20,000). The cash received £3,000 is therefore £1,000 more than expected. The amount of £1,000 is recorded as an increase in the ownership interest.

(b)

Biscuit Manufacturing Company
Balance sheet at 31 December Year 4

	£
Fixed assets	
Machine at cost	nil
Current assets	
Cash	95,000
Total assets	95,000
Ownership interest	
Ownership interest at the start of the year	76,000
Profit of the year	19,000
	95,000

Biscuit Manufacturing Company
Profit and loss accountfor the year ended 31 December Year 4

	£	£
Revenue		
Sale of biscuits		40,000
Expenses		
Wages, ingredients and running costs	(17,000)	
Depreciation less gain on disposal	(4,000)	
		(21,000)
Net profit		19,000

(c) There is apparently a gain on disposal because the cash collected is greater than the net book value of the asset. In reality, all that has happened is that the estimate of depreciation over the asset life is, with the benefit of hindsight, a marginally incorrect estimate. Perfect foresight at the outset would have used £3,000 as a residual value, rather than £2,000, in calculating the annual depreciation charge. However, it is known that accounting involves estimates so it would be inappropriate in most cases to attempt to rewrite the profit and loss accounts of the past. Accordingly all of the 'gain' is reported in Year 4, as a deduction from annual depreciation.

C8.3 Souvenir Company

(a) Straight-line depreciation

Machine cost £16,000, estimated residual value £1,000, so depreciate the difference, £15,000, over five-year life to give annual depreciation of £3,000.

End of Year	Depreciation of the year (b)	Total depreciation (c)	Net book value of the asset (£16,000 − (c))
	£	£	£
1	3,000	3,000	13,000
2	3,000	6,000	10,000
3	3,000	9,000	7,000
4	3,000	12,000	4,000
5	3,000	15,000	1,000

(b) Guess a rate which is at least twice the percentage applied on a straight-line basis (i.e. in this case guess 20% × 2 = 40%).

Calculation of reducing balance depreciation (as in Exhibit 8.3):

Year	Net book value at start of year (a)	Annual depreciation (b) = 40% of (a)	Net book value at end of year (a − b)
	£	£	£
1	16,000	6,400	9,600
2	9,600	3,840	5,760
3	5,760	2,304	3,456
4	3,456	1,382	2,074
5	2,074	830	1,244

(The residual value at the end of Year 5 should ideally be £1,000, so a first estimate which arrives at £1,244 is quite reasonable.)

(c) The net book value at the end of Year 5 is £1,000 and therefore disposal at £2,500 gives an apparent gain of £1,500 which is best described as caused by overdepreciation of earlier years. The effect on the accounting equation is that the asset of machine decreases by £1,000 while the asset of cash increases by £2,500 so that overall the ownership interest increases by £1,500.

(d) The net book value at the end of Year 5 is £1,000 and therefore disposal at nil scrap value gives an apparent loss of £1,000 which is best described as caused by underdepreciation of earlier years. The effect on the accounting equation is that the asset of machine decreases by £1,000 with no increase in any other asset so that overall the ownership interest decreases by £1,000.

Chapter 9

Test your understanding

A9.10 Use lower of cost and net realisable value on each category separately:

Description	Basis	Stock value
		£
Engine	Cost	6,500
Chassis	Net realisable value	1,600
Frame	Net realisable value	4,600

A9.11 The recorded stock will increase by £18,000 and the ownership interest will increase by £18,000 (reported as a reduction in the cost of goods sold).

A9.12 The asset of debtor will be reduced by £154,000 and the ownership interest will decrease by £154,000 (reported as an expense of cost of bad debts).

Application

B9.1

(a) The FIFO approach to the issue of units for sale, where:
   (i) the calculation is carried out at the date of sale; and
   (ii) the calculation is carried out at the end of the month without regard for the date of sale.

Date	Number of units purchased	Unit cost	Number of units sold	Cost of goods sold (i)	Cost of goods sold (ii)	Stock (i)	Stock (ii)
				£	£		
Jan. 5	100	£1.00					
Jan. 10			50	50			
Jan. 15	200	£1.10					
Jan. 17			150	50			
				110			
Jan. 24	300	£1.15					
Jan. 30			200	110	100		
				115	220		
					115		
	600		400	435	435	230	230

	£
Sales 400 × £2	800
Cost of goods sold	435
Profit	365

Stock = 200 × £1.15 = £230

(b) The LIFO approach to the issue of units for sale, where:
   (i) the calculation is carried out at the date of sale; and
   (ii) the calculation is carried out at the end of the month without regard for the date of sale;
   and

Date	Number of units purchased	Unit cost	Number of units sold	Cost of goods sold (i) £	Cost of goods sold (ii) £	Stock (i)	Stock (ii)
Jan. 5	100	£1.00					
Jan. 10			50	50		50	
Jan. 15	200	£1.10					
Jan. 17			150	165		55	
Jan. 24	300	£1.15					
Jan. 30			200	230	345	115	100
					110		110
	600		400	345	455	220	210

either (i):

	£
Sales 400 × £2	800
Cost of goods sold	345
Profit	455

Stock = (50 × £1.00) + (50 × £1.10) + (100 × £1.15)
= 50 + 55 + 115 = 220

or (ii):

	£
Sales 400 × £2	800
Cost of goods sold	455
Profit	345

Stock = (100 × £1) + (100 × £1.10)
= 100 + 110 = £210

Note that in all cases the Cost of goods sold plus the unsold Stock = £665.

(c) The average-cost approach to the issue of units for sale, making the calculation at the end of the month without regard for the date of sale.

Date	Number of units purchased	Unit cost	£
Jan. 5	100	£1.00	100
Jan. 10			
Jan. 15	200	£1.10	220
Jan. 17			
Jan. 24	300	£1.15	345
Jan. 30			
	600		665

Average cost = £665/500 = £1.108

	£
Sales 400 × £2	800
Cost of goods sold 400 × £1.108	443
Profit	357

Stock 200 × £1.108 = £222

B9.2

Group of items	Basis	Stock value
		£
A	Cost	1,000
B	Net realisable value	800
C	Net realisable value	1,900
D	Cost	3,000
Total stock		6,700

Chapter 10

Test your understanding

A10.9 The liability to the supplier will increase and the ownership interest will decrease (recorded as an increase in the cost of goods sold).

A10.10 The recorded asset of cash will decrease and the recorded liability to the supplier will decrease.

A10.11 First the original incorrect entry must be reversed. When the entry was made, it was treated as an increase in the ownership interest and an increase in the asset of debtor. This error must be reversed by decreasing the ownership interest and decreasing the asset of debtor.

Then the correct entry must be made which is a decrease in the ownership interest and an increase in a liability to the landlord.

Application

B10.1 The aim of the calculation is to show the cost of telephone used during the year.

	£
Cash paid	3,500
Less rental in advance for July, one-third of £660	(220)
Add calls for May and June, two-thirds of £900	600
Expense of the period	3,880

The rental paid in advance will be shown as a prepayment of £220 in the balance sheet and the calls made during May and June will be shown as an accrual of £600 in the balance sheet.

B10.2

		Asset	Liability	Ownership interest: profit of the period
Date	Transactions with security company	Cash	Security company	Security expense
Year 1		£	£	£
Mar. 31	Invoice received £800		800	(800)
Apr. 5	Security company paid £800	(800)	(800)	
June 30	Invoice received £800		800	(800)
July 5	Security company paid £800	(800)	(800)	
Sept. 30	Invoice received £800		800	(800)
Oct. 5	Security company paid £800	(800)	(800)	
Dec. 31	Invoice received £800		800	(800)
	Totals	(2,400)	800	(3,200)

B10.3 The tax charge reduces the ownership interest and is shown as an expense of £8,000 in the profit and loss account. The accounting equation remains in balance because there is a matching liability of £8,000 recorded. However, the liability is split as £6,000 current liability and £2,000 deferred liability to reflect different patterns of payment of the overall liability.

Problem solving and evaluation

C10.1 The year-end is 31 December Year 1.

Item	Description	Amount		
		£		
1	Invoice dated 23 December for goods received 21 December.	260	Increase asset of stock.	Increase liability to supplier.
2	Invoice dated 23 December for goods to be delivered on 3 January Year 2.	310	Nothing recorded – this will be an asset and a liability of the following year.	
3	Foreman's note of electricity consumption for month of December – no invoice yet received from electricity supply company.	100	Decrease ownership interest (expense of electricity).	Increase liability to electricity supplier.
4	Letter from employee claiming overtime payment for work on 1 December and note from personnel office denying entitlement to payment.	58	Nothing recorded in the financial statements because it is not yet clear that there is an obligation (might be a contingent liability note).	

Item	Description	Amount		
		£		
5	Telephone bill dated 26 December showing calls for October to December.	290	Decrease ownership interest (expense of telephone calls).	Increase liability to phone company.
6	Telephone bill dated 26 December showing rent due in advance for period January to March Year 2.	90	Nothing recorded – this will be an expense of the following year.	
7	Note of payment due to cleaners for final week of December (to be paid on 3 January under usual pattern of payment one week In arrears).	48	Usually nothing recorded if payment in arrears is normal, since the corresponding payment from January Year 1 will be included in the year's expense.	
8	Invoice from supplier for promotional calendars received 1 December (only one-third have yet been sent to customers).	300	Decrease ownership interest £300 (expense of calendars).	Increase liability to calendar supplier £300.
			Increase stock of calendars by £200.	Reduce expense by £200.
9	Letter dated 21 December Year 1 to customer promising a cheque to reimburse damage caused by faulty product – cheque to be sent on 4 January Year 2.	280	Decrease ownership interest (expense of damage).	Increase liability to customer.
10	Letter dated 23 December promising donation to local charity – amount not yet paid.	60	Decrease ownership interest (expense of donation).	Increase liability to charity.

Chapter 11

Test your understanding

A11.6 Reduce revenue by £40,000 (two-thirds of £60,000) and increase balance sheet deferred income by £40,000. Effect on profit and loss account is to reduce reported profit. Reason is application of the matching concept. The £40,000 deferred income will be transferred to profit and loss account over the next two years.

A11.7 Increase expense of provision for repairs by £50,000 (reporting as an expense in the profit and loss account) and create a liability under the 'provisions' heading. Effect on profit and loss account is to reduce reported profit.

Application

B11.1 The profit and loss account would show an expense of £8,000 provision in Year 1 and an expense of £9,000 provision in Year 2. The actual amount of expenditure as shown in the question would be set against the provision in the balance sheet.

Date of repair	Profit & loss expense	Balance sheet provision in total before expense charged	Actual expense matched against provision	Provision remaining in balance sheet
Year	£	£	£	£
1	8,000	8,000	4,500	3,500
2	9,000	12,500	8,000	4,500
3	*500	4,500	*4,500	nil

*The actual cost in Year 3 is £5,000 but there is only £4,500 provision remaining, so the extra £500 must be charged to profit and loss account as an unexpected expense.

Note that the total amount charged to profit and loss account is £17,500 and the total amount paid out for repair work is also £17,500. The accounting entries in the profit and loss account are an attempt to spread the expense on the basis of matching with revenue, but the total must be the same over the three-year period, whatever matching approach is taken.

Date of repair	Profit & loss expense using provision approach	Profit and loss expense using actual repair amount paid
	£	£
1	8,000	4,500
2	9,000	8,000
3	*500	5,000
Total	17,500	17,500

B11.2 The grant will initially be recorded as an increase in the asset of cash and an increase in the balance sheet liability item headed 'deferred income'. The deferred income is transferred from the liability to revenue over three years (so that the ownership interest increases evenly over the three-year period).

Chapter 12

Application

B12.1
(a) Increase the asset of cash by £50,000. Increase the ownership interest by the nominal value of shares, £50,000.

(b) Increase the asset of cash by £75,000. Increase the ownership interest by (i) nominal value of shares £25,000 and (ii) share premium £50,000.

(c) Increase asset of property by £20,000. Increase ownership interest by revaluation reserve £20,000.

B12.2
(a) Decrease asset of cash by £20,000. Decrease ownership interest by £20,000 as a reduction in the owners' claim on the business.

(b) Increase current liability of dividend payable £30,000. Decrease ownership interest by £30,000 as a reduction in the owners' claim on the business.

B12.3 Nithsdale Ltd

	£000s	(a) £000s	(b) £000s	(c) £000s
Cash	20	70.0	20	80
Other assets less liabilities	320	320.0	320	320
	340	390.0	340	400
Ordinary shares (400,000 of 25 pence each)	100	112.5	125	105
Share premium	40	77.5	40	95
Reserves of retained profit	200	200.0	175	200
	340	390.0	340	400

B12.4 If the directors decide that they wish to incorporate the revaluation in the balance sheet, then the asset will be reported at £380,000. The difference between the previous recorded book value £250,000 and the new value £380,000 is £130,000. This is an increase in the ownership interest and will be reported as a revaluation reserve as part of the total ownership interest.

B12.5 In this case the value has decreased by £10,000. This is a reduction in the value of the asset and a decrease in the ownership claim. On grounds of prudence the loss should be reported in the profit and loss account immediately and the recorded book value of the asset should be reduced.

Chapter 13

Application

B13.1

(a) **Hope plc**

(i) **Liquidity**

Ratio	Definition in words	Hope plc Workings	Result
Current ratio	Current assets : Current liabilities	2,360 : 1,330	1.77 : 1
Acid test	(Current assets − Stock) : Current liabilities	(2,360 − 620) : 1,330	1.31 : 1
Rate of usage of stock (closing stock only available)	$\dfrac{\text{Cost of sales}}{\text{Average stock held}}$	$\dfrac{2,750}{620^*}$	4.44 times
Debtors collection period	$\dfrac{\text{Trade debtors}}{\text{Credit sales}} \times 365$	$\dfrac{1,540}{6,200} \times 365$	90.7 days

*Assuming the opening stock is the same as the closing stock.

(ii) **Analysis of management performance**

Ratio	Definition in words	Hope plc Workings	Result
Return on shareholders' equity	$\dfrac{\text{Profit after tax}}{\text{Share capital + Reserves}} \times 100\%$	$\dfrac{692}{1,380} \times 100\%$	50.1%
Return on capital employed	$\dfrac{\text{Profit before interest and tax}}{\text{Total assets − Current liabilities}} \times 100\%$	$\dfrac{1,172 + 252}{2,780} \times 100\%$	51.2%
Net profit on sales	$\dfrac{\text{Profit before interest and tax}}{\text{Sales (turnover)}} \times 100\%$	$\dfrac{1,172 + 252}{6,200} \times 100\%$	23.0%
Gross profit percentage	$\dfrac{\text{Gross profit}}{\text{Sales (turnover)}} \times 100$	$\dfrac{3,450}{6,200} \times 100\%$	55.6%
Total assets usage	$\dfrac{\text{Turnover}}{\text{Total assets}}$	$\dfrac{6,200}{1,750 + 2,360}$	1.5 times
Fixed assets usage	$\dfrac{\text{Turnover}}{\text{Fixed assets}}$	$\dfrac{6,200}{1,750}$	3.5 times

(iii) **Gearing (leverage)**

Ratio	Definition in words	Hope plc	
		Workings	Result
Debt/equity ratio	$\dfrac{\text{Debt} + \text{Preference share capital}}{\text{Ordinary share capital} + \text{Reserves}} \times 100\%$	$\dfrac{1{,}400}{1{,}380} \times 100\%$	101.4%
Interest cover	$\dfrac{\text{Profit before interest and tax}}{\text{Interest}}$	$\dfrac{1{,}172 + 252}{252}$	5.6 times

(c) **Investor ratios**

Ratio	Definition in words	Hope plc	
		Workings	Result
Earnings per share	$\dfrac{\text{Profit after tax for ordinary shareholder}}{\text{Number of ordinary shares}}$	$\dfrac{692}{900}$	76.9 pence
Price/earnings ratio	$\dfrac{\text{Share price}}{\text{Earnings per share}}$	$\dfrac{1{,}100}{76.9}$	14
Dividend cover (payout ratio)	$\dfrac{\text{Profit after tax for ordinary shareholder}}{\text{Ordinary dividends}}$	$\dfrac{692}{330}$	2.1 times
Dividend per share	$\dfrac{\text{Dividend payable to ordinary shareholders}}{\text{Number of issued shares}}$	$\dfrac{330}{900}$	36.7 pence
Dividend yield	$\dfrac{\text{Dividend per share}}{\text{Share price}} \times 100\%$	$\dfrac{36.7}{1{,}100} \times 100\%$	3.34%

Chapter 14

Application

B14.1
D Ltd Operating cash flow

	£m
Operating profit	12
Add back depreciation	1
	13
Deduct increase in stock	(4)
Deduct increase in debtors	(3)
Add increase in creditors	5
Cash flow from operations	11

B14.2
E Ltd Operating cash flow

	£m
Operating profit	16
Add back depreciation	2
	18
Deduct increase in stock	(1)
Add decrease in debtors	3
Deduct decrease in creditors	(2)
Cash flow from operations	18

Problem solving and evaluation

C14.2 Trend analysis: Safe and Sure

Safe and Sure

	Year 3	Year 4	Year 5	Year 6	Year 7
Group turnover	309.1	389	474.1	600.3	734.6
Group profit	74.4	90.4	114.5	147	177
Tax	−27.2	−33.9	−44.3	−52.4	−62.2
Group profit after tax	47.2	56.5	70.2	94.6	114.8
Dividend	−12.7	−16.4	−22.4	−27.8	−33.7
Retained profit in the group	34.5	40.1	47.8	66.8	81.1
Earnings per share	4.88	6.23	8.02	9.71	11.74
Dividends per share	1.32	1.69	2.31	2.85	3.45
Share capital	19.4	19.4	19.4	19.5	19.6
Reserves	160.8	195.3	265.4	326.5	415.2
Capital employed	180.2	214.7	284.8	346	434.8
Ratios					
Net profit to sales	24.1%	23.2%	24.2%	24.5%	24.1%
Tax charge as % of pre-tax profit	36.6%	37.5%	38.7%	35.6%	35.1%
Dividend cover	3.70	3.70	3.47	3.41	3.40
Growth in turnover	n/a	25.9%	21.9%	26.6%	22.4%
Growth in eps	n/a	27.7%	28.7%	21.1%	20.9%
Growth in dividend per share	n/a	28.0%	36.7%	23.4%	21.1%
Return on shareholders' equity	26.2%	26.3%	24.7%	27.3%	26.4%

Commentary: The company has exceeded its annual growth target of 20 per cent in each year for which calculations can be made. It has also exceeded that growth rate for dividends. The dividend cover is relatively high, indicating a policy of retaining new wealth to finance expansion. With the expansion the company has maintained its rate of return on shareholders' equity. It is likely to be attractive to investors if future prospects are similar to the historical trend.

Index